Encyclopedia of
WORLD
RELIGIONS

Encyclopedia of
WORLD RELIGIONS

Judaism, Christianity, Islam, Buddhism, Zen, Hinduism, Prehistoric & Primitive Religions

octopus
in association with
Phoebus

CONTENTS

First published in 1975 by
Octopus Books Limited
59 Grosvenor Street, London W1

ISBN 0 7064 0433 5

© 1970-71 BPC Publishing Ltd

© 1975 BPC Publishing Ltd.
This book has been produced by
Phoebus Publishing Company
in co-operation with
Octopus Books Limited

Distributed in USA by
Crescent Books
a division of Crown Publishers Inc
419 Park Avenue South
New York, NY 10016

Distributed in Australia by
Rigby Limited
30 North Terrace, Kent Town
Adelaide, South Australia 5067

Produced by Mandarin Publishers Ltd
14 Westlands Road, Quarry Bay, Hong Kong

Printed in Hong Kong

THE DAWN OF BELIEF

Comparative Religion

The term 'comparative religion' has gradually become the established designation for the discipline more correctly described as 'the comparative study of religion'. Among English-speaking scholars comparative religion generally includes what Continental scholars tend to regard as two separate subjects, the history of religions and the phenomenology of religions. But these subjects are essentially interrelated, for no serious comparative study of religion can be undertaken without both a sound knowledge of the history of the religions concerned and a wide acquaintance with the variety of forms in which religious faith and practice have found expression.

Religion, in two of its basic concerns at least, can be traced back to the very beginning of human society. The peoples of the Old Stone Age ritually buried their dead and practised fertility rituals. Then religion was doubtless largely the practical expression of deep-felt emotions awakened by the mysteries of birth and death. Some reasoning about these issues must certainly have informed the ritual action, but in the absence of written records we can know nothing of its nature or content. However, it would seem improbable that these remote ancestors of our race would have been mentally capable of looking critically at their religious customs and asking how they had originated.

Evidence of such ability is clearly found in the earliest writings known to us, which date from the third millennium BC in both Egypt and Mesopotamia. On the so-called Shabaka Stone, now preserved in the British Museum, a text in honour of Ptah, the god of Memphis, the earliest capital of Egypt, briefly tells how religion started. Ptah, it claims, 'created the gods, he made

the cities . . . he set the gods in their cult-places, he established their offerings, he founded their shrines'. The claim is a naive assertion by the priests of Ptah that their god was the creator of all the other Egyptian gods, and that he had arranged for their ritual service. However, despite its naivety, the claim has a great significance. It shows that already in Egypt people were interested in the origin of religion. A similar significance attaches to a Sumerian text of about the same period which tells how the gods had to labour to provide their food until the wise god Enki made men of clay, to be their servants. In other words, according to ancient Sumerian thought, the purpose of the human race was to feed the gods by sacrifices and house them in temples.

These primitive theories, if such they may be called, about the origin of religion were in no sense adversely critical of religion as an institution. Indeed, they obviously regarded it as being of divine origin, and constituting the reason for the existence of human society. It was, characteristically, in the world of Greek culture that a sceptical appraisal of religious origins first appeared. The philosopher Xenophanes of Colophon, writing in the 6th century BC, perceived that the conception of deity is essentially conditioned by ethnic factors, as well as being basically anthropomorphic. He pointed out that the Thracians thought of their gods as Thracians, with grey eyes and red hair, whereas the Ethiopians naturally conceived of theirs as having negroid features. And he cynically remarked that horses and oxen, if they could carve, would undoubtedly represent the gods in their own animal forms.

Xenophanes was followed by many other thinkers who could detach themselves from the religious beliefs and practices of their environment, and speculate freely on the nature and origin of religion as a human institution. One of the most notable of these

thinkers was Euhemerus of Messene (c 300 BC). He hit upon a novel means of propounding his theory. In a fictitious travel-narrative, he described how he had found an inscription on an island in the Indian Ocean which revealed that the Greek gods had originally been great kings who were subsequently deified. This theory, known as Euhemerism, is not entirely without foundation, although it is not a sound explanation of the origin of the chief gods of ancient Greece. A remarkable instance of its truth is the deification of Imhotep; but it is unlikely that Euhemerus knew of this instance.

The religious syncretism of the Graeco-Roman world also prompted a comparison of deities. Already in the 5th century BC, the historian Herodotus had identified certain Egyptian and Greek deities; but the most notable example of this practice occurs in the beautiful description of the Egyptian goddess Isis by the Latin poet Apuleius (2nd century AD) in his famous romance *The Golden Ass*. Isis reveals herself as the Great Goddess, who is worshipped by many peoples under various names (Minerva, Venus, Ceres and many more) but under her true name of Isis by the Egyptians.

The famous saying of the Latin poet and philosopher Lucretius (1st century BC) epitomizes his evaluation of religion: *tantum religio potuit suadere malorum*, 'so great is the power of religion for evil'. According to Lucretius, religion arose out of the exploitation of man's fear of death and the unknown by unscrupulous priests and seers; and he laboured to free his fellow-men from this evil by arguing that death is personal extinction, beyond which there is nothing more to fear.

The great variety of religions that competed for allegiance in the Graeco-Roman world, and their tendency to mingle with each other, led other thinkers to find less sceptical explanations of religion's origin. For example, Maximus of Tyre (c 125–

185 AD) argued that since God, the Creator and Sustainer of the universe, is both ineffable and invisible, men have been obliged to worship him under whatever form has seemed intelligible to them: hence the Egyptians worshipped animals and the Greeks conceived of God in human form. Sallust (c 363 AD) rationalized many myths; for example, he explained that of Cybele and Attis in terms of her being a life-giving goddess and Attis the creator of 'things that come into being and perish'.

Such attempts to explain the origin of the complex mythology of Greek religion ceased with the triumph of Christianity and the defeat of paganism. And since Christianity dominated the medieval society that followed the break-up of the ancient world, the origin of religion was no more a subject for speculation. For Christianity saw itself as the only true religion, and its origins were divinely revealed in the Bible. So far as the 'false religions' were concerned, it was enough to condemn Judaism as the miserable remnant of a faith that had failed to understand God's purpose, to account for Greek and Roman paganism as the invention of the Devil, and to denounce Islam as a damnable heresy. There were some attempts by individual Christians to study Islam for missionary and disputative purposes, a notable example being Raymond Lull; the medieval Crusades, however, represented the typical Christian reaction to the religion of Mohammed. Of the great religions further east, medieval Christians had scarcely any knowledge, owing to their geographical isolation – it is significant of the degree of their ignorance that the story of the Buddha filtered through in such a garbled form that the founder of Buddhism was believed to be two godly persons, Barlaam and Joasaph, who were duly canonized as saints in the Eastern Church and were venerated as such.

The re-awakening of interest in the other religions of mankind had to await the humanism of the Renaissance and the development of maritime exploration. Thus the new passion for classical antiquity in the 15th and 16th centuries caused statues of pagan gods to be highly prized, and the Renaissance artists began to depict the gods of Greece and Rome in splendid human form instead of as demons, as did the artists of medieval Christendom. Through trade and missionary enterprise contact was gradually established with the great and ancient civilizations of India and China, and many European scholars came to admire the cultural achievements of these eastern peoples. Trade and colonization also made Europeans acquainted with the cultures of the primitive peoples of Africa, Australasia and the Americas.

Already by the 17th century the stimulus of all this new knowledge about other religions was bearing fruit. In 1724 a Jesuit scholar, Joseph Lafitau, who had served as a missionary in Canada, published a book entitled *Moeurs des sauvages amériquains comparées aux moeurs des premiers temps*. The work constitutes a veritable landmark in the study of religion; for in it Lafitau noted similarities in the religion of the American savages, the ancient cults of Bacchus, Cybele and Isis and Osiris, and Catholic Christianity. These similarities seemed to him to point back to a common origin, to a single original revelation.

The 18th century saw other notable studies in comparative religion. In 1760 Charles De Brosses, in a work entitled *Du culte des dieux fétiches, ou parallèle de l'ancienne religion de l'Egypte avec la religion actuelle de Nigrite*, sought to explain the animal-headed gods of Egypt in the light of the religious practices of contemporary savages. Even more revolutionary perhaps was the attempt of Charles-François Dupuis, in 1795, in his *Origine de tous les cultes*, to discern behind the figures of Christ and Osiris, of Bacchus and Mithras, a common tendency to personify the sun in its annual course through the heavens.

These attempts to rationalize the complex phenomena of the religious ideas and practices of mankind prepared the way for the more scientific approach of later times. The commercial and political domination, which the leading European nations had gradually built up in Asia and Africa, was also producing a rich academic harvest. Art treasures and manuscripts brought home from the East provided the material for scholarly research, encouraging especially the study of oriental languages. Notable pioneers in this field were Anquetil-Duperron, who in 1771 produced the first translation of the *Zend-Avesta* into a Western language and thus provided the key to the study of Zoroastrianism, and Sir William Jones (1746–94), whose Sanskrit studies opened the way to the sacred literature of India. Early in the 19th century the decipherment of the long-forgotten languages of Egypt and Mesopotamia was gradually achieved, so making possible for scholars the interpretation of the earliest religious texts of mankind.

This linguistic preparation for the scientific study of religion was accompanied by the accumulation of an increasing mass of data about the beliefs and ritual practices of the so-called primitive peoples of Asia, Australia, Africa and the New World. Much of this information was first acquired incidentally by Christian missionaries who sought to convert the peoples concerned; but gradually special investigation was undertaken as the sciences of ethnology and anthropology were established and developed.

The comparative study of religion in the 19th and early 20th centuries was characterized by the rise and decline of various 'schools' of thought, which sought to explain the origin and essential nature of religion according to some preconceived principle of interpretation. This phase in the development of the discipline was doubtless inevitable, because theological interest in the subject was then predominant. Thus Friedrich Max Müller (1823–1900), who may justly be regarded as the pioneer of the scientific study of religion, attempted to explain the origin of religious myths through comparative philology. He argued that language-analysis will often provide the key to the origin of a deity. The following example shows his method: the Sanskrit word *dyaus*, which originally meant 'bright', came to denote the (bright) sky. Since thunder was heard from the sky, the Aryans, who spoke Sanskrit, would say the *dyaus* (the sky) thunders. This usage led to the personification of *dyaus* as the Power manifest in the sky, and so on to the concept of a sky god Dyaus, who announced his presence by thundering. Max Müller traced religion itself back ultimately to 'an ineradicable feeling of dependence' upon some higher power that was innate in the human mind. Its expression in mythology

was essentially due to an inherent 'disease of language', in the manner described. Müller did much invaluable work for comparative religion, particularly in editing the *Sacred Books of the East*, a series of translations which made the literature of Hinduism, Jainism, Buddhism, Zoroastrianism and Confucianism available to English-speaking students.

Anthropology soon concerned itself with the question of the origin of religion. For there was a tendency with the early anthropologists to assume that the beliefs and ritual practices of the so-called primitive peoples represented the earliest forms of religion. Out of this new science came one of the most notable theories of the origin of religion, 'animism' as propounded by Sir Edward Tylor.

The other great exponent of the anthropological approach to the study of religion at this early stage of its development was Sir James George Frazer. In *The Golden Bough* he defined religion as being 'a propitiation or conciliation of powers superior to man which are believed to direct and control the course of nature and of human life'. But he maintained that religion emerged after magic. At the earliest stage of human culture, according to Frazer, 'man essayed to bend nature to his wishes by the sheer force of spells and enchantments'. When experience taught him that magic did not work, man resorted to prayer and

The temples of ancient religions reflect the beliefs of the people who worshipped in them *Above* Roman temple at Dougga in North Africa *Opposite* To the Egyptians a temple represented heaven, and rites performed inside it were believed to ensure security for the land and its people; worshippers moved gradually from the strong sunlight of the secular world through the deepening darkness of great halls into the intense blackness that shrouded the shrine that contained the god's image: one of the pylons at the entrance to the temple of Amun at Karnak *Left* The Acropolis in Athens, dominated by the Parthenon. This temple is a supreme example of the architectural perfection with which the Greeks honoured their gods; the cult image usually dominated the interior of each temple

sacrifice to 'mollify a coy, capricious, or irascible deity'. Frazer also showed how agriculture had profoundly influenced man's religious ideas and practices. It inspired the two basic concepts of the fertility goddess and the vegetation spirit, who annually dies and rises to life again.

The early years of the 20th century saw a great proliferation of theories about the origin of religion. The dominance of anthropology led to emphasis being placed upon the communal aspect of primitive society and a diminution of the importance of the individual within it. Hence the origin of religion was sought in communal consciousness. The distinguished French sociologist Emil Durkheim interpreted totemism as a factor of basic import for understanding the social origins of religion. In the totem deity he saw the personification of the clan itself in the form of an animal or vegetable. Unconscious of themselves as individuals, its members were inspired with a sense of their integration with this deity during their worship and service of it.

The emergent science of psychology also contributed to the speculation about the beginnings of religion. Sigmund Freud (1856–1939) found the origin of religion, or its primordial form, in 'an infantile obsessional neurosis' which centred on the primal father-figure. He conceived of human society as originally comprising a 'primitive horde', ruled over and con-

13

A. F. Kersting

Michael Holford

trolled by a father who kept all the females for himself and repelled his growing sons. The sons, who both hated and admired their father, finally united in killing and eating him, to absorb his strength and virility. Then, stricken with a sense of guilt, they invented rites of expiation, which involved totemism, taboo and all the other institutions of primitive society. This presentation of the Oedipus complex as the source or cause of religion had the support of no archeological or anthropological evidence, but it excited much interest and won great publicity.

Freud's distinguished successor C. G. Jung (1875–1961) greatly concerned himself with the psychological interpretation of religion, although he was more interested in its basic forms than its origin. The latter he traced to 'a peculiar attitude' of the human mind to its experience of environmental factors that are variously powerful, dangerous or helpful. He sought in myths, as evidence of the collective unconscious, for 'archetypes' or primordial images that have exercised a formative influence upon human thought and behaviour. Jung's influence in the field of religious studies is still immense.

From the fact, noticed by Andrew Lang (1844–1912), that many 'primitive' peoples believed in a supreme Creator god, designated as a 'High God' or 'All-Father', Wilhelm Schmidt (1868–1954) deduced that the earliest form of religion was monotheism. This belief resulted from early man's rationalization of his experience of the natural world. Schmidt set out this thesis in a 12-volume work entitled *Der Ursprung der Gottesidee* (1926–55; there is an English epitome, *Origin and Growth of Religion*, 1931). He maintained further that polytheism was a degenerate form of the primeval monotheism. Schmidt's interpretation was congenial to Christian theology; but it is not borne out by the evidence of Paleolithic archeology.

Another interpretation of the origin of religion which has much commended itself to theologians is that presented by Rudolf Otto (1869–1937) in his book *Das Heilige* (1917), which was translated into English as *The Idea of the Holy* (1923). Otto was particularly concerned to show that religion did not originate from early man's rationalizing of his experience of his natural environment, as earlier scholars had assumed. Instead, according to Otto, man is endowed with the ability to sense the 'numinous'. This term was derived from the Latin word *numen*, which meant a supernatural non-personalized entity. It constituted something that was in essence 'wholly other' from all normal objects of human experience. The presence of the numinous was sensed under two different forms of manifestation, the *mysterium tremendum* and the *mysterium fascinans*. The former induced the feeling of terror associated with the eerie and uncanny, and was essentially 'awe-ful'. As the *mysterium fascinans*, the numinous exercised a strangely compelling force, drawing those who experienced it on to a closer communion. Otto sought to show that the idea of 'the holy' stemmed from such experience. For that which was associated with the presence of the numinous had to be treated with circumspection; it became 'holy', and contact with it was carefully controlled by taboos. Otto accounted for the various forms of primitive religion, such as a belief in a multitude of spirits, totemism and the cult of the dead, as due to man's subsequent rationalization of his numinous experience.

Otto was certainly justified in emphasizing

the importance of non-rational emotive factors in religious faith and practice; but his thesis rests upon assumptions about the experience of primitive man for which no possible means of verification exist. It is, moreover, difficult to conceive of human experience divorced from ratiocination.

Great insight into the fundamental springs of religion was shown by the philosopher A. N. Whitehead (1861–1947). In contradistinction to those who sought to find the origin of religion in the corporate consciousness of a community, Whitehead stressed the essentiality of personal experience. He wrote: 'Religion is what the individual does with his own solitariness' (in *Religion in the Making*, 1927) and he saw it as a 'transaction from God the void to God the enemy, and from God the enemy to God the companion'. He distinguished four basic aspects or factors of religion: ritual, emotion, belief, rationalization, and he evaluated them as four successive stages in the evolution of religion.

In 1935 a series of essays entitled *Myth*

and Ritual, edited by S. H. Hooke, initiated a new line of interpretation for the religions of the ancient Near East. A theory has been suggested (in *History, Time and Diety*, 1965) that religion stems from the time-consciousness of man.

Such variety of interpretation can be perplexing for newcomers to comparative religion; but the histories of other subjects are equally strewn with the debris of rejected or outmoded theories, and conflict of opinion is generally evidence of vigorous critical thinking that makes for progress. Comparative religion, however, has also been subjected in the past to the pressure of non-scientific interests. Since religion concerns the fundamental issues of human life, many people have sought in its comparative study for the revelation of some desired truth. Such interests are understandable, and they are still felt; but they must not be allowed to obscure the fact that comparative religion is essentially a discipline concerned only with the scientific investigation of the religions of mankind.

Speculation about the springs of religion long preceded the acquisition of archeological data concerning the earliest forms of human culture. Indeed, it has only been in the more recent decades of the present century that the study of prehistory has become established as a scientific discipline. We are better situated today for knowing something of the earliest forms of religion than were

previous generations though we cannot, of course, penetrate back to the actual origin of religion, which could scarcely be documented by archeological data. But we can form some idea of the religious beliefs and practices already existent at the dawn of human culture, c 30,000 BC. Our knowledge can, inevitably, be only of an inferential kind from archeological material, since no written records then existed, or would exist until some 27 millennia had passed.

The fact that the Old Stone Age peoples not only buried their dead, but placed food and equipment of various kinds in the graves indicates that they envisaged some form of life after death. In other words, these burial customs show that, in contrast to all other animals, man was already concerned about death. This means that he was able to abstract himself from the business of living and ponder on the phenomena of its cessation. It means also that he did not accept the physical evidence of death as attesting the definitive end of a human person. For in some crude way he thought that the dead still needed the necessities of life, and that it was the duty of the living to provide them. A certain variety of burial customs suggests also some variation of ideas about the state of the dead. We can infer that, from the very appearance of man in the archeological record, the cult of the dead was already an established practice. How this practice started we cannot tell;

but it is significant that the so-called Neanderthal Man, a sub-human precursor of true man, also buried his dead ritually.

On many Paleolithic sites carved figurines of women have been found. They exhibit two notable characteristics: the maternal features are grossly exaggerated while the faces are left blank. A clue to the significance of these figurines is provided by a similar, but larger, figure in bas-relief which was found as the central object of a Paleolithic rock-sanctuary at Laussel in the Dordogne area of France. Generally known as the 'Venus of Laussel', this figure has the same features as the figurines but holds a bison's horn in its right hand.

The emphasis upon the maternal attributes and the blank faces of these figures suggest that they were not intended to be portraits of individual women, but attempts to portray 'woman' as the source of life. Such an intention is intelligible, since the phenomenon of birth provided primitive man with visual evidence of the emergence of new life from the maternal womb. The importance of the production of new living beings to these Paleolithic peoples needs no stressing. And it is easy to understand their awe and respect for the mystery of maternity. There is reason for thinking that a figure such as the Venus of Laussel is an anticipation or prototype of the Great Mother Goddess of the later religions of the ancient world, which we shall consider presently.

A. F. Kersting

Prehistoric Religion

What prehistoric men thought can never be known with certainty, because they did not write it down. The bits and pieces they left behind them – bones, tools, weapons, works of art and the rest – can be interpreted in many ways and are the fragmentary records of different groups of men in different circumstances over a period far longer than recorded history.

However, some deductions can perhaps be drawn from the burial practices and tools of the man-like creatures who preceded true man on the earth. Neanderthal men buried their dead with care, with food and equipment and often, it seems, with affection. This suggests belief in an afterworld of some kind, in which the dead were not entirely

cut off from the living. It also implies the presence of one factor which distinguishes man from other animals, the knowledge of his own inevitable death, which in turn implies a sense of time.

The deliberate manufacture of tools also implies a sense of time, because it means planning for the future. A sense of time implies a feeling for order, for events following one another in succession, which may have carried with it the concept of a rough general pattern behind human existence. We are born, we live for a while and we die. The same is obviously true of the animals. The realization of order and the observation that 'all flesh is grass' may have pointed to the conclusion that whoever or

whatever is responsible for the order of Nature is not human or animal but something superhuman and superanimal, though it (or they) may be given many human and animal characteristics.

Evidence of some sort of religio-magical cult, dating from c 100,000 BC, has been found in caves in the Alps where the skulls of bears had been placed on stone slabs in what looks like a ceremonious arrangement. It may be that a creature's head was already thought to contain the essence of its being, and the rituals of later bear-hunting peoples suggest that the intention was to appease some supernatural power for the killing of a bear, to make sure that there would be no decline in the supply of bears for hunting. Whether or not this is the right explanation, the finds indicate that certain places were being treated as special, set apart, holy. Later, there is plenty of evidence for the use of caves as sacred places.

People whose control over their environment is limited are naturally likely to try to establish good relations with their own ancestors, from whom they have inherited such techniques as they possess, and with whatever powers control the order of Nature which provides food and children, or which sometimes disastrously fails to provide them. In the Upper Paleolithic period (c 30,000 to 10,000 BC), after the arrival on the scene of *homo sapiens* himself, burials became more elaborate and ceremonious, and there is strong evidence of concern for fertility in the 'Venuses', small figures of women, some highly stylized and others comparatively realistic, with the breasts, thighs and buttocks grotesquely emphasized. The swollen pregnant bellies of many of these figures and their blank, featureless heads suggest that they were not meant to portray women but 'woman' in general, and woman in her role of mother. They may have been worn by women as amulets to ensure fruitfulness and they may have represented a Great Mother, the source of all life.

The Upper Paleolithic is also the period of the magnificent cave art which may have been meant to promote fertility in human beings and animals, as well as to assist early man in his hunting. The art indicates belief in a supernatural order of reality which man must try to influence if he and his quarry are to eat, live and beget. It also implies a magical attitude to symbolism and mimicry, that the real can be influenced through the simulated.

Scenes in some of the caves show human figures dressed in animal skins and masks, and dancing. There is an example in the cave of the Trois Frères in France, where a man disguised as a bison is dancing and apparently playing a musical instrument. Ahead of him are two peculiar animals, a reindeer with what look like human arms, and a creature part-bison and part-reindeer which is looking back at him. Professor Maringer asks, 'What else can this odd scene be but a magic performance, wherein sorcerer and "animals" alike are human hunters in disguise? And what was the disguise for if not to compel animals to bow to the hunters' will?'

An alternative possibility is that the dancing figure in a bison's skin is a deity, a Lord of Beasts, and that the other two creatures mingle parts of different animals because they stand for 'beasts' in general, the whole world of animal life which the god controls. The Trois Frères cave is also the home of the famous Dancing Sorcerer, who again can be interpreted as perhaps a magician, perhaps a god, or perhaps both – a man acting the part of a god.

Neanderthal man did not wear ornaments, so far as is known, but the later Paleolithic peoples did. They made necklaces of animals' teeth or cowrie shells, for instance, and carved bracelets from mammoths' tusks. It seems likely that ornaments contained an ingredient of magic, as they have tended to do ever since. The teeth may

Opposite **That spirits inhabit all aspects of Nature, that every tree or hill or stream has a soul, is one of the oldest human beliefs: Indian tree spirit c 2nd century BC** *Below* **The care with which prehistoric man buried his dead implies a belief in some kind of afterworld in which those who had died were not entirely cut off from the living: burial cave at Tellem Mali in the Sudan (*left*) and (*right*) chamber tomb in County Meath, Eire, c 2000 BC; a linear pattern is carved on the lintel**

have carried with them the qualities of the animals from which they came, and the cowrie shell has long been an emblem of woman and fertility because of its shape. The same principle may have applied to weapons. For example, the figure of a jumping horse was carved on the end of a spear-thrower found at Bruniquel in France, presumably to give it the propelling energy of the horse's leap.

The 'Neolithic revolution', as it is called, the gradual development of cultivating crops and breeding animals, instead of gathering and hunting, originated in Asia in the ninth millennium BC, or earlier, and had spread to most of Europe by c 3500 BC. The picture now becomes, if anything, even more obscure than before and the course of the transition from what is known of the Paleolithic to the religions of societies with written records is not at all clear.

It seems evident that as agriculture and stockbreeding are gradually established, the plants on which men and herds depend for food become crucially important. The annual cycle of Nature becomes a dominating factor in men's lives and a focus of religious and magical attention. Seedtime and harvest are the two great occasions of the year, and are likely to be celebrated with festivals and rites intended to ensure a good crop.

The sky also becomes important, because sun, rain and wind affect the growth of crops and because the calendar, which suc-

cessful agriculture demands, is worked out by reference to events occurring in the sky. (Reverence for the sky and its forces may easily have existed long before, though there is no evidence of sky worship in the Paleolithic). Later on, we know that there were ideas of Sky Father copulating with Earth Mother, and of rain penetrating her, so that she would bring forth harvests for men and pasturage for beasts. These ideas must have begun to develop earlier, but how, where and when is uncertain.

Paradoxically, the Neolithic advance in control of the environment may have created a greater sense of dependence on supernatural powers than before, because the farmer's attitude is likely to be more passive than the hunter's. He relies more on the slow workings of forces which are still largely beyond his control, and less on his own resources of courage, quickness and skill, as in the chase. Hunting's perspectives are relatively short-term and farming's are relatively long. The sense of an order behind Nature, of man's dependence on it, and of the perils of disorder in the shape of drought, famine, destructive storms, pestilence, may have been strengthened by the longer perspective of farming communities.

Most Neolithic societies buried their dead with greater pomp and circumstance than before, especially those who had been powerful in life, and sometimes with extravagant toil, as in megalithic burials in Europe,

C. M. Dixon

implying a deep respect for the powers of the dead and probably the belief that they influenced the growth of crops from the earth in which they lay buried. Representations of the mother goddess are often found in burying places and she seems clearly connected with the earth.

As Earth Mother, the goddess would need to be impregnated, so that she would conceive and bear her annual yield. In some societies the masculine principle in fertility is represented by carved phalluses, and in some, apparently, by animals, especially the bull. At Catal Hüyük in Turkey, for instance, the shrine of a mother goddess, dating from c 6000 BC, was adorned with representations of bulls' heads, human heads and the breasts of women, and with human skulls. Farming communities in the Danube area made female figurines and effigies of bulls and other male animals. Later, the ancient world knew many great bull gods, respon-

sible for the fertility of fields as well as herds and frequently connected with sky.

Another pattern, presumably already developing in the Neolithic, was the tendency to personify the life of vegetation as a god who was both the son and the lover of the Great Mother and who died and rose again each year, as the plants did. This concept sprouted a rich harvest of mythology and ritual in the ancient world.

As men began to master new techniques, inventions and discoveries were fitted into a religio-magical context. The discovery of yeast, for example, made it possible to bake bread and brew beer, both commodities which had a long history of symbolic connections with the gods and the otherworld. The rise of metallurgy with the development of working in copper, bronze and iron gave the smith the uncanny powers of one who was as much magician as craftsman. Writing was regarded as an invention of the gods and the preserve of priests. Improved control of the environment was still disrupted by what we call accidents, which less sophisticated people put down to supernatural interference. Greek potters in historical times, for instance, still fixed hideous masks on their kilns in order to frighten away the demon who liked to crack the pots while they were being fired.

In the East the development of towns, states and armies, of male dynasties and priesthoods, tended to diminish the Great

Mother's status in favour of the great male gods of the sky who loom large in the civilizations of the ancient world, the gods who created the universe, who made man, who established order and put down disorder. In Europe the invasions and conquests of warrior peoples, whose deities were gods of the sky, had the same effect.

All these developments occurred over long stretches of time and their details are concealed from us, but there was evidently considerable continuity. The prehistoric Earth Mother, in her various local incarnations, was the ancestress of goddesses of historical societies. A striking example of continuity from prehistoric to historic was found at Eridu in Mesopotamia, which in the ancient world was the home of the great god Enki, lord of waters.

Above Skull, c 6000 BC, from Jericho: the facial features were modelled in plaster, possibly as an indication that the individual retained his personality after death **Opposite** To the Asaro tribe of New Guinea earth is a symbol of success in battle: they therefore cover themselves in mud for victory **Below left** Ruins of Mohenjo-daro and (**below right**) of Harappa: the chief cities of the Indus valley were established in about 2000 BC by an agricultural people who worshipped fertility gods; rituals to ensure fruitfulness, one of prehistoric man's basic concerns, were among the earliest religious ceremonies

J. Allen Cash

William Macquitty

The Mother Goddess

Not very long ago the suggestion was made that a certain bestseller in the field of religious literature would be a book entitled 'God is a Woman'.

The history of religion reveals a panorama of gods and goddesses, higher and lower spiritual beings, among whom personifications of the earth occupy a prominent place. As a rule these personifications bear all the attributes of female sexuality and motherhood. Sometimes they are paradoxically believed to be virginal. Often, still more paradoxically, they combine within themselves attributes of generosity and grace and also those of horror and destruction. If human love is one of their areas of influence, the senseless urge which leads men into war is another.

Their icons and images may be of the order of the Venus de Milo, an idealized form of female beauty; or, equally, they may suggest a mind diseased — skinny, skull-festooned hags, their fangs dripping with the blood of generations of men. Clearly the mother goddess of human history is no romantic figure, but rather one in which opposites combine, in which the giver of life is clearly seen as the being who also takes it away, and in which promises are hollow and temporary, and hope a mockery.

The tension and paradox appear to have been almost universal. From Scandinavia to Melanesia, goddesses in which precisely these characteristics predominate have been worshipped, feared and propitiated. This universality has led some scholars to suggest that what we are in fact seeing is the reflection of a human psychological trait which is always and everywhere the same, though clothed in slightly different images and symbols. This psychological interpretation is not without its risks, however. The Paleolithic 'Venuses' for instance cannot simply be equated with medieval figures of the Virgin Mary. The figure of the mother goddess in India is not the same as the Great Mother of the Mediterranean world, however much they may appear to have in common. The hypotheses of Freud and Jung must not be made to carry more weight than they can bear. As well as similarities, there are significant differences.

Among man's earliest artefacts, dating from the late Paleolithic period, are coarse and crude figurines of pregnant women, their breasts and hips grotesquely enlarged. These, it has been supposed, represent in human form that concern with human reproduction that was a pattern of man's condition of survival on the face of the earth. It is not known whether these in any sense represent what one might regard as mother goddesses.

It is interesting, though, that these figurines are seldom more than approximately human. Apart from their lack of proportion, their faces and other personal characteristics are hardly even hinted at. This same characteristic is found in female figurines from Bronze Age peasant cultures and many of the earliest urban cultures, for instance those of north-west India. Excavations made on Indus Valley sites have revealed many such artefacts, often smoke-stained in such a way as to suggest some form of household worship. If this is a continuous line of development, it would seem to suggest something more than merely 'good-luck charms' or magical amulets. The pattern is consistent, at all events: a female figure with rudimentary features, but with prominent breasts and hips, often dressed in a girdle and necklaces, and wearing a head-dress.

Even today the visitor to an Indian village may be surprised to find that the temples of the great gods, Shiva and Vishnu, are regarded by the people as being of less importance than the little shrine of the local goddess, or Grami Devi. She may have many names, most of which are not found in the standard textbooks on Hinduism. But she is 'of the earth', and directly responsible for the fertility of the fields surrounding the village. She may be linked mythologically with the consorts of the great gods, Parvati, a consort of Shiva, Kali his wife, or Lakshmi who was Vishnu's wife, but to all intents and purposes she is the guardian of the village and the one to whom the people turn for everyday purposes. She has her festivals and her particular responsibilities, and it is probable that her nature and function have not changed for more than 5000 years.

However, the most authoritative evidence concerning the worship of mother goddesses comes from the Mediterranean area, from Iran in the east to Rome in the west, and covering Mesopotamia, Egypt and Greece. Indeed, in this area, the names and functions of the great goddesses were so inter-changeable as to make comparative study a highly complex undertaking. The primary identification of the goddess with the fruitful earth is unquestionable, but starting from Mesopotamia there is an involved pattern, in which celestial elements combine with those of the underworld in such a way as to suggest that the Great Mother may be a composite figure, as complex as the human mind.

The Semitic names for the greatest mother goddess were Inanna in Sumeria, Ishtar in Babylon and Astarte or Anat among the Canaanites. Commonly identified with the planet Venus, her most typical title is 'queen of heaven', though she is also known as 'mistress of all the gods' and 'the lady of the world'. In time, she gathered to herself the attributes of a host of other goddesses, so that in Mesopotamia the word *ishtar* came to mean simply 'goddess'.

She was believed to be the giver of vegetation; a hymn contains the words:

'In the heavens I take my place and send rain, in the earth I take my place and cause the green to spring forth.' She was the creator of animals, and the goddess of sexual love, marriage and maternity. In another hymn it was said: 'I turn the male to the female, I turn the female to the male; I am she who adorneth the male for the female, I am she who adorneth the female for the male.' Her worship was frequently connected with the practice of sacred prostitution.

Two other characteristics of the Semitic mother goddess are worth mentioning in this context. The first concerned her connection with a male figure who could be described as son, brother or husband. The best known of these figures was Tammuz (Sumerian Dumu-zi), a god of vegetation and in particular of the growing corn. Every year a festival was held at which his 'death' and 'resurrection' was celebrated. The vegetation god was believed to die and rise again annually, and in the myths of the descent of the mother goddess into the land of the dead there is a dramatic image of the search of the mother for her lost son and lover, the search of the earth for the temporarily lost fertility which the new spring restores. A Sumerian version of this myth, *Inanna's Descent to the Nether World,* is one of the earliest examples.

Inanna descends, perhaps in order to free Dumu-zi; she approaches the subter-ranean temple of Ereshkigal, god of the dead, through seven gates, at each one of

which she has to remove part of her clothing, until she finally stands before him naked. An interesting feature of this myth is that on her return, she brings with her all manner of evil and malevolent beings: 'They who preceded her, they who preceded Inanna, were beings who knew not food, who knew not water, who eat not sprinkled flour, who drink not libated wine, who take away the wife from the loins of man, who take away the child from the breast of the nursing mother.' Similar myths were current all over the Semitic world, for instance in Canaan, where the mother goddess Anat attacks and conquers Mot (death) in order to free the fertility god Baal.

The cult of the mother goddess moved

Opposite Known by many names, the mother goddess in India is a deity of many aspects, some of which are beneficent and others terrible. Worshipped as Parvati, the consort of Shiva and daughter of the Himalayas, as Sati 'the good wife', and as Bhairavi 'the terrible', she is also Ambika, the source of all life: statue of Ambika, 11th century AD *Below* Crude figurines of women with prominent breasts and grotesquely enlarged hips are among man's earliest artefacts and have been found all over the world; it is possible that these represent the fertility that is essential if man is to survive: model of a temple, found in Malta, for the worship of a fertility goddess: the ground plan resembles a huge fat woman that is similar to the artefacts in their distortion of the essential features

Above Gaia who, in Greek mythology, created the sky, mountains and sea: terracotta statuette from Tanagra, Greece. Similar figurines seem to have been connected with the great mother goddess, the mother of all living, who also ruled the dead *Right* Coatlicue, the great earth mother of the Aztecs

westward, perhaps through Cyprus and Crete, into Anatolia and Greece. Significantly, the most popular image of Venus, the Greek Aphrodite, depicts her emerging from the sea on the coast of Cyprus, while her consort, Adonis, is a Semitic figure, with a Semitic name. In her purely Greek form, as Aphrodite, the goddess's cult was fairly decorous, but on the borders of the Greek world, in Corinth, sacred prostitution was practised.

However, on entering the Greek culture, the cult of the mother goddess encountered another similar cult deriving from the Indo-European culture. In Iran, Anahita the goddess who 'purifies the seed of males and the womb and milk of females', described in sculptural terms as 'a beautiful maiden, powerful and tall', was worshipped. Her cult spread through the Persian Empire, and she gradually coalesced in various ways with Athene, Aphrodite, and the Anatolian Cybele. It was Cybele who eventually came to be honoured in the Roman Empire as the Great Mother of the gods, a temple being erected to her honour on the Palatine Hill in Rome in 204 BC.

The cult of Cybele remained, even after its adoption in Rome by the Romans, the responsibility of native Phrygians, who wore their hair long, dressed in female clothes, and celebrated the goddess in wild orgiastic dances to the point of exhaustion. It is believed their consecration to the goddess sometimes involved self-emasculation.

Although this type of worship was not unknown in Greece, particularly in connection with Dionysus, worship of the mother goddess took more decorous forms.

Another popular form of the worship of the mother goddess in the Roman Empire was that of the Egyptian goddess Isis. Originally the wife of Osiris, identified with the dead pharaoh, she was the mother of Horus, the living pharaoh, who gave birth to her son after having conceived magically on the body of her dead husband. One common representation of Isis is as a mother suckling the infant Horus, thought by some to be a prototype of later Christian images of mother and child.

Indeed, the queen of heaven, the universal mother, was known by many names in the ancient world. For example there is Artemis or Diana, the huntress and mistress of animals: in Acts, chapter 19, there is recorded a celebrated encounter between Paul and devotees of 'Artemis of the Ephesians', a local, many-breasted form of what may have originally been a moon goddess. There was the Anatolian goddess Ma, whose priests were known as *fanatici* (servants of the *fanum* or temple) and from whose wild excesses comes the word 'fanatic'. Farther north, there were Celtic and Teutonic tribal goddesses.

In Northern Europe, the goddess Freya was said to have had sexual relations with all the male members of the pantheon, and as goddess of the dead shared with Odin the custody of warriors slain on the field of battle. This is the same kind of ambivalence that is to be observed in most mother goddesses; because the earth receives the dead in corruption and also gives birth and sustenance to crops, men and animals, the connection between the mother goddess and the kingdom of the dead is common. In Greece, for instance, the dead were sometimes called 'Demeter's people'.

The coming of Christianity to the Mediterranean countries and Europe had the effect, on one level, of devaluing the indigenous cults by demoting the ancient deities to the rank of demons. In the case of the Great Mother, however, popular belief reasserted itself by transferring many of her attributes to the Virgin Mary.

In much the same way, local deities often came to be identified with the saints. This interesting development can be paralleled in many parts of the world. Its roots are certainly psychological: the hold of the Great Mother on the mind of an agricultural people was too strong to be broken overnight. Legends and attributes came to be attached to the name of Mary, in her role as the Mother of God, which lack all scriptural support, but which clearly correspond to needs in the popular mind.

At Bethlehem for instance there is, or used to be, a cave known locally as the 'milk grotto'. Legend has it that the Holy Family once took refuge in the cave, and that as Mary nursed the infant Jesus, a drop of her milk fell on the floor. Because of this, it was believed that to enter the cave would cure barrenness in women, and increase their milk and even the milk of animals. It seems clear that this particular cave was once the shrine of a local form of mother goddess, and that the legend is merely a Christianization of the site.

It is worth emphasizing that doctrines and dogmas concerning the Virgin Mary have always been formulated as a result of popular religious practices. On the theological level, as long as God and Christ were thought of in terms of the dispensation of justice, both appeared remote and, the nature of man being what it is, frightening. The Virgin, on the other hand, was unquestionably human, although elevated to near-divine rank and crowned Queen of Heaven. Who better to intercede for sinful mankind at the judgement seat? In this, she was in effect doing what the mother goddess, whatever her name, had always done.

Mankind's worship of, and reverence for, the divine figure of the mother, is a religious phenomenon far deeper than creeds, councils and dogmas. It reflects man's profound need for security in a frequently unfriendly world, his own inadequacies and his own fears. In it can be seen the tension between good things and evil, between the gift of life and the fear of death, personified in the goddess who gives and takes away, who creates and destroys, but who is never as aloof and unconcerned as her consort, the sky god. As long as man retains any of his roots in the earth, reverence for the earth — whether personified or not — will remain, and the Great Mother will still have human children.

Opposite The supreme deity of Crete was feminine 'single in essence, but of many forms', one of which was guardian of the royal palace: the prince may have ruled as her consort. 'Prince of the Lilies' detail from a wall-painting at the ruined palace of Cnossus

PRIMITIVE RELIGION

Africa

The continent of Africa contains some 6,000 different tribes. So complex are African languages, races, cultures and religions that anthropologists cannot yet agree about many of the facts that are available to them.

It follows that where there are so many sorts of men, there are many gods, or concepts of God, and many religious sects with their peculiar rites, magical practices and traditional myths. Some idea of the enormous diversity involved can be seen by comparing the Egyptian Copt, a tall, fair-skinned Christian, with the Bushman of southern Africa, a stunted, black-skinned pagan. Both are Africans, and both are typical in their way of African racial types, cultural groups and religious beliefs.

But there are certain basic concepts which underly all African religions; and these concepts, far from being the mumbo-jumbo popularly associated with medicine-men, witch-doctors, black magic, fetishes, ju-jus and the rest of it, are still a powerful spiritual and social force.

To most Africans, God in one of his many manifestations, or called by one of his many names (there are over 200 principal epithets ranging from 'the Everlasting One of the Forest' to 'He who roars so loud that the nations are struck with terror') is an ever-present being; and his priests (medicine-men and witch-doctors) are recognized leaders of the tribal community.

Estimates give the number of non-Christians and non-Moslems in Africa as 157,031,000, or over half of the total population. In earlier times, before the true character of African traditional beliefs was

Nuba wrestlers cover themselves with ashes, partly to reduce slipperiness but also because they believe that the ashes give them extra vigour. The belief that ashes, like fire which created them, carry new life and strength is widespread all over the world

understood, these people were called simply 'heathens'. They were poor benighted savages who 'bowed down to wood and stone'. The more accurate term used today is 'pagans', from the Latin *paganus*, a word which originally meant a peasant or countryman.

The African pagan (like the pagan everywhere for that matter) believes in a polytheistic system in which a chief god presides over lesser deities, rather as a king ruled over his domain in ancient times. Nearly all African cults had their Supreme Being, called by a hundred different names which vary from tribe to tribe. But no matter what the chief god is called, he is invariably conceived of as the Maker of the World, the Master of Human Destiny, an omnipotent and omnipresent 'king of kings' and 'lord of lords'. And under the rule of the Supreme Being are all the lesser godlings, each with his special function.

The question that has puzzled observers since white men first arrived in Africa is whether this Supreme Being, whatever his name, is an abstract idea — a sort of creative energy which animates and pervades the universe, but has no direct relationship with man; or whether this god is a personal being, like the Jehovah of the Hebrews, or the 'Our Father' of the Christians. It is, perhaps, typical of the difficulties inherent in a study of African religion that no native has come forward to clarify the question; and that white men can only make their observations from the outside, with no help at all from written scriptures, texts or recorded ecclesiastical history.

Yet all observers who have managed to make contact with pagan Africans agree that the idea of a Supreme Being, though vague, is universal, even among the most primitive of peoples, like the Bushmen of the Kalahari Desert. It is also clear that the worship of this Supreme Being is, on the whole, a lackadaisical affair. The Creator of the Universe is, after all, bound to be

somewhat indifferent to a mere human and his problems.

On the other hand, the lesser gods — the spirits of the earth and the ghosts of departed heroes — are thought to be much more sympathetic.

They can be flattered, wheedled and even threatened. A not unusual African prayer will go as follows: 'You are useless, you gods! You give us only trouble! You are a bunch of so-and-so's! What do we get from you? Nothing!'

It is evident that this 'personalized' relationship with the deity is not confined to African pagans. Christians, in particular Roman Catholics, often approach God through such intermediaries as the Virgin, the Apostles, local saints, martyrs, and others. And in the Moslem religion, Mohammed and his fellow prophets (including Jesus Christ) are the buffers, as it were, between humble man and Almighty God.

The African, surrounded from birth by all the wonders and terrors of nature, logically pays more heed to sun, rain, storms, rivers and animals than we do, as these objects are his immediate friends or enemies. From the dawn of time primitive man discovered objects of reverence and fear all around him. The former had to be thanked; the latter placated. This was the origin of all religious activity and remains the cardinal principle of African paganism. And if we remember that, in the beginning, men noticed that their enemies — crocodiles, snakes, lions and the like — were quiescent once they had caught and devoured their prey, we can begin to understand the origin of human sacrifice. Such sacrifices were common throughout the continent of Africa until quite recently, and nobody knows the extent to which they are still practised today.

Nature worship, then, is perhaps the most significant aspect of African paganism,

John Bulmer/Camera Press

them for favours, or even argue with them. The ghosts themselves are present in some peculiarly personal belonging or frequented place – their hut, or the log they sat on at council meetings, or the tree they rested beneath. The well-known 'stool huts' of the Ghanaian kings are explained in these terms. The stools symbolize the 'soul' or personality of the departed kings and are preserved for many generations. Moreover, whereas our ideas of personal life after death are often comparatively vague, the African has a firm belief in reincarnation, a belief no doubt founded on the physical resemblance of a child to his parents and grandparents. Eventually one of the ancestors returns from the spirit world to enter the body of a newly-born child.

Summarizing the main tenets of African paganism, we can conclude that there is an underlying concept of a Supreme Being who made the world and presides over the destiny of mankind; that this world is full of spirits enshrined in natural phenomena and dead ancestors; and that there is no final 'death', but an active after-life together with an eventual return to earth in a reincarnated body.

Moslems make up the second largest religious group in Africa, estimated at 97,934,000, the majority in North Africa which is almost wholly Mohammedan, especially in view of the predominance of Arab nations in this part of the continent.

The Arabs began their conquest of Africa in the 7th century and had wiped out almost all traces of Christianity within a hundred years. Only the Coptic Church of Egypt and Ethiopia survived – small communities of Christians who were to be cut off from their brethren in the outside world for almost ten centuries.

There is no denying the immense appeal of Islam to the nomadic people who inhabit the lonely wastelands of the Sahara – 3,000,000 square miles of mountain ranges and sand seas. Islam originated in the desert among desert people, and its prophet Mohammed conceived its spiritual and moral code in terms of desert needs. It is an eminently practical religion, well-suited to the actual conditions obtaining in Africa, where polygamy, for instance, is recognized by all unprejudiced observers as a necessary institution. By way of contrast, Christianity, with its emphasis on original sin and sexual inhibitions, is comparatively unsuited to the African temperament and life though of course many continue to embrace it

Once North Africa had been conquered by their armies, Arab traders and merchants began their penetration of regions which even the Carthaginians and Romans had not explored. These traders were primarily after loot in the form of ivory, gold and, above all, slaves. And wherever they went, the Arab traders took with them the new religion, an absolutely uncompromising faith and fervour which left subject peoples no alternative: one was either a believer or an infidel. And this often meant, in prac-

and it is found in a hundred different forms throughout the continent. We are familiar with it in the animal gods of ancient Egypt; and among those gods, the crocodile and serpent were accorded special veneration. They still are in parts of Africa. It is difficult for Western man, with his inbuilt horror of snakes, to understand the African's attitude; yet our obsessions about reptiles are perhaps more illogical and less 'scientific' than primitive man's regard for these lowly creatures. After all, there are more beneficent serpents than maleficent, and we often kill our friends in our ignorance.

The African is more cautious in his approach; and instead of indiscriminately killing all snakes, whether poisonous or not, he tries to placate the 'snake spirit' itself. Python worship, for instance, is characteristic of several West and East African tribes.

Less than a hundred years ago, travellers described the python 'temples' where these snakes were fed, watered, venerated and

even danced to. The python god was given many wives who brought food and water to him and made him comfortable with grass mats and a decorated house. In return, his spirit watched over the tribe and, in the person of the priest, forewarned the community of dangers, accidents and the like. The penalty for killing a python was death by burning, and in 1864 the explorer Sir Richard Burton saw a python-killer burnt alive in his hut, from which he escaped only to be clubbed to death by priests.

Another fundamental fact of African paganism is the firm belief in life after death. No one dies from natural causes in any case. He ceases to live because he has been 'interfered' with – perhaps by human enemies, perhaps by evil spirits. Hence, when he 'passes over', this does not mean that he has gone for good but, to the contrary, he continues to take part in the communal life, now in his spirit form.

Africans, however, do not 'worship' these spirits so much as consult them or ask

tical terms, a choice between life and death.

Millions of pagan Africans all over the continent chose to 'co-operate' with the fierce and well-armed invaders, as they were to 'co-operate' with the Portuguese Christians during the 17th and 18th centuries. At the same time, the Moslem concept of the One God was, as we have seen, not alien to African thinking.

Moreover, Koranic law (as opposed to Christian morality) did not basically conflict with tribal custom. It recognized the institution of slavery, for instance – an institution which was actually an economic necessity in non-industrial, non-mechanized societies. But Islam controlled and to some extent softened the cruel system by introducing laws regulating the treatment of slaves, concubinage, the status of the resulting children, and the rights of slaves as human beings, particularly if they chose to be converts to the true religion and thus embrace Islam.

The bulk of the Negro population who suffered from the cruelty of kings and chieftains must have welcomed the new laws. Before the arrival of the Arabs, the best that a Negro captured by a rival tribe could expect was a lifetime of intolerable serfdom or, if he was a young man, castration. The more likely fate was to have a leg chopped off and to be left to die. A number of European travellers in central Africa scarcely a hundred years ago give eyewitness accounts of this treatment of prisoners taken in tribal wars. The Arab traders, with an eye to the Mediterranean markets, considered this practice a waste of manpower; and wherever they converted people to their faith, they introduced a more humane relationship between master and slave.

In addition, the Arabs being themselves a non-industrialized people did not upset the simple economy of Negro life by introducing the machines and paraphernalia of western civilization. But they did bring many needed arts and crafts which enabled the primitive tribes slowly to improve their standard of living.

The results are obvious throughout Moslem Africa. Islam is a living force with strong political overtones. Once converted to the Mohammedan faith, the African can seldom be converted to Christianity, and most missionaries now openly admit that it is a waste of time to try to proselytize in Islamic countries like Morocco, Algeria, Libya and Mauretania. Wherever Islam has had a few centuries to take root, it gives

the impression of being wholly integrated into the spiritual, social and political life of its African converts.

From about 100 AD to 600 AD the Christian Church in Africa was one of the great bulwarks of the faith, a church with millions of adherents, hundreds of bishops, and an imposing list of martyrs and leaders. This powerful organization covered the whole of northern Africa from the mountains of Ethiopia to the shores of the Atlantic. Yet it was wiped out almost overnight (except for the Copts) by the conquest of the Arabs from the 7th century onwards. Christianity was unable to obtain a new foothold on the African continent for the next thousand years.

Today, the Christian Church claims a total of 68,208,509 members, of whom 29,100,000 are Roman Catholics, 17,500,000 belong to the Coptic and Eastern Churches, and 21,608,509 are Protestants. The handbooks that provide these statistics warn that they should be accepted with caution, since it is almost impossible to take an exact census in many parts of Africa.

None the less, the figure of over 68,000,000 adherents is an imposing one, as Christian missionaries have only been at work in Africa since about the end of the 15th century, when the Portuguese began their explorations and conquests of the Dark Continent.

One of the objectives of these conquistadores was, in their own words, 'the exaltation of the Catholic faith', and priests invariably accompanied the armies and navies of the invaders. They had consider-

able success in terms of numbers, for we hear that one Jesuit priest on a short tour through the Congo in 1531 baptized 1,500 Negroes, using a hose for the purpose. A number of native kings were also persuaded to divorce all their hundreds of wives save one, no doubt with disastrous results to the tribal organization.

But unfortunately for the success of the missionaries, the European slave-traders were simultaneously busy exporting millions of Africans overseas to the New World – an estimated 100,000,000 having been shipped out as slaves between 1441, when the trade began with the arrival of the Portuguese, until 1888 when it officially ended. The black men were not unnaturally puzzled by the assurances on the part of the missionaries that they were children of God on the one hand and slaves of white men on the other. The problem was summed up by a Jesuit priest who worked in the Congo from 1881 to 1887. 'The Negro saw, and compared with his rude intelligence, the teaching and the works', he writes. 'They did not coincide. While the Christian missionary proclaimed the lofty dignity of the child of God by grace, the Christian trader merely counted one more "piece" for his gang.'

However, brave and truly Christian men like Livingstone continued with their work, and they have been followed by thousands of evangelists who have penetrated into every corner of Africa within the last hundred years. Today, through churches, chapels, mission schools and hospitals, the African is in daily contact with Christianity in its more practical form.

Opposite **Christian cross-bearer in procession, during the Queen's visit to the Sudan in 1965. There are said to be over 68 million Christians in Africa, though it is impossible to take an exact census in some parts of the continent** *Right* **Typically arid landscape in the Sudan. The African's reliance on Nature for water, food and all the necessities of life is the basis of Nature worship, the most significant aspect of African paganism, found in many different forms all over the continent**

Leni Riefenstahl

Australian aborigines, their bodies painted, as part of a highly secret ritual of purification: from Arnhem Land in northern Australia

Each local group with its own food-gathering country is self-governing. It is an enlarged family, consisting of a man and his brothers and their children and son's children, whose wives come from, and whose sisters marry into, other local groups. In aboriginal thought the living members of such a group belong to their own country, not because they are descended, as we would say, from the migrating band which settled there, but because they were brought there by that band – in spirit form. And there, in a water-place or in some other natural feature associated with the migrating group, they sojourned ever since until they entered their mothers' wombs to be born, or indeed, to be reincarnated. And after death, they return to those same spirit 'homes'.

The pioneers in that period long ago lived, hunted, made implements and performed ceremonies just as their representatives do today. Time, however, has fashioned the pioneers in heroic mould, endowing them with extraordinary powers, so that their actions, especially the exploits of their leaders, provide an explanation of the world as it now is. By striking mountains with ritual staffs or by hurling their boomerangs, the heroes cut gaps through them. In some regions, their whirling boomerangs with hurricane-like effect laid flat a road through thick timber. Striking the ground with a staff, as Moses did at the rock in Horeb, they caused water to rise as in a well. They appeared now as humans, and now as animals or birds. They travelled through the air or under the ground. But above all, by their actions, now copied in ritual, they caused plants and animals, birds and fish to appear, and human beings too. In their journeyings, spirit children were born from the women or emanated from the bodies of the heroes, just as in ritual today, the bird-down and paint flies off the actors' bodies as they vibrate themselves rapidly. Finally, when they died, their spirits went into a water-place, or remained in their dead bodies or their limbs changed into rock or earth, trees or anthills; and there they remained as a 'reservoir' or home of emanating or pre-existing spirits of the generations yet to be born.

What the aborigines believe about their own origin and their birth from generation to generation, they also believe about animals and birds, reptiles and fish, insects and plants, and indeed also about inanimate things such as rain, wind and fire. Many of the heroic figures who gave the land its features, and from whom men and women arose, were in essence both human and animal or plant. This explains why they could appear and behave now as humans, and now in another form. Indeed, it is often difficult to know whether the mythical exploit is being performed by man or animal.

Even today, when an aborigine says he is, for example, wallaby, he means what he says. He and the wallaby species are 'one

Australasia

Australia

The Australian aborigines are a very dark chocolate-brown people, with narrow heads, sloping foreheads, deep-set eyes, broad noses, and black, wavy to curly hair. Archeological and anthropological research suggests that they came originally from the south-eastern Asian archipelago region. Following population increase, some groups moved southwards, crossing the narrow water spaces in the simplest boats. In the course of centuries they reached the Sahul Shelf, which was then a land bridge between Timor, New Guinea and the southern continent. Eventually, some 20–30,000 years ago, one or more groups were on what, after the subsidence of the Sahul Shelf, became the northern shores of Australia.

The basic requirement of each migrating group was permanent drinking water, within range of which its members could obtain food by hunting and gathering what nature provided, for the aborigines were neither gardeners nor herdsmen. When the numbers of a group so increased that they could not obtain sufficient food within their accustomed range in bad as well as good seasons, some of them hived off to live around another water-place. This hiving-off process was repeated until all Australia was occupied. In the course of time, separation resulted in variations in language and customs. Neighbouring groups, however, who kept in close touch with one another, retaining a common language, became tribes. They often had a tribal name, but never a central authority such as a council or a chief to give them a focal point.

flesh' and one in the unseen world, for they and their forbears had a common origin. The man-wallaby hero of the 'creative' time, called the Dreamtime or the Dreaming, was by his very nature and actions the source of both a line of human beings and also a line or species of wallabies. Both emanated from him and ever since the human line or clan has been named wallaby, and has been linked with wallabies in ritual and belief. When the hero 'died' his body changed into a stone, a tree or some other object; it became and has remained an inexhaustible centre of life-cells or pre-existing spirits, which go forth to be born in human or wallaby form.

The land is dotted about with spirit centres for human beings and natural species of phenomena, each along the paths followed by the heroes. A woman passing unwittingly near such a centre, and realizing soon after that she has conceived, will be told by her husband that a spirit child from that centre, wallaby, bandicoot, pigeon, plum tree or whatever it is, has entered her body on 'the incarnation road'; or a man 'finds', that is, sees in a vision of the day or night, a spirit child which then follows him to his camp and to his wife.

With regard to natural species and phenomena, the men of each local group, who are related in the father-son line, constitute a secret lodge. Their task is to cherish the myths, chants and ritual, the sacred sites and symbols connected with particular Dreamtime heroes, who were, or gave rise to, a particular animal, plant or natural object. After initiation, they are shown the sites and symbols amidst much solemnity, and taught the ritual. Thereafter, at the prescribed time of the year they must anoint the sacred relics with blood or red ochre and fat, and perform the prescribed ritual which re-enacts the heroes' travels and exploits. Then the life-cells or 'spirits' of the animal or plant or whatever it is, will go forth and increase the species in its due season. Similar sites and rituals are associated with rain, fire and the heavenly bodies, ensuring water, warmth and light for man.

This system of mythology and ritual is called totemism. A person's totem denotes the particular animal, plant or object to which he stands in a special relationship. Usually, he neither injures, kills nor eats it unless he is in dire distress. Usually, too he must not marry a person of the same totem,

for those of the one totem are like brothers and sisters. The totem – the animal or bird or indeed a plant – by behaving in some unexpected way before his waking eyes or in a dream, warns him if danger is near, strengthens him when he is sick, and turns his mind towards absent relations if they are in trouble.

Above all, if a man's totem involves him in ritual duties, his responsibility is great. He is a custodian of the totemic sanctuary and of the ceremonial objects and the ritual connected with it. For him and the members of the totem-lodge, the chanting and acting are the break-through of the creative Dreamtime, and the symbols (outwardly artefacts of wood, stone or other material) are sacramental signs and means of its presence. Thus, in a performance, the chanting goes on and on; the decorated actors appear; but they are no longer the men of a few hours previously. They are now the heroes of the Dreaming. Excitement rises. The chanting becomes louder and louder and the rhythm more vigorously marked, until singers rise up, draw blood from themselves, and dance a prescribed and very energetic backward slide, until at a sign all is over.

In another ritual, while the singers 'chant the journeyings' of the kangaroo ancestors through the desert country, the young men are anointed with human blood; and then when the song has brought the kangaroo clan almost to the end of the journey, the young men silently and quickly form a human pyramid. The climax is near: the dust rises up from the heavy beating of the rhythm sticks on the ground; the chanting is intensified and an actor, the headman Dreaming Kangaroo, springs on to the top of, and over, the pyramid, which represents a great sandhill that the kangaroo totemic band had to cross.

In these and hundreds of similar rituals the dramatic effect is striking. Actors, singers and onlookers alike feel that the life-giving, the creative, the timeless past is present, embracing all. It is the Dreaming, for just as in our dream life, action is not limited by space, time and apparent power, so it was and is in the time-state of the Dreaming: the Eternal-Now.

Only the most obtuse observer would not be affected by the awe with which the men of a secret cult, a totemic lodge, approach the sanctuary of the transformed relics, or of

the symbols of the Dreaming, and silently, carefully and reverentially handling them, break into chant. Then and there we recognize that the aborigines' inner religious experience is deep and vital. We recognize too, that they sense an abiding and life-giving reality through their myths, rituals and symbols. To them these are a heritage treasured through generations of the initiated, and interpreted to each generation by the elders of each cult-lodge.

Many of the sacred chants may seem uninspiring to the outsider, as he reads literal translations. Verse after verse, scores of them recount monotonously and repetitively everyday, ordinary happenings. The heroic ancestor or the totemic party move here, move there, cross a sand-hill or over a plain; they gather food; they see a bird or an animal and perhaps hunt it. They see another 'Dreaming' group and avoid them; they quarrel and they fight; but they also reveal their supernormal powers, especially of moving through the air or under the ground, and of changing into other forms, of men acting as animals, and animals as men. But the very 'everydayness' and repetitiveness of the actions are not boring. It is the singers' and actors' own life writ large, for it was the powerful Dreaming heroes who so lived, and whose power is still present through myth, ritual and symbols.

Very many myths are recorded in this way, or by the aboriginal narrator telling in broken English the story of the heroic past. But how different when the recorder is thoroughly versed in the tribal language and culture! Then the brief verses come to life; their poetic expression is revealed and their grip on the people understood. Such a recorder is the linguist T. G. H. Strehlow, who lived as a child on a Mission among the Aranda of Central Australia, and for the past 30 years and more has been studying the tribe's chants, myths and rituals. Here is one example of his work. A group of honey-ant people left its old home at Ljaba to go on a long journey west to another honey-ant centre.

Coming eventually to a curve in the mountain range, and realizing that Ljaba would therefore be hidden from their view, they looked back and saw the 'pale purple peaks which surround it' but, like a pall of smoke, a haze was enfolding the hills. They were sad because they did not expect to see their

Initiation

The lad had made no sound that I could hear, all through his ordeal, no movement that I could see. He looked almost a sickly green from giddiness and suppressed fear. The old warrior bending over him thrust his dirty fingers into the boy's open mouth, feeling, tugging, jerking at a front tooth.

With his bony fingernails soon stained with blood he forced back the gum from the tooth, jerking and tugging to loosen it a bit. I saw the boy's eyes close tightly as his face screwed up, but he did not murmur. The old fellow then withdrew

from his matted hair a stone punch, a naturally cylindrical stone about five inches long and as thick as a finger. Our workmen use a similar tool, but it is of steel and they do not use it for punching out a tooth. The old man placed the punch end hard against the tooth, then struck it sharply with a stone. At the sharp click there was an instant shouted 'Wah! Ai!' from all hands. Silence, while the old fellow placed his punch on the tooth for the next blow.

I had almost heard the tooth crunch agonizingly

in its socket. The lad kept his eyes tight shut, and now he could not quite control the shivering of his body. But he had made no sound. The old man raised his arm again. 'Click!' echoed by the roar and stamp of feet. The boy shivered violently now, but still he made no sound. Again that click but this time, to a triumphant roar of 'Wah! Ai! Wah! Ai!', the operator held up a bloody tooth.

Ion L. Idriess
Our Living Stone Age

home again. As tears ran down their cheeks, they chanted:

> Enfolded by plains lies Ljaba,
> Beyond the far horizon lies Ljaba.
> Enfolded by plains lies Ljaba,
> Dimmed by the enveloping mists.

They moved on but to this day, when Northern Aranda men perform the honey-ant ritual of Ljaba, 'tears come into their eyes as their low chant trembles on into the hushed pulse of the night':

> Enfolded by plains lies Ljaba,
> Beyond the far horizon lies Ljaba.

Once again they are with the heroes of old; indeed, they *are* the heroes of old, journeying west from their totemic spirit home which is dimmed in their eyes by the enveloping mists.

Through most of the interior of Australia, the mythological heroes, singly, in pairs or in groups, in human or totemic form, journeyed back and forth over vast distances, often criss-crossing each other's tracks. When their courses were finished they sank into the ground or became stones, trees or other objects which have remained as memorials and sources of life.

In Eastern Australia, however, especially along the coast and the great Darling and Murray river system, the leader and culture giver of old, often with his wife and brother or son, or with a group, arose from the earth, or just appeared, origin unknown. In some versions, he landed from the sea. He travelled southward, establishing groups and tribes; furnishing them with implements and weapons; naming natural species; arranging the totemic system and rules of marriage; and teaching the tribes rituals, especially those of initiating young men. And when his work was finished, he went up to the sky.

He was known by different names, of which Biral in the north, Baiame and Goin in New South Wales, Nurundere in the lower Murray River region and Bundjil in Victoria were the most widespread. But these names were possibly not his real names. In the 1930s it was noticed that the few remaining initiates would only reveal with much diffidence what they regarded as the sky being's real, secret name. He was, however, generally referred to as the All-Father, or 'our father', whose voice was heard in the thunder and whose symbol was the bullroarer, a flat strip of wood tied to a string which makes a roaring noise

when whirled around above the head.

Baiame could be visited by medicine-men, the 'clever men' as their fellows called them. They were men of 'high degree', who having been initiated like every other male, then passed through a vivid experience of death and rising again, which was preceded by training, fasting and discipline. This experience, according to some accounts, also included being taken to the sky where they saw the All-Father and received magical substances. These included quartz crystals, which enshrined the colours and essence of the rainbow. In some regions they were obtained by medicine-men in pools at the foot of the rainbow, a great snake who linked earth and sky, and who was a source or channel of life-giving power.

Every male, however, had to be 'made' Baiame (or Biral, Bundjil and so on) to become fully a man, for only then did he know, though dimly, his whence and whither and why. The ground where he was initiated and where the teachings and symbols of Baiame were revealed, represented Baiame's sky world. Frequently, this inner sanctuary at the end of a secret path, was on an elevated position, such as a hill-top. In some districts, too, the trees around it, and also

around burial places, were engraved with patterns of waved lines or diamonds, indicating the upward road to Baiame's world, which the spirits of the dead would eventually follow.

Unfortunately, this 'sky-hero' cult predominated in Eastern Australia, which was quickly subjected to European settlement. No one observed its rituals in their original completeness; no one studied its myths and doctrines. Its religious significance was not suspected. There were no material signs of religious observances, such as altars or temples, and questions failed to elicit a belief in a deity. And by the time anthropological field research was begun in Australia, the All-Father cults of Eastern Australia had almost ceased to exist.

Although the sky-hero cult is limited to Eastern Australia, all over Australia the sky world is the scene of activity of transformed and translated human and animal heroes of the Dreaming. This is understandable. The aborigines' existence depends on sufficient rain to ensure growth and increase of plant and animal, and on the light and warmth of the sun. Their routine of economic and social activities is correlated with the sun's recurring seasonal variations, and with the phases of the moon. But being ignorant of science, they see heavenly bodies and phenomena as the outward appearances and actions of persons like themselves, though endowed with greater powers, who having finished their earthly courses, went 'on top'. There the rainmen noisily roll their stones which are the thunder clouds, hurl down stone axes which are thunderbolts, and pour down water. The sun, a female, lighting her fire each morning, and the moon, a male, rekindling and waving a torch, each in its cycle sinks down into a 'hole' in the horizon and then rises up again.

The cycles of the heavenly bodies and the seasons must have contributed to the aboriginal idea of time as a continuing cycle. For them the present is not just the effect of what happened in a past Dreamtime but is that Dreamtime here and now. Time does not go on and on in serial order, but returns on itself. So too, human souls do not arise one from the other in a biological line but appear and reappear from the spirit-homes. In some tribes this is the effect of the moon's success in rising again after regularly waning away into 'death'.

In aboriginal experience and thought the sky on top and the earth below are one interconnected system, one world. This indeed is how it seems during the clear nights of inland Australia. Except during rain, the aborigines rest and sleep in the open, with nothing between themselves and the sky; only space. But space is not void; the shooting stars are spirits of the recently dead moving through it. And as one lies looking upward, the Milky Way and the constellations come nearer and nearer until they and the horizon are one.

Other stars and groups of stars are subjects of myths and have their own Dreaming explanations. In the region south and east of Broome in Western Australia, two dingos 'arose' out of the ground; they became gigantic men as tall as the sky. They are the *Baga-djimbiri*. As they travelled along the coast, they named animals and plants, and made springs of water by driving sacred pointed boards into the ground; they saw, but avoided, some women in the west who were digging for locusts; they cooked wattle seed, after realizing that trying to eat it uncooked was a mistake; they lost a hitting stick which local men later saw and copied, and which is represented in the sky as the pointers to the Southern Cross; they instituted the initiation rite of circumcision with the stone knife. A large bullroarer which they whirled flew into the sky to become a black patch in the Milky Way. In their travels they also speared a large kangaroo which hopped up to be the Coal Sack beside the Southern Cross. And so the two Baga-djimbiri went on until one day they laughed at a native cat-man. He and his group speared them. Their bodies became water-snakes, and their spirits went up above; they are the Magellan clouds.

This is a typical myth. Gazing upwards and restfully as sleep steals over them, the aborigines retrace the Dreaming in the sky. They see again the deeds and experiences on earth of those early ones who, translated to the sky, hunt and work, dance and sing, or simply shine there forever.

Mythological systems vary in Australia. New sets of beliefs and rituals have been developed here or there, or else introduced from outside. The two most interesting new cults are in the Northern Kimberley area and in Arnhem Land.

In the former region, in the Dreaming, the ancestors of the clans arrived on the coast led by individuals called Wandjina, each with his own name. They moved in groups about this very rugged country, meeting with varied experiences, some of heroic magnitude, until each band or clan settled down in a particular part of the region. In time the Wandjina died, and he, she or they became a painting on a cave or rock shelter in the clan country. The Wandjina was usually represented lying down, bust or head only, but the mouth was (and is) always missing.

The spirit of the Wandjina went into a nearby water-place, from which it would issue to vitalize its painting. For the Wandjina were and are Dreaming. Associated with rain, the rainbow and the sky, and therefore with the cycle of the seasons, their potency is ever present. Man's duty, clan by

Opposite above left The head of a totem group after a ceremony, with blood and eagle's down on his body. Important totem rites are performed only by men; women are excluded *Opposite above right* The singing and dancing out of myths are partly intended to hand on the stories to the younger men. Every few moments there may be a pause while the old men explain the meaning of each part of the ritual *Opposite* The singers and dancers work up to a high pitch of excitement, sometimes cutting themselves until the blood runs *Right* Cicatrization, often part of an initiation ceremony. Pepper is rubbed into wounds cut into the skin, so as to leave raised scars. It is essential that the initiate must show his manhood by making no sound, in spite of the pain; he bites on a wooden ball in his mouth

The Magician

(An aborigine named Kurkutji described how two spirits, Mundadji and Munkaninji, gave him magical powers. He came on them in a cave, where Mundadji caught him by the neck and killed him.)

Mundadji cut him (Kurkutji) open, right down the middle line, took out all of his insides and exchanged them for those of himself, which he placed in the body of Kurkutji. At the same time he put a number of sacred stones in his body. After it was all over the youngest spirit, Munkaninji, came up and restored him to life, told him that he was now a medicine-man, and showed him how to extract bones and other forms of evil magic out of men. Then he took him away up into the sky and brought him down to earth close to his own camp, where he heard the natives mourning for him, thinking that he was dead. For a long time he remained in a more or less dazed condition, but gradually he recovered and the natives knew that he had been made into a medicine-man. When he operates the spirit Munkaninji is supposed to be near at hand watching him, unseen of course by ordinary people. When taking a bone out, an operation usually conducted under the cover of darkness, Kurkutji first of all sucks very hard at the stomach of the patient and removes a certain amount of blood. Then he makes passes over the body, punches, pounds and sucks, until at last the bone comes out and is then immediately, before it can be seen by the onlookers, thrown in the direction of the spot at which Munkaninji is sitting down quietly watching. Kurkutji then tells the natives that he must go and ask Munkaninji if he will be so kind as to allow him, Kurkutji, to show the bone to them, and permission having been granted, he goes to the spot at which he has, presumably, previously deposited one, and returns with it.

B. Spencer and F. J. Gillen
The Northern Tribes of Central Australia

clan, is to retouch the paintings with ochres and pipeclay each year as the wet season approaches, thus ensuring that they are whole; then the power of the Dreaming becomes operative, as in the days when the Wandjina walked on the earth. The rains will fall, vegetation will grow, animal and bird life will abound.

In addition, in order to express their specific desires and duty, the ritual headmen of each clan paint or retouch designs representing the clan's totems, particularly natural species which contribute to the tribe's food supply. This painting and retouching is part of an increase ritual which includes chanting and recounting of the myth.

The most striking complex of myth and ritual is in the northern third of the Northern Territory. Elsewhere in Australia male figures are dominant in mythology. Women, when present, usually play subordinate roles: but not so in Arnhem Land. There the myths centre on the Great Mother who arrived from the sea and, moving from place to place, gave birth to groups of human beings in what became the countries of particular clans and tribes, each with its own language. In some myths she also gave rise either as emanations from her own person or through ritual acts performed by herself, to the life-cells or entities of natural species.

A male consort or companion or brother is sometimes mentioned, but he is well in the background. In spite of this, in the rituals and in some of the myths, a great snake plays an important part. He is the Python, the Rainbow or Lightning Snake. 'When he raises his lengthening body from the springs, billabongs and rivers to the sky, flashing and roaring, the rains and floods come, and with them the wet season and the promise of life and increase for nature and man.' For as the wet season proceeds, the Mother, the Earth, brings forth food for man.

There are local variations of this basic theme. In north-eastern Arnhem Land the Mother's role is taken by two sisters, the Djanggawul, who with their brother came to the Gulf of Carpentaria coast by canoe from Beralgu, the island of the dead. In one version of the story, they are called the Daughters of the Sun, which left its home to rise up for them and warmed their backs as they rowed and rowed on to the Place of the Sun at Port Bradshaw. And yet they were also the Daughters of the Morning Star, which guided them as they paddled their way across the sea through the night:

On the sea's surface the light from the Morning Star shines as we move, shining on the calmness of the sea. Morning Star, sent by the dancing Spirit People; those people of the rain, calling out as they dance with out-stretched arms.

And as each night drew to its end, the rays of the Star reddened and then paled away before the rising sun. The epic of the Djanggawul is a great revelation of the poetic genius of the aborigines.

Another variation is the widespread cult of the Mother Kunapipi, the ritual of which has striking parallels to elements in the classical mystery religions of Europe. Coming from across the sea, Kunapipi landed either in the lower Roper River or the Victoria River area. She was accompanied by a band of left-handed boomerang throwers who cleared a road through the timber, and also by a group of desirable young women. These were her first-born children but she gave birth to many more at various places in her travels. She also performed the now popular Kunapipi secret ritual, in which those who are to be initiated at one stage enter a crescent-shaped trench, which symbolizes Kunapipi's womb, from which they emerge ritually reborn. While still in the womb each is given a wooden bullroarer to swing. As he does so, his spirit double enters it, and remains with the bullroarer in the trench when the initiate is 'reborn'. After the bullroarer disintegrates, this spirit double goes to the place of 'shades', the spirit centre, there to wait until the individual's death and burial ritual. The latter frees the flesh-soul which then joins the double and becomes one with it again, and so awaits reincarnation.

In their mythology and thinking, aborigines have not come to grips with the ultimate problem of the origin of the world and of life. The earth and sky exist. The Dreaming heroes merely change the outward shape of what is. Rivers and valleys, hills and rocks, anthills and trees, are formed by their movements and in some cases by the transformation of their own bodies. Similarly, the heroes themselves are not created. They too exist; they appear from the ground, the sea, the sky, and bring with them the pre-existent life-entities or spirits of all that will be, man or animal, bird or fish, insect or plant. Beyond that, all is mystery.

But the aborigines have tried to come to terms with the contingencies which face all human beings: death and disease. The aged must die and wait resignedly to 'finish'. The person wounded in a fight might die: there is nothing mysterious about it; and he can be revenged. The failure of many infants and young children to survive is accepted: they will be born again. And there is nothing suspicious about ordinary aches and pains; if bad enough they are treated with folk medicine.

The aborigines know nothing about germs and viruses or other natural explanations of sickness and death. They seek causes which they understand, namely, men (sometimes women) or spirits. In other words, the individual is sick, or has met with a serious accident, or has died because he is the victim of black magic. Some person of evil intent may have performed a magical rite on his footprint, or burnt and stabbed a small 'image' of him, singing the prescribed chant, thus causing him to burn inwardly and die. The important feature is the 'singing' and the intention or projection of the performer's desire. This is most clear in 'bone-pointing'. A pointed bone or stick, usually with a piece of wax at the throwing end, is directed and jerked towards the victim to the accompaniment of action and chant. The projection of magic power must not be undertaken lightly. In one region, the performer must take care that the moon or sun is behind him and that there is no waterhole in front of him, or else he will be struck himself.

A major element of some initiation ceremonies is knocking out a tooth. A bar of wood is inserted between the teeth of the initiate and another piece is used as a hammer, the blows being directed on to a small piece of wood placed directly against the tooth

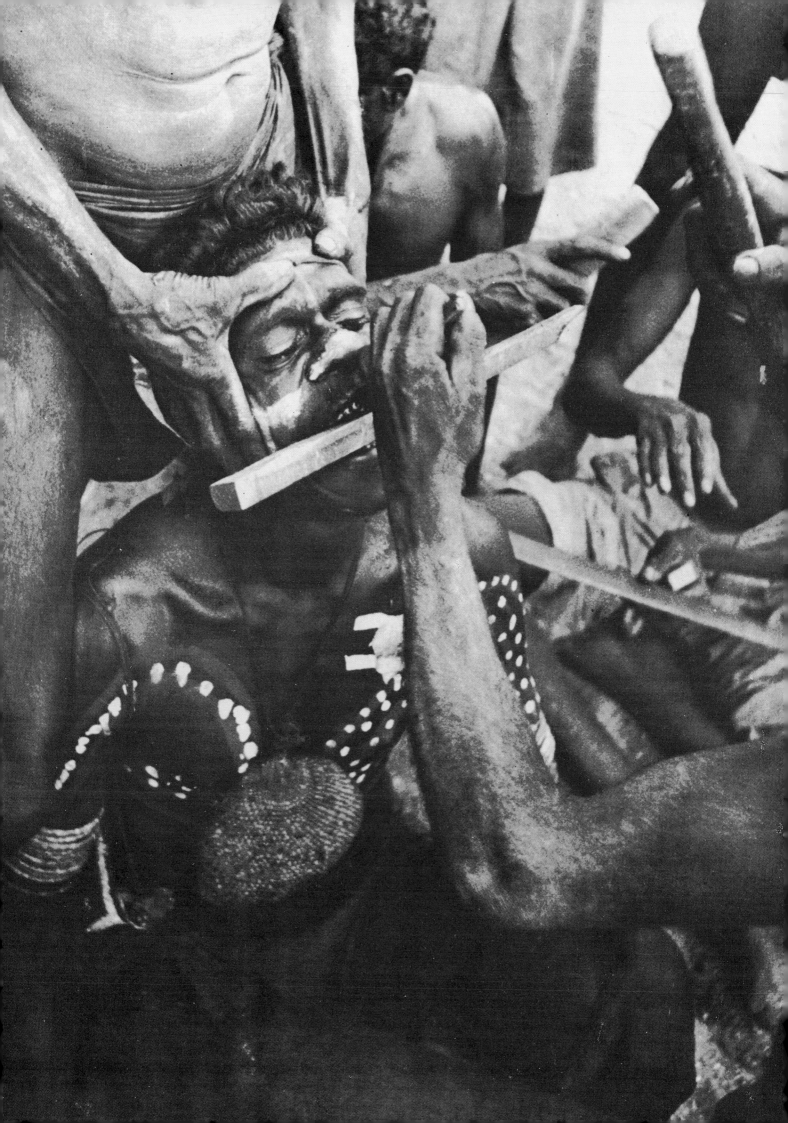

University Museum of Archaeology and Ethnology, Cambridge

New Zealand

The Maoris are a Polynesian people whose ancestors arrived in New Zealand from eastern Polynesia, possibly in the 9th century AD. These population movements were not planned, rather they were accidental voyages made by adventurous seamen, defeated warriors or wind-blown fishermen. It is known that by the 11th century they had explored much of the east coasts of both main islands of New Zealand, which stretch over 1000 miles from the subtropical North Cape to the temperate southern tip of the South Island.

These early settlers ingeniously adapted their tropically derived culture to the colder and more varied New Zealand environment. Of their familiar plants, only the *kumara* (sweet potato) grew really successfully. The settlers brought with them the dog and the rat. They made their clothing from flax and their more durable tools from suitable local rocks, especially basalt, argillite, nephrite and obsidian. They were expert fishermen and cleverly exploited certain local plants for food, notably fern root, which became a staple ingredient of their diet. By the time Captain Cook first visited New Zealand in 1769, the tribes had evolved a sophisticated seasonal economy within the limited productive areas.

Traditional Maori religion can be seen as the means whereby the people perceived and came to terms with the varied environment of sea coast, forest, swamp, tussock flat and mountain that they encountered in New Zealand. They believed in a pantheon of numerous gods, which some scholars have divided into four groups. It is still sometimes claimed that at the head. was a Supreme Being, Io, but the evidence is not very convincing. On the other hand, there were a number of less esoteric gods, the children of Rangi (sky) and Papa (earth), the original parents. These were the gods of the forest, peace and agriculture, war, the ocean, wind and storm, uncultivated food, earthquakes, and also the god of evil. Through myth they provided the ultimate sanctions for human behaviour and attitudes. There were also lesser gods known only within a limited area, and usually restricted to one tribe, such as Maru, a war god. Finally there were tribal ancestral spirits, who were believed to have great influence over the affairs of their living descendants. The ordinary Maori commoner usually felt closest to the members of the last two groups.

Gods were approached by means of ritual offerings and incantations (*karakia*, which is also a generic word for magic). Here, for example, is a translation of part of a karakia used at the kumara harvest:

> This is the spade that descends,
> This is the spade that reverberates,
> This is the spade that resounds,
> Penu, Penu, the spade Penu.

This extract is typical in its reiteration of a particular phrase and in its reference to a particular phenomenon, in this case the spade, Penu, sacred in tribal tradition.

The major gods were consulted only on more important occasions, such as before war or in the preparations for building a canoe. These rituals were mostly left to priests (*tohunga*), who underwent intensive education during their youth in a *whare wananga* (school of learning). One meaning of the word tohunga is 'skilled', and the influence of the priest was often due as much to his practical as his esoteric knowledge. A tohunga of Tangaroa (god of fishermen) for example, often possessed much information about fishing techniques. As well as obtaining the favour of the god through ritual, he could advise the commoner on the best methods and places for catching different varieties of fish.

Because of his influence over supernatural forces, the priest was considered sacred or *tapu* (taboo). His sanctity was proportionate to his knowledge and to the relative importance of his particular god. When, as was often the case, the tohunga was also of high birth, his power and prestige could become enormous. He might also be skilled in sorcery (*makutu*).

The significance of Maori religion and magic lies in its social context. Kinship was the most important organizing force in prehistoric Maori society. It was the basis for the family group (*whanau*), whose members, ranging through three or four generations, formed a residential unit. A number of whanau, with common ancestry, comprised a *hapu*, which controlled a definite stretch of tribal territory, with its own fishing and forest rights, and owning such valuable objects as canoes. Finally, each individual was a member of one out of about 50 tribes, all of whose members acknowledged descent from a common ancestor, sometimes a mythical hero with supernatural powers. In this way, kinship bound the individual to a series of groups interconnected both socially and symbolically.

Hapu chiefs (*rangatira*) were descended in a direct line from the founding ancestors and were thus tapu. They were believed to possess special inherited powers which endowed them with a strong influence over supernatural forces through ritual.

The concept of tapu was thus extremely important. The word can be translated as 'holy' or 'sacred', since the power of tapu was derived from the gods. All free men had such power, to varying degrees, the amount depending on status. Women, unless of high

Left Carved godstick of Maru, a Maori war god: godsticks were used to request the help of a god; the image attached to a string was thrust into the ground while the priest, intoning a prayer, tugged at the string to attract the god's attention to the needs of the worshipper *Opposite* Detail from the beautiful carved lintel of a Maori house; the three-fingered motif is present, while the protruding tongue is a sign of defiance against evil

status, were only tapu during menstruation or childbirth. Tapu was regarded with reverence but also with fear, since infringement would result in misfortune, even death, from outraged spirits. It could be transmitted by contact and so, for example, everything a chief touched shared his sacred qualities. It was dangerous, even disastrous, for anyone else to have contact with these things, unless he was equally tapu. A high-born Maori was surrounded by restrictions, lest he should endanger both his own holiness and that of others. The activities of the chief were particularly circumscribed. Contact with cooked food, which was regarded as profane, would make the food vessels unfit for general use. Any such contact would also threaten the chief's sanctity, since cooked food was often used in tapu-removal ceremonies. The chief was therefore fed by an attendant.

An interesting case is recorded of a high-born and powerful priest who could not travel by the public paths, in case he rendered the route unfit for others to use. There are also accounts by reliable European observers of death following accidental infringement. For instance, it has been reported that on one occasion a Maori ate some food which, unknown to him, was the remainder of a chief's meal. As soon as the man learnt what he had done, he was seized by violent convulsions and cramps, and died before sundown. This episode illustrates an interesting difference between Maori and Christian attitudes towards the wrongdoer. The Christian believes in the existence of hell. The Maori, although believing in an afterlife, had no such concept. Supernatural punishment was direct and often immediate.

Tapu customs imposed many difficulties on the Maori commoner. Not only did he live in physical danger of accidentally breaking certain forms of tapu, but he could also suffer quite considerable material loss. For example, the visit of a high-born chief to a settlement would be dreaded and his movements within it anxiously watched, in case his shadow happened to fall on a food storehouse. If this occurred, the house and its contents would have to be destroyed.

The practice of cannibalism is best understood in terms of the Maori belief that spiritual powers could be transmitted by physical contact. In war, many of the defeated — men, women and children — would be killed and eaten. Normally death and the attendant funeral ceremonies (tangi) involved much tapu observance. But this attitude did not apply outside one's kindred. Thus, imbued with tapu, the successful warrior acquired further status by overcoming enemies of equal or higher status. Their tapu was reduced to nothing by the act of cooking their bodies as food. Usually, a corpse 'contaminated' its surroundings by its great tapu. By dismembering and eating the war dead the victors enhanced their own victory.

The tapu concept operated not only within society, but also directly in its environment. Most objects could be sacred. For example,

the forests were protected. Birds were 'the children of Tane', the god of forests, and the fowler invariably observed numerous magical practices. Before hunting, he carried out a ritual at a special sacred post, and throughout the day he was careful not to use certain words connected with fowling, lest the birds be warned of his intentions. Neither feathers nor dead birds were left lying around, nor was cooked food taken into the forest, for these could pollute its resources. Similarly, trees were felled carefully and ceremoniously, for to cut or even chip a living tree without due ritual precaution was to invite misfortune. Similarly, when fishing, both men and their equipment were sacred, unable to be touched or even approached by unauthorized people, especially women and slaves.

The more elaborate items of equipment, such as canoes, storehouses and fishing nets, were treated with special care and reverence. Nothing, however, was more valuable to the Maoris than land. This was not only the main source of livelihood and prestige, but was also a tangible link between past, present and future generations, held in trust by the living with the consent of their ancestors for their mutual descendants. A chief who attended the signing of the Treaty of Waitangi, at the time of British annexation in 1840, expressed this view well: 'We are not willing to give up our land; it is from the earth we obtain all things; the land is our father; the land is our nobility; we will not give it up.'

The tapu rituals which accompanied cultivation, notably of the sweet potato, reflected this deep-seated attitude. From planting time to harvest, the kumara was surrounded by ceremony. Neither women nor cooked food were allowed on the plantations, and those working there were careful to observe stringent precautions to maintain the integrity of their sanctity. It is also interesting to notice that the Maoris invoked tapu restrictions to prevent over-exploitation of their food resources. If a patch of forest, a stretch of river or a fishing area showed signs of depredation, a chief would indicate that it was temporarily declared tapu by leaving some of his possessions, usually old clothes, in a prominent position nearby.

Tapu must not be regarded as an irrational superstition. It was a comprehensive expression of religious belief with a highly practical significance for prehistoric Maori society. It gave sanction to the leadership of the chiefs. It did much to ensure the proper use of food resources. In these respects, therefore, it contributed to the maintenance of law within the tribe. More broadly, it helped to 'place' the Maori securely within a physical and mental environment which had many interrelated points of contact with his numerous gods.

Christianity destroyed these traditional Maori beliefs, though this did not occur quickly. The first Christian sermon was preached by Samuel Marsden on Christmas Day 1814, in the Bay of Islands, North Auckland; an area more influenced by

European contact at that time than any other part of the country. But progress was slow. As the historian Keith Sinclair says in his *History of New Zealand* (1969): 'It was nine years before the first Maori was baptized — a girl about to marry a European; eleven before the next and death-bed conversion. No substantial progress was made until the eighteen-thirties.'

After that, Maori attitudes changed relatively quickly. The traditional social order was destroyed, and with it the complex and all-embracing nature of Maori religion. After the British annexation of 1840, conversion was very rapid. The new world of the European trader, settler and administrator called for different attitudes. The previous changes in Maori society, following initial European contact, had been contained within its traditional framework. With the subsequent rapid growth of European settlement and its insatiable demand for land, the Maoris became defensive. While many adopted Christian standards of behaviour, local deviations began to occur. As early as the 1830s, a millennial cult, *Papahurihia*, emerged in the Bay of Islands, which rejected Christianity as such, but contained elements of the Old and New Testament.

Rather similar reactions to Christianity also occurred later in the 19th century, during and after the Maori Wars (1856–70), when the profound Maori-European antagonism over land took a particularly bitter form. In 1862 a resistance movement began to develop which was also a new religion, compounded of Christian, Jewish and Maori elements. Called the *Hauhau* after their rallying cry, they regarded themselves as chosen people, who through faith, and pitiless war on the settlers, would regain their traditional heritage. The main fighting died down by 1870 although guerilla warfare lasted until 1872, with much savagery on both sides. During this time Te Kooti, a notable rebel leader, founded the Ringatu Christian Church, which contained certain Hauhau features.

The Ringatu Church is not the only specifically Maori Church existing today. In 1918 a faith healer called Ratana established a Church bearing his name, which particularly appealed to the rural and urban poor. It is interesting to note that he was opposed to belief in tapu. Both Churches have provided considerable moral encouragement to a people who took many years to recover from the effects of the Maori Wars in the context of a rapidly urbanizing society.

It is not surprising that so much Maori traditional ideology is now consigned to history. As J. E. Ritchie said in *The Making of a Maori* (1963): 'Only sickness and death, violence, and serious accident, waken responses from that past world of supernatural completeness, and then only for a few.'

Opposite left Chimbu man wearing a feather head-dress takes part in a ritual dance before visiting a pig-killing ceremony **Opposite right** Carved, painted figures representing clan spirits, in a men's ceremonial house in New Guinea

Melanesia

A group of Pacific islands lying south of the equator, Melanesia includes New Guinea and Fiji, and the Admiralty, Solomon, Santa Cruz, New Hebrides, New Caledonia and Loyalty islands. In this area it is possible to pass, in not much more than an hour's flying time, from a centre where most traditional beliefs have been discarded for a generation or more to an outpost among people whose life has been only superficially influenced by contact with Europeans. In discussing the Melanesians, therefore, it should be remembered that the use of either the past or the present tense can be misleading: what is true of one section of a tribe may no longer be true of another.

When first seen by Europeans the Melanesians were at a cultural level equivalent to the Neolithic period of Europe. They used tools of stone or shell, finished by grinding, and most of them still live by gardening, growing mainly tropical root crops. Social and political units are usually small and democratic, hereditary chieftainship being unusual, and warfare was endemic. This general cultural uniformity accompanies an extraordinary diversity in language and considerable physical variation, reflecting a complex ethnic history.

Their world is thickly populated by spirits, which are everywhere, in trees, river pools, in the sea, in animals, and which affect human life at every turn. They are of two kinds: the ghosts of the dead, and spirits that have never inhabited human bodies. There is no concept of great gods in charge of activities such as fishing, craftsmanship or war, still less of an ultimate

Creator. Religion is a strictly practical matter and consists basically in making contact with a spirit who will befriend and help a human. The two sorts of spirits exist side by side, but their relative importance varies. Ancestral ghosts are always venerated, though in some parts it is the spirits of non-human origin that have the real importance. But spirits can move from one group to the other, for after a time the human origin of a powerful ghost may be forgotten.

In the central and southern Solomon Islands important ghosts, called *tindalo*, often enter an animal, and the place associated with the creature becomes sacred. A man may announce during his life what creature he will enter, sharks being especially favoured. A notorious man-eating shark may become associated with a famous ancestor, and a man who escapes from it will be thrown back out of fear and respect for the spirit. Sea spirits are believed to shoot the living with magical arrows in the form of flying fish, and a man struck by a fish as it skims above the surface will therefore be likely to die. On the other hand sea spirits send shoals of bonito (a fish which is an important item of diet) and help the living in other ways. For this reason, in the Solomon and Santa Cruz groups figures of ancestral spirits often have some attributes of fish or are depicted holding them.

Spirits are much concerned with the observance of custom, any breach of which angers them and brings misfortune to the people. The fear of such consequences forms

the sanction which upholds native morality and the delicate balance of society, and its breakdown has been one of the most unfortunate results of European contact.

At the basis of Melanesian religion and magic is the fundamental concept of *mana*, supernatural power which has been compared to a charge of electricity; although it can be controlled and directed to human ends it is always dangerous. Inanimate objects can have it, possession of it being indicated in many cases by an unusual appearance or quality. Men too have mana: outstanding success or exceptional force of personality prove that it is present. This power, however, always derives ultimately from a spirit, at least in eastern Melanesia; it seems to do so less clearly in New Guinea.

The belief that mana can be transferred helps to explain three practices which occurred widely though sporadically in Melanesia: headhunting, cannibalism and human sacrifice. Headhunting often seems to be connected with the notion of acquiring mana from an enemy group. The Marind-anim of southern West Irian (Indonesian New Guinea) believe the capture of a head to be necessary before a boy can be given his adult name, though on the other hand the peoples living near the estuary of the River Fly, not far away in Papua, state that the head is regarded merely as a trophy won in battle. Cannibalism seems to have a similar ritual basis, not always acknowledged; but the fact that peoples as far apart as the Kukukuku of New Guinea and the Fijians believe that it is dangerous

Axel Poignant

Masks representing spirits are made in many parts of Melanesia. Their significance, like their style, varies from place to place. Often they are worn only by initiates and may not be seen by others. Women and uninitiated boys sometimes believe (ostensibly, at least) that the masked figures are in fact spirits, or that the sounds of special instruments such as bamboo flutes are their voices. The men, though conscious of the deception, yet feel a mystical identification with the spirits which they represent.

Initiation rites are widespread. In some places initiation is undergone by all boys at a certain age, usually about that of puberty. In others there is a series of ceremonies. The rites admit boys into the responsibilities and privileges of manhood. The secrets of the cults and of the cult objects are revealed to them, the myths are recounted, food taboos may be lifted, and where the men's house is an institution boys move to it and leave the company of women; for there is often a feeling that femaleness is dangerous to men. The rites often include physical ordeals, such as circumcision, the piercing of the nasal septum (the cartilaginous division of the nose) and beating with stinging or thorny plants. In parts of eastern Melanesia initiation is not automatic. It may be by purchase, and then confers privileges. Sometimes the initiate is regarded as being ritually reborn, and his rebirth may be enacted.

Though in principle the distinction between religion and magic may be clear, in practice it is apt to become blurred. The Rev. R. H. Codrington, a missionary in eastern Melanesia a century ago and a very acute and accurate observer, has discussed the way in which a prayer, the outcome of which is uncertain, merges into a spell (a magical procedure) when it is believed that the words automatically produce the result. Magic permeates Melanesian life, and belief in it is very persistent.

Magic is white or black — good magic or sorcery — but here too the distinction is not always clear. Harmful magic directed against a fellow-clansman is bad, but directed against a man of a hostile tribe it is wholly admirable. Sorcerers are greatly feared. Their methods vary in different parts of Melanesia. As a generalization it is probably true to say that the sort of magic which depends on obtaining some substance closely connected with the victim — nail parings, excreta, a morsel of food — is more typical of eastern Melanesia. A form widely feared in the northern parts of Australian New Guinea is called, in pidgin, sangguma.

to handle human flesh, and used special implements when eating it, shows that it is not regarded merely as another sort of meat.

Human sacrifice was less general. Where it occurred, as in the Solomons and the New Hebrides, it was usually connected with an occasion on which mana was required, such as the launching of a war canoe or the performance of the culminating ceremony in a great cycle.

An object which is· dangerous because it has mana is taboo. The place associated with a spirit is therefore taboo, or a chief, by virtue of his mana, can impose a taboo on the produce of a garden or the use of a certain path.

Except in Fiji there are no orders of priests. A man· who has a special relationship with a powerful spirit may profit considerably from the demand for his services, but he continues to lead a normal life as a

gardener, fisherman or craftsman. An important element in his expertise is often a knowledge of the correct form of words to use in invocation of the spirit; and in connection with the invocation small sacrifices or offerings are frequently made.

In most parts of Melanesia there are, in addition to such personal approaches to individual spirits, ceremonies in which the whole community participates. These are often to honour a group or class of spirits. Among the Elema at the head of the Papuan Gulf such ceremonies formed a cycle which took years to complete. Masks of painted bark cloth represented the spirits, and the celebrations included feasting, drumming and dancing. The people of northern New Ireland periodically perform ceremonies in honour of the recently dead, for which elaborate masks and carvings known as malanggan are prepared.

Above Cult house decorated with magical objects including chains, tassels and the figures of birds **Opposite** White magic in Melanesia can serve many purposes, such as promoting success in important activities, bringing rain, or healing the sick; from a European point of view healing procedures can combine both medical and magical elements: witch-doctor treating a patient

It is believed that the sorcerer has the power to introduce a sharp object into the victim's body without leaving a visible wound. The Tifalmin, near the source of the Sepik River, believe that the sangguma men – always from another tribe – shoot their victims with magical arrows. If the arrows are not removed by an expert, who works by manipulation and massage, the victim dies. In the Banks Islands a length of bamboo was filled with magical ingredients, including a relic of a dead man, and directed at an enemy, the end being covered with a thumb until he came into view. Codrington relates instances when the wrong person crossed the line of fire.

White magic can serve many purposes: healing, promoting success in important activities, averting or bringing rain. Healing procedures can be, from a European viewpoint, both medical and magical. The Tifalmin massage a painful place with the flat bone of a river turtle which is found only at lower altitudes. The bone is a magical object, and the treatment is accompanied by muttered spells, but clearly the massage itself may be beneficial. Every Tifalmin man possesses charms which bring luck in his activities. Nearly all are obtained by trade with peoples who live in the foothills. These charms are of kinds which do not occur in the Tifalmin valley: fossils are in great demand, and also bones of animals not found in the mountains. The power of the dead is illustrated by the practice of temporarily burying in a garden, to ensure a good crop, the jaw bone of an ancestor who was a famous gardener.

The differences in belief and social and political structure between Melanesia and Polynesia are reflected in their mythologies. Some resemblances to the Polynesian system can be traced in eastern Melanesia, but Melanesian myths contain nothing similar to the creative activities of the Polynesian pantheon. It is true that certain heroes of the Banks Islands and the New Hebrides – Qat and Tagaro – stand head and shoulders above the minor spirits.

According to one account Qat at first made men and pigs in the same form, but later made pigs go on all fours and men upright to distinguish between them. In another he made men and women of wood and brought them to life by dancing in front of them. But Qat himself had a mother and companions. Tagaro resembles Qat in many ways. He is probably the Poly-

Head of one of the colossal stone images on Easter Island; these figures, weighing up to 50 tons, were cut from compressed ash quarried from the crater of an extinct volcano. They represent ancestors, and stood in burying-places

nesian god Tangaroa adapted to a Melanesian cosmogony.

There are some resemblances between Melanesian and Australian views of the origin of things, but their significance should not be over-estimated. Like the Australian aborigines, many Melanesians believe in a time before men existed when supernatural beings were active, often forming the natural features that are now seen today. Totemism, so highly developed in Australia, is more vaguely conceived in Melanesia, but there are many traces of it.

Many stories concern the origin of men. In some New Guinea myths the first people came out of a tree or from the ground. Sometimes the 'first man' finds women on earth, or stories of the 'first people' refer to other people apparently already existing – an inconsistency which does not worry the tellers, for the myths really explain the origin of a clan or a tribe rather than of all mankind, a reflection of the fragmentation and isolation of many of the Melanesian groups.

Peoples living as far apart as central New Guinea and the Solomon Islands have stories of descent from snake-ancestors, or from women who married snakes.

Myths concerning the release of the sea from the ground and the separation of the lands are widely spread. Often the sea burst out as the result of the foolishness, curiosity or greed of someone who failed to do as instructed.

A number of stories centre round the origin of death, for it is widely believed that at one time people lived for ever. A common group of tales, current as far apart as New Britain and the New Hebrides, tells that once people sloughed their skins when they grew old, and appeared young again. For various reasons a woman re-assumed her old skin, in one version because her child did not recognize her and cried; since then people have died.

It is believed everywhere that the soul or spirit survives after death, though it may be only for a time. Usually there is a land of the dead, on a distant island or mountain or under the ground, and there is often a prescribed route which the dead must follow. Commonly they have to pass a spirit guardian who tests them in various ways. If they fail to satisfy him or outwit him they may be destroyed and cease to exist.

The destination of the dead does not depend on their moral conduct during life. There is no equivalent to heaven and hell. What matters is the performance of rituals by surviving relatives, the observance of custom, the status of the dead man. If he was a great warrior, an orator, a leader, people will remember him and will call on him for help, and he will survive in the spirit world. If he was a nonentity in life he will be a nonentity after death and will soon disappear. In Malaita the ghosts of such people turn into ants' nests which are eaten by the great ghosts, but when those latter are finally forgotten they too turn into ants' nests and are eaten.

Micronesia and Polynesia

The origin of the Polynesians and Micronesians, who people almost every speck of inhabitable land in the Pacific north and east of the area called Melanesia, has been argued since Captain Cook's voyage of discovery in the 18th century. The evidence shows that their ultimate links are with Asia, but recent research suggests that they became a distinct group in the area of eastern Melanesia and western Polynesia, and then spread eastwards to the central groups and north to Hawaii, south-east to Easter Island and south-west to New Zealand and the Maori. The Micronesians, especially in the west, have been influenced by later immigrations from Asia.

The history of these peoples is very relevant in a religious context. When it was believed that they left Asia as a distinct ethnic group, it was natural to look for origins of their religion and mythology among the ancient Asiatic civilizations: their metaphysical ideas were compared with those of the Vedic Aryans, for instance. Now interest centres as much on the relationship of their ideas with those of the Melanesians, with whom they seem to share a common origin.

Like the Melanesians, the Polynesians when whites discovered them were at a 'Neolithic' cultural level, using ground stone or shell for their cutting tools. In most of the islands they subsisted mainly by gardening but, especially on the small atolls, they also depended heavily on the sea.

Their religious and metaphysical ideas were, by comparison with their simple material culture, sophisticated, complex and poetical. All Polynesians had myths about the beginning of the world.

Whatever its origin, once created the world evolved. At first the sky father and the earth mother lay embraced, and their offspring, the gods, were born into the darkness between them. Finally one (often Tane) decided to separate them, and thrust the sky up into its present position, allowing light into the world.

Most of the great gods are found throughout Polynesia, but their names and attributes differ in the various groups, and some islands had deities unknown elsewhere. The New Zealand Maori seem to have had a supreme Creator called Io. The name occurs again (as Ihoiho) in Tahiti. One has to distinguish between Io as a true Creator of all things, and the gods who bring order out of chaos. Tangaroa was especially the god of the sea, but in the outlying groups became of minor importance.

Tu (Ku in Hawaii) was a war god. In the Society Islands he was associated with Ta'aroa in the creation myths, but his function as war god was usurped by Oro, a son of Ta'aroa, who became the supreme deity. But in Hawaii Ku, in various forms, was supreme.

Rongo was widely known in central and eastern Polynesia, alternative forms of his name being Lono in Hawaii, and Ono in the Marquesas Islands. He was an agricultural god, in whose honour harvest festivals were celebrated; he was also patron of singing and music. In a Hawaiian legend he sailed away, overcome with grief at the death of his wife, but promised to return one day in a canoe laden with food. The Hawaiians took Captain Cook for the returning Lono, and their disillusion led to his death.

Goddesses were of less importance. Hina or Hine appears in many forms. According to the Maori tale, Tane created Hine from the sand of the sea-shore as a mate for himself, and took their daughter Hine-Titama, the dawn maiden, as his wife. When she discovered their dual relationship she fled to Po, the underworld, and so originated death. Hine in her different aspects was the goddess of death and the underworld and, as the first woman, a source of fertility. She was also associated with the moon and with women's crafts.

The great gods were too remote to take much interest in the daily affairs of ordinary people, which were the concern of numerous lesser deities: local or family gods, or those who watched over certain crafts or activities. Some were sons or descendants of the great gods, others were deified ancestors. The two classes merged, for chiefs were themselves descended from gods.

The Polynesians felt that all creation – gods, mortals and Nature – was one. Natural and supernatural were equally real, and equally significant, aspects of experience. The whole of creation was pervaded by a force, known as *mana*, which showed itself in power, efficacy, success, skill, fruitfulness, prowess. It was beneficial if rightly directed, but always dangerous. Religion was concerned with controlling and directing mana, with increasing it where it was needed, with shielding man from its dangers. The moral content in Polynesian religion was slight. What mattered was not probity or standards of conduct but the correct performance of ritual. Breaches of custom might offend the gods and be punished, but punishment could be averted by offerings. There is no clear distinction between religion and magic, since both aim to control and make use of mana, though in general religion works for social ends whereas the aims of magic would often be considered antisocial.

Chiefs were directly descended from the gods, and were therefore charged with mana. A chief who was descended from a god through an unbroken line of oldest sons was not only the senior in a political or social sense; he also possessed the most potent mana. The mana of a chief was the mana of his people, as he was the main link between his tribe and the gods and the non-physical world. Because any diminution of this force was a matter of general concern, it was essential that the blood be kept pure. A Hawaiian chief of the senior line therefore married his sister.

The chief had obligations to his people as well as autocratic power over them. He had to ensure that his mana was not diminished and that commoners did not come to harm by accidental contact with it. The consequent restrictions could be extremely onerous.

One of the means by which mana was manipulated, and danger from it avoided, was the now well-known institution called taboo. The word covers a number of related concepts. A chief and anything connected with him were taboo, because contact was dangerous (often fatal) to his inferiors and because at the same time it diminished his mana and therefore that of his people. This kind of taboo was automatic and unavoidable; but a chief could use his mana positively to impose a taboo, on a place, an activity, the consumption of a certain food.

These taboos derived from sacredness. Another type derived from pollution. Women, especially, were charged with this kind of power; their reproductive organs and functions were the greatest danger to sacredness. Death, sickness and women (especially at childbirth and menstruation), were contaminating; all who came into contact with them were in peril. At childbirth and periodically, therefore, women retired to special huts in the bush.

A man contaminated in this way, or by contact with excessive mana, could be restored to a state of *noa*, or normality, by ritual and by means of the cleansing agents, fire and water. In the same way a crop which had been under taboo, or a new canoe or house which acquired mana during the making, had to be made noa before they became free for general use.

The Polynesian sense of the unity of all creation probably explains the licence which characterized certain harvest festivals, and the performances of societies of entertainers such as the Arioi of Tahiti. These were religious in nature and consisted of recounting creation myths, singing, drumming, miming and dancing. As they proceeded they became more and more erotic, the tempo accelerated, and finally all present (or in some accounts, only the lower grades) succumbed to a frenzy of sexual abandon. The gods were believed to be present enjoying these performances, and as the people copulated so did the gods, and all Nature was fructified.

Unlike the Melanesians, the Polynesians had specialist priests who varied in grade and function, though on great occasions the chief himself often officiated. The temple priests, often of noble rank, were in charge of ritual. They presented sacrifices to the gods, conducted ceremonies, released from taboo those who had come into contact with divinity. They were the repositories of sacred learning, and some groups ran schools in which chiefs' sons were instructed in the sacred lore. The second kind were the inspirational priests, subject to possession by their god who spoke through them. They were consulted before all important enterprises. Others, considered inferior, were mediums who were able to contact spirits, and who were consulted in case of sickness,

to detect thieves and on similar occasions.

The presence in most of Polynesia of temples or sacred enclosures is another point of difference from Melanesia. In Tonga and Samoa the graves of chiefs served the purpose, but in the eastern groups temples were more elaborate. The Society Islands had family, district and royal temples, and temples associated with occupations such as canoe-building and fishing. They often had stone platforms, superimposed and stepped back at each level, and a walled forecourt. A stepped platform in Tahiti was 44 feet in height. Some temples in Hawaii and Tahiti provided sanctuary for criminals, or refugees in time of war.

Figures representing gods or spirits, many important deities, are found widely in Polynesia. In the Marquesas and on Easter Island they represent ancestors, and the figures in human form from Tahiti also seem to be of ancestral spirits or perhaps minor deities, in many cases the familiars of sorcerers. In this island the great gods were represented by blocks of wood covered with closely-plaited coconut-fibre cord set with red feathers, red being the sacred colour. These figures were not in themselves sacred, but became so when the god or spirit descended into them. Nor did they necessarily represent the deity's actual appearance. In some islands gods were symbolized by paddles, clubs or intricately-carved batons.

In ritual, forms of words were all-important. Exactness was essential; any error not only made the ceremony ineffective but could endanger the life of the priest. This was especially so when, as sometimes happened, the ritual consisted of repeating the precise words of the god.

Ritual was almost always accompanied by sacrifice. First-fruits — from the gardens, or of fish when a new season began — were offered to the god whose creatures they were, as an act of conciliation. Pigs were commonly sacrificed on important occasions, but at a family meal the offering would be merely a few morsels of food.

In Tahiti and the Marquesas human sacrifices were made before a war, and in Hawaii when an image of Ku or a new war canoe was made. The Hawaiians also placed a victim at the foundation of a sacred building. It seems that the soul, tied to the site by ritual and by the presence of the body, became a guardian spirit.

The fickleness of Polynesian gods is illustrated by the Tahitian practice of making offerings near a besieged enemy to lure his gods away. A deity's followers were equally fickle: a god who failed his people would be abused, insulted and abandoned. This perhaps explains the changes in function and status of deities, and the willingness with which most Polynesians adopted Christianity.

The Polynesians believed that the soul could leave the body without causing immediate death, and that dreams were the experiences of the wandering soul. In sickness it could be caught and restored by experts, but it might also be trapped by enemies. In Pukapuka, an atoll of the

Cook group, a priest whose god had been offended would make a trap consisting of a series of coconut-fibre rings and suspend it from a tree over the offender's house. If a bird or insect flew through one of the rings the offender's soul was captured.

Sorcerers had other means of destroying people by attacking their souls. Hair, nail-parings, or fragments of food left by the victim could be burnt or buried with magical objects, and his soul would then be extinguished. The sorcerer could also send an evil spirit to attack his soul.

Sickness could be sent by a god to punish a transgression, or by discontented spirits of the dead who had not been accorded the usual ceremonies. In either case a propitiatory rite and an offering might bring about a cure. Since the progress of the soul to the next world, and its status and survival there, depended on rites performed by the living, it was justifiably annoyed by neglect.

Sorcerers derived their power from spirits or used them as their agents. In Hawaii a sorcerer could create his own powerful familiar. The body of a dead person was obtained, the bones and hair preserved, and regular offerings made to the spirit to build up its power. Such a familiar might destroy its creator if it was not regularly sustained by offerings.

After death the ghost soon began its journey to the land of the dead. Usually this was to the west, and most islands had a place at the western end from which souls were thought to leave. In western Polynesia the afterworld was called Pulotu, but in the eastern groups it was often Hawaiki, the homeland. The souls of commoners, or those for whom the rites had been omitted, often failed to overcome the dangers of the journey or to survive for long in the afterworld, but chiefs and eminent people could expect immortality.

The less fortunate souls might go to Po, which sometimes meant extinction and sometimes an underworld, ruled by Miru. In the Cook Islands Miru was an ogress who cooked and ate the souls of ordinary men. The Marquesas had three underworlds, ranging from pleasant to wretched, and the soul's destination depended on the rites and offerings made on its behalf, and also, no doubt, on rank and prowess.

Apart from cosmogonic myths, and legends concerning the wanderings and origin of the peoples of the different islands — many of which undoubtedly have historical foundation — there are numerous tales about the adventures of heroes and heroines, about the pranks of tricksters, about ogres and demons. A favourite hero, often regarded as a demigod, is Tahaki. He is the epitome of the great chief: brave, resourceful, handsome, full of mana, gracious and at ease, proud but patient. His adventures do not show him as perfect. That would be dull. He has his faults, he is occasionally foolish, his numerous love affairs do not always go easily.

Tahaki's grandson Rata is a hero of a different kind, a great seaman and adventurer, headstrong, quick-tempered, determined. His mother, Tahiti Tokerau, was abducted by one Puna, who plucked out her eyes to serve as lights and buried her head downwards in the sand so that her feet could be supports for the baskets of Puna's wife. When Rata grew up he determined to rescue his mother. He built a great canoe with the aid of wood spirits, who had at first been angered by his action in cutting down a tree but relented when they heard of his project. Finally, after numerous adventures, overcoming monstrous guardians and other dangers, he slew Puna and released Tahiti Tokerau. Several chiefly lines claimed descent from Rata.

Probably the most popular hero was Maui. Born prematurely and discarded by his mother, he was rescued and reared by the gods. After learning everything they could teach him he rejoined his mortal family. The stories of his adventures are innumerable. He feared no one and respected no one. No institution or taboo was sacred to him. In a society as rigidly hierarchical and strictly governed by etiquette as the Polynesian, the Maui stories must have provided a welcome safety-valve.

Many of his escapades are simply tricks or jokes, in which he makes the pompous or the great appear ridiculous, or outwits the clever. But some of his greatest feats were of benefit to man. He lassoed the sun, which used to race across the sky, and so gave people the day as we know it, with time to work and cook meals. He stole fire, which man had lacked. He fished up islands from the depths of the ocean, according to some accounts with a hook made from his grandmother's jaw-bone (and therefore possessing great mana).

His last adventure, though it led to his death, was his greatest: he tried to save humanity from having to die. Accompanied by his friends the birds he sought out Hina, the goddess of death. He found her asleep. Warning his companions to keep silent so as not to wake her, he attempted to kill her by crawling between her thighs into her body and emerging from her mouth. When only his legs were still visible the ridiculous sight was too much for the wagtail, which let out an uncontrollable chuckle. Hina awoke, closed her legs together, and Maui was crushed.

The mythology and religious and magical ideas of Micronesia form a less cohesive and clear-cut pattern than those of Polynesia. Cosmogonic myths are relatively unimportant. Certain groups had a Creator being, and the concept of an original chaos or void is present, but many Micronesians seem to have regarded the world as always existing: the task of the Creators was to make it habitable. Stories of the separation of earth and sky are fairly common. As in Polynesia, islands were drawn up from the sea by semi-divine fishermen, whose names are sometimes variants of Maui. There are stories about the snaring of the sun, the obtaining of fire, and other themes popular in Polynesia and other regions.

Many tales concern man-eating monsters

Axel Poignant

Carved figures in the courtyard of the temple of Honaunau in Hawaii; the deified bones of the chiefs were at one time buried there, and it was a sanctuary for criminals and for refugees at times of war

or ogres, ferocious but stupid, who are often overcome by children: a theme common in Melanesia. Another group explains the origins of food taboos: for example, there is the story of the porpoise girl who came ashore at night to watch men dancing, removing and hiding her tail. A man found it, thereby preventing her return to the sea, and married her. After a while she found its hiding place and went back to the sea, warning her children that they must never eat porpoise meat, since they would be in danger of indulging in cannibalism if they did so.

Ancestor worship seems to have been a more conspicuous element in religion than it was in Polynesia. Supernatural beings who were not of human origin were less prominent in cult, and their spheres were less clearly defined. Among the most important families of gods were those concerned with canoe-building and seafaring, as one would expect in this part of the world.

Everywhere sacrifices and offerings were made, but human sacrifice was apparently absent. Ritual, and the priesthood, were less highly developed; and possession by a god was unusual, though there were mediums who communicated with the spirits of the dead or with lesser deities. Representations of gods or spirits were rather rare in their culture.

In general chiefs were not considered sacred and though they were treated with great respect their powers were more limited than in Polynesia.

America

North America

A study of American Indian religion shows that its complexity developed in line with the development of civilization. The basic units were the spirits of ancestors and personifications of forces of Nature such as wind, rain, thunder, and sun and moon. Every natural object might have a spirit which could be contacted. There were greater powers of creation and destruction worshipped among such people as the Eskimo, who regarded a Great Mother who lived under the sea as a giver of life in addition to sun and moon.

With the Eskimo, as with all other tribes, there was the need for day-to-day aid from the spirits. The nature of coming events was revealed through ecstatic visionaries, generally known as medicine-men because of their special functions as faith-healers. The main worship of the great natural forces usually took the form of a tribal ceremony at the appropriate season of the year. There was a great deal of self-torture by young men seeking to ensure success in war through pain. Most of the ceremonies lasted for four or five days, and everywhere the tribes had sets of carefully prescribed dances and chants to dramatize the occasion.

All American Indian religions were deeply influenced by the passage of the seasons. It was a necessity for the hunting tribes to be aware of the migrations of the animals, buffalo or salmon; and if at least the moon

in which the migration could be expected was known, there would be time to prepare traps and snares, and gather supplies of arrows and spears. As a result, the successful medicine-man was likely to be a good astronomer.

The stars were lights in a world above the earth. Some wise men said they were the camp fires of the tribes in the sky. The sky land was a wonderful place, it was always summer there, and the souls of men and animals lived together without need to hunt and kill one another. There the sun had his house and the moon, who was often thought to be the younger brother of the sun, went on his regular journeys. Some of the stars were identified with deities, and the planets were thought to be great divine beings who wandered through the heavenly fields eternally acting out the drama of their lives. In particular, Venus usually had a dual character, being evil as the evening star and a power for good as the morning star.

The Pawnee a century ago still remembered the last occasion on which they had sacrificed a girl to the morning star. It was an ancient ceremony performed infrequently in times of trouble when the aid of this star was required. Being a cultured people, they would not sacrifice one of their own tribe but sent out a special expedition to kidnap a girl from one of the surrounding tribes. Once the captive had been taken she was treated with

every consideration, given fine clothes and good food, and was never told the fate which awaited her. When the time came she was led out to a frame in the open air. Stripped naked, and painted half black and half red, she was tied to the framework. Then the young men danced and shot arrows at her. She was killed quite quickly and it was thought that her spirit would go to the morning star and intercede for the people. It was because they needed her help in this way that they had treated her well during the days of captivity.

Almost every tribe paid reverence to the morning star because this brilliant planet which heralded the sunrise was thought to have something miraculous and fortunate about it.

From the Dakota come many star legends, and here the red star Aldebaran, one of the brightest in the heavens, took on a heroic aspect. This young star was the child of the sun and the lady Blue Star. One day he saw approaching him a white buffalo calf (the Pleiades) and wanted to hunt it. He looked around to find a sapling to make a spear, and pulled one up. He opened a hole in the sky world and looked down on the prairies and saw the Indians hunting game. The buffalo calf came near and charged so that he tumbled through the hole in the sky and fell to earth. There he was found by a poor old woman who was gathering firewood. She took him back to her home where she treated him well. People called him Old Woman's Grandson.

On earth he killed many strange monsters which had been troubling the Indians. He stopped the clashing rocks which killed everyone who travelled along the trail which led between them, by sending his dog to dash through the opening, after a huge bonfire had been lit on top of one of the peaks. The stone began to melt, and as the rocks tried to crush the dog they stuck together; they are now a natural rock arch through which people can pass in safety.

Then there was a terrible drought, and Old Woman's Grandson discovered that a great serpent had come up onto the land and was drinking all the rivers. He took his firesticks with him in a canoe, and was duly swallowed by the monster. He then made a fire and burned up its heart. When it was dead he cut his way out through the carcass, and released a great stream of water which became the Mississippi.

He saw the white buffalo calf again and knew that he must hunt it once more and follow his destiny. So they ran across the prairie and came to the edge of the sky

Above Clothing was not regarded as a necessity by the Indians, who thought of garments primarily as indicating social status and personal importance: warrior *(left)* and a woman of Florida *(right)*; they both wear body paint, applied in formal designs **Opposite** Sacred building of the Natchez Indians; the bodies of their dead were dried and kept on frames. 16th century watercolours by John White, now in the British Museum

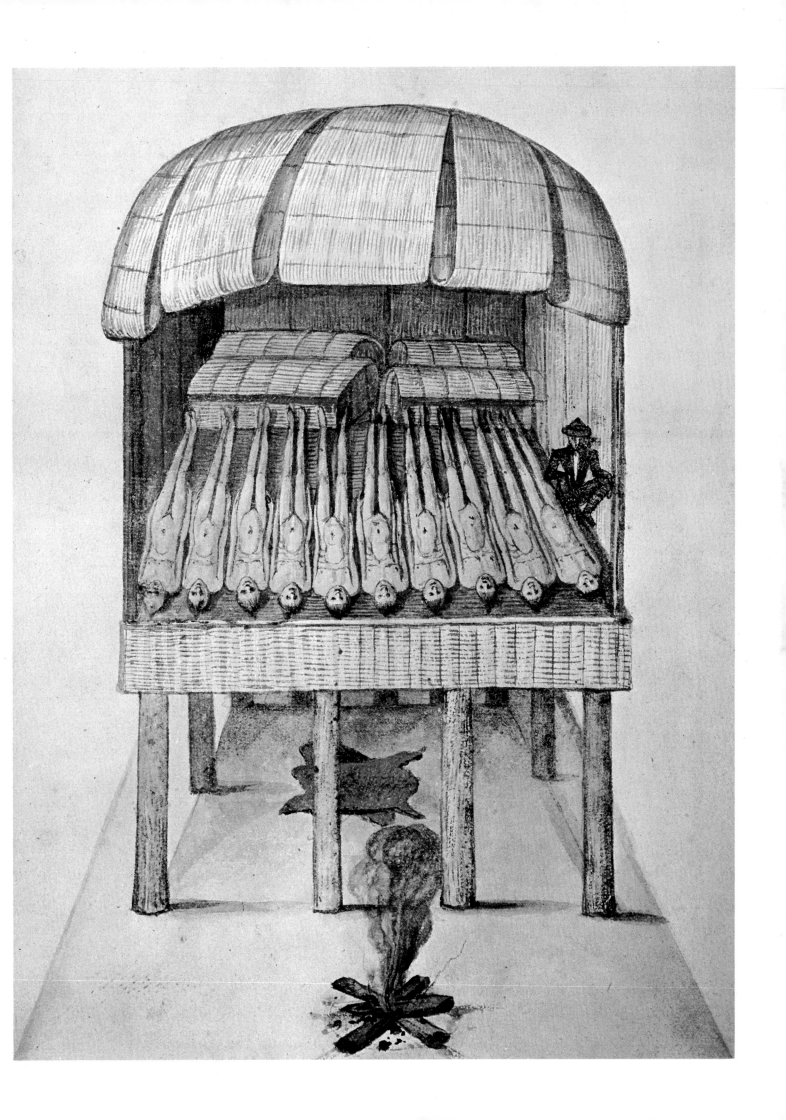

south of the Great Lakes cultivated tobacco, and it was regarded as a way of making contact with the Power Above, whom white men call the Great Spirit. The smoke of the tobacco went upwards bearing prayers and wishes from people on earth, but the American Indian developed no tobacco habit. It was used at conferences to bring about a state of peaceful intent so that discussions could be started without anger. Thus it was used in the pipe-of-peace to symbolize the quiet friendship which would replace war.

In the south-eastern United States there was a charming legend of the origin of tobacco. A young man and his beloved were walking one summer, naked except for their moccasins as was usual in very warm weather.

They found a patch of scented grass and lay down together. Each was beautiful, and admiring each other they joined together in sexual partnership. It was so beautiful an experience that they remembered it and at the same time the following year they returned to seek the place where such happiness was found. There they found a strange plant growing with beautiful scented flowers. It was the first tobacco plant, the bringer of peaceful happiness. Hence for all future people tobacco was to be a holy plant and the bringer of peace.

Hallucinatory drugs were but rarely used among the North American Indians. Only in the 19th century was the mild narcotic, peyote, connected with a cult, introduced from Mexico. It became an important source of visions for the participants in the Ghost Dance cult but it seems that the expectation of the dreams was more important than any narcotic contained in the peyote. Much more important in rituals were the emetics which cleared the stomachs of those seeking visions, before which the whole person had to be emptied and cleansed. Many quite ordinary people participated in the great ceremonies, at least at the beginning of the year, and danced and took the magical drinks. They chose to take part because of a personal need of enlightenment from the powers above.

Women might occasionally come as assistants to the religious ceremonies, but they usually did not take part actively in the ritual. It was not for them, they thought, to participate in the sky ceremonies. Within themselves they held the powers of the Earth Mother who gave them the blessing of motherhood, and the magic which brought peace to their menfolk. When they painted themselves it was more for beauty, than for the symbolism in which their more brilliantly painted husbands gloried and indulged so often.

Because of the wide differences in cultural needs, a considerable variation in religious beliefs may be observed among the pre-Columbian groups of Indians. On the whole this is most closely represented in the creation myths. The more primitive groups generally regarded the first ancestors as having been created by the Power Above,

sometimes by direct bringing into being; but in other myths they were thought of as having been carved or modelled by divine powers and given life by a special god who might be an adversary of the Great Creator.

Among some peoples several different explanations were given of the origins of the ancestors. In general the more advanced agricultural peoples developed a religion which saw their forefathers as emerging from a prehuman animal condition. These legends usually tell of an emergence in stages from one land beneath the earth to another, ever ascending towards more perfect humanity and the light of the sun. The Pueblo and Navaho Indians believed their homeland to have been the first created place, where they had always existed.

Most of the tribes had a belief that mankind had once been threatened by a terrible flood. Whether this is a folk-tradition from the days when the ice sheets were melting is not clear, but it seems to have been current among many tribes before they came into contact with Europeans, though later the legend was slightly altered to suit the book of Genesis and the story of Noah. The Mandan of the upper Missouri preserved a ring of planks which they believed to be relics of the Great Canoe in which their ancestors gathered on a hill top, just before the encroaching waters were stayed and then began to recede.

All American Indians had faith in charms and amulets, which were revealed in visions. The dreamer would find a similar object in his waking life and keep it in his personal medicine bag. Some objects were so sacred that they were kept in tribal medicine bundles which were passed from hand to hand over the centuries. It was the spirit and the symbol, not the object, which had power for the Indians.

After the 16th century the Plains tribes, who became dependent more on their hunting ability than on the gardens tended by their womenfolk, were obsessed with rituals of hunting and war. The young men were organized into religious confraternities which, by means of prayer, self-torture and dramatic representational dance, encouraged the guardian spirits to bring the tribe abundance of food, and victory in adversity. The leaders were elderly chiefs who knew the proper ritual for every occasion in all its complex detail. The young initiates wandered naked and alone in the prairie, fasting until they were given visions in which they saw their future spirit protectors. These directed them into ways of life which, in effect, determined which magic society they should join.

The rituals of these hunting tribes were more public, and more of a mass festival, than those of the agricultural people who tended to hold their principal ceremonies within a sacred house where they were visible to initiates only. Among the Pueblos the rituals were performed in circular underground chambers called *kivas*, which were decorated with paintings of the gods concerned in the ceremonies. Among the

where they chased onwards and at last returned home in peace. Old Woman's Grandson was once more in his starry home and was greatly honoured because he had helped the Indians to live without fear.

The earth itself was thought to be a great turtle floating in the endless ocean. Some tribes believed it had been brought to the surface directly by the gods, others thought that diving ducks had brought earth from beneath the sea and piled it on the back of the great turtle, until a mountain was made from which earth spread to make the plains and valleys.

Special animals and birds were reared as sacrificial offerings and messengers to the gods. The Pueblo sacrifice of tame eagles once a year is a case in point. All tribes

Hamlyn Group Library/British Museum

Above The Chippewa of the north believed in Great Spirit who presided over the forces of Nature; the snowshoe dance was performed to thank this being for sending the first snow of winter, which enabled men to hunt game more easily as they were able to skim over the snow wearing snowshoes *Opposite* Carved kachina doll, painted to resemble one of the supernatural beings impersonated by masked dancers in Pueblo tribal ceremonies; these symbolic dolls are given to children to enable them to recognize the gods depicted

Iroquois the meetings were held in long houses of elm bark which were reserved for the tribal elders.

Such segregation of ritual from the mass of the tribe was bound to lead eventually to the growth of religious orders, in which a priesthood of men dedicated to certain deities was developed. The temple with its subsidiary buildings and priest-houses, which was the end product of this development, was only fully developed in Mexico. Among the northern Indians, such people as the Natchez of the lower Mississippi valley developed a structured society in which the highest class was of chiefs and priests who were called 'suns'. They led the nation in war and directed all tribal activities. The priests were specialists within the upper social group, and tended the temples, performed ceremonies including sacrificial offerings to the gods, and made deities in wood and clay.

Somewhat similar but less highly organized cultures flourished among the Creek, Cherokee and Choctaw Indians of the hill country of the south-eastern United States. They lived in villages built along trackways which joined one town with

another. These tribes were advanced in a Neolithic phase of culture, having well-organized plantations of maize, beans, pepper and squash. There were sufficient deer and wild pigs to give some meat in their diet, and fishing was abundant in the many rivers of their country. They had to resist forays from their neighbours and even from the more distant tribes of the prairies, some of whom, like the Pawnee, were related to them. They built temples on mounds, and their gods were served by specialist priests. The passage of the year was marked by a regular series of ceremonies which were expected to bring blessings from the powers of sky and earth.

Everywhere the sun was the most important visible entity, and the moon a changeable secondary power. The earth and her fruits were holy and offerings were made. On the whole, rituals for the sun and sky spirits involved self-inflicted pain, and earth ceremonials involved sexual rituals which included public intercourse by chosen young people. In such ceremonies there was no idea of decency or indecency; the action was holy and part of the world of Nature through which came all the gifts from the gods to their human supporters.

A quite distinct culture in North America was centred on the North Pacific coast where a high degree of comfortable village life was achieved without the practice of agriculture. The reason for this unusual state of affairs was that abundant supplies of sea food and wild berries made it possible for people to settle in permanent villages. They carved wooden utensils, built houses and dug canoes out of the great trunks of Douglas fir trees. There was a strong belief in the relationship

between human and animal relatives, and tales concerning these were told in the form of ceremonial plays during the winter nights. The idea of the totem was more important in this region than in any other part of North America.

Most tribes believed that spirit protectors in the form of animals could be acquired by young men through fasting and self-torture. Such animal-souls occasionally took possession of a skin carried by the owner, and acted as oracles ever ready to help with advice and even a little magic. In some ways they may be compared to the familiars that were said to help European witches.

There was much variation in language and costume in the widely scattered tribes. There were some 700 languages, which were divided into slightly more than 20 linguistic groups, some of them as different in type as are Latin and Mandarin Chinese. Communication between tribes was often conducted in sign language which became a regular inter-tribal code of signals in areas like the Great Plains. Some peoples used picture writing and sometimes symbolic objects such as strings of wampum beads to convey history and information. But it was not until the early 19th century, under European influence, that the first truly American Indian alphabet was invented, adapted to suit the Cherokee language.

Clothing was also influenced by the European settlers, and pictures of the 19th century show that the skin gowns of the squaws on the prairie reflected something of European fashion. But none of the American Indians felt clothing to be a necessity. Rather it was a way of marking social status, and proclaiming individual importance.

Mexico and Central America

The Aztecs were a group of American Indians speaking Nahuatl, a language of the Siouan family. They came originally from North America but may have been in Mexico for several centuries before they became a powerful tribe. The language was also spoken by the Toltecs, who controlled most of Mexico between 750 and 1000 AD.

Southern Mexico had been a civilized country long before the Aztecs built their great city state. As early as 900 BC there had been a civilization of importance on the southern curve of the Gulf of Mexico. This was a development which appeared quite suddenly among tribes of primitive farmers whose villages depended on maize cultivation. When this early Olmec civilization declined, it was succeeded in south-western Mexico by another culture, developed by the Zapotecs, who continued from the 2nd century BC until 1480 AD, when they were brought into the Aztec Empire.

On the highland plateau of Central Mexico a new civilization arose around the city of Teotihuacan (Teo-tee-wa-kan) the Place where the Gods were Made. Here great pyramid temples were built for the Sun and Moon and the Wind-and-Rain. The city was probably the home of nearly a million people. The paintings and sculpture from Teotihuacan show that much of later Aztec religion was already in existence by the first century AD. Teotihuacan had a great many contacts with surrounding Mexican tribes, and its art style is found throughout the whole area of the later Aztec Empire.

After the fall of Teotihuacan in the 6th century AD, there was a period of confusion, which ended with the development of a war-like empire based at Tula (or Tollan) the Place of Reeds, 20 miles north of what is now Mexico City. The Toltecs, who ruled from Tula, gradually controlled all civilized parts of Mexico. But soon after 970 a civil war broke out. The fighting was excessively fierce and a terrible pestilence broke out. By the end of the war the Toltec Empire was finished. Some leading Toltecs had escaped to Yucatan, far to the south, and tradition says that only 20 noble Toltec families survived on the Mexican plateau.

These Toltecs were important because they were descended from the god Quetzalcoatl (Kwet-zal-co-atl) the Precious Twin, who was the planet Venus as Morning Star. But the name can also be read as Feathered Serpent, which refers to Quetzalcoatl as the wind god whose breath rippled the leaves and grasses as if they were the green plumes of the earth serpent. Quetzalcoatl was blessed by the Creator, and his descendants alone among the Mexican nobility had the right to rule the country.

After 1000 AD the Mexican city states were constantly at war with one another. Some tribes reached a high level of civilization but others were poverty-stricken and still wore skins and hunted with bows and arrows.

Among the latter were the ancestors of the Aztecs. It was in 1168 that the leaders of this small tribe came to a ruined temple where they heard a message from a talking image of their tribal god Huitzilopochtli (Wit-zil-o-poch-tli), Blue Humming Bird on the Left, the bright sun god at the height of his path in the sky. They were sent on a pilgrimage which lasted nearly a century. They were promised that one day they would find an island in a lake with a rock on which there would be a cactus. On the cactus they would see their god in the form of a shining eagle holding a serpent in his talons. This would be the place where they were to settle and build a city from which they would rule all Mexico.

After many tribulations the Mexica, as they called themselves, were defeated and ensnared by the king of Colhuacan. The tough Aztec tribesmen were soon sent to help in a war against the surrounding tribes. They killed all the enemies they saw because they would not bring back prisoners to be sacrificed to the gods of their oppres-

sive ruler in Colhuacan. Instead they cut off one ear from each victim, and put them in packs on their backs. When the king upbraided them as cowards who could not capture any prisoners for his gods, they silently poured a torrent of human ears over his feet.

The king was shocked and afraid. He dismissed the Aztecs and told them they could settle freely on an islet in the Lake of Mexico. So they went to the rocky islet among the swamps. There their leader found a stream beside a rock, and on the rock was the cactus and the shining eagle of Huitzilopochtli. Their long pilgrimage was over. The year was 1325.

It was not until 1375 that an Aztec war chief assumed the title of Tlatoani and so asserted his independence as the 'Speaker' of the will of the Aztec people. In 1440 the fifth chief of the Aztecs came to rule Tenochtitlan (Cactus Rock) as they called Mexico City. The Mexica now dominated the whole of the Valley of Mexico, and had allied themselves with the neighbouring cities of Tezcuco and Tlacopan. Their chiefs had sought out princesses of pure Toltec descent as their brides, so that they could inherit the divine right to rule which belonged to the descendants of Quetzalcoatl. The new ruler of the Aztecs was given the title of Uetlatoani or Great Speaker for the several tribes over whom he had dominion. His name was Moctecuzoma Ilhuicamina (Moc-te-cuzoma Il-wi-ca-mina), meaning Noble Strong Arm, He Who Aims at the Sky. During his reign the Aztec armies continued their conquests and first reached the shores of the Mexican Gulf.

In 1484 the Great Speaker Tizoc (He who offers his own Blood to the Gods) laid the foundations for the rebuilding of the ancient temple to Huitzilopochtli. He took prisoners and sacrificed some to the god. The annals say that this was the first sacrifice of human captives on a large scale. In fact it had long been felt to be necessary to kill a few captives, rarely more than 20 at even the greatest ceremonies.

Tizoc died before the temple was completed. The great building was to be finished and dedicated under his successor, the Great Speaker Ahuitzotl (Ah-wit-zotl) or Water-Opossum, a magical creature believed to be the cause of death by drowning.

Ahuitzotl was a patron of the arts, and a great lover of music. He had more wives than any other Mexican ruler, and rejoiced

Above Tonatiuh, the sun god: originally his heaven was reserved for those who had achieved fulfilment on earth, but the Aztecs made it the abode of warriors: Aztec relief, c 1500 AD **Opposite top** Mixtec sacrificial knife made from chalcedony, 14th century AD **Opposite** Aztec skull, encrusted with turquoise mosaic: possibly a representation of the black Tezcatlipoca, god of 'black magic and devilry'

in flowers, beautiful birds and animals. Yet his name became a synonym of horror and cruelty. When the great temple was dedicated he took 20,000 captives and had them all sacrificed in four days by eight teams of priests. The year was 1487, only five years before Columbus sailed into the West Indies. Ahuitzotl died in 1502 when the Spanish had just settled in Cuba. His successor was Prince Strong Arm, the Noble Lord; or by his Aztec name, Moctecuzoma Xocoyotzin.

By this time almost all of civilized Mexico was under Aztec domination. Traders went far afield, bringing turquoise from New Mexico, gold from Panama and precious feathers from Guatemala. Even the independent priest-kings of the Zapotecs had surrendered. But when Moctecuzoma (Montezuma) died in 1519, his city was occupied by the Spanish troops of Hernando Cortes. The god had fulfilled his promise of glory and had now deserted the Aztecs; and it was left only for the brave young Prince Falling Eagle (Cuauhtemoc) to lead a hopeless resistance against the white men.

During their years of expansion the Aztecs had been, in their way, an enlightened people. They not only married princesses of Toltec descent but also sought out knowledge of past arts and crafts. They hired teachers from the Mixtecs, who knew a great deal about Toltec customs and included many fine artist-craftsmen among the tribe. The work of Aztec artists was almost entirely concerned with religion and it is possible to understand the inner meaning of many of their best works because captive Aztec nobles gave much information to Spanish missionaries after the Conquest.

The religion which they described was already an ancient one when the Aztecs first settled on Cactus Rock. It was an expression of the inner spirit of Mexico, the result of generations of philosophical thought by American Indians who had built up a new kind of life from the discovery of agriculture right up to the evolution of great cities.

Basically they believed that beyond the world and the gods of nature there must be a

Supreme Creator, whom they named Omete-cuhtli (Omey-te-cu-tli) which means Two-Lord. As Creator he was thought to be two persons in one, for no creation could take place without the co-operation of male and female. Sometimes he is shown as a pair of very old people, and sometimes as a single being dressed half as a woman and half as a man.

It seems that Ometecuhtli was the product of thought by learned philosophers. Most of the Mexicans looked to the central fire-place in their homes as the shrine of the oldest of the gods. They called him Ueuet-eotl (Old Old God) and saw in him a symbol of the continuous creation of fire (equivalent to life) and the destruction of used-up things. He was a fountain of change at the heart of everything. His place in the heavens was the Pole Star, the pivot of the universe. The oldest image of this god, shown as an aged man seated with a fire-bowl balanced on his head, comes from the ruined pyramid of Cuicuilco, near Mexico City. It dates from more than 2000 years before the Spanish conquest of Mexico.

The Mexicans believed that 13 domed heavens circulated around the pivot of the universe. There was one for each of the visible planets, the sun, the moon, the clouds, the lightnings, the heat, and the rain; all contained within the dome of the fixed stars. Under the flat surface of the earth there were thought to be nine underworlds, the lowest of which were the lands of the dead.

As the central hearth-fire in the house was the pivot of earthly life, so the souls of the dead who eventually entered the fire in the lowest region of the universe ascended to a point where the Creator might send them back to earth. But this again was a philo-sophic idea. Most people appear to have expected a long stay in the underworld, which was after all a very happy place where people in the form of skeletons enjoyed a normal social life, presided over by the Lord and Lady of the Dead.

To the philosopher this multi-layered universe was like a single drop of water in the hand of the ineffable Creator, Omete-cuhtli. But in general the Aztecs believed, much as did their Red Indian forbears, that the world was the back of a gigantic living creature.

The Aztec legends described Mother Earth as a strange monstrous being like a gigantic alligator. Long ago, the black Tezcatlipoca (Tez-caat-li-po-ca) or Smoking Mirror, so named from his symbol, a black obsidian mirror which appeared to smoke when the magicians looked into it to descry the future, had drawn the earth up from the great waters of creation. As he put his foot into the waters, the monstrous alligator snapped at it but the foot was not torn off until the terrible god of magic and youthful energy had drawn the earth monster from the waters and

Left The god Quetzalcoatl was the Lord of Life and Death, and god of the wind: only his descendants, the Toltecs, had the right to rule over the Aztecs

Human Sacrifice

It is difficult for us to come to a true understanding of what human sacrifice meant to the 16th century Aztec: but it may be observed that every culture possesses its own idea of what is and what is not cruel. At the height of their career the Romans shed more blood in their circuses and for amusement than even the Aztecs did before their idols. The Spaniards, so sincerely moved by the cruelty of the native priests, nevertheless massacred, burnt, mutilated and tortured with a perfectly clear conscience. We, who shudder at the tale of the bloody rites of Ancient Mexico, have seen with our own eyes and in our days civilized nations proceed systematically to the extermination of millions of human beings and to the perfection of weapons capable of annihilating in one second a hundred times more victims than the Aztecs ever sacrificed.

Human sacrifice among the Mexicans was inspired neither by cruelty nor by hatred. It was their response, and the only response that they could conceive, to the instability of a continually threatened world. Blood was necessary to save this world and the men in it: the victim was no longer an enemy who was to be killed but a messenger, arraigned in a dignity that was almost divine. All the relevant descriptions . . . convey the impression not of a dislike between the sacrificer and the victim nor of anything resembling a lust for blood but of a strange fellow feeling . . .

Jacques Soustelle
Daily Life of the Aztecs

---

made her back into the dry land. Since then the god has had but a single foot and his lonely footprint in the heavens is the constellation of the great Bear. According to another story, his foot was cut off when the doors of the underworld closed on his leg.

Tezcatlipoca was lord of the four directions on earth, East, South, West and North. He was also lord of the Nature gods when these other gods were developed.

A popular legend told of a cave in the universe where the Mother of the Gods gave birth to starry offspring. They were the 400 northerners, the 400 southerners, and the planets. Then she became pregnant again. The children were upset and planned to destroy the new child. Only the golden moon girl wanted to protect her mother.

When the new child was born, it proved to be a monstrous sun-before-the-earthly-sun. It was Tezcatlipoca armed as a warrior. He destroyed all the stars. Then, seeing his sister among the slain, he realized that her head might yet live, so he cut it off and cast her into the sky, where the head with golden bells on her cheeks can still be seen as the Moon. Each day when the sun emerges in our real world, we see that the stars of night are slain, but they are reborn as the moon comes among them, grows pregnant and then meets her ever-recurring end.

Once the earth was established, the gods created men. Three times the human race became too self-opinionated and had to be destroyed, at about 2000-year intervals. They were destroyed by the fire, the waters, the winds. Now the present human race, who were made by the gods from the beloved maize plant which is still the sustenance of mankind, are being tested.

The end of this universe will come from a terrible earthquake. Whether after this fourth sun, the earth will be re-populated by another better race remains to be experienced in the future.

On each re-creation a new sun was made by the gods. At the beginning of the present creation they made a great offering place at Teotihuacan. There they met for four days, waiting for one of them to cast himself into the fire. At last from a distance there came a miserably ill and poverty-stricken god. He had no reason to continue as he was, so he voluntarily cast himself into the fire. Blazing, and blue with magic power, he flew into the heavens as Tonatiuh (Ton-a-tiyu) the Lord of Fate, the sun. The sun appeared every day, and each day had its separate fate for people, so the count of time which the fortune tellers used was based simply on the sun.

The sun was very brave, the source of all brightness and glory. He had his special heaven for brave warriors who had been sacrificed and for women who had died in childbirth. These warriors, dressed as eagles, lifted the sun to the top of the sky every morning; the women lowered him down each evening into the underworld.

All the time the sun was thirsting from great heat. So he had to be nourished and cooled by offerings of the red cactus-fruit (which meant human hearts and blood). Only a few need be sacrificed to keep the sun moving in the sky, but the sacrifice must never be neglected or the human race would die from the fire caused by a motionless sun.

Of all deaths the most glorious was to be sacrificed to the sun. The sun himself sacrificed his victims in the sky as he rose and the stars died. On earth the stars were represented by the spotted quails, which were killed every morning at sunrise. Sometimes people saw at this lucky time the little brother of the sun, Piltzintecuhtli (the Divine Princeling), the planet Mercury.

Sometimes the Great Star was visible, in the form of the morning star lifting up the sun. This was a symbol of Quetzalcoatl, the god of the air and of human civilization also.

The other planets were also gods; and so were the major stars. The groups of stars through which the sun passed were the houses of 13 gods. These were very like our 12 signs of the zodiac, though the Mexicans knew that there were 13 moons in any one year, but that one of them was always incomplete. Thus there was always a relationship between earthly events and the shapes in the sky where the gods had their palaces.

Earth was the domain of the powerful and demonic Tezcatlipoca, who had four forms. He was the yellow Tezcatlipoca as god of the sunrise in the East, of bravery and growing crops. The blue Tezcatlipoca was the fertility spirit and the patron spirit of the Aztec nation. In the West he became the red Tezcatlipoca, who died by being skinned alive so that maize could be given to mankind. In this form he was Xipe Totec, Our Lord the Flayed One. In the North he was the black Tezcatlipoca in the land where the sun never shone, where he became the ruler of all forms of black magic and devilry.

This religion suited warriors and astronomer-priests but it had little meaning for the farmers who produced the food on which the people lived. Most Mexicans were small farmers, feeding their own families and growing cotton for their own clothing. They needed to propitiate the rain and wind, the spirits of vegetation and the kindly Earth Mother. Probably their religion was more ancient than that of the warriors to which it became wedded in the complex Aztec theological system. Their traditions were fully integrated into the other system, however, and certainly by Aztec times the whole complex of beliefs presented a kind of unity. It was no more logical than an exciting dream; and that may well be because the gods of Mexico were really those factors within the depths of the human personality from which our dreams normally spring. Always, without any very conscious thinking about it the Aztecs linked the world of nature with the sequence of human life, and projected their thoughts onto a very human pantheon of deities, regarded with all the affection and fear with which humans regard

---

The Essence of Fear

Coatlicue (Co-at-lee-kway), the 'Lady of the Serpent Skirt', and mother of Huitzilopochtli, was thought of as powerful and awesome, so the task of the sculptors was to transmute those qualities into stone. The great statue in Mexico, whose head is twin serpents, whose necklace human hands and hearts, whose feet and hands are viciously armed with claws and whose skirt is a mat of writhing snakes, brings into a dynamic concentrate the manifold horrors of the universe. A smaller carving, simpler and less detailed, produces this same effect, implying that the very essence of fear was honoured and worshipped.

G. C. Vaillant
The Aztecs of Mexico

their neighbours, particularly of the non-human kind.

The almost passive centre of the farmers' religion was the maize plant. It had many spirits, but was basically the maize god Cinteotl (Sin-tay-otl). This divine power within the basic foodstuff of ancient America was nurtured by Mother Earth. He loved pretty Chalchihuitlicue, the flirtatious mistress of the rain god Tlaloc, and was cleansed by the winds sent by Quetzalcoatl.

When the first green ears appeared on the maize, the girls took some and danced with their hair thrown loose and with naked breasts, for the maize was now the pretty young goddess Xilonen. Later, when the maize was to be harvested, bundles of ears were made up to represent the maize spirit, and were carried ceremonially to be enshrined in the granaries for next year's sowing. Then some of the grain was chewed by the girls so that it would ferment in water and so become a delightful kind of light beer. Great magic was worked by the priests so that each year the maize could be protected from its natural foes. Maize was life, and the rhythm of planting and reaping conditioned the whole concept of the meaning of the passage of time in Mexico. At the harvest festival the girls wore necklaces and headbands of brightly dyed popcorn, as if it were the most delightful of flowers, and indeed so it was.

The priests in Aztec Mexico were the most important example of social mobility. Warriors sometimes, by feats of great bravery, might move across barriers and become members of the tribal nobility; but priests might come from any social class. Young candidates were sent by their parents to a training school. They were questioned very carefully by the priests, because such a life meant much hardship and demanded a great love of learning. The tests were the same for children of the meanest serf and for those of the greatest noble.

Once boys entered the temple service they went through much hardship, sleeping on the ground and being woken up for night ceremonies. They became inured to spending long hours in chanting poetic history and theology, and learning the knowledge of the stars and of medicine. They must frequently perform acts of personal offering by cutting their ears and tongues to give blood to the gods.

The black-painted junior priest ate little and simply and never cut or cleaned his hair or nails, but acquired knowledge and wisdom as he progressed. He might become an interpreter of magical symbols or an artist or, if he were good enough, he might become a sacrificing priest who graduated from taking out the hearts of quails to performing a similar operation on the hearts of living men.

The priestly way was a strangely savage life of deep learning; a kind of ferocious holiness. At the head of the priestly organization were the High Priest of the Rains and the High Priest of the Winds. Their titles show that whatever deities they were actually serving, their office was to preserve the life and fertility of the land.

There were also religious women, who were usually employed in making vestments of beautiful weaving and featherwork for the servants of the gods. They were expected to carry out the cleaning of the temples and also to cleanse humans from disease, just as the goddess Tlazolteotl

Above left The sun had to be nourished with offerings of the 'red cactus fruit', human hearts and blood, according to Aztec belief. If this sacrifice was neglected the sun would stop moving and the human race would die from the resulting fire: to be sacrificed to the sun was considered a glorious death. Illustration from a manuscript in the Museo de America, Madrid *Above right* Aztec water goddess tempting Quetzalcoatl, like the earth waiting for fertility from the 'breath of life', the wind which brought the refreshing rains *Opposite* Modern Peruvian witch-doctors, like their earlier Inca counterparts, are thought to be able 'to converse with the spirits of the air, and the creatures of the earth'

could do with her magic. They had a considerable knowledge of herbal medicine, which was aided by the national passion for taking a sauna bath as a form of spiritual purification. It is clear from the painted books that some of the priestesses were elevated to the rank of Sacrificers, who took human hearts for the gods.

Another group of religious servants were those whom the gods seized upon and caused to utter prophecy. These were people who saw visions, or heard the voices of the spirits of the dead or the voices of the gods. Many of them would have been trance mediums of great power in our day. But any person who showed an abnormal mental condition was thought to have received a divine inspiration. A passage in a manuscript called the Codex Laud, at Oxford, compares the highly trained astronomer-priest to the inspired prophet. One has command of the moving stars but the other has command of the breath of life.

There were a vast number of omens to be observed, which were recorded soon after the Spanish Conquest of Mexico by Father Sahagun. But almost any event might be treated as an omen by people who thought that life was determined for them by outside powers. There were a great number of things to be learned from the flight and behaviour of birds. The cries of an owl at night were considered to be ominous and the movements of lizards and serpents were also of interest. The rattlesnake conveyed messages from the earth goddess.

There was also a good deal of interest in the weather and the directions of the winds, which was natural in an agricultural community. The peasant was always aware of the reliance of the community on the powers of nature. But it was realized that these powers might well be capricious. The water goddess, for instance, was described as a brilliant and capricious young woman.

In the home of this goddess, where she lived with her husband Tlaloc, the god of all sources of water, there was continuous warm drizzle and brilliant rainbows shone over the masses of flowers and sweet smelling shrubs. They had four servants, the Tlaloques or Little Rains. These were cloud spirits who reclined in the rolling vapours, carrying different kinds of rain. One came from the East and brought the golden spring rains to fertilize the soil; another from the South brought warm blue rains to make all things fruitful; a third from the West brought the red rains which made the plants sleep as winter came; lastly the northern rain was dangerous, for he came from the realm where the sun never shone and so his rains brought destruction and were mostly hailstones.

What would the rain do without the winds? The Aztecs said of Quetzalcoatl that as god of the wind he came to sweep the way for the rains and in this form he was a breath of life which made the vegetation of the earth sway like a serpent covered with green feathers. When his time of power was well advanced, the naughty water goddess decided to tempt him. She stripped naked and sat before him with her beautiful vulva opened, like the earth waiting for fertility from the breath of life which was the wind. The somewhat grotesque painting of this in the Codex Laud also combines the idea that the goddess of whirlpools tempted the wind and so caused the great breakers on the sea in hurricanes.

But Quetzalcoatl was also the morning star and his path, first rising in the heavens and then sinking, was also linked with the fertility myth. And it was the key of the story of the divine King Quetzalcoatl.

The divine king brought blessings to the earth, improved agriculture, made the arts flourish and covered palaces with jewels and precious feather decorations. He taught a philosophy of gentleness and austere asceticism, offering blood from his ears and limbs daily to the gods in the outer heaven. But when the revolutions of time brought the stars into a pattern which meant that his planet was setting, he was tempted. The goddess approached him and visited his court, bringing with her many magicians and enchanters, among whom was the black Tezcatlipoca. At a festival she offered the god-king a bowl of alcoholic pulque prepared from the agave heart. Then as he became intoxicated she offered him magic mushrooms and induced a trance-like ecstasy in which he abandoned his austerity and raped her.

On awakening, appalled at his break with the ascetic code of priestly behaviour, Quetzalcoatl left Mexico. He gave over his power to Tezcatlipoca and sailed into the sun, where his heart burnt up and ascended again as the morning star. Already there was a confusion between the god and the first king of the Toltecs, who was dedicated to the worship of Quetzalcoatl. The truth is that the concept of the god Quetzalcoatl was very ancient indeed but because it concerned an earthly king it was a myth which could be applied to any period in the past.

In the Quetzalcoatl myth, an account of wind and rain and the passing seasons, which promoted fertility and then passed on, had expanded into a universal parable of the human condition. We all follow this path of development, which ends in loss of energy and eventual death. We also share something of all primitive religion within our own personalities, for the gods of old Mexico, and of many other places, are expressions of images which lie deep in the structure of the human personality.

These natural gods, in spite of their raw and often horrific appearance in Mexican art, inspired great devotion and trust in the populace. The religion was not just a formality but a reality which people lived. It was a re-presentation of the natural universe of which they were part. The sense that mankind was an active part of the life of the whole universe was the driving force behind their artistic output, whether it was a great image for a temple, or a little pot for use in the home.

In the Aztec version of the final collapse of Mexico we find that not all the population fought the Spaniards. They moved only when led by the great nobles to whom they owed allegiance. Mostly they suffered passively, and acted bravely when called upon by the brilliantly feathered war leaders. Though decimated by the smallpox which killed the noble Cuitlahuac, who succeeded Moctecuzoma, the Aztecs continued to give battle with their Stone Age weapons against Spaniards clad in steel and armed with cannon. The young Cuauhtemoc was their last elected war leader. But finally he surrendered as the last buildings in the city of Cactus Rock were torn down. Later, when he made a brave effort to achieve freedom he was captured and strangled. But Cuauhtemoc became the national hero of modern Mexico; and his mother tongue, the ancient Nahuatl language, has become the language of poetry in Mexico.

Camera Press London

South America

Within four centuries the Inca family expanded from rulers of part of a small town to a semi-divine tribe of which the head, the Sapa Inca, ruled an immense empire which they termed *Tahuantinsuyu,* the Four Quarters, to imply that their father the sun god destined them to rule the entire known earth. In the mid-11th century, about the time of the Norman Conquest of Britain, a family of American Indians came from the East and ascended the mountains into a civilized country which had broken up into warring tribal troups. Their legend tells us that they were commanded to find the very centre, the navel or *Cuzco,* of the earth. To ascertain this they carried a wedge of gold, symbol of a sun ray, and at each stopping place they placed the wedge upon the ground to see if it would sink into the earth and disappear. This at last happened when Inca Manco and his sister Mama Occlo, who were the only survivors of the family, came to a little mountain town near the headwaters of the Apurimac river.

At the time of the Inca arrival Peru was divided. The mountain peoples were heirs to three previous empires. The earliest originated around Chavin de Huantar well before 1000 BC and its characteristic art styles enable archeologists to show how it dominated much of the northern part of the Peruvian Andes. It has a close artistic relationship with the peoples of the more southerly part of the Peruvian Coast around the Paracas Peninsula, where there was a typically Peruvian cult of the dead, important people being sun dried after death, and then wrapped in great quantities of elaborately embroidered cloths. The strange art of these peoples was obsessed by the forms of serpents, pumas and condors, sacred animals representing earth, mountains and sky. A slightly later development of this religious art centred around Nasca on the southern half of the Peruvian Coast and was expressed in the creation of beautifully painted pottery, which in the early centuries AD included the first near realist figures of human beings in Peru.

Further to the north, again in the early centuries AD, another culture had arisen. These Mochica people lived in city states, were apparently often at war with each other, and built temples on great pyramidal mounds of brick. Their pottery is well modelled and painted simply with terracotta colours on cream, and here also arose true portrait modelling. Presumably this was part of the cult of the dead for the best vases are all found in the pits in the coastal sands where the mummified bodies of people were buried with their household treasures.

The people of the highlands seem to have developed separately and by the 6th century AD formed into two rather similar groups around the northern city of Huari and the famous southern one of Tiahuanaco near Lake Titicaca. In the 8th century or perhaps a little later, the Tiahuanaco people defeated the tribes around Nasca and imposed their culture upon them. But the conquest did not last, and eventually Tiahuanaco itself fell in some catastrophe beyond our knowledge. Similarly the Huari power broke up. In the 10th and 11th centuries central and southern Peru and all the highland regions fell into a chaos of small conflicting tribal states. Only on the northern half of the coast was there much development. The Mochica towns were taken over by a warrior group who came on balsa rafts from the north, led by a great king known as the Great Chimu.

Chimu culture prospered exceedingly and from the 12th to the 15th centuries the kingdom was centred around the great city of Chan Chan. On that rainless coast it was built of mud brick covered with brilliantly painted plaster. The artisans worked in gold, silver, turquoise and crystal. Women created beauty in workshops, weaving quantities of clothing for the townspeople. Irrigation of the narrow river valleys passing through the arid coastlands made the plantations of maize, beans, pumpkins, melons and chilli peppers fruitful and rich. These people worshipped the stars and forces of Nature, but above all they adored the moon god, Si, who spared them from the fierce heat of the sun and guided their fishing boats over the calm seas on moonlit nights. From all the evidence they were a rich comfortable people, loving colour and jewellery. Their fertility festivals were gay and often enough thoroughly and happily pornographic, to the shocked indignation of their highland neighbours, the Incas, who were becoming a powerful force to be reckoned with by the late 14th century.

Camera Press London

Michael Holford

Above In honour of their great father the sun, the Incas celebrated elaborate festivals of feasting and rejoicing: wooden beaker showing a ceremonial procession *Opposite* Headhunting was prevalent in Peru before the advent of the Spanish; it was believed that the possession of another man's head increased the new owner's spiritual powers: llama wool fabric depicting warriors grasping shrunken heads *Top* Many Christian festivals among the Sierra Indians of Peru contain practices which are relics of forgotten Inca beliefs. At the feast of Corpus Christi, dancers wear masks bearing both the cross and the ancient Inca symbol of the sun

The Inca city of Cuzco had been growing in importance, and the Inca family claiming descent from the sun god actively worked to spread their rule. The Inca was so holy that he could not be born from normal human parents. He was always the firstborn son of the divine marriage of the previous Sapa Inca with his sister (some say first cousin) the Ccoya, who was of equally pure lineage from the sun. In the male line there was only one breakdown – the Prince Yahuarhuaccac, He Who Weeps Blood. It seems that the growth of Inca power in the Cuzco Valley roused the jealousy of a group of Highland tribes known as the Chanca confederation. The young Inca was terrified of the power of the confederated armies and he lost a battle. His own family had him killed and appointed his brother to rule. The new ruler dared first to state the gravity of their plight by taking the name of Viracocha, the Creator. Only under that protection could they hope to win. In a series of outflanking raids and unexpected attacks the Inca forces destroyed the Chanca confederacy and Inca Viracocha found himself in command of all the mountain tribes around Cuzco. In another generation the Incas spread their rule over the whole Peruvian part of the Andes, including the sacred though by now thoroughly ruined ancient city of Tiahuanaco.

Eventually the clash with the Chimu kingdom developed. The ruling Inca was becoming elderly but he sent his son Prince Tupac to conduct the campaign. After some fighting the Chimu capitulated. The Inca made their burden light, taking all the gold in the country for the glory of the sun god, but allowing the Chimu to retain silver ornaments. The Chimu were permitted to worship their own gods, but every temple had to support an oratory to the sun which made it quite clear that his children, the Incas, were

the real rulers of the country. The Chimu crown prince was taken to Cuzco to learn Inca ways. He was treated well and married to an Inca Princess, which made sure that his children would also be of proper Inca descent.

The capture of the Chimu kingdom made the Incas masters of all the civilized areas of Peru. Under the great Tupac Yupanqui when he became Sapa Inca, the Inca armies faced a movement of tribes from Argentina, so he decided to spread the Empire down to Chile. His son Huayna Ccapac turned northwards and captured the Cara kingdom of southern Ecuador and took the Cara princess as one of his hundreds of junior wives. He was so in love with her that he decreed that on his death Huascar, his son by his sister, should be Supreme Inca in Peru, but that his son by the princess, Atahuallpa, should rule the northern section of the Empire. As things turned out, on the death of Huayna Ccapac, the two princes engaged in a terrible civil war. The true heir, Huascar, was taken prisoner and shut up in a cell in Cuzco and the false Atahuallpa called himself the Supreme Inca. Peru was paralysed because the people realized that this was no true child of the sun. Just at this time the Spaniards arrived. In a short campaign they captured Atahuallpa, and murdered him; but not before he had had Huascar, the true heir, killed. Thus in 1533 fell the divine sun kingdom of the Incas.

In their years of power the Incas achieved a great deal. Believing themselves to be directly descended from the sun god they felt it to be their duty to spread the benefits of divine rule throughout the lands which they controlled. They improved the road systems and arranged for storehouses of food and clothing in all parts of Peru so that in times of catastrophe there was always a reserve for the people. They greatly extended the use of the coloured knotted cords by which they transmitted messages instead of writing. Most important of all from their point of view was the establishment of a sun temple in every town of their dominions.

In Cuzco the great sun temple was surrounded by smaller buildings which held the lesser gods of all the peoples of the empire, as if they were servants waiting to obey their master. There was only One more powerful than the sun. Inside the sun temple was a wall covered with gold. Upon it there were figures of the sun, moon, thunder, and rainbow. The first humans were there and the first Inca. Then there were the constellations of stars and in their midst an open blank space, which astronomers now know as the 'coal sack' because of its comparative blackness in the Milky Way. This centrepiece of the golden wall was always empty. It represented the mystery of the Creator, Viracocha, the Breath of Life who was everywhere unseen but eternally giving life, even to father sun. The temple was so placed that once a year the rays of the rising sun shone through the doorway and lit up the golden wall with living burning light. On that occasion the Sapa Inca was alone in the temple. He was without his crown and barefoot, having meditated all night and prayed that the sun, which was now at its furthest point away from his kingdom, should return to spread light and life again. Outside, the people of the city had spent a night of penitence without fire and food, weeping for their past evil-doings. The priests had worked magic over a black llama so that it would take the sins of the peoples on its back before being driven away into the mountains.

Then when the returning sun had shone upon the golden wall the Inca put on his diadem and his golden sandals. After he had sacrificed a pure white llama the people burst into songs of rejoicing and the city was filled with processions, singing and dancing. On that occasion strangers kept outside the city for fear. From the royal storehouses food was distributed and every individual was given a vase holding about half a gallon of maize beer. After the day of rejoicing was over the streets of the city were lined with people in a quiet, happy stupor, for the drunken Peruvian preferred sleeping to fighting. They were happy that once again the sun was returning through the skies, every day shining higher and higher, until the day came when he sat on his stone throne in every town and cast no shadow because he was right overhead, showering blessings on the four quarters of the earth ruled so wisely by his son, the Sapa Inca.

In addition to the great powers of Nature the Peruvians found magic in all manner of things which they thought were lucky charms. They collected strangely-shaped stones, reverenced unusual animals, and found an aura of power in the dried bodies of the dead. Wise men knew how to interpret the language of animals and predict the future from the flight of birds. On occasions of great disasters they might offer a few human sacrifices, but normally they made little presents of food and small animals and birds to their gods. They well understood that sometimes the powers of Nature were terrible, but they accepted that the Nature gods took their own human victims as they pleased. Famine might be sent by the gods but the storehouses of the sun and the Inca existed to return the divine bounty to help the afflicted people.

Under the Incas social organization was thorough. Every event in a village was recorded on the knotted string *quipus*, or cords, and sent to the town for the archives. Abstracts of these reports were knotted up and sent to the supreme administration in Cuzco. The Inca was in his massive stone palace for all great festivals, but he also travelled widely inspecting towns, ordering the construction of roads, bridges and storehouses, and impressing his people that all were interdependent in the kingdom of the sun. The taxes for the Inca and the sun god, each taking a third of the harvest of every field, were largely returned in the paternalistic welfare service. Only his direct servants, the High Priest and his closest

relatives might look closely on his face. Others threw themselves down and turned their faces to the earth as the divine king passed close to them.

It appears that people discussed the Inca as an individual, and on a very few occasions protested against new regulations, but on the whole they regarded him as a natural phenomenon, a divine sun child sent to guide them in the pleasanter paths of life.

In such a society marriage was important because good family organization was the basis of the state. Once a year in every district there was a great ceremony in which young couples were married. They had only a very small choice of partners, but there seems to be little record of domestic un-happiness. They accepted the chosen part-ner whom they had almost certainly known from childhood, reared their families, looked after the flocks, cultivated the fields, and made pots and wove cloth for the home.

Gold funerary mask of the Chimu people, who were conquered by the Incas: they worshipped the stars and the forces of Nature, but especially the moon god who guided their fishing boats 'over the calm seas on moonlit nights'

For the family of the Inca himself, however, arrangements were different. Each Sapa Inca was married to his sister who was the sacred queen, the Ccoya. In addition he was expected to take many more wives. The daughters of defeated chiefs were often taken into the harem of the Inca, an honour which bound their family in allegiance. Important tribal areas were kept happy within the empire if their noblest young ladies bore children of Inca descent.

In the general field of religion there were the functioning priests from the High Priest of the sun right down to the cleaners in the temples. A third of the wealth of the country secured their welfare and was used to keep the store rooms full in readiness for times of shortage. In Cuzco there was a college for young ladies who were chosen from all the kingdom for their intelligence and beauty. They were known as the Virgins of the sun. They wove beautiful clothing for the Inca and for the priests and temples. Some of them remained dedicated to the service of religion all their lives; but most were married off to nobles and visiting rulers. They became the gifts of the Inca to those whom he delighted to honour.

The position of women in Inca Peru was of equality with men, but within the sphere of women's work. They were not warriors and roadmakers, but no men made pottery or wove cloth. Everywhere in the empire the woman and mother was treated with respect and honour, and the Ccoya was queen of women's employment just as the Inca was king over the male side of life. Some women became professional healers. They had a deep and scientific knowledge of herbal medicine, and knew the value of massage and of bone-setting. There were also many women as well as some men who were inspired by spirits and who gave advice when in a state of trance. They were supposed to be able to converse with the spirits of the air, and the creatures of earth.

There is nothing else in history to com-pare truly with Inca Peru. It is an example of a divine kingship taken to the ultimate extreme. By good fortune the individual Incas seem to have been men of very high character with a real care for the welfare of their kingdom. They used the thousands of cousins in the Inca family as a disciplined and closely knit civil service. The organization of every facet of life made administration easy, but it was also scientific. There was not much freedom, yet very few revolts. Progress was not great because there was enough food, clothing and entertainment for everybody and no one wished to introduce innovations into a contented, divinely-inspired civilization. On the whole the gods and mankind had found a *modus vivendi*, a way of living that was mutually acceptable, for a few generations. But at the beginning of the 16th century came the strange end, with the Divine Inca deposed and murdered by his more earthly brother; and then a total change when the bronze age theocracy was taken over by the feudal iron-using Spanish invaders from over the great oceans.

Michael Holford

THE ANCIENT WORLD

Egypt

Two factors have conspired to give ancient Egypt its unique appeal: its religion and the fact that its climate has so wonderfully preserved the relics of this religion for us. Religion permeated the whole life both of the individual Egyptian and of Egyptian society. It found expression in such a rich variety of forms that Egyptian religion provides the best introduction to the historical and comparative study of religion. Almost every aspect of religious faith and practice is found in this ancient religion: polytheism, henotheism (the worship of a single god), monotheism (belief that there is only one God), mythology, magic, ritual, divine kingship, mighty temples and mysterious tombs, a professional priesthood, illustrated religious texts, a wisdom literature and religious scepticism. It also embraced the most elaborate funerary cult, magical resurrection and a complex afterlife, and the earliest conception of a judgement after death. Although now extinct, Egyptian religion was the longest-lived religion yet recorded; it was already in being in 3000 BC and it survived until the forcible suppression of pagan cults by the Christian emperor Theodosius in 384.

Egyptian religion is well documented. There is an abundance of texts inscribed on the walls of tombs, temples, obelisks, statues and stelae (stone memorial slabs), or painted on coffins or written on papyrus scrolls. They range in date from the Pyramid Texts of c 2400 BC, or the Book of the Dead, to texts of the 4th century AD. Monuments such as pyramids, temples and tombs have often been so well preserved that their ritual use can be easily traced.

Temples and tombs were adorned with ritual scenes, and tombs with depictions of the underworld, all of which provide a vivid picture of Egyptian deities, worship and belief about the next world.

The immense duration of Egyptian religion makes it necessary to know something of the course of Egyptian history, especially since Egyptologists use their own chronological scheme in making reference to various periods. This scheme is founded on a dynastic framework; the dynasties concerned are royal, but it is not certain why the various groups of monarchs are so related to each other. The dates given here are approximate, since only rarely can an Egyptian date be definitively established. The Thinite Period (3200–2780 BC), comprising Dynasties 1–2, marks the beginning of the united kingdom of Upper and Lower Egypt under pharaonic rule. The Old Kingdom (2780–2280 BC), comprising Dynasties 3–6, was the pioneering period of Egyptian civilization, known as the Pyramid Age. The First Intermediate Period (2280–2052 BC), comprising Dynasties 7–10, was a time of social revolution when royal power was seriously weakened. At the time of the Middle Kingdom (2052–1778 BC), comprising Dynasties 11–12, the political centre had moved to Thebes in Upper Egypt; this was a period of great literary activity. The Second Intermediate Period (1778–1567 BC), Dynasties 13–17, was a time of national eclipse, when Egypt was subjugated by Asiatic invaders. The New Kingdom (1567–1085 BC), Dynasties 18–20, was the period of Egypt's greatest imperial expansion; Tutankhamen was a minor king of the 18th Dynasty. The Late Period (1085–330 BC), Dynasties 21–30, was a period of national decline, when Egypt suffered from Assyrian and Persian invasions; the last native Egyptian pharaoh was Nectanebo (359–341 BC). During the Ptolemaic or Hellen-istic Period (330–30 BC), Egypt was ruled by Greek (Macedonian) monarchs, the last of whom was the famous Cleopatra. After her death, Egypt was incorporated into the Roman Empire; this was the Roman Period (30 BC–641 AD). The main pattern of its religion continued, with the Roman emperors taking the place of the pharaohs, until it was finally suppressed in favour of Christianity in 384 AD. Certain elements of the ancient faith passed into Coptic Christianity, which survived the Islamic conquest of Egypt in 641 AD and the subsequent conversion of the Egyptian people.

Two natural features have always dominated life in Egypt, namely, the River Nile and the sun; from them stemmed two of the basic themes of ancient Egyptian religion. Egypt has been aptly described as a land having length but no breadth. The description is not quite accurate, because the Delta area is certainly extensive; but south of Cairo, Egypt really consists of two strips of irrigable land on either bank of the Nile, with the desert stretching away on each side. The land consequently divides into two distinctive parts: Lower Egypt, comprising the Delta area, and Upper Egypt, formed of the long narrow Nile valley. The fertility of the land depends absolutely upon the annual flooding of the Nile and the careful control and conservation of its life-giving waters. This entails the construction and maintenance of elaborate irrigation works. Consequently a strong centralized government, uniting Upper and Lower Egypt under one rule and able to direct the country's labour resources, has always been essential to the economic and social well-being of the people. Such a government was first established about 3000 BC by princes of This, in Upper Egypt, and the achievement was so important that the Egyptians looked back to this union of Upper and Lower Egypt as the starting point of their national life and characteristics as a people.

Because the pharaoh (a title derived from *per* meaning 'house' and *aa* meaning 'great') was so essential to the well-being of the land, he came to be regarded as divine. According to a tradition that arose in the Old Kingdom, he was believed to be son of the sun god, and therefore the deity's representative upon earth. The pharaoh was accordingly regarded as the owner of Egypt (in Egyptian *Kemi*, the 'black land'), and the mediator between the people and the sun god. A royal insignia and ritual proclaimed his unique status. When he died, or rather ascended to the sky to join his divine father, his body had to be enshrined in a great tomb, served by a mortuary temple. The pyramids were the distinctive tombs of the pharaohs of the Old Kingdom.

Because the sun so insistently dominates the daily scene in Egypt, it was venerated under the name of Re (Egyptian-Coptic for 'sun') as the supreme state deity, intimately associated with the monarchy. Known as the 'Great God', Re was conceived under various highly imaginative forms. As Re-Horakhti, an ancient falcon or falcon-headed sky god called 'Horus of the horizon' was associated with the sun god. Re-Horakhti was represented in art as a falcon-headed man, crowned with the solar disc; sometimes this form of the deity was depicted as the solar disc, encircled by two serpents, between the outstretched wings of a falcon.

As the sun at dawn, Re was represented as a beetle (*Khepri*) or a beetle-headed man. This strange concept had a subtle significance. 'Khepri' derived from the word *kheper*, meaning 'to become or exist', so that Re-Khepri indicated both the rising sun and the sun as the self-existent creator of the universe. The declining sun was Re-Atum, shown as an aged man of wise counsel; the word 'Atum' conveyed some idea of 'completion'. Atum was the god of Heliopolis, the old centre of sun worship.

Since Re, as the state god, was essentially connected with the kingship of the pharaohs, it was inevitable that his cult should be affected by political changes in Egypt. During the Old Kingdom period, he was worshipped as Re-Atum in his ancient home at Heliopolis, where his temple was supposed to mark the primeval hill where he began the work of creation. When the political capital was moved to Thebes in Upper Egypt, during the Middle Kingdom, Re was associated with the local god of Thebes, Amun. Amun-Re was represented in art as a man wearing a cap, surmounted by two plumes and the solar disc. The great pharaohs of the New Kingdom were zealously devoted to Amun, building at Thebes for his worship huge temples, richly endowed, so that Amun became in effect the sole state god. This exaltation of Amun eventually produced one of the most interesting, though obscure, episodes in the whole of Egyptian history.

It appears that the priests of Heliopolis, the ancient cult centre of Re-Atum, attempted to combat the exaltation of Amun by promoting the worship of Re untrammelled by association with another god. Accordingly they proclaimed the Aten, the sun's disc, as the symbol of supreme deity. Meanwhile at Thebes the enormous power acquired by the priesthood of Amun had begun to challenge the royal power. When Amenhotep IV (1372–1354 BC) ascended the throne, he gradually set about supplanting Amun as the supreme deity by the Aten. This king, who soon changed his name to Akhenaten ('Pleasing to the Aten'), was a strange genius whose devotion to the Aten bordered on fanaticism. He moved his capital from Thebes, the stronghold of Amun, to a new city named Akhetaten ('Horizon of the Aten'), where he built a magnificent temple to his god, similar in plan to that at Heliopolis. He expressed his devotion in hymns to the Aten and he had himself frequently portrayed, together with his beautiful wife Nefertiti and their children, worshipping the Aten, whose descending rays, ending in hands, bless the pious family. He took measures to repress the cult of Amun, even to the point of causing the deity's name to be removed from monuments. However, the attempt to reform Egyptian religion did not survive the heretic king, and his successor Tutankhamen (1354–1345 BC) was obliged to submit to Amun's supremacy and bring the court back to Thebes. The memory of Akhenaten was execrated and his monuments destroyed. The ascendancy of the Amun priesthood reached its inevitable conclusion in about 1080 BC when Herihor, the 'First Prophet of Amun', took over the royal power at Thebes.

The third main theme of Egyptian religion was constituted by the funerary cult which centred on the god Osiris. This was essentially concerned with the spiritual needs of individuals, which were not served by the state religion. Osiris, the divine hero who died and rose again, had an intimate personal appeal and, since it was believed that resurrection to eternal life could be achieved through ritual assimilation to him, he came increasingly to dominate Egyptian religion; his cult was the longest lived of all those of the Egyptian deities.

The earliest texts record a multiplicity of gods and goddesses. The majority were local deities but some achieved a nationwide recognition. Amun is a case in point: the political supremacy of Thebes made him the supreme state god. Most local deities, like Bast, the cat goddess of Bubastis, and Sebek, the crocodile god of the Faiyum, had their chief sanctuary in their place of origin, with which they remained essentially associated; sometimes their cult might be accorded a limited observance in one or two other places. The origin of these local deities is unknown. The fact that many of them had animal forms or animal heads has suggested the theory of their derivation from ancient totems; but there is no certain evidence that totemism existed as an institution in early Egypt, and many other local deities cannot be explained in this way.

Of the major deities after Re, Osiris and Amun, whose worship was generally observed throughout the land, Horus and Isis enjoyed the widest recognition. Horus was a complicated deity who, under certain forms, actually achieved the status of a state god.

His solar aspect as Re-Horakhti, under which he was associated with Re the sun god, was paralleled by another of equal importance but of confusing significance, especially since the two aspects became combined in one single deity. In the Osirian mythology Horus is the posthumous son of Osiris, who avenges his father's death and inherits his kingdom. Since the Egyptians identified a deceased king with Osiris, and his son and successor with Horus, the latter came to be regarded as the divine prototype of the reigning pharaoh.

In the Osirian mythology the god Seth figures as the murderer of Osiris and the opponent of Horus, who finally overthrows him. This god, who seems originally to have been associated with storms and the desert, and so regarded as a strong and fierce being, gradually became the Egyptian god of evil. Seth is generally depicted as an animal-headed man. The animal has never been certainly identified; it has a long curved muzzle, almond eyes and sharp pointed ears. The Greeks later identified Seth with the monster Typhon.

The other chief deity of the Osirian mythology who can claim to have become, with Osiris, one of the two most popular deities of Egyptian religion, and later of Graeco-Roman society, was the goddess Isis, the wife of Osiris and mother of Horus, the daughter of Geb and Nut.

Ptah, the god of Memphis, always enjoyed a position of dignity in the Egyptian pantheon, because Memphis had been the ancient capital of the land and continued an important city. He is represented in art invariably in human form, tightly wrapped in a robe like a mummy; he wears a skull cap and holds a curiously shaped staff or sceptre. The priests of Memphis attributed to him the creation of all things, including the other gods. Memphis was also the cult centre of the Apis bull, a primitive symbol of procreative vitality, which was associated with Ptah as the manifestation of 'his blessed soul'; later the Apis was also associated with Osiris.

The Egyptians deified the earth as a male deity, Geb; but often he was represented as a goose. In the Heliopolitan story of the creation, Geb originally lay in close embrace with Nut, the sky goddess, until

In Egypt the god Osiris was killed and restored to life but his 'resurrection' was not a resumption of earthly life for he did not leave his throne in the land of the dead. Like each Egyptian king, who became an Osiris after death, he was connected with the Nile flood and the fertility of the earth; with the ascent and descent of the sun, and with life after death *Opposite* The mummy of Osiris receives the deceased from the jackal-headed Anubis, the underworld guide

separated by Shu, the god of the atmosphere, and so creation began. The Pyramid Texts indicate that Geb was once venerated as the oldest of the gods, and the pharaohs were regarded as his successors, sitting on the 'throne of Geb'. A very different deity was Thoth, who was associated with the city of Hermopolis but acquired attributes that made him significant to all Egyptians. His appearance is one of the strangest among the many strange Egyptian deities, for on a human body he has the head of an ibis bird. Thoth was regarded as the god of wisdom and the divine scribe; he is generally represented holding the reed pen and colour palette of the Egyptian scribe. He assumed an important role in the judgement of the dead, where he recorded the verdict when the heart of the deceased was weighed. The Greeks identified Thoth with Hermes and, as Hermes Trismegistus ('Thrice-great Hermes'), he was the source of the mystic revelation incorporated into the so-called Hermetic literature of the Graeco-Roman period.

A god who deserves special mention, though he was not numbered among the greater gods of Egypt, is Bes. He was represented as a squat, dwarf-like figure with a large grinning face. He may justly be called 'the poor man's god' because of his great popularity, despite his having no cult centre. Bes was the patron of fun and music, and helped women in childbirth. In many ways he could be regarded as the god of good luck; numerous amulets shaped in his image have been found.

The Egyptians were most obviously polytheists; but there is also evidence of a tendency to henotheism, if not monotheism, among them. Most notable is the use of the expression 'the Great God' in their wisdom literature and certain inscriptions. The use of this expression, without further qualification, is significant; it shows that the Egyptians recognized one supreme deity who needed no distinguishing name. It seems certain that in the earlier period the title 'Great God' referred to Re, the sun god; later Osiris may sometimes have been so designated. Akhenaten's concept of the Aten certainly merits the description 'monotheistic'. But it seems likely that the worship of any specific Egyptian deity in its local sanctuary was a kind of henotheism; during the service, the deity concerned was conceived of as the 'one' god, there and at that moment.

Egyptian religion does not appear to have been so rich in mythology as was the religion of the contemporary civilization of Mesopotamia. It had indeed its creation myths and the fundamentally important Osirian myth. Three other myths are known which concerned Re and certain goddesses. One told how Re grew old and mankind rebelled against him. To punish them, Re sent forth his eye in the form of his daughter Hathor. So destructive was the goddess that the sun god had to make her drunk in order to stop her work of slaughter, for otherwise mankind would have been wholly exterminated. A variant version of this myth concerned the fierce goddess Tefnut, who lived as a lioness in the Nubian desert. Re, whose daughter she was, wanted her to return to him and he sent Shu and Thoth, in disguise, to persuade her to come back. On the return journey she transformed herself into a beautiful goddess at Philae, and revealed herself as Hathor at Dendera, which was her chief cult centre. The third myth told how the goddess Isis acquired her magical power. She made a serpent and caused it to bite Re. No god could cure Re in his agony; then Isis appeared and offered to relieve him on condition that he revealed his secret name to her. The tormented sun god was forced to comply and the knowledge she gained gave Isis her great power. There are a number of tales, such as that of the Two Brothers, which are full of supernatural details, but they are not true myths.

Religions are concerned not only with the deities who personify and explain the various manifestations of power that men encounter in the world, but also with human nature and destiny. The ancient Egyptians' concern with their personal destiny found expression in their elaborate mortuary cult. This cult presupposed a very complicated view of human nature. The individual person was conceived as a mixture of the physical and spiritual, made up of several constituents. The *ka* was a kind of *alter ego* or double, created at conception together with the person whose ka it was. Egyptian texts give conflicting information about the nature of the ka and where it existed during the lifetime of the individual concerned. In art it was depicted as an exact replica of the individual, from whom it was distinguished by the ka symbol — shown as two arms extended upwards — which was set on its head. Provision had to be made for the ka at death; in fact the tomb was called the *het ka*, the 'house of the ka', and it contained the ka statue in which the ka dwelt. 'To go to one's ka' was a euphemism for death. It is uncertain whether the Egyptians thought of the ka as a non-material entity; it seems to denote some vital force essential to the existence of the individual person.

The ka cannot properly be described as the soul. The *ba*, another constituent of human nature, had more claim to this description, though not in the sense of the 'soul' as the inner essential self according to the Greek idea of the *psyche* or the Hindu *atman*. In their concept of the ba, the Egyptians expressed their belief that at death a free-moving entity separated itself from the body but remained in close proximity to it. They represented the ba as a human-headed bird, giving it a male or female face according to the sex of the deceased. In the funerary papyri the ba is often depicted as perched on the portal of the tomb or flying down the tomb shaft to revisit the embalmed body lying in the sepulchral chamber below. Another important constituent of the person was the *ib* or heart. This was sometimes referred to as the 'god in man', since it was regarded as a kind of witness or censor of the conduct of the individual within whom it resided. The heart had a vital role in the judgement after death. The individual's shadow and name were also important to his being, though of lesser significance compared with the other entities. At death, the Egyptian trusted that the proper performance of the mortuary ritual would then automatically transform him into an *akh* or glorified soul.

Important as all these constituents were to the whole person, the body was always regarded as essential to life: this was why it was so carefully embalmed to preserve it from the disintegration caused by death. With their elaborate conception of human nature and the care given to ensuring eternal well-being after death, it is remarkable that the Egyptians never seem to have been curious about the purpose of human life in this world. In this lack of concern they contrast notably with the Mesopotamians, in whose mythology the origin and purpose of mankind was a primary topic.

Egyptian ideas of how and where the dead spent their afterlife are fundamentally confused. This confusion is already present in the Pyramid Texts (c 2400 BC). It doubtless went back to predynastic times and stemmed from different local traditions. Three conceptions of the afterlife can be distinguished. What is probably the most primitive envisaged the dead as living on in their tombs, equipped with various everyday necessities and nourished on daily food offerings made by their relatives. In the Pyramid Texts the existence of a celestial realm of the dead is described. The idea takes two forms: that of ascending to heaven to join the sun god Re in his solar boat on his daily journey across the sky; or of ascending to join the 'Imperishable Ones', the circumpolar stars. The idea of accompanying the sun god became the more generally accepted view. The third conception was associated with Osiris and his realm, which was called the *Duat* or *Ament* (the West).

This realm was subterranean and was situated beneath the western horizon, which in Egypt was constituted by the western desert. The dead had to journey there, encountering many hideous monsters and fearsome obstacles on the way. This land of the dead was imagined as an idealized Egypt, where the blessed dead lived happily the same kind of life as in the Nile valley. Special guidebooks to the next world were provided for the dead: the Book of the Two Ways described alternative land and water routes, both equally perilous; the Book of Gates divided the Duat by 12 gates; the Book am Duat told of the 12 time-divisions taken by the sun god on his nightly journey through this underworld. What is particularly significant, in all this complex imagery and practice concerning the dead, is that the Egyptians continued, century after century, to embalm their dead and to furnish their tombs as though the dead really did live in them, once they had passed on.

The immense duration of Egyptian religion, and the impressive continuity of its traditional pattern of faith and practice, suggest that the Egyptians unthinkingly accepted an ancient priestly tradition, generation after generation. But there is evidence that this was not wholly so, and that there were those who could look critically at their ancestral faith, especially the funerary cult.

The expression of such sentiments is significant; for it shows that there did exist at least a minority who could doubt the truth of their traditional religion and the effectiveness of its ritual technique for the achievement of a blessed immortality. Yet this faith was able to continue its serene tradition without the suppression of such heretical scepticism. That it did so attests the strength of two things: the spiritual satisfaction which the average Egyptian got from his faith in Osiris, and the practical nature of his philosophy of life. The Greek historian Herodotus, who visited Egypt in the 5th century BC, records an Egyptian custom at banquets of showing the guests a model of a mummy with the admonition: 'Gaze here, and drink and be merry; for when you die, such will you be.' This curious custom was prompted by no spirit of cynicism or levity; it reflected the practical evaluation of life that characterized the Egyptians. They feared death, but they believed that they had the means of reversing its threat of personal extinction and they accordingly made provision to secure this immunity. But such preoccupation with death and the afterlife did not induce pessimism or prompt a this-world-denying attitude. The Egyptians sought to extract the most joy possible from life, while preparing for death and mindful of the judgement that faced them thereafter.

The legacy of Egypt's ancient religion cannot be accurately assessed. The famous American Egyptologist J. H. Breasted believed that Akhenaten's monotheism influenced Moses and found its fruition in the Hebrew concept of one single God, who is the creator and sustainer of the universe. The connection cannot be proved and the assumption that it did exist has not been generally accepted by scholars. More certain is the influence of Egyptian wisdom literature on the Jewish Book of Proverbs. The elements of Egyptian religion which passed into Coptic Christianity were chiefly related to the world after death; such elements included the idea of a judgement immediately after death and of the assessment as being made by weighing the soul on scales. And the Egyptian elements have yet to be fully evaluated in the Hermatic literature, where the god Thoth figures prominently under the name of Hermes.

Akhenaten, who sought to promote the worship of the Aten, the sun's disc, above the worship of Amun, frequently had himself portrayed sitting in the sun's rays. These rays, ending in hands, bless the devout pharaoh as they reach his head

Mesopotamia

In the ancient world religion was not a distinct or optional activity but the attitude to life which gave it cohesion, meaning and pattern. Mesopotamian religion, like Hinduism, had its roots in prehistory and was not attributed to a specific founder. Despite the three thousand years over which the evidence extends, and the several distinct groups of peoples concerned, there is a sufficient continuum to justify treatment of the whole of the evidence as belonging to one cultural stream, and to speak of Mesopotamian 'religion' rather than 'religions'. Some distinction can be seen between the systematized theology of the scribes, which provides the bulk of the evidence, and the popular religion, but since evidence of the popular religion appears only incidentally and allusively, little specific can be said of it.·

Mesopotamia here means the pre-Christian cultural area approximating geographically to the modern state of Iraq. In the context of ancient times the southern part of this region is known as Babylonia, the northern as Assyria.

The earliest evidence of the occupation of southernmost Mesopotamia comes from c 5000 BC. By 3500 BC this region was settled by the Sumerians. This ethnic group, of unknown origin, initiated a cultural revolution which gave the world writing, cities, and a corpus of religious practices and concepts. From their original area of settlement in southern Babylonia, where their city states flourished during the third millennium, Sumerian cultural influence permeated as far north as the area later known as Assyria, but was less marked there than in the south.

The period 2750 to 2500 BC saw considerable immigration into Babylonia of peoples from the Arabian desert, speaking the Semitic language Akkadian, who in the course of their assimilation to the higher Sumerian culture profoundly modified it, not least in religion. Further Semitic immigration brought about, by c 2000 BC, the disappearance of the Sumerians as an ethnic or cultural entity, and in the north overlaid the aboriginal inhabitants of Assyria with a mainly Semitic culture.

The beginning of the second millennium was marked by the rise of a number of Akkadian-speaking city states, of which Babylon under Hammurabi ultimately achieved supremacy. Before 1000 BC political supremacy had passed to Assyria, which with brief intermissions remained predominant until shortly before the fall of Nineveh in 612 BC.

The Sumerians and their successors employed as their principal writing material tablets of clay, inscribed by impression with a stylus. Such tablets, virtually indestructible, have been found in hundreds of thousands. Many of them contain texts directly or indirectly related to religion, myth or magic, one of the principal sources being libraries collected by Assyrian kings, particularly Ashurbanipal (668–629 BC) at Nineveh.

Ancient man saw the universe in the form of conscious forces, which were conceived of in some specific shape. Such personification was originally not necessarily in human shape, since some of the most primitive concepts of divine powers invested them with animal aspects. Some aspects of the forces active in the world, certainly those thought of as universal gods, must have been personified by the Sumerians before their settlement in Mesopotamia. In addition, each early Sumerian settlement had its own local deity (sometimes identified with a universal deity), with attributed characteristics depending on the dominant features of the locality and community. As society developed, the deities of different settlements were brought into relationship, whilst additionally specific aspects of agriculture and technology (for example, corn or brickmaking) became personified in a deity. Thus arose a considerable pantheon, the names of its members being compiled in god lists before the middle of the third millennium. Genealogies of the gods (theogonies) were developed to explain the relationship between deities.

In one group of theogonies Enlil is the first god, deriving from several generations of vaguely defined primeval beings. In other theogonies, this role falls to An (Akkadian Anum), with Enki (Akkadian Ea) as his son. These two concepts were theologically combined, so that heading the pantheon in its developed form there stood a triad of universal gods: Anum, the sky god and king of the gods; Enlil, 'Lord Wind', originally a wind and mountain god; and Enki (Ea), god of wisdom, originally 'Lord Earth'. Though Anum was nominally king of the gods, executive power was in the hands of Enlil, who often in practice usurped the supremacy. In the mythology of historical times the sphere of Ea's activity was the cosmic sweet waters (Apsu) beneath the earth, probably as a result of the Sumerian Enki absorbing the attributes of a divinity of an earlier stage of religion.

A second group of deities comprised the moon god Nannar (Sin); the sun god Utu (Shamash); Venus, known in Sumerian as Innin or Inanna, 'Lady of Heaven', and in Akkadian as Ishtar; and the weather god, who was of less importance in a purely Sumerian context than to the Semites, amongst whom he was called Adad. These four gods, manifestly related to the diurnal period, are specifically described as sleeping during part of the day. Since in the latitude of Babylonia the crescent of the new moon is seen on a level axis like a boat, Sin was said to ride across the sky in a holy ship. Though, like the other great gods, thought of also anthropomorphically, he bore the epithet 'Brilliant Young Bull', and in a myth took that form to impregnate a cow.

The sun god rode across the heavens in a chariot drawn by mules. It was to him that prayers were addressed by those who lived by the ancient pre-agricultural pursuits of hunting and fishing, although all civilized men bowed to him at his rising. Seeing all that happened on earth, he became god of justice and the divine lawgiver, and also controlled omens. He was sometimes thought to pass through the underworld at night.

The importance of Adad, the weather god, increased as one left Babylonia, a region watered almost wholly by irrigation, and moved north-westwards into areas dependent upon rain. Because of the sound of his voice in thunder, Adad was associated with the bull: he was also represented by the lightning symbol.

Inanna-Ishtar, a very complex figure, Queen of Heaven and Earth, the only prominent goddess of historical times, seems to have personified the vital forces of the crises of life. She could be felt as the loving mother who had suckled the king, or as the goddess controlling sexual powers, or as goddess of battle. She was also associated in myth and popular religion with a consort Dumuzi (Tammuz), a fertility deity who was annually lamented when he was temporarily absent in the underworld.

Other deities of major significance included Marduk, originally an aspect of the sun god. As god of Babylon, he ultimately achieved supremacy in the Babylonian pantheon, assimilating the characteristics of Enlil; he was also equated with a god Asallukhi, in which context he was regarded as god of magic. Nabu, god of Borsippa, the nearest city to Babylon, was (probably for this geographical reason) regarded as Marduk's son; he was also patron of the scribal profession. The latter function had earlier been attributed to a Sumerian goddess Nisaba, and the conflict between the two concepts was resolved by Nisaba being (by the first millennium) regarded as Nabu's wife. In Assyria it was Ashur, originally the Assyrian tribal god, who ultimately usurped leadership in the pantheon, bearing the title 'the Assyrian Enlil'. Another god who became of particular significance in Assyria was the warrior god Ninurta, son of Enlil.

The great gods, whilst regarded as being concerned with the life of Babylonia and Assyria as a whole, might at the same time be thought of as having their abode particularly in a certain city or cities.

Inanna-Ishtar—was a difficult and complex personality in Mesopotamian religion. Queen of Heaven, and of Earth as well, she came to represent the most important events in life. She was mother, and by extension goddess of sexual forces, and also goddess of battle. In her sexual role she was a forerunner of Venus, originally a goddess of gardens and flowers, but eventually the embodiment of female allure and sexuality: *Venus* by Titian

Mansell Collection

Sonia Halliday

Greece

The history of Greek religion reflects an uneven, halting but recognizable development from magic to officially sponsored religion; from an epoch when men had not clearly separated themselves from Nature and natural forces to a time when gods and goddesses were worshipped in human shape. However, the uniformity of this process should not be overestimated. For magic continued to be inseparably associated with religion, especially in the realms of popular cult, just as birds, beasts and flowers continued to be identified with particular gods and goddesses.

The traditional polytheistic religion of classical times incorporated, in varying forms and with varying emphasis, many survivals from earlier periods, including the Minoan and Mycenean periods of the Bronze Age, especially in Nature-religion and fertility cults. Broadly speaking, the Greek religion of classical antiquity was an amalgamation of early Aegean with later Indo-European elements, the latter having been contributed by people who spoke Greek as one of the Indo-European family of languages.

However, realization of this is comparatively recent. A hundred years ago there were no accepted objective criteria, in the form of buildings, pottery, jewellery and armour, which were relied upon to form an independent witness of the realities of the world which emerges in the Homeric poems. The history of Greece was thought to have begun with the first Olympiad in 776 BC, and everything that went before including the Homeric Age, was legend or myth.

Now, however, what is sometimes described as the Aegean civilization has been discovered by archeologists. In consequence, the objective criteria of Greek pre-history reach back to the beginning of the Iron Age (roughly 1000 BC), and through the two millennia of the preceding Bronze Age into the earlier Neolithic period.

This vast change in outlook is mainly the result of the work of two men, Heinrich Schliemann and Sir Arthur Evans. Schliemann's excavations at Troy, Mycene and Tiryns proved that there was some historical reality behind the Homeric epics. Sir Arthur Evans began to excavate the Bronze Age palace of Minos at Cnossus 70 years ago.

The abiding mystical concepts derived from Cretan religion are significantly marked by the influence of a mother goddess and a dying god, associated with the bull, who later became worshipped as 'Cretan-born Zeus'. This Zeus, who died and was born again, was different from the Olympian Zeus of the familiar Greek pantheon. He was much more comparable with the Greek Dionysus, also a bull god and a dying god. These two different concepts help us to establish distinctions between the Minoan and the Mycenean phases of earlier Greek religion.

The historian Herodotus records that the poets Homer and Hesiod were the first to compose theogonies, poems dealing with the origin of the gods, and gave the deities their epithets, allotted them their offices and occupations, and described their forms. It is probable that these traditional Greek theogonies derived from the Greek epics which were rooted in the Mycenean period of the late Bronze Age.

Traditional mythology recorded legends about conditions before the Mycenean pantheon of the Olympic gods became paramount. Before this time, the Titans, the children of Uranus and Gaia (Heaven and Earth) held sway. To prevent Cronus, the youngest Titan, from swallowing his baby

Above left Poseidon, whose dominion was the sea: bronze statue c 460 BC **Above right** Hermes, god of travellers and the messenger of Zeus, was also responsible for guiding souls on their way to the underworld **Opposite** Both Zeus and Jupiter, his Roman counterpart, were renowned in mythology for their many love affairs; Semele, the mother of Dionysus, was loved by Zeus but was consumed by the fire of his thunderbolt, when the god appeared to her in his divine form: **Jupiter and Semele**, painting by Gustave Moreau

son Zeus, his wife Rhea bore him secretly in Crete and substituted a stone wrapped in swaddling clothes for the infant, who was subsequently reared in hiding. The legends about the birth of Zeus in Crete were responsible for the specific epithet of the supreme god as 'Cretan-born'. This epithet and the oriental connections of his mother Rhea, indicate that he was an old Minoan god, involved in the same basic pattern of oriental ritual which prompted the myths of Ishtar and Tammuz, Isis and Osiris, Venus and Adonis. It is probable that Greek-speaking people who arrived in Crete gave the name of their sky god to an old Minoan deity whose ritual and character can be guessed from the evidence of later times.

The Olympian Zeus was the leader of the traditional Greek pantheon. There is reason to suppose that the hierarchical organization of the gods and goddesses as portrayed in the Homeric epics reflects the actual social conditions of the Mycenean period. The Homeric Greeks (the Achaeans), burst the bonds of their own ancestral tribal organization and adapted their control of Bronze Age techniques to warfare. The martial character of the Myceneans of the later Bronze Age is exemplified in their fortification of their urban centres, in marked contrast with the unfortified cities of Minoan Crete. Similarly, the Achaean chieftains of the Homeric poems dominate the battlefield.

The heroic age of ancient Greece, as it is portrayed in Homer, represents the violent and ruthless conquest of an older, sophisticated, peaceful and refined civilization by warlike adventurers. Its richest and most important centres were away from the mainland, especially on the island of Crete; so the greatest prizes were out of reach until the Achaeans became sailors.

After 1400 BC the leadership of the Aegean world passed to mainland Mycene; and the Mycenean pantheon presumably spread its influence as the Mycenean social and economic system penetrated widely from its mainland centres. The ensuing social conflict, and fusion of peoples and customs, was paralleled by increasing complexity in cults and in mythology, and in the composition and organization of the pantheon. The most dramatic form of this process was a struggle, never quite resolved, between the old concept of a mother goddess and the newer concept of a dominating male god, Zeus.

Under the monarchical leadership of Olympian Zeus, the gods and goddesses were gathered together in a single heavenly stronghold. Their dwelling-places, built by Hephaestus, surrounded the central palace of Zeus. Although the authority of the supreme male god had become fairly stable, it was not unchallenged. In fact Hera, wife of Zeus, was amongst those who intrigued against his authority.

This Homeric picture of the Olympian hierarchy is paralleled by the Homeric picture of earthly conditions. Even in the midst of war, Agamemnon, the leader of the Greek expedition to Troy, could claim only a loose kind of authority: his control was often disputed by his fellow-chieftains. This instability has its analogy in the inability of the Achaeans to establish a centralized, enduring Bronze Age economy similar to the older oriental type.

There is, too, a lack of uniformity in the Homeric accounts of the Olympian system. In two passages of the *Iliad* Zeus is living alone on Olympus. In one passage he hurls a thunderbolt, in the other he sends a storm. It is highly probable that Olympus itself was a kind of generic term for 'mountain'. However, in a well-known evocative passage of the *Odyssey*, the heavenly Olympus is described in a way that is more appropriate to the Minoan Fields of the Blest than to a lofty, mountainous seat of storms and rain.

The growth of the Olympian pantheon was a process of tribal federation which led to military kingship. The mortal prototype of the weather god who was lord of storms, rain, lightning and thunder, and reigned in a mountain fortress, was the Mycenean overlord. The companions of the god, with their differing functions, at first lived apart from him but eventually, although they kept their traditional functions, they went to live with the Olympian overlord in his stronghold and were subject to his will.

The Twelve Gods who were early united into a sort of official Olympian society were normally Zeus, Hera, Poseidon, Demeter, Apollo, Artemis, Ares, Aphrodite, Hermes, Athene, Hephaestus and Hestia. There were sometimes modifications to the list, as when Dionysus replaced Hestia in the representation of the Twelve on the east frieze of the Parthenon in Athens.

Dionysus has a place of special importance in Greek religion, essentially popular and non-Olympian. However, the cults which he personified and which played such a major role in historical times, had their counterparts elsewhere in much earlier times. Explaining why the cult of Dionysus was conspicuously absent in Crete, M.P. Nilsson observed in *Minoan-Mycenaean Religion*: 'The reason why Dionysus does not appear in Crete can only be that he was not needed there, the religious ideas of which he was the herald having already been applied to the Cretan Zeus.'

The copious amount of legendary material regarding the birth of Zeus in Crete emphasizes its pre-eminence compared with other birth-stories of Zeus. However, the very existence of such a remarkable birth-story, and the cults associated with it, inevitably meant that places other than Crete were also credited with being the site of Zeus's birth. These included Messenia where Zeus was reputed to have been reared by nymphs on Mount Ithome; Arcadia which, apart from Crete, made the strongest claims, with a legend that Cronus had swallowed the stone on Mount Thaumasius and that Zeus was born and reared on Mount Lycaeus; and Olympia, which was said to be Zeus's birthplace in a legend of the founding of the Olympic Games.

It was quite consistent that the dying god, Zeus of Crete, should not only have had his sacred marriage to Hera commemorated in an annual ceremony during which sacrifices were offered with traditional wedding rites but that his death also should have been mourned. This explains why the legend of Zeus's tomb, supposedly located at various places in Crete including Cnossus, Mount Ida and Mount Dicte, has endured from ancient to recent times.

There are a number of versions of the inscription on this legendary tomb, which suggests that 'Zan', the old name for Zeus, was certainly well known in Crete, and also that the cult of Cretan Zeus was involved with, if it did not actually develop from, an earlier cult of Minos. A common link was an annual festival celebrating a god like Adonis or Tammuz, at which this god was eaten in the form of a bull. The evidence for the tomb, relatively late though it may be, indicates that Cretan Zeus was looked upon as a dying god, with the implication that he died annually and was born again.

Initiation, which may well have originated in the Bronze Age, continued to play a major part in various Greek cults and in social life generally. The death and rebirth of an initiate tended to be dramatically represented, often with a contest and some kind of ordeal. It was not only the god, or his animal symbol, who continually died and was born again. A similar pattern persisted in the training of the youth of the Greek city-states in classical times.

The late appearance and subordinate status of a male Minoan deity served to emphasize the over-riding importance of the Minoan goddess. In Neolithic times there seems to have been no concept of a male divinity in human form. He emerged later, as a secondary deity, but the tendency to raise him to a superior status was clear by the end of Minoan times. With the decline of the mother goddess, the bull became associated with the Minoan kingship, which perhaps had important functions in relation to the governing of the calendar. Hence the bull became a symbol of the sun, and both were fertility symbols. Bull-worship and snake-worship remained associated with traditions of the prehistoric Bronze Age kingship.

The Minoan goddess is a central feature of Minoan religion, just as the palace was a central feature of Minoan social life. In surviving monuments and artefacts she is shown in association with animals, birds and snakes; with the sacred pillar and the sacred tree; with poppies and with lilies; with the sword and the double axe. She appears to have been huntress and goddess of sports, she was armed and also presided over ritual dances; she had male and female attendants, and she held sway over mountain, earth, sky and sea, over life and death. She was household goddess, vegetation goddess, Mother and also Maid.

There are many examples of figurines from Minoan Crete, including votive images from sanctuaries, cult idols from shrines, and statuettes which have been recovered from graves and tombs. The various attitudes assumed by these figurines, which

The so-called mask of Agamemnon, leader of the Greeks in the siege of Troy according to Homer: gold funeral mask of a prince of Mycene, the great fortress-city of pre-classical Greece. The organization of the gods and goddesses portrayed in Homer reflects the social conditions of the Mycenean period

include the 'gesture of benediction' familiar in portrayals of the mother goddess, sometimes recall the postures of a sacred dance. The sitting or squatting position of early specimens could well represent the attitude actually assumed for childbirth. Hence the differing gestures depicted by later statuettes could also have been supposed to have had a beneficial influence on childbirth and on the growth of crops.

As puppets, the images had clear associations with birth and with death, accounting for their presence in graves and tombs. As votive offerings, they represented worshippers appealing for the protection of the goddess in sickness or childbirth, an initiation, marriage or bereavement; or the statuettes could represent the goddess herself. Figurines dating from the earliest times onward have been discovered in Greece, showing that the ancestral idols of magic did not easily yield to the more recently established deities of religion.

By Minoan times the bull, the dove and the snake had already acquired special prominence. Large numbers of votive offerings included figurines of oxen, goats, rams, swine and dogs. There is no doubt that the birds that are so often portrayed in Minoan religious contexts, perched upon double axes, columns, trees or idols represent divine manifestations. In fact, the birds of the domestic shrines are not mere votive offerings but real representations of deity; and the idea of birds as manifest forms of the spirits of the dead was persistent in later Greek religion.

The most conspicuous Minoan domestic cult was that of the snake, especially in connection with the so-called snake goddess. Snake cults are world-wide, and are associated with the belief that snakes are incarnations of the dead. They also signify immortality because they cast their skins and renew themselves, personifying the ability to be reborn. Both dreaded and revered, snakes became beneficent, guardians of the house. Snake-worship was common in later Greek religion and indeed plays a part in modern Greek folklore, even up to the present day.

All these powerful traditions seem to have played their part in the formulation of the mother goddess as an abstract and unifying principle, both one and many. It was perhaps in the Cretan palaces of the Bronze Age that the Neolithic figurine developed most rapidly into a female deity in human form, still attended by magical and totemistic symbols, in the form of trees and stones, animals, birds and flowers.

Rome

Roman religion has no equal in the ancient Mediterranean although its type of polytheism is shared throughout pre-classical and classical Europe, North Africa and the Near East. Polytheism was never a mode of theology as we understand it today. A formal body of dogma and an organized congregation or network of congregations have no place in a study of Roman paganism. Even the notion of religion remained outside the ancient cognizance.

The Latin word *religio*, whose original definition is obscure, meant 'awe', 'scruple' and also 'superstition', although the Romans sometimes acknowledged the last as a distinct and extreme attitude. One's devotion and sense of obligation to the divine could be expressed by the idea of *pietas*, which was by no means due merely to the gods. It was a bond of obligation which could be felt in accordance with blood-ties, ethnic solidarity or contractual agreement. Whereas pietas and similar notions reflect a personal recognition of a deity's existence, the worship (*cultus*) of a deity manifested itself in sacrifices, gifts and utensils (*sacra*) which shared with other sacrifices, gifts and utensils the common denomination of the *ritus* that was normally designated by its ethnic origin. Hence, such modern expressions as 'Greek rite' have a very long history.

Some Roman gods were worshipped in a non-Roman rite. For instance, a sacrifice to Saturn took place in the 'Greek rite'. In this case the Roman officiant did not cover his head with his toga but poured the wine while bare-headed. Normal Roman ceremonial practice dictated a covered head – evidently to avoid ominous sights. Constant flute music was also required – evidently to avoid ominous sounds. The 'Roman rite' of Italy implied a covered head, flute music and other practices which distinguish it from the rites of diverse communities and peoples. Theoretically rites were as numerous as there were clear ethnic divisions. The various rites are an integral part of Roman imperial religion.

Occidental religion tends to concentrate man's attentions upon one deity and to prescribe norms of behaviour that constitute morality, but little in the way of moral precept emerges from pagan religion. Further, a modern focus upon the single deity tends to narrow our attention on the breadth of Roman religion. While the importance, not to say power, of the Roman gods cannot be denied, the role of these gods can never approximate the omnipotence and unity of Western man's one god. Some Roman gods did not even begin as gods but as forces, activities and spheres of influence beyond man's ken and control. The one god acknowledged today has received superhuman attributes, that is attributes which are human though somehow better than human. Creating, knowing, loving and the like can be understood only in human terms. For the Romans a god enjoyed human shape, but religion involved much besides man-like gods. The history of Roman religion exhibits traces of non-gods becoming gods, so that we must admit the possible growth of a notion of deity. However, this growth derived its material from religious forces, powers and entities otherwise outside the nature of the world, if not outside knowledge or fear.

The majority of Roman gods rarely received cult as the simple god. Rather, the gods usually bore an epithet or surname which distinguished them from others whose realm of efficacy differed. Consequently the universality of one pagan god was never possible. From place to place his epithets evinced his peculiarity. The gods of the Romans may conveniently be divided into groups of natural forces and their phenomena, physical activity, single abstract conceptions, deities of a given place and, finally, divinities of unknown origins. Among the gods of Nature stand Jupiter, Mars and Ceres. Jupiter was once the sky and the day. So he might be worshipped as a god of the sky and be called Thunderer or the like after some heavenly appearance. Mars belongs to the forces of springtime, and so his cult was concentrated in March.

Ceres ruled the growth of crops and vegetation in general. Her origin leads naturally to the next group, the type of physical activity. At an earlier stage Ceres was no goddess. *Ceres* or *cerus* was a verbal noun from the root 'to make grow' (*creare*) or 'to grow' (*crescere*). It was Growth itself. By the classical period Ceres had acquired all the attributes of a fertile lady and had narrowed her attentions upon agriculture, with the notable exception of her invocation at a wedding. She was identified with the Greek grain goddess, Demeter, as early as the 5th century. Indeed her oldest Roman temple may have been totally the result of Greek influence. Be that as it may, Ceres in cult and in story rarely exhibits a purely Roman background.

Venus represents the same type of deity. She began as the physical activity of coaxing and luring, but was early assigned a role in keeping watch over vegetable gardens. In some parts of central Italy the same priestess served both Ceres and Venus. A third such deity was Juno, whose name must be related to the word 'youth', a period of animal life which she as a goddess preserved and prolonged. In many instances the Romans forgot the origin of such 'gods'.

These divine types differ in origin very little from the manifest abstraction which never, or only occasionally, assumed a human form that could overwhelm the deity's beginnings to such a degree that a Roman could not understand its principal function. In this category are Tellus, Dis, Fides and Salus. Tellus signifies the earth, which is anything but an abstraction. However, *tellus* was most certainly the state or essence of earth, 'earthness', rather than a natural power such as growth or physical activity such as coaxing. The sole major festival of Tellus was named for the slaughter of pregnant cows, which were cremated so that the bountiful ash might be employed in fertilization. Tellus was enriched and was not in itself a force or deity. However, under Greek influence the 'earth' became a mother goddess.

Dis shows affinities with Tellus and also influence from a Greek quarter. Dis belonged to the underworld. His name means 'rich', which was thought a suitable translation of the Greek Pluto. Whereas Tellus received annual sacrifices, the underworld's Dis received sacrifice every century (*saeculum*) at the splendid and gorgeous Secular Games. Tellus had one Roman temple which had been vowed in wartime on account of an earthquake. Her old cult was performed in the open away from temples. Dis had the one altar, buried except for a few hours every century. Evidently neither deity was represented by a man-like statue, although the Romans considered one a goddess and the other a god. Tellus remained quite Roman in cult in spite of learned attempts to equate her with the Earth of Greek mythology. Dis, on the other hand, was an integrated foreigner.

The many deities invoked at the Secular Games exhibit a miscellany of Roman, Italic and Greek gods, worshipped by prayers and with utensils emanating from equally diverse quarters. The core of the ritual went back to the middle of the 4th century BC. The Games were controlled by the Fifteen Men (formerly Ten Men) For Sacrificing, a powerful priesthood in charge of imported state cults. The cult of Tellus, however, was carried on by the chief pontiff and the Vestal Virgins, the oldest civil priests of Rome. Yet Tellus, 'Earth', and Dis, 'Rich', share similar beginnings and interest in the soil's goodness.

Of the same type are Fides Publica and Salus. The former, 'the People's Trust', had a very old cult and precinct. The latter, 'Welfare' or 'Safety', received a temple very late although the notion of the people's well-being dominated many areas of the civil religion. Both were acknowledged as gods to the extent that they were given temples, but neither had a human representation and, so far as we know, they were female only because of their grammatical gender. Ceres, Venus, and probably Tellus, originally, had a neuter grammatical gender and became 'feminine' in the process of becoming deities with functions seemingly appropriate to women.

Ops offers herself as an example. The grammatically feminine word means 'abundance', 'resource' and 'provender'. On 25 August she received worship from the Vestal Virgins at the King's House. On 19

70

The mythical founders of Rome, Romulus and Remus, were the sons of Mars and a mortal maiden. Cast adrift on the Tiber, they were rescued by a she-wolf: painting by Rubens

December fell her oldest civil festival, which the Romans recognized as a ceremony for a deity generous in the bestowal of natural resources. Hence, she was honoured after the harvest and in the dead of winter. Yet this 'goddess' could not withstand the tendency to anthropomorphism and became in the popular mind the wife of Satúrn, for no better reason than the occurrence of his great festival on 17 December, two days before hers. The one temple Ops certainly had was probably not very old. Sacrifice at the King's House suggests that originally the cult was only domestic.

Many gods and goddesses enjoyed temples, precincts, chapels or altars in Rome. However, such honours did not necessarily imply a conception of a man-like deity. Even statues sometimes did not blur the Romans' understanding of the god's primitive existence as a force or activity.

Very early Romans applied 'Father' and 'Mother' as cult titles. What was akin to the Roman imagination was the myth-creating belief in marriages among gods and their offspring. Most divine marital and filial ties the Romans transferred from Greek to Latin poetry. So far as we can ascertain, the Roman gods passed celibate lives before Greek ideas were introduced.

A very different force is met in the divinity which the Roman community wished to ward off. On 25 April every year a civil priest offered sacrifice to the force of the rust blight, Robigus, which might strike the crops. The rites were held at places five miles from the city, apparently in order to

keep the rust from crossing some archaic boundary. More unusual, indeed unique, was the altar dedicated on the edge of the city to Verminus, god of cattle worms. The rearing of this altar by a prominent patrician was prompted by a great plague in 175 BC, which wrought death among the cattle and the men such that corpses were heaped untended in the streets. The Romans explicitly speak of Robigus and the like as 'gods'. However, they clearly never saw them as beneficent deities. They sought their benevolence, and in this context there is much truth to the view of Roman religion as perpetual appeasement of natural forces.

Because the primitive religion, which the Romans conservatively kept, closely adhered to the agricultural economy of its decidedly unintellectual practitioners, most festivals, ceremonies and deities betray and reflect the lives of tillers and herders, within the cycle of the year. If the well-being of a people is not reckoned only in its battles, it is reckoned by its material resources. In this context Romans sought a right relation with their gods or, more specifically with natural forces and activities, in terms of their society. Hence the state religion took little account of deities of trade and manufacture, who did indeed exist and in some later cases thrived apart from the major civil cults.

A history of Roman religion would need to trace the development of an agrarian religion into an imperial religion that borrowed and modified gods and cults from many peoples within its vast empire and upon its fringes. Sometimes old deities changed and added to their own attributes those of other gods with whom they were identified. Sometimes the alien god was introduced with or without a slight Roman veneer. Later stages in Roman religion may reflect merely the Latin outcropping of some Etruscan, Greek or Near Eastern religion. Although inherently interesting and equally Roman phenomena, the borrowings remained just borrowings, unless we are to except Christianity.

The civil calendar has the oldest stratum of Roman religion. This calendar was an official almanac of religion which the state priests were bound to observe, even though the first serious Roman student of his religion (Varro, in the 1st century BC) tells us how knowledge of some cults had deteriorated till only the name was known. The basic features of the calendar's liturgy roughly parallel the farming year in central Italy. The planting, promotion of growth, harvesting, storing of crops fall at their appropriate moment. February is given over to cleansing and March to decorating as the year ends and begins. December and January betray some signs of festivals of lights, but generally the Romans seldom took their eyes off the ground to gaze at the heavens. They left that task to others when they wanted it done.

The calendar comprised festivals for sacrifice and festivals for games. The simplicity of sacrifice also reflects the people's earliest economy, despite occasional attempts at modernization which show garish and wanton luxury. More recent and foreign were the sumptuous games that included athletic contests, chariot racing, theatrical drama, ballet, gladiatorial fights and wild animal hunts.

Every manner of diversion imaginable to the ruling class, or later to the emperor, was offered the people in the name of the gods. Such generous magnificence gave to the people what was otherwise lacking in their lives. Neither intellectual pagans nor fiery Christian preachers could bring an end to what was an agreed disgrace but also a lively and highly diverting spectacle.

Less glamorous and more common were the routine sacrifices in the hands of the state priests. Roman cult was rarely ever personal or congregational. Almost all civil sacrifice fell to the priests named for life or to annually elected officials. The priestly class at the top was identical with the ruling class. A priest came from the social elite and rarely felt his religious duties to be in conflict with his political ambitions. An official clergy as we understand it did not develop. This lack does not indicate the absence of priestly expertise. On the contrary, the normal expectation of priesthoods by members of the same clans presupposes traditional religion preserved by these clans.

Empty of moral content and gradually losing all semblance of relevance to the priests' prevailing social condition as an imperial elite, ancestral Roman religion lapsed into a formalism unusual in its consequences. Native scruple and aristocratic ambition made religious acts the object of bitter political quarrels so long as the aristocracy ruled. Temples, statues, altars and gifts came to the gods because of aristocratic munificence. Religious formalism promoted a religious legalism that ultimately converted the Roman mind into one of the keenest instruments of legislation and jurisprudence, if the soul were not imbued with lofty dreams. When Roman religion reached the stage of formalism, it had already lost its monopolizing hold on the Roman spirit. This does not mean that religious enthusiasm quit the Romans. Rather it was not to be found in the grand state cults.

The most important priesthoods were the panels of pontiffs, augurs and Ten Men For Sacrificing. The pontiffs oversaw many aspects of sacral law and jurisprudence. The chief pontiff served the state in the capacity of religious spokesman in the formal conduct of religion and frequently presided over meetings of the pontifical college which included the one priest-king, the flamens and the Vestal Virgins. The pontiffs, and more particularly the chief pontiff, regularly decided matters of law and sacrilege put to them.

The augurs were charged with constant surveillance of the well-being of the land and people from a religiously technical point of view. Their technical expertise also had political ramifications, for they could disrupt public assemblies and void elections by proclamation of some religious miscarriage or detection of an ill omen. Foreign cults and rites were entrusted to the Ten Men For Sacrificing.

Some deities, but by no means all, enjoyed the services of their own priest, called a flamen, and the flamens exhibit an early stage of Roman religion, as with Jupiter. Another kind of priesthood was the sodality, the Luperci and the Salii being representative examples. The Luperci, divided into two bands, performed a purification of the Palatine Hill on 15 February. Garbed only in loincloths, they struck unclean objects with a strip of goatskin called 'Juno's cloak'. The Salii, also divided into two bands, performed throughout March on behalf of Mars, whose divinity was associated with the new year of growth and war.

Ordinary religious ceremonies included the dinner or the sacrifice. A sacral supper might be offered only to the god or gods, and every September Jupiter alone received a dinner of the harvest fruits. Extraordinary situations could demand a banquet for a group of deities. Equally efficacious were regular suppers of which men and a god partook. While in later times invitations to a sacral dinner might be limited to priests and magistrates, early universal custom respected inclusion of all worshippers. This kind of ceremony differs from the sacrifice, which was usually a total offering of one food to a god. However, some of the food might be distributed to worshippers after a sacrifice. The Romans gave their gods what they themselves ate. Animal victims were the pig, sheep or cow, rarely the goat and only in one known case the horse. The animal had to be ritually pure. Otherwise, some attention might be paid to the animal's selection according to sex and colour. Besides animals the Romans offered foodstuffs of grain and fruit or wine and milk. Incense was introduced very early and was presumably acquired locally long before the oriental frankincense was imported. Burnt sacrifice was made on an altar, which might be a stone hearth or turf specially cut and piled for the ceremony.

Cleansing ceremonies were many. A common type was the procession of a pig, sheep and bullock (suovetaurilia) around the area to be purified and their slaughter for the good of the soil. Borders and boundaries had such singular significance that some rituals presupposed the retention or expulsion of men and deities along some well-defined holy limit. Like other ancient peoples, the Romans firmly believed in the divinity of a given place or some social unit. Sometimes the local god was called simply Genius of This Place or God Who Watches Over This Place. Otherwise the deity had the name of the place itself. Any sojourn in a place prompted sacrifice if not a more permanent gift. Also the full range of governmental offices and communities as well as the multitude of military units worshipped their several Genii or the like.

The Romans were keenly aware of the strength that the land imparted to its inhabitants. When they conquered and wholly absorbed another people, the Romans ritually summoned the chief local god (or gods) from the conquered land to Rome where the alien god was properly domiciled. Further, the vanquished town and its farmland might be placed under a perpetual curse by uprooting its boundary-markers, sowing salt in its furrows and consigning the town and land to gods of the underworld with prayer to Jupiter and Tellus, Heaven and Earth. This ceremony was called devotio, as was that personal act of self-dedication whereby a general would literally sacrifice himself to the enemy and thus gain a victory for his people. Devotio was but a particular kind of vow or promise which Romans were wont to make in a moment of stress or need. Many religious donations from high and low stemmed from the vow (*ex voto*). The customary form for keeping one's promise was to pay or loosen the vow (*votum solvere*). Romans seldom offered what was not due. The gods received according to their deserts and merits.

Most Romans left the celebration of civil gods to the state priests. At home and within the tradition-bound clans private worship continued unabated for centuries. Indeed, the extent, variety and tenacity of private cult demonstrates how gods were so deeply

An early 15th century plan of Rome from the Duc de Barry's Book of Hours, now in the Musée Condé at Chantilly, France

rooted in pagan hearts. The primitive centre of the household cult was the hearth. The name of the goddess Vesta means no more then the hearth-fire. Vesta's public cult of the City's fire kept by her virgins grew as her domestic cult declined.

Other domestic deities were the Penates, Lares and Genius. The Penates were gods of the food cupboard (*penus*). The Lares occupied the hearth but also functioned elsewhere in Rome. The Genius typifies the house cult and the Roman mentality. The word signifies the procreative force of the male householder. It was honoured at least on every birthday by libations of wine.

The Genius joined the Lares in a small shrine with an artificial hearth set in every dining-room and was often portrayed between the two Lares. He was a model householder, wearing a toga and holding in one hand a horn of plenty and in the other a wine-saucer.

Although some ancient authors give the impression that the domestic gods received little more than perfunctory attention, the physical remains, especially those of Pompeii, eloquently counter such an impression. Every household had its altar. Besides the painted or sculptured Lares and Genius are found a variety of statuettes.

THE GREAT FAITHS

Religions East & West

'The Kingdom of God is within you'. This is an aspect of Christianity which since the Reformation has been by and large allowed to lapse. More and more emphasis has been put upon the god 'out there' or 'up there', the God of judgement and justice. Protestant Christianity (apart from the Quakers and similar dissident sects) has tended to separate God from man, and so in the long run it has made God irrelevant to man. This is the reason why Protestant Christianity is everywhere in retreat and why modern man is groping towards a form of religion which will reunite God with man, eternity with time.

The religions of the world may be roughly divided into two types — the prophetic and the mystical. Each type derives ultimately from one nation — the prophetic from the Jews, the mystical from India. In addition, China must count as an independent religious phenomenon which, however, belongs to the Indian 'type' by which it was profoundly influenced.

To the prophetic type of religion belong Judaism itself and its daughter religions, Christianity and Islam. These religions all originated in the Near East, Christianity spreading mainly throughout Europe. Islam replaced it in Asia Minor and North Africa, but its greatest expansion was towards the East when it displaced Zoroastrianism in Persia and made deep inroads into India and beyond. If we speak of 'prophetic' religion as 'Western', we must remember that Islam constituted an integral part of this 'Western' block, not of the 'Eastern'. The great religious divide is not the Bosphorus

which separates Europe from Asia, but the Hindu Kush which separates the lands of the Moslem Iranian nation from India on the one hand, and the Gobi Desert which separates them from China on the other. Thus, if we persist in using the words 'Eastern' and 'Western', we must understand that in the religious context we mean Europe and the Middle East by 'Western'; India and the Far East by 'Eastern'.

In prophetic religion the first assumption is that of a personal God who rules the universe and who communicates his will to man through Prophets and Lawgivers. This God is directly and personally concerned with the right ordering of *this* world and with the right and 'righteous' relationships he wishes to exist between man and man: hence he is the Lawgiver *par excellence*, operating in time and space in a concrete situation the centre of which is man. Though himself the Eternal and therefore exempt from all conditions imposed by time and space, he manifests himself in act. As Pascal said, 'he is the God of Abraham, the God of Isaac, the God of Jacob, not of the philosophers and the learned'. He is a personal and 'living' God who manifests his will in history.

The God of 'Eastern' religion *is* the God of the philosophers — so much so indeed that to call him God at all can only mislead, for he is not a person, *it* is a principle: it is the principle of unchanging Being which is yet the source of all becoming, the stillness that is yet the source of all activity, the One from which all multiplicity proceeds. In Chinese it is called the Tao, the 'Way', in the Indian languages it is *Brahman*, unchanging, One, dependent on nothing, free.

All réligions aim at 'salvation' of some sort, and this implies that there is both something or someone which can be 'saved' and also something *from* which it can be saved. For prophetic religion this 'something' is usually sin or evil, for the mystical religions it is the human condition as we

know it, subject to birth and death, old age and decay — the tyranny of time and of this world in which we live. This longing to have done with life as lived and experienced on earth is typically and admirably expressed in an ancient Hindu prayer:

> From the unreal lead me to the real!
> From darkness lead me to the light!
> From death lead me to immortality!

Immortality and the 'real' are one and the same thing: they are not of this world, for they are what does not and cannot change. 'Immortality' does not mean 'life ever-lasting', for it does not last at all: it just *is*. It is the real as contrasted with the unreal, the eternal as contrasted with the transient. The essential experience is that of the 'salvation' or rather 'liberation' of the soul from the bondage of time, space and matter.

What then is the nature of the soul if by this word we understand that thing in man which can be so liberated? It is emphatically not what Christians understand by that word: it is not the responsible element in man which can be 'saved' or 'damned' because salvation and damnation are the reward and punishment allotted to the doers of good or evil deeds. The 'soul' or, as the Hindus prefer to call it, the 'self', cannot be saved or damned because it has nothing to do with 'doing', only with 'being'. 'Doing' in Sanskrit is *karma,* and it is karma which binds you to the never-ending round of impermanent existence. 'Liberation' means to have done with 'doing' and 'having' in order that you may simply 'be'.

Brahman is Being: Brahman is conscious-ness: Brahman is joy. So too, you and I, in our inmost selves, are Being, consciousness, and joy. We do not know this because we are ignorant of the true nature of things: we identify ourselves with body, senses, mind, the 'ego', or even with what we in the West call 'soul', of which conscience is an essential part. This is to fail to see things as they

At the highest level of eastern religious thought, God is abstract, but orientals have also pictured their gods in human form and have glorified the physical body, in contrast to the ascetic, body-denying tendencies also found in some faiths: temple sculpture, c 1000 AD, at Khajuraho in India

really are; and so liberation means also to free oneself from a false view of things.

Brahman is the same changeless principle which both pervades the universe and dwells in the consciousness of every man. To 'become Brahman' is to realize that one's true being is independent of this world, of mind and emotion and feeling just as much as of the body and its desires. To 'become Brahman' means to realize that the point without magnitude within the human heart is the same as the ground of the cosmos:

As wide as is this space around us, so wide is this space within the heart. In it both sky and earth are concentrated, both fire and wind, both sun and moon, lightning and the stars, what a man possesses here on earth and what he does not possess: everything is concentrated in this (tiny space within the heart).

This is what is usually called pantheism; but it does not mean that everything is indiscriminately and indifferentiably divine, but that all things are divine in the sense that the same eternal spirit, Brahman, is fully present in them all. 'Liberation' means to *experience* the presence of this unchanging being both in yourself and in all Nature – hence it is possible to say that one's inmost self and the highest Brahman are one: 'This finest essence – the whole universe has it as its Self: That is the Real: That is the Self: That *you* are.'

This 'Highest Self' is usually regarded as far transcending anything that can be called personality and the experience of identity with this impersonal absolute means the loss of anything you can call 'I', the dissolving of the hard contours of personal existence into the wide expanse of unqualified being, just as a river loses its identity once it flows into the featureless ocean. And yet in the ancient Hindu texts Brahman is not always conceived of as being simply the changeless One behind the ever-changing many, for it sometimes appears as the creative ground of the universe, the 'Lord' of the universe.

This is indeed the great unborn Self which consists of understanding. . . In the space within the heart lies the Ruler of all, the Lord of all, the King of all. He neither increases by good works nor does he diminish by evil ones. . . For it is he who makes him whom he would raise up from these worlds perform good works, and it is he again who makes him whom he would drag down perform evil works. He is the guardian of the worlds, the sovereign of the worlds, universal Lord. Let a man know: He is my Self.

Here the identification of the essence of man and the Absolute which is at the same time God is complete. This is not the Judaeo-Christian God who stands over against you as a judge, it is not even the 'Kingdom of God' that 'is within you'; it is a God who transcends all personal gods and yet is identical with you as you exist in eternity. Moreover, this is not something that must be accepted on faith alone, it is something that all can experience if their dispositions are right and if they are suitably trained. It may sound absurd, but it is an experience that is attested all over the globe and at all stages of human development. Once experienced, this vision of the one undying reality behind all that comes to be and passes away cannot be doubted, for to have glimpsed it, if only for a moment, brings the conviction that death itself is an impossibility. The danger is that

it introduces you into a world where all action is transcended and in which there can therefore be neither good nor evil. This too is the experience which the Buddhists call 'Enlightenment'.

The Hindus were and are incurable metaphysicians. Though all admit that this experience is not explicable in words, this did not prevent them from trying to explain it philosophically. Some said it proved that all things are inseparably one and that all multiplicity is an illusion: others went to the other extreme and claimed that there are two orders of being – the eternal and the transient – and that liberation means no more than the final separation of the eternal element from all that is not eternal. All this the Buddha rejected as being irrelevant to the saving experience itself which for him meant the 'snuffing out' *(Nirvana)* of all worldly existence and the actual experience of 'what is unborn, does not become, is not made or compounded'. This Nirvana, the blowing out of the flame of life and of anything we are pleased to call a 'self' (for the Buddha will have nothing to do with a 'self' of any kind whether individual or universal), is the realization of the Changeless. This again is an experience that may be had here in this life: it is something that is present in all of us. For most of us it is hidden away so that we do not even suspect its existence. The Buddha, however, is there to show us the way, the Noble Eightfold Path which is the only sure way to the cherished goal and which is based on a strict morality of self-lessness and self-abnegation.

Both Hinduism and Buddhism see salvation as a release from *this* world into an unconditioned form of existence in which all change and all action are transcended. That is because they believe in the transmigration of souls, the endless repetition of lives more or less miserable to which, but for the possibility of 'liberation', there would be no foreseeable end. Their tendency is to see this world as a prison from which the spirit of man must escape. The Chinese did not believe in transmigration, and their attitude to this world is therefore very different. The Supreme principle is the Tao – the 'Way' – the 'way' things work, that is; and man's salvation consists in his attuning himself to and uniting himself with this Tao. Since the Tao is the principle that makes things what they are, man must not resist it. Like Brahman the Tao is the single reality that operates in all things, though remaining still and unperturbed itself all the time. Hence to be at one with all things is to be at one with the Tao, or the basic principle behind all.

When Buddhism came to China it too was transformed: the original rigid separation of eternity from this world of space and time was abolished. The result was Zen in which 'enlightenment' is seen much as the Taoists and early Hindus saw it – as the realization of the interconnectedness of all things in the one absolute 'ground'. Enlightenment may come after long practice either gradually or quite suddenly. The experience, as with the Hindus, is one of Being, heightened consciousness, and joy. In it there is nothing that a Christian would recognize as God; it is simply the discovery of a changeless principle within yourself, it is your own true being which no one, not even God, can take away from you. 'Salvation' lies squarely in your own hands: and in this surely lies the attraction of Zen and the whole 'Eastern' tradition to post-Christian man.

Eugen Kusch

Picturepoint London

Judaism

A significant factor in the understanding of Judaism is that it centres around a people, rather than an individual. Important though Moses or Abraham or Isaiah is for Judaism it is quite possible to imagine the Jewish faith without any of these. But it is as inconceivable to have Judaism without the Jewish people as it is to have Christianity without Jesus.

It has been estimated that there are around 12 million Jews in the world today, 5 million in the United States, $2\frac{1}{2}$ million in the State of Israel and the remainder distributed over the rest of the world. Some of these have no religious belief whatsoever but the majority do subscribe to the faith known as Judaism, though with many differing emphases in matters of both belief and observance. One large division (an ethnic rather than a doctrinal one) is between Oriental Jews together with those hailing from Spain and Portugal, and Jews from other parts of Europe. The former are known as Sefardim (from the Hebrew name for Spain, *Sefarad*) and the latter as Ashkenazim (from the Hebrew name for Germany, *Ashkenaz*). The differences between these two groupings are in minor liturgical rites, customs, ceremonies and popular foods.

Another division is between Zionists, who see the main future for Jews in the State of Israel and who tend to look upon the Jews as a nation, like the English or the French, and the non-Zionists, who see Judaism purely as a religion, and in non-nationalistic terms. This does not rule out the existence of many religious Zionists and there are even a few anti-Zionists. Still another significant division is between Orthodoxy and Reform; the main difference between these two groups concerns the nature of revelation and the permanent binding character of the ceremonial law.

The Jewish place of worship is the synagogue, from a Greek word meaning simply 'place of assembly'. Some Reform synagogues are called 'temples', chiefly because Reform Jews, unlike the Orthodox, do not believe that the Temple in Jerusalem will be rebuilt in the days of the Messiah and

animal sacrifices again offered there, so that the synagogue has now taken the place of the ancient Temple. In the modern synagogue the rabbi and the cantor – the reader of the prayers to music – officiate at the services, but there is nothing in Jewish teaching to prevent any Jew from officiating at any service, including the marriage service. The rabbi is not a priest. The word rabbi means 'teacher' or 'master' and his chief function is to be an expounder of the Jewish religion. There is, in fact, no priesthood nowadays in Judaism, except for vestigial remains of a very peripheral order. Jews claiming descent from the Temple priesthood, who frequently have the name Cohen, from the old Hebrew name for 'priest', recite the priestly blessing 'May the Lord bless you and keep you' in Orthodox synagogues on the great occasions of the year, but otherwise very little is left in present-day Judaism of the hereditary priesthood.

In fact, until the 14th century there were no professional rabbis, the Jewish teachers earning their living by practising such crafts as that of physician while teaching Judaism without fee in their spare time. The rabbis of an earlier period were drawn from every walk of life. Some of them were businessmen, others smiths or cobblers. The sole qualification was proficiency in the Torah.

There is to be observed in Jewish history a definite substitution of an aristocracy of learning for the older aristocracy of the priesthood. This received its most dramatic expression in two sayings dating from as early as the 2nd century: that only the son of a king can be a prince and only the son of a priest can be a priest, but the crown of the Torah lies in a corner and anyone capable of so doing can don it; and that a bastard learned in the Torah takes precedence over an ignorant High Priest. Love of learning and respect for things of the mind has been a distinguishing feature of Judaism so that a non-believing Jew like Freud could still feel himself strongly attached to Judaism.

The most obvious way of describing a religion is to state the beliefs it expects from its adherents. There are, however, notorious difficulties when one tries to describe Judaism in this way. There has never been in Judaism any proper machinery for the formulation of dogmas, no synod or body of representative Jewish teachers to decide authoritatively and categorically what it is that a Jew must believe in order to be a Jew. This has resulted in an extremely wide range of diverse views among Jewish theologians.

It would be wrong to conclude, as many 19th century scholars were in the habit of doing, that Judaism has no dogmas, that a Jew can believe what he likes and still remain an adherent of Judaism. This is clearly an absurd position to adopt: as Solomon Schechter (d.1915) pointed out,

it would make the central idea of Judaism the dogma of having no dogma. What does emerge from a study of the classical sources of Judaism – the Bible, the Talmudic literature produced in Palestine and Babylon during the first five centuries AD, and the medieval Jewish writings – is a kind of consensus of opinion among believers as to the distinguishing features of Jewish belief.

With these reservations the 13 principles of the Jewish faith can be examined as formulated by the greatest Jew of the Middle Ages, Moses Maimonides (1135–1204). These are the nearest thing to a Jewish catechism. They have been printed in many prayer books and are recited daily by the pious. But many modern Jews do not accept them without considerable qualifications and there are other beliefs, such as that of the divine election of Israel, for example, which are not included among the 13 but which many Jews would consider to be basic. Maimonides's principles are: belief in the existence of God; in his unity; his incorporeality; his eternity; and that God alone is to be worshipped; belief in the prophets; that Moses is the greatest of the prophets; that the Torah is from heaven; that it is unchanging; belief that God knows the deeds of men; that he rewards the good and punishes the wicked; belief in the coming of the Messiah; and in the resurrection.

The first five principles have to do with the nature of God. Maimonides's choice of principles was chiefly in response to the particular challenges of his day and the second, third and fifth principles are fairly obviously directed against Christianity. While in the Middle Ages and later there were to be found Jewish teachers of note who were prepared to acknowledge that the Christian doctrine is not tritheism and that Christianity is not 'idolatry', Jews have been unanimous in declaring the doctrine of the Trinity, and especially the doctrine of the Incarnation, in which Jesus of Nazareth is the Second Person in the Trinity, to be a breach of pure monotheism and therefore incompatible with Jewish belief. The Jewish declaration of faith is the *Shema,* 'Hear, O Israel; the Lord our God, the Lord is One' (Deuteronomy 6.4). The Jewish child is taught to recite the verse as soon as he can speak. The devout Jew recites it daily, in the morning and at night. The dying repeat it as life's last affirmation.

There has been a wide spectrum of belief regarding the nature of God, from the negative theologians who wax eloquent in declaring how little one can say of God as he is in himself (some of these observe that one cannot, strictly speaking, say

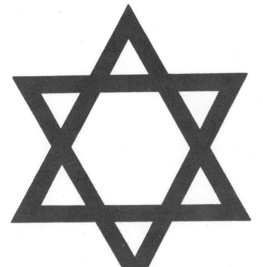

The idea of the Jews as the chosen people has been partly responsible for the persecution and hostility they have encountered: Mohammed ordering the execution of Jews, from a 16th century Turkish manuscript

دیدیم ایکی مسلمان بر جهودی اولدردلر ابن هشام ایدرزول تاجرکم

حصه بلمس ندی انی اولکون اولدردی قرنداش حویصه اولکونک

that God exists, since 'existence' is a term too heavily laden with human associations) to the Jew of simple faith who is not bothered at all by the problem of anthropomorphism. Even the belief that God can, if he so chooses, assume a bodily form (as in the legend, when he appeared on the altar in the Temple to consume the sacrifices in the form of a lion of fire) is not, according to some theologians, sufficient to cause those who hold it to be excluded from Judaism. Maimonides does, indeed, declare such persons to be heretics and his third principle states this emphatically but some of Maimonides's critics, while themselves rejecting any belief in God's corporeality, feel that the anthropomorphisms in Scripture encourage this belief so that although the sophisticated understood these in a non-literal sense the more naive believers cannot be condemned for holding opinions which, for them, have the full sanction of holy writ.

God is beyond time and space (the fourth principle) and the universe is subordinate to him. He is both transcendent and immanent. He is apart from the world and yet involved in it. Judaism rejects both deism, which denies God's immanence in the universe, and pantheism, which denies his transcendence and identifies God with the universe.

Prayer and worship are to be offered to God alone (the fifth principle). Even prayer to God through an intermediary is forbidden.

In the Hasidic movement, or Hasidim, which arose in the 18th century one does, however, find the idea of prayer through an intermediary, the hasidic saint or master. This was one of the reasons why the movement met in its early stages with such vehement rabbinic opposition. But the prayers are never offered *to* the holy man. It is rather that he prays on behalf of others who present their petitions to him; the hasidic movement believed that the prayers of the holy teacher can accomplish that which sinful men are incapable of achieving by themselves.

The sixth to the ninth principles (belief in the prophets of whom Moses is the greatest, and in the heavenly origin and unchanging character of the Torah) are concerned with revelation. The seventh and ninth principles appear to have been particularly stressed by Maimonides as a response to the claims of both Christianity and Islam that a greater prophet than Moses had arisen and that Judaism, though once valid, had been superseded. Until modern times, with very few exceptions, Jewish teachers held that the books of the Hebrew Bible (the 'Old Testament') were divinely revealed to man, albeit in differing degrees. The Pentateuch (the Torah proper) was thought of as being divinely dictated by God to Moses. The manner of the divine communication was, to be sure, variously understood in the Middle Ages (Maimonides himself held that all the people heard was an inarticulate sound which Moses put into words) but the content was conceived of as the very words of God. The prophetic books of the Bible (and this includes the historical books with the exception of Ezra, Nehemiah and Chronicles) were written by the prophets under the impact of prophecy (a lesser degree than the inspiration vouchsafed to Moses) while the books of the Hagiographa (including Psalms and Proverbs) were thought of as conveyed by the still lesser degree of inspiration known as the holy spirit. This is expressed in Jewish practice by forbidding the placing of the books of the Hagiographa on top of the prophetic books and the prophetic books on top of copies of the Pentateuch. The Torah was seen as twofold: firstly the written Torah, or the Pentateuch and the other books of the Bible, and secondly, the oral Torah or the teachings held to have been conveyed by God to Moses by word of mouth, together with those elaborations and applications now found in the rabbinic works produced during the first five centuries AD, the most important of which is the Talmud. There are two Talmuds; the Palestinian edited around the year 400, and the more authoritative Babylonian edited around the year 500.

Orthodoxy holds fast to the position that the present text of the Pentateuch is the word of God, infallible, sublime, created before the world came into being. Both the written and the oral Torah are from God in a direct sense with the corollary that the precepts of the Torah in their rabbinic interpretation are eternally binding upon Jews and immutable. In the Orthodox view all biblical criticism, whether 'higher' or 'lower' (that is, literary criticism and textual criticism) is heresy because it expresses doubts as to the correctness of the present text and because it sees the Pentateuch itself as a composite work produced at different intervals and with contradictions between the Codes of Law found therein.

Reform Judaism, on the other hand, accepts the new picture of the Pentateuch and the rest of the Bible which has emerged as the result of modern historical investigation and criticism. Reform holds the view that a radical re-interpretation of what revelation means is now called for and abandons the idea of an immutable law. A compromise position between Orthodoxy and Reform is represented chiefly in the United States by Conservative Judaism, to which the precepts are binding not because they were given by God in the direct sense in which Orthodoxy understands it but because God is seen, as it were, in the process as a whole. The real source of authority is the tradition of the Jewish community of believers, just as the Church in Catholicism is for Christians.

To illustrate the differences an example can be given from the dietary laws, such as abstinence from eating pork and shell-fish. Orthodoxy insists on the observance of these laws as God-given ordinances. Reform leaves such observances to the individual conscience but holds in any event that it is the moral rather than the ritual and ceremonial law which is permanently binding. Conservative Judaism believes that the binding character of these laws derives not so much from any kind of direct divine communication but because the laws have evolved through the historical experiences of the Jewish people and are therefore part of the divine-human encounter in human history and can serve in the present, as

Above In accordance with Levitical law, every Jewish male must be circumcised on the eighth day after his birth. Originally a rite of initiation, it is now practised mainly for health reasons: *Circumcision of the Children of Israel*, by the 18th century Italian painter G. B. Tiepolo *Opposite* Satirical drawing of the Jews of Norwich which appeared in the Jews' Roll, a list of tax payments in Henry III's reign; antisemitic feeling ran high in medieval Europe and in England Jews were afforded protection only on payment of exorbitant taxes

they have done in the past, in furthering the ideal of holiness in daily living. With regard to the ethical law there is complete unanimity among all sections of Jewry that this has binding force for all time.

The tenth and eleventh principles (that God knows the deeds of men and rewards or punishes them accordingly) are accepted in outline by all religious Jews, although there is considerable difference of opinion as to the exact nature of divine Providence and as to how reward and punishment are to be understood. Does the doctrine mean that God rewards directly in this life those who keep his laws and punishes those who do not, or does it mean that virtue brings its own rewards and similarly vice its own punishments?

Does it mean that there is reward and punishment in the afterlife and if it does, what is the nature of heaven and hell? Is there a hell at all and, if there is, is it a place or a state of remoteness from God? Is punishment in hell eternal or only for a period? On these questions there are still differing answers among Jews.

The twelfth principle refers to the belief mentioned frequently in the Bible that the day will come when this world will be perfected, when war and hatred will be banished from the earth, and when the Kingdom of God will be established and all men will recognize him as their Maker. The Orthodox belief is in a personal Messiah (a word meaning 'the anointed one', in reference to the practice of anointing kings with oil), a human being of great renown but in no way divine who will be a descendant of King David and who will be sent by God for this purpose. Non-Orthodox opinion since the last century has tended to place all the stress on the dawning of the messianic age and to reject the doctrine of a personal Messiah as savouring too much of the magical. The basic idea is that God will eventually intervene in human affairs so as to bring about the perfect society envisaged.

In the last century many Jews tended to interpret the doctrine in purely naturalistic terms, that better education and social reforms in the Western world will themselves bring about the millennium. The horrors of this century have made such a belief in automatic human progress towards the desired goal remote and even ludicrous, though this theory is by no means dead. It has been related by many to the events which led up to the establishment of the State of Israel. The fact of the holocaust in Europe in which 6 million Jews died and the setting up of the State of Israel have both encouraged religious Jews to see the new State as having messianic dimensions. A number of religious Jews today tend to look upon Israel as 'the beginning of redemp-

tion', believing that the first steps have been taken towards the realization of the age-old messianic vision. At the same time they believe that the world still needs redemption and that the full realization, in which the perfect society under God will be established for all mankind, is still awaited and will only be achieved when God himself intervenes. It should be noted that the messianic belief concerns events here on earth. Whatever the Jewish views on the afterlife, Judaism believes that God will not permanently abandon this world to chaos and that one day mankind here on earth will find its complete redemption.

The last principle, about the resurrection of the dead has also been variously interpreted. Originally the doctrine of the resurrection referred to the dead rising from their graves and living again here on earth. It was closely connected with the messianic hope. After the advent of the Messiah the resurrection would take place on earth. As its name implies, the doctrine means that death is really death and resurrection a new birth of the body. In the course of time, however, the doctrine of the immortality of the soul came into Judaism. There may be traces here and there in the Bible of the doctrine that the soul lives on after death but these are few and vague. When the two doctrines — of the resurrection and the immortality of the soul — were fused, as eventually happened, the official view became that when a person dies his soul lives on in another realm until the resurrection, when it is reunited with the body on earth.

Maimonides seems to have been embarrassed by the whole idea of the body living on and, indeed, by the basic notion of the resurrection. In his earlier writings he is very indefinite about the idea and towards the end of his life he put forward the view that the resurrection is only for a time and that it is the soul alone which inhabits eternity. The ultimate bliss for the righteous is, in the words of the rabbis, to bask forever in the radiance of the divine presence. The references in the classical sources, of which there are many in the post-biblical period, to the world to come are both to the soul's fate in the afterlife and to the resurrection.

Reform Judaism, and for that matter even some Orthodox interpreters, prefer to think, as Maimonides seems to have done, of the doctrine of the immortality of the soul as the really significant part of this principle. Many modern Jewish thinkers accept this with the proviso that it does not refer to the mere survival of a nebulous 'soul' but to the continuing existence of the total human personality which, it is claimed, is really what is implied in the doctrine of the resurrection. It must also be appreciated that Judaism is not a religion of salvation, in other words, Judaism sees this life as good in itself, and not only as a means of acquiring eternal life. Life would be worth living even if this world were all man can hope to have. The paradox inherent in Judaism as a religion that is both this-worldly and other-worldly was finely expressed by the 2nd century teacher who said: 'Better one hour of good deeds and repentance in this world than the whole life of the world to come but better one hour of spiritual bliss in the world to come than all the life of this world.'

Judaism is a people-centred religion but it is not an exclusive religion. Converts are accepted although they are required to show clear evidence of sincerity. Moreover Judaism does not believe that salvation is only possible for Jews but that the righteous of all peoples have a share in the world to come. The idea that the religion depends on the peoplehood of Israel is frequently expressed, in the Biblical idiom, by saying that God has chosen Israel. This notion presents difficulties all of its own and is liable to misconceptions. There is nothing racialist about the doctrine that Israel has been chosen to serve God and all mankind. The convert to Judaism, whatever the colour of his skin and whatever his background, becomes a full member of the Jewish community.

Yet tensions inevitably exist between the universalism taught by Judaism — God as the Father of all mankind – and the particularism inseparable from the idea of divine election. Some modern Jewish thinkers, notably Mordecai Kaplan in the United States, have found the doctrine so open to misrepresentation that they have suggested it be dispensed with entirely. But the majority of religious Jews prefer to live with the tensions, trying to further the richness of the idea of Israel as God's covenant people without losing sight of the fact that, as Judaism itself repeatedly stresses, God loves all men.

That this is no idle dream can be seen from the contribution Judaism has made in the past to civilization. Judaism's daughter religions, Christianity and Islam, have received many of their most significant beliefs and institutions from Judaism: the doctrine of the one God, the patterns of worship in church and mosque, the reading of the Scriptures, the teachings of the prophets. The stories of the book of Genesis, for instance, with their strong moral sense have been a powerful aid in the moral education of children of both Jewish and other faiths. Movements of social reform and freedom from tyranny have found inspiration in the Old Testament passion for justice and the narrative of the deliverance from Egyptian bondage. Words like *Hallelujah* and *Amen* have become part of the vocabulary of worship for millions. The rhythm and concreteness of Hebrew prose and its powerful idioms have influenced, through biblical translation, all the European languages.

Jewish practices are of two kinds, the ceremonial and the ethical. On the ceremonial side there are colourful rituals both in the home and the synagogue. The sabbath and festivals are celebrated with joy. These always begin at nightfall and end at nightfall. On the eve of the sabbath two candles are lit as a symbol of peace in the home and increased spiritual light. The master of the house recites a benediction over a cup of wine in which he praises God for creating the world and giving his people sabbath rest. Tuneful table hymns are sung during the meal, the whole family joining in. The sabbath is a day of rest and of spiritual refreshment. Orthodoxy adheres strictly to the laws prohibiting all kinds of creative activity on the sabbath in acknowledgement of God as Creator and giver of life's blessings. Some Orthodox Jews refrain even from switching on electric lights on the sabbath. Orthodox Jews do not ride on the sabbath, do not write, engage in business, smoke or carry anything in the street. Reform Judaism has relaxed many of these laws but has not lost sight of the ideal of the sabbath as a day devoted to spiritual pursuits.

During the sabbath service in the synagogue a scroll of the Pentateuch is taken from its place in the Ark at the eastern end of the synagogue and carried in procession around the building while the congregation stand. The scroll must be written by hand and there are detailed traditional rules which the scribe must observe while carrying out his sacred task. It is adorned with silver ornaments, especially bells which tinkle while it is being paraded. A portion is read from it each week; this portion is divided up and members of the congregation are given in turn the honour of reading from the scroll (or, since many cannot read the Hebrew nowadays, of having it read for them by a competent reader). In this way the whole of the Pentateuch is read each year. The reading of the complete scroll is concluded in the autumn of the year. On this occasion no sooner is the reading complete than it begins again. The

persons given the great honour of reading the last portion and the first of the new cycle are called respectively: 'Bridegroom of the Torah' and 'Bridegroom of Genesis'. These two invite the rest of the congregation to festivities to mark the event.

The Jewish calendar is rich in festivals. The three pilgrim festivals (so called because in Temple times people would ascend to Jerusalem, then in joyous pilgrimage to the Temple) are the Passover in the spring, Pentecost seven weeks later, and Tabernacles in the autumn. Passover is in celebration of the Exodus from Egypt, when God led the enslaved people out of Egyptian bondage; in their haste to depart they had not time to bake their bread properly, so that they were obliged to eat unleavened bread. On Passover eve, in a delightful home ceremony, the family partake of unleavened cakes and they eat bitter herbs as a reminder of the bitterness of slavery, and they drink wine, in joy at the new-found freedom. At this meal the *Haggadah* (literally 'the telling') is recited. This is a dramatic presentation of the Exodus culled from biblical and other sources, in the course of which the youngest child present asks four questions regarding the unusual ceremonies he sees and the father and the rest of the company reply. Pious Jews refrain from eating leavened bread during the whole eight days' duration of the festival.

Pentecost is a celebration of the giving of the Torah, that is, of the revelation on Mt Sinai, as told in the book of Exodus. During the synagogue service of the day the portion from Exodus describing this tremendous event and containing the Ten Commandments is read from the scroll. Tabernacles celebrates the dwelling of the Israelites in 'booths' in the wilderness after they had gone out of Egypt. Many Jews build a booth in their gardens, the roof of which is open to the sky but lightly covered with foliage or straw, in which they eat all their meals for the seven days of the festival. On this festival a palm branch and other plants are taken in the hand during the recitation of Psalms in the synagogue in thanksgiving for God's bounty.

Historically considered, the three pilgrim festivals were originally agricultural feasts pure and simple but the genius of Judaism transformed them into festivals celebrating historical events. Some Jewish thinkers today see this as part of a long process in which religion was gradually freed from subservience to place. Unlike many pagan gods the true God is not bound to single spots on the earth's surface and he manifests himself through human history.

The New Year festival in the autumn is a solemn occasion, the major portion of the day being spent in prayer. In the home on the eve of the festival an apple is dipped in honey and eaten at the festive meal, while prayers are offered to God to grant a sweet and good year. The central feature of the synagogue service on this day is the blowing of the ram's horn, the oldest musical instrument known to man. Many ideas have been read into this ceremony, the best-known of

The annual feast of the Passover celebrates the Exodus from Egypt when God rescued the enslaved Jews from Egyptian bondage. Today on Passover Eve, Jews eat bitter herbs, to remind them of slavery, and drink wine, in celebration of their freedom: 13th century Haggadah illustration of the plagues of Egypt, which finally induced Pharaoh to let the children of Israel leave and go to settle in the Promised Land

which is that the piercing sound of the horn affords a shrill warning to man to awaken himself to his duties and responsibilities in the year ahead. Another explanation is that trumpets are blown at the coronation of a king and at the beginning of the New Year God is hailed as king of the universe.

On the tenth day after the New Year festival there falls the great fast of Yom Kippur, the Day of Atonement. Devout Jews fast for 24 hours, partaking of no food or drink whatsoever and spending the better part of the day in prayer. The Day of Atonement is a day of pardon. Jews confess their sins and throw themselves on the divine mercy. But solemn though the day is, it is in a way a joyous occasion because on it man is reconciled to his God and to his fellows. The name 'Black Fast', which is sometimes given to it by non-Jews, is a misnomer. In

fact, the readers of the services and many members of the congregation dress in long white robes symbolizing purity and divine compassion.

Two minor feasts are Purim (literally 'lots'), celebrating the deliverance of Jewry from the machinations of Haman as recounted in the book of Esther, and Hanukkah (literally 'dedication') celebrating the deliverance of the people in the days of Antiochus and the re-dedication of the altar, as told in the books of the Maccabees. On Purim the book of Esther is read amid jollification. On each of the eight days of Hanukkah candles are kindled in the Menorah (candelabrum), one on the first day, two on the second and so on for the feast. Legend has it that when the soldiers of Antiochus profaned the Temple there was only one small jar of pure oil left uncontaminated. This was used for kindling the Temple Menorah and although there was only sufficient for one night it burned by a miracle for eight days. The miracle of the oil became symbolic of the victory of the spirit which is the main theme of the Hanukkah festival.

The most vivid description of what Judaism demands of its adherents is found in the book of Deuteronomy (6. 4–9):

Hear O Israel: The Lord our God is One Lord; and you shall love the Lord your God with all your heart, and with all your soul, and with all your might. And these words, which I

The Torah refers by extension to the whole range of Jewish teaching *Above* In the synagogue part of the Torah is read each week *Below* At a children's village in Israel the class learns to read from the Torah *Opposite Jew with the Torah*, a painting by Chagall; the persons having the honour of reading the first and last portions of the Pentateuch each year are called respectively 'Bridegroom of the Torah' and 'Bridegroom of Genesis'

Telaviv Museum/A.P.A.G.P. Paris

command you this day, shall be upon your heart; and you shall teach them diligently to your children, and shall talk of them when you sit in your house, and when you walk by the way, and when you lie down, and when you rise. And you shall bind them as a sign upon your hand, and they shall be as front-lets between your eyes. And you shall write them upon the posts of your house, and on your gates.

The passage is repeated in slightly different words in Deuteronomy, chapter 11. At an early period in Jewish history the last verses were taken literally so that to this day the devout Jew has these two passages inscribed on parchment and fixed in a little case (the *mezuzah,* 'doorpost') to the doorpost of his house, reminding himself of God's law whenever he enters and leaves his house. Similarly, the passages, together with two others, inscribed on parchment, are placed into little boxes known as *tefillin,* meaning 'attachments' or 'phylacteries'. They are affixed with leather straps to the left arm, opposite the heart, and to the head and worn during prayer; they symbolize the Jew's dedication of mind, heart and hand to God's service.

Ritual observances, important though they are in the scheme of Judaism, are far from being the main features of the Jewish faith. At the heart of Judaism is an ethical affirmation. This is that man can imitate God by practising justice, righteousness and holiness and by showing compassion. This is the way to be God-like. It is for this reason that those biblical passages which breathe the spirit of passionate concern for the downtrodden and which speak in the most urgent terms of the pursuit of justice have always been favourite Jewish

texts; such as those enjoining concern for the poor and needy, for the hired servant and for the stranger; the spirit of neighbour-liness, and just and upright dealings. There are innumerable examples of this constant demand for sound ethical conduct as the basis of human life and such teachings were not seen by the Jewish teachers as mere preachment but as divine imperatives. The rabbis, the post-biblical teachers, elaborated on these precepts, discussing in great detail, for example, the question of fair prices and fair and unfair competition in business, of the laws against overcharging and having false weights and measures, of the prohibition of misleading others and the need for a community to take adequate care of its poor and needy, of regulations between employers and employees, masters and servants, parents and children. Even animals have their rights and have to be treated with kindness. A distinguished 18th century rabbi when asked if it is permitted for a Jew to hunt animals for sport replied that he could not imagine a Jew wishing to do any such thing.

Jewish ethical teaching is not confined to laws and deeds alone. Character formation is of the utmost significance. There has grown over the centuries a vast moralistic literature produced by Jewish teachers and studied by Jews regularly, inculcating the formation of good character traits and the rejection of vicious tendencies. Hatred of one's neighbour, sloth, pride, lust, anger, spite, envy and jealousy, are to be fought against, while compassion, kindliness, benevolence, the love of learning and of one's fellow-men are to be pursued vigorously. In the words of an 11th century Jewish moralist, Judaism certainly knows of 'duties of the limbs' but even more

important are the 'duties of the heart'. It was in this spirit that the Talmud contains a passage in which it is said that there are three distinguishing marks of the Jewish people: they are compassionate, they are bashful, and they are benevolent.

The conflict in man's soul between his higher and lower nature is described by the Talmudic rabbis as a conflict between the 'evil inclination' and the 'good inclination'. By the evil inclination they mean man's ambitions and his bodily instincts. These, though called 'evil' because they can lead to such, are essential to life and provide it with its driving power. With some exceptions Judaism is not an ascetic faith but it holds strongly to the need for self-control. Its ideal is neither life's denial nor its exploitation but its sanctification. In a rabbinic homily the Torah, the law of God, is compared to a plaster on a wound. While the healing plaster is on the wound the wounded man can eat and drink safely and freely and the wound will not fester. As Judaism sees it, man should not try to live as a hermit or a recluse. He should live in society and be of constant help to his fellows, he should marry and have children, he should enjoy life as a precious gift from God, but he should always be aware of the call to higher things and see himself, in the marvellous imagery of Jacob's dream in Genesis, as a ladder with its feet firmly planted on earth but its head in heaven.

This short survey of the Jewish faith can be fittingly concluded with a Talmudic tale about the great teacher Hillel who lived 2000 years ago. A prospective convert to Judaism came to Hillel and asked the sage to teach him the whole Torah while he stood on one leg. Hillel replied: 'That which is hateful unto thee do not do unto thy neighbour. This is the whole of the Torah'.

Christianity

Christianity takes its name from its founder, Jesus Christ. Christ is not a name but an adjective meaning 'the anointed one' and derived from the Greek *Christos* which is itself a translation of the Hebrew *Messiah*, the one chosen and anointed by God. Jesus is a Hebrew name, Jesus was a Jew, and the designation Jesus Christ points to two cardinal facts about the rise of Christianity. It sprang from Judaism, and in the early centuries it had its widest dissemination in the Hellenistic world, the Mediterranean area where Greek cultural influence was strong.

Many of the central concepts of Judaism were incorporated into Christianity: as Jesus said, he had come not to destroy the law and the prophets but to fulfil. The Old Testament, the name given by Christians to the Jewish scriptures, asserts the oneness of God: 'Hear, O Israel, the Lord thy God is one god.' An intransigent monotheism has been both the glory and the tragedy of Israel. In the ancient world this insistence set the Jews apart from their neighbours even in a political sense, as the gods of the various peoples were expected to recognize each other. In particular, Israel came into conflict with rulers who claimed to be gods themselves. This claim was made by Alexander and his successors, by the Egyptian pharaohs and by the emperors of Rome, and this claim the Jews resolutely rejected. They were the only people in antiquity who refused to place a pinch of incense on the altars of the emperors and the only people who were tacitly granted exemption from this universal demand.

There are religions of Nature, religions of contemplation and religions of history, and Judaism was centred in history. Religions of Nature see the divine in the recurrence of the seasons, and particularly in the processes of fertility. Their rites call for the sacrifice of infants to win the favour of the god and to stimulate the fertility of the earth; sometimes also for the emasculation of men and the perpetual virginity of women or, in reverse, for sacred prostitution. Ancient Israel met such practices in Canaan and sought ruthlessly to stamp them out.

Religions of contemplation seek the divine by turning within, until meditation is consummated in ecstatic union with the Ultimate. Judaism knew of dreams and visions but not the rapture of the mystic who loses his identity in the abyss of the godhead.

Religions of history see the divine rather in events, in the mighty acts of God as he raises up and casts down. Frequently they look forward to a great coming event, a cataclysm which will terminate the present world order and introduce a new and blessed era. For the Jews the new era was to be the restoration of Paradise, to be inaugurated by an inspired leader, the Messiah.

If the coming day of the Lord was to be light and not darkness, Israel must do God's will. Some believed that this consisted in the performance of the rites of the Temple. But when the Temple was no longer accessible, as a result of the captivity of the Jews in Babylon, in the 6th century BC, the law (called the Torah) with all its requirements of circumcision, kosher food, sabbath observance and the like became the focus of Jewish piety. The prophets, however, deprecated formalism of this sort.

By the time of Jesus the Jews, who had been an oppressed people for seven centuries, were under the yoke of Rome. Many of the peoples of the Empire rejoiced that Rome had given them security through the establishment of a universal peace but the Jews were resentful. The flower of their youth had been squandered in Rome's earlier civil wars and the Roman belief in the divinity of the emperor was contrary to Jewish belief in the sole rule of God.

There were three parties among the Jews. The Sadducees were willing to collaborate with the occupying power, the Zealots fomented rebellion, and the Pharisees would neither fraternize nor rebel but kept the law and waited for vindication at the hands of God. Those who committed themselves to political passivity in this way were all the more ready to dream of an intervention from heaven. A deliverer would come, whether he was 'the righteous one' of the Dead Sea Scrolls, a Messiah on earth, or the Son of Man appearing on the clouds of heaven.

Into this society was born Jesus the Galilean, a loyal Jew who observed the feasts by going up to Jerusalem.

There are no writings from his pen. The gospels which tell of his life and teachings were not composed until some 30 or more years after his death (commonly dated to the year 33 AD) and some portions of the Christian scriptures, called the New Testament, may date from as late as the end of the 1st century or even the beginning of the 2nd.

Some historians have questioned even the very existence of Jesus, despite the difficulty in that case of explaining the rise of the Christian religion. Marxists have maintained that Jesus was a myth of the proletariat, though there was no proletariat in the modern sense in that day. Some have suggested that Jesus was a Nature myth, a personification of the dying and rising of the seasons, for he rose from the dead in the spring. But the early Christians clearly did not see him in this light, and in fact they took care not to commemorate the Resurrection on the day of the spring equinox, because that was the day on which the Nature god Attis arose after the death of winter.

Other historians have said that Jesus did indeed exist but of one fact only can we be quite sure, that he was crucified. There are variants in the accounts of all the other events of his life.

Such scepticism has diminished of late, for we are unable to account for the ways in which the early Christians differed from their Jewish forbears unless it is accepted that Jesus instituted changes. The essential picture in the New Testament is reliable, the more evidently because the authors recorded unpalatable sayings of Jesus. For example, the Church was confronted by a group stemming from John the Baptist, giving them good reason to disparage John. Yet they recorded Jesus's words, 'There is none greater born of woman than John.'

The cross itself was also a source of offence. Why revere a criminal executed by the most shameful of all deaths? Some in the early Church tried to eliminate the dilemma by denying that Jesus had a real

Daily Telegraph Colour Library

Left The first expansion of Christianity was into the Greek-speaking world of the eastern Mediterranean, where the Greek Orthodox Church continues to flourish: an Orthodox priest in the Church of the Nativity at Bethlehem, built on what was believed to be the site of Christ's birth *Opposite* Some historians have maintained that the only thing we know for certain about Jesus is that he was crucified, though such a degree of scepticism is now out of fashion, and the essential picture given of his life in the New Testament is generally accepted as reliable. God looks down from heaven, while St John supports the Virgin Mary who mourns over the dead Jesus: from the Rohan Book of Hours, in the Bibliothèque Nationale, Paris

body at all. He merely looked as if he did and on the cross he cried out 'as if in pain'. But the main body of the early Church would have none of this. Their creed asserted that 'he suffered under Pontius Pilate, was crucified, dead and buried.'

If Jesus was a Jew, loyal to the tradition of his people, and if he was not a rebel against Rome, why was he crucified? The answer is that he alienated all parties: the Sadducees because he scorned them for collaborating with the Romans; the Zealots because he would not rebel; the Pharisees because he differed from them as to what was meant by fulfilling the law. He held that the Great Commandment was to love God and your neighbour, rather than to refrain from certain foods, or to observe the Sabbath to the neglect of human obligations. In particular, Jesus consorted with outcasts, prostitutes and tax-gatherers. Assuring them of God's forgiveness, he even undertook to forgive their sins himself. He seemed, then, to be guilty of blasphemy, by usurping the role of God. Jesus certainly spoke of God as his Father, and he appears to have thought of himself as the Messiah who would redeem Israel, not by arms but by suffering.

Jesus was conscious of standing at the pinnacle of history, about to usher in the new Paradise of God. His challenge to the priests at Jerusalem, when he defied their authority by casting out of the Temple those who changed foreign coins into Temple currency, brought the wrath of the hierarchy upon him; but because he already enjoyed a popular following, the rulers of the people feared to lay hands on him. They were not empowered to put him to death without Roman consent, and the only charge which Rome would entertain was that of political insurrection.

Jesus could hardly be accused of committing an overt act of rebellion, and the charge finally made against him, and fixed to his cross in Hebrew, Greek and Latin, was that he had claimed to be the 'King of the Jews'. From the point of view of the Jews, therefore, his real offence was blasphemy, but to Pontius Pilate, the Roman official, he was guilty of inciting rebellion.

After his crucifixion, Jesus was alleged by his disciples to have risen from the dead. Some historians feel that there were three stages in the growth of this tradition. First came visions of the risen Jesus, then the stories that his tomb had been found empty, and finally the belief that he had ascended bodily into heaven. But however the Resurrection may have been conceived or experienced, the followers of Jesus were convinced that their master was still alive.

This faith created the Church. Such a statement may seem too strong, for other religions have originated without a founder who rose from the dead. But it is certain that the faith of the early Christians rested on the belief that Christ had conquered death and had broken the power of the demonic forces in the cosmos. He had given men a new power to surmount their

own perverse propensities. Another vivid element in the early Christian faith was that Christ would soon return as the Son of Man upon the clouds of heaven, to set up a new order, whether on earth or in heaven.

Inspired with this faith, all the disciples became missionaries. Christianity had its first following among the Jews, to whom Peter was missionary, but Hellenist converts, who spoke Greek, soon became more numerous. As a result, the New Testament has come down to us not in Aramaic, the language of Jesus, but only in Greek. St Paul, the missionary to the Gentiles, was largely responsible for Christianity's development away from its origins in agrarian Palestine and into the urban Hellenistic world. His missionary journeys throughout Asia Minor made this region the most heavily Christianized until the time of the Emperor Constantine in the 4th century AD. He also travelled to Rome where, according to a strong tradition, he was martyred during Nero's persecution of the Christians in 64 AD.

Paul came nearer than any other New Testament writer to formulating a Christian theology. A Jew himself, he naturally accepted the Jewish picture of God as the Father. Jesus is not called God by Paul, but he is said to have been on an equality with God and to have humbled himself, taking the form of a slave and becoming obedient even to the death on the cross. For this reason God 'has highly exalted him and bestowed on him the name which is above every name, that at the name of Jesus every knee should bow, in heaven and on earth and under the earth, and every tongue confess that Jesus Christ is Lord . . .' (Philippians, chapter 2).

Paul's statement that Christ humbled himself was taken to mean that he emptied himself of his full power and glory, a view which facilitated the later claim that he was both God and man. As man he had divested himself of some of the prerogatives of deity.

In the gospel of St John there is a more precise statement of the doctrine of the Incarnation, the doctrine that God became man. In the prologue to that gospel we read that, 'In the beginning was the Word.' The English 'Word' translates the Greek *logos*, which means the rational principle, both dormant and active, in the entire universe. This was the principle in accordance with which God created the world, and this logos became flesh in Jesus. The Latin word for 'flesh' is *carnis*, hence becoming flesh is called 'incarnation'. Other religions teach that men have become gods: Christianity that God entered into flesh and became man.

Paul was the greatest theologian among the early Christians: the greatest leader of the churches is believed to have been Peter. The Roman church looked upon Peter and Paul as the co-founders of their church and Peter, as well as Paul, is assumed to have suffered martyrdom under Nero. There is a tradition that Peter became the first bishop of Rome but this has not been established for certain. The bishop was at first merely

the pastor of a local group of Christians. The Roman congregation soon acquired a leading position among the churches, partly because it was in the capital of the Roman Empire but even more because it was the most reliable source of the Christian tradition, since it was founded by the two martyred apostles, after whom there had been an unbroken line of succession in the bishopric.

Christian morality at that time was heroic rather than ascetic. In many respects, Christianity carried over the ethic of Judaism. But in contrast to both Judaism and paganism, Christianity stressed the gentler virtues: mercy, compassion, consideration, tenderness, self-sacrifice and love, sheer love, with no consideration of recompense.

At certain points, this early ethic was affected by the expectation that Christ would soon return. Because Paul believed that the current world order of society would only last a short time, he taught that no one should try to change his status, whether he was a slave or a free man. The early Church, therefore, sought to ameliorate the lot of the slave and Christianize the relationship of master and man, but did not call for universal emancipation.

By the same token, the married and the unmarried should remain as they were, except that marriage might be allowed to those who could not abstain from sex. This grudging concession was later given an ascetic turn and led for centuries to virginity being considered superior to marriage. The only point at which the early ethic called for a drastic change in social attitudes was with regard to war. No Christian author condoned killing in war until the time of Constantine. Various reasons were given for this pacifism, the main one being Christian love. However, some leaders of the Church allowed Christians to do military service, provided they did not kill. This was possible during the two centuries of the great Roman peace, when the army was generally engaged in what today would be police work.

Christianity seems to have emerged as a religion in its own right, recognizably distinct from Judaism, by the time of Nero's persecution in 64 AD. Once this had happened, Christians forfeited the exemption from taking part in the worship of the emperor, which was tacitly granted to the Jews. The Christians, quite as emphatically as the Jews, would give divine honour to no man. This refusal was one of the main reasons for their persecution until the time of Constantine. In addition, their rejection of all pagan gods was interpreted as atheism and the pacifism of the great majority of Christians was thought to be a danger to the state.

During the first three centuries the Church continued to spread, especially around the shores of the Mediterranean and inland along the courses of rivers such as the Tiber, the Po and the Rhone. As Christianity expanded and the number of

When he was about 30, Jesus was baptized in the River Jordan by his cousin John the Baptist, according to the gospels; after the ceremony the Spirit of God descended on him in the form of a dove, and a voice from heaven declared 'This is my beloved son, with whom I am well pleased'. This illustration is from an 18th century Ethiopian manuscript in the British Museum

its adherents increased, divisions arose within the Christian body.

Reference has already been made to those who argued that Jesus did not have a real body but only the appearance of a body. The same claim was made by the Gnostics; because the body is material and evil, Jesus could not have had a body and could not have been incarnated in flesh. Equally the material and therefore evil world could not have been created by God, but by a malevolent god or spirit, a 'demiurge'.

The Church strove valiantly to conserve belief in the humanity of Jesus and the creation of the world as good by God. The early Creed affirmed 'I believe in God the Father Almighty, the Maker of Heaven and Earth.'

A question of discipline caused a schism in the Church after the great persecution by the Emperor Decius in 250 AD. Many members of the congregations and even some bishops had been frightened into sacrificing to the Roman gods. When the persecution ceased they wanted to be restored to communion within the Church, for already great importance was attached to receiving the body and blood of Christ in the form of bread and wine; the rite that was later called the Mass. Most members of the Church agreed to readmit the lapsed after suitable penance but splinter groups, who believed in the strict enforcement of rules, seceded.

The conversion of Constantine in 312 AD marked the turning point in the status of the Church in the Roman world. One of the contestants in the struggle for the position of emperor — a struggle that had divided the Roman world — he overcame his rival in Rome at the battle of the Milvian Bridge.

Picturepoint London

Constantine was convinced that victory had been given him by the risen Christ. Although it seems strange that he should have looked for triumph in war from the Prince of Peace, there can be no question of his sincerity. He had nothing to gain politically by proclaiming his conversion; at that time only about 15% of the population in the West was Christian. In 323 AD he became ruler of the entire empire. When he became a Christian he had to give up being a god and the cult of the deified emperor came to an end.

Constantine declared the day on which Christ rose from the dead a public holiday and called it the Sun's Day – previously he had been a worshipper of the sun. Northern Europeans followed Constantine's lead with such names as Sunday and Sonntag.

Under Constantine there was not precisely a union of Church and State but there was a close affiliation. This became closer under the later emperors in the Byzantine East. Legislation was passed favouring orthodox Christianity and penalizing dissenters. The Jews suffered some restrictions, the pagans more, and the heretics most. The heretics were driven out, the pagans died out and the Jews alone survived, although they were treated as aliens in a Christian society.

Ethically, the greatest change in Christian thought during and after the time of Constantine was in the Church's attitude to war. This was partly because of the martial victories of Constantine, the defender of the faith, and partly because of continuing pressure from the barbarians. Most Christians adopted a modified version of the classical theory of the just war. In the West St Augustine, at the turn of the 4th and 5th centuries, taught that the motive of the just war was love and that its objects must be the vindication of justice and the restoration of peace. Its conduct should be as humane as possible. Monks and the clergy should not fight.

After the fall of Rome in 410 AD the political unity of the Roman empire was shattered, despite a partial and temporary recovery under Justinian (c 482–565 AD). Various Teutonic tribes established themselves within the empire, some of whom were already Christians but Arians, members of a heretical sect. Others were pagans. The conversion of both to orthodox Christianity was the work partly of the papacy, partly of the monastic orders.

Monasticism had developed in Egypt, especially in the time of Constantine. As the masses began to flock into the Church, the more ardent spirits withdrew to the desert. At first they were hermits who renounced the society of men, but later communities of monks were formed. From the outset celibacy was demanded of monks as it was, later, of nuns. Monasticism gradually became part of the structure of the Church. St Jerome combined monasticism and scholarship, devoting himself to the translation of the scriptures. Monks often became bishops.

Eventually, a vocational division arose. The bishops or secular clergy (from *saeculum*, the world) served the parishes, while the monks or regular clergy (from *regula*, the rule of the monasteries) engaged in contemplation and prayer, did missionary work and, later on, dispensed hospitality.

In the West the papacy, centred in Rome, became immensely powerful politically, because government had broken down and although the Byzantine emperor in the East still claimed jurisdiction over the West, he lacked the resources for dealing with the barbarians.

In the mid-8th century the kingdom of the Franks, to the north, recognized the bishop of Rome as the civil ruler of a strip of Italy running from Rome over the Apennines to Ravenna. Meanwhile the Benedictine monks, followed later by other orders, crossed the Alps and took over unused land. There they created self-sustaining communities and became centres from which the task of converting and educating the pagans was carried out.

The expansion of Christianity and the Church's involvement in society brought changes and corruptions. A religion cannot expand without adapting itself to the language and customs of its converts, and while this process may win converts it may at the same time pervert the religion. The pacifism of early Christianity disappeared completely in the Middle Ages, with many kingdoms, all professing Christianity, fighting between themselves. The saints were militarized. St Peter was honoured not because he had acknowledged Christ, but because he had cut off the ear of the high priest's servant. St George, St Andrew, St David and St Michael assumed the roles of the war gods of antiquity.

Wealth was corrupting. A monk described the history of western monasticism in this sequence: piety produces industry, industry creates wealth, wealth destroys piety, piety in its fall dissipates wealth. Each of the great monastic orders enjoyed at least two centuries of vitality. Enfeeblement followed, and new orders arose in an effort to recover the original spirit. The papacy, too, experienced periods of efflorescence and of decay.

The 11th century was marked by a great movement of reform, led by men from the north who had little feeling for the Mediterranean world, and who desired to cleanse the monasteries, purify the Church and give direction to society. The Western (Roman) and the Eastern (Byzantine) Churches finally separated in 1054 AD. The Cistercians supported monastic reform and restored the original Benedictine emphasis on manual labour. Priests, like monks, were required to be celibate, and the clergy were told to put away their wives. Princes were called upon to swear to observe the Truce of God, resulting in fighting being reduced to a summer sport.

This great reform, called the Gregorian after Pope Gregory VII, resulted in the papacy of the 13th century functioning as a

Above Easter procession in Malta with the figure of Christ carrying the cross which he bore for every man *Opposite* Procession of the Penitents of Perpignan, in France, carrying the image of Christ crucified. The custom of doing public penance on Good Friday is a common one in many parts of the world

world government more effective than any before or since. The pope was the Lord above the nations. Intellectual life flourished, universities were founded, St Thomas Aquinas brought about a new synthesis of Christian theology and Aristotelian philosophy, while Gothic architecture gave expression to piety reaching for the stars, and beyond to the very throne of God.

But reforms, if they misfire, can bring new corruptions. The Christian princes broke the vows they had made to observe the Truce of God, and the only way to reduce warfare between Christians of the West proved to be by diverting their belligerence toward the infidels in the East. The peace movement ended in the Crusades. The imposition of clerical celibacy resulted in clerical concubinage, which was rife by the time of the Reformation in the 16th century. The papacy's success in controlling Europe politically involved the popes in political machinations to such an extent that by the 15th century, the papacy was in danger of becoming a secular city-state.

So far as property was concerned, the Church in the Middle Ages had approved of rent but not of usury. However, as the Church itself became increasingly wealthy, the doctrine that a money-lender should receive compensation for the gain that would have accrued had he used the money himself, was accepted. In domestic relations the emphasis in marriage was on children and faithfulness, rather than on falling in love.

The Church had been without serious divisions in the West from the early 5th to the 12th centuries. Education during this period was scant and intellectual interest even scantier. But with the relative failure of universal reform, small groups arose in the 11th and 12th centuries, resolved to carry out, among themselves, the changes that had proved impracticable in the Church as a whole. Southern France and northern Italy swarmed with sects.

In the late Middle Ages the papacy was weakened by divisions, as a result of which there were sometimes two, or even three, popes at the same time. Church councils were called which threatened to supplant the papacy as the governing organ of the Church, but the popes regained control.

The opening years of the 16th century, eventually a period of vast upheaval, were characterized by an interlude of tolerance. The heretical sects of the Middle Ages had been suppressed and the Church felt sufficiently secure to suffer criticism. In fact there was much to criticize. Clerical concubinage was rife, and was tolerated to such an extent that a tax was laid on concubines. The bureaucratic machinery needed for the papacy to play its universal role had to be paid for, and the financial extortion by the Church that resulted was deeply resented, especially when the Renaissance popes spent money on wars and were so secularized as to make treaties with Turks against Christian princes. Excommunication lost its spiritual force when it was used against rulers because they had failed to

make financial contributions to the papacy. Many people tried to influence God through external practices such as pilgrimages, the cult of relics, the intercession of the saints, and of the Virgin.

Then came the great reformation movement, of which one aspect was Martin Luther's attack in 1517 upon the whole system of indulgences. These granted remission of penalties for sin, not only on earth but also in purgatory, and sometimes offered the forgiveness of sins. These indulgences were supposed to transfer the unused extra credits of the saints, who were better than they needed to be for their own salvation, to those whose accounts were in arrears. The recipient of the indulgence made a financial contribution to the Church.

Luther's attack was directed against the religious aspect of the system rather than the financial. He did not believe that anyone had any extra credits, as no one could ever be good enough to earn salvation. God's forgiveness of, and favour to, those who have sinned is a sheer act of grace mediated to men through the sacrificial death of Christ.

The main effect on the Roman Catholic Church was to tighten the dogma, the discipline and the bureaucratic structure of the Church. The secularized papacy of the Renaissance came to an end. The popes became as austere as the Puritans. Clerical celibacy was enforced and dogma was more rigidly formulated. This was the work of the Council of Trent, in the years between 1545 and 1563.

The violent conflicts of Roman Catholics and Protestants in the 16th and 17th centuries brought to the fore the problems of Church and State and the problem of religious liberty. In effect, the solution was a system of religious liberty on a territorial basis, which carried with it the right of emigration. One region was to have only one religion and those who could not in conscience subscribe to it were not sent to the stake or the dungeons of the Inquisition but were free to emigrate.

This was not an ideal solution, and only lasted for a short time. As France learnt through the expulsion of the Huguenots, it is disastrous for a country to lose many of its finest citizens.

There are various reasons why religious pluralism within the single state was eventually tolerated. One was sheer weariness of war. The Thirty Years' War in Germany in the 17th century left cities with inhabitants dead of starvation in the streets with grass in their mouths. Another factor was trade. Holland was particularly sensitive to this consideration as she was the market-place of the world, and if she restricted her commerce because of religious beliefs, her prosperity would suffer.

The deepest considerations were religious. The champions of religious liberty pointed out that faith cannot be constrained, that sincerity cannot be forced. Compulsion may make men into martyrs or hypocrites. It cannot make them into genuine converts. To

burn a man because he refuses to save his life by renouncing his convictions is to burn him for telling the truth, that is, what he believes to be the truth. Sincerity does not necessarily make a man right, but insincerity makes him necessarily wrong.

Since the 18th century, Christianity has gradually been moving towards overcoming its own divisions. At the same time it has been wrestling with new scientific and social developments. Until recently this was more true of Protestants than of Roman Catholics. After the Council of Trent, the Catholics continued to enhance rather than diminish their claims on behalf of the papacy, and at the same time felt a greater alienation from the contemporary world of thought. Protestants were more open to new ideas, even at the risk of making so many concessions as to depart radically from the Christian tradition.

One area of controversy has been natural science. The Catholic Church suppressed Galileo; and Luther and Calvin rejected the views of Copernicus on biblical grounds. However, many Protestants accepted his views and his writings were allowed to circulate. The theories of Newton and Galileo did not trouble the Protestants, and they accepted the new astronomy as an impressive commentary on the text 'the heavens declare the glory of God'. Serious conflict began only in the 19th century when geological discoveries cast doubt on the biblical account of the creation of the world in six days. Some scientists attempted to reconcile the two points of view by assuming that a day meant 1,000 years or even longer, and that God created the world in six of these periods. But biblical scholars retorted that the word 'day' in the book of Genesis meant 24 hours. Genesis conflicted with geology, and geology won. Liberal Protestants came to regard the book of Genesis as inspired mythology, not as a scientific treatise.

The doctrine of organic evolution was more disconcerting because it affected the understanding of man. If man is biologically descended from lower forms of life, among whom Nature is red in tooth and claw, is man ineradicably predatory and warlike by nature? If animals are mortal and man immortal, when in the scale of ascent did man become immortal? Some theologians have suggested conditional immortality, asserting that not all men are immortal but only those who are capable of living in the atmosphere of the spirit.

The application of historical techniques to the Bible raised the problems of uncertainties as to the texts and discrepancies between various accounts. These problems were passionately pursued from the 18th century onwards, especially in Germany and mainly by Protestants. Catholics were not granted freedom in the field of biblical study until the time of Pope John XXIII and the Second Vatican Council, which opened in 1962.

Politically, Protestantism has been hospitable to, and has contributed toward,

The early Christians expected that their master would soon return in glory on the clouds of heaven to set up the kingdom of God on earth, and his coming was awaited with joyous expectancy: 19th century painting on a ceiling of the Rila monastery in Bulgaria

political democracy, largely as a result of the Puritan revolution in England and America. The Catholic Church, which is organized as a hierarchy, has preferred on the whole to deal with highly centralized governments. This situation has been modified in the United States where Catholics have recognized that both democracy and the separation of the Church and State might be advantageous to the Church. Had there been an autocratic government and an established Church in the United States, neither would have been Catholic.

Modern theology is centred on the doctrine of the Trinity: the Father, the Son and the Spirit. In the case of God the Father, some schools of thought emphasize his immanence, as a being who pervades the universe. This was true of Protestant Liberalism. Others stress transcendence, the belief that God exists beyond and apart from the universe.

Mystics, on the one hand, who are stupefied by the overwhelmingness of God, and scientists on the other, who are aghast at the immeasurable universe, shy away from all concrete language about God, especially from all personal adjectives. Many theologians turn to Christ as the focus of their piety because they 'can walk with Him and talk with Him'. In Pietist movements there has been a saccharine Jesus cult. Yet others emphasize the Spirit which lies at the heart of all rules and structures and doctrines. Believing this, they may sever themselves from any organized church and be led beyond Christianity to a combination of all religions.

Christianity expanded phenomenally during the 19th century, its greatest numerical gains having been among primitive peoples. Although it has made no serious inroads into the ranks of the world's other great religions, Christianity has influenced other faiths, which have adopted Christian attitudes without acknowledging formal adherence to the faith.

Mithraism

During the period between 1400 BC and 400 AD Persians, Indians, Romans and Greeks worshipped the god Mithras. The god was particularly important in the old polytheistic religion of the Persians between the 8th and 6th centuries BC and again in the Roman Empire in the 2nd and 3rd centuries AD. No direct evidence remains of Persian paganism, and if we wish to get an idea of this polytheistic religion we must fall back on reconstruction from texts of a later period. Plenty of material is available, however, and many points can be discovered which are very probably accurate.

There are four important sources for Mithraism. The first is a cuneiform script tablet from Boghazköi in Turkey which contains a contract between the Hittites and the Mitanni, an Iranian-speaking tribe in Mesopotamia c 1400 BC. In this contract, Mithras is invoked as a god before whom an oath may be sworn. Secondly, there are some Indian texts in which the god Mitra appears as a 'friend' and as a 'contract', and has connections with the sun. Unwillingly, he participates in the sacrifice of the god Soma, who frequently appears in the form of a bull or as the moon. Thirdly, great hymns of praise (*yashts*) were written, probably in the 5th century, in honour of Mithra and the goddess Anahita. The Mithraic yasht extolled the god as the Lord of Contract, who in war grants victory and in peace prosperity. Finally, the Roman monuments reveal some important aspects of Mithraic mysteries that spread to far-flung areas of the Empire.

By comparing these sources we may infer that in Persian paganism Mithras was a god of friendship and of contract and had close connections with the sun. These three points are interrelated, as contracts are the basis of friendship among people; as a witness to contracts the sun has often been called upon, as he is all-seeing. The sacrifice of bulls was also part of the Mithraic cult. It is closely connected with Mithras as god of contracts, as in ancient times contracts were sanctioned through common sacrifice and a common feast. According to Plutarch, Mithras was the 'mediator'. This corresponds to what we know about the old Persian Mithras. The contract as a bond between humans, friendship and feasting after the sacrifice which was a unifying force, and the sacrifice itself linking men with the gods are all examples of Mithras's role as a mediator. Mithras, the sun, was in old Persian times also closely connected with kingship. People swore oaths by the king and by the sun. Kingship also incorporated above all else the idea of law and order at a time when the abstract concept of the state was still unknown and there were no written laws. Order was visibly present in the person of the king; the king was the law, and when he died chaos erupted, as law and order were gone.

The Persian social system was feudal, in the sense that there were no abstract legal rights and duties but only reciprocal personal obligations between man and woman, parents and children, lord and peasant, and so on. Mithras, who represented law and order, was the divine exponent of the Persian system as god of contracts and of all reciprocal relationships.

Persian religion was completely changed by the life and teaching of Zoroaster. The exact period of the prophet's life is uncertain; at the latest it was about 550 BC, perhaps considerably earlier. Zoroaster taught that there was but a single god, Ahura Mazdah and he totally rejected the other gods of the old Persians. The Persian word *daivas,* which originally meant 'gods', has since Zoroaster signified 'evil demons'. Zoroaster fought passionately against polytheism and against Mithras. He protested against the bull sacrifice, the principal festival of the Mithraic religion. In later generations, the doctrinal teaching of Zoroaster was gradually interspersed with elements of the older polytheism, and the wide gap between the two religions was bridged by compromise. After Darius, who died in 486 BC, the Persian kings were Zoroastrians. But the aristocracy probably continued to be attached to Mithras and the old gods. Despite this difference of opinion, the Persian kings seem to have made allowance for those social groups who did not want to replace the old cults entirely by Zoroastrianism. Indeed, the kings were practical politicians, and considerate of the feelings of their subjects. In the 4th century BC the Kings Artaxerxes II and III mentioned Mithra and the goddess Anahita in their inscriptions. But by this time, Zoroastrianism was the dominant factor in the blending of the two religions and we hear no more of the Mithraic bull sacrifice.

After the destruction of the Persian Empire by Alexander the Great nothing more is heard about the Persian worship of Mithras. Yet over three centuries later Mithras was worshipped in the states between the Parthian Empire and the Graeco-Roman world, for example in Armenia, where Mithras was again god of kings and feudalism. In a Mithraic ceremony, King Tiridates I submitted to the Roman Emperor Nero in the 1st century AD and made his kingdom a fief under Nero's control. Mithras was also the god of the kings of Commagene, to the south of Armenia. It is likely that Mithridates of Pontus (1st century BC), the great enemy of the Romans, worshipped Mithras; his kingdom included the northern coast of modern Turkey, and the Crimea. Finally, we know from Plutarch that the pirates of Cilicia, the south coast of Turkey, also worshipped Mithras during this period. On the other hand, Mithras was of no importance in the Greek-populated areas of Asia Minor. The Persians were the national enemies of the Greeks and their god Mithras had no chance of success with the Greeks.

It is an open question whether the Roman Mithras mysteries were the same religion as the Persian Mithraic cult. The Persian religion changed to accommodate the different conditions of the Roman Empire. Certainly, many elements of the old religion were retained, but at the same time the Roman theology contained elements unknown to the Persians. For example, the Romans took their doctrine of the fate of the soul from Plato's philosophy. One could say that the Roman mysteries were a completely new religion. It may be that there were one or more founders of the new cult, dating from perhaps c 100 AD. The dated Roman Mithras monuments start from c 140 AD.

It is puzzling how this religion came to Rome. It is unwise to postulate that its spread can be compared to the spread of the Christian mission, for the Mithras mysteries were addressed to entirely different social strata, to the soldiers and officials in the imperial service, and only men were initiated into the cult. It has been suggested that the Mithraic cult spread slowly, by way of Syria and Asia Minor, and then came to Rome by sea. However, this theory is contradicted by the hostility of the Greeks in Asia Minor towards the god. It has also been suggested that the Roman legions became acquainted with the cult of Mithras on the Persian frontier and that when troops were moved from the eastern front to Europe they brought Mithras with them to the west. It should be remembered, however, that a religion would only have been able to spread in the army of the Roman emperors if it were regarded favourably by those at the top. It is therefore probable that the founder, or founders, of the Roman Mithraic mysteries must have been active in Rome itself, and that he or they must have enjoyed the benevolent encouragement of higher generals, perhaps even of the *praefectus praetorio,* the commander of the Praetorian Guard. The Mithras cult was probably introduced into the legions from above, by officers who were posted from their headquarters in Rome to legions on the frontiers of the empire.

The geographical distribution of archeological finds supports this hypothesis. Many Mithraic remains have been excavated in Rome and in areas of military conflict on the frontiers, such as the Euphrates, Danube, Rhine and in Britain; but almost none have been found in the pacified provinces such as Gaul or Spain, apart from the Mithraeum or temple in Mérida, Spain, the seat of the Roman governor.

There are numerous Mithras initiation inscriptions that do not originate from soldiers but from officials in the imperial service, particularly from freedmen who were able to obtain very influential positions in finance and customs administration if they proved their worth. Such men worshipped one god only if it did not pre-

Ohrmazd, the principle of truth and light, on horseback, tramples on Ahriman's snake-covered head. Zoroastrians, who fought against Mithraism, believed that the perpetual struggle would end in the triumph of Ohrmazd. Rock relief at Naqsh-i-Rustem, Iran

judice their career. It is characteristic of the Mithraic cult that it was a religion of loyalty, of respect for the social system, unlike Christianity which was a religion of rebellious aloofness from the state, and of revolutionary hope in the Last Judgement.

The Mithraic sanctuaries in the Roman world were underground grottoes. The ceiling symbolized the heavens, and the cavern the world. The chambers were never very large, with space for barely 100 men. Around the central chamber there were sometimes labyrinthine systems of artificial passages, as beneath the church of

St Clemente in Rome. There was always a spring in the cavern. The Mithraic monuments were certainly not built secretly below ground, but a hole was dug in the same way as when a cellar is constructed, perhaps behind a high fence.

There were seven grades of initiation into the Mithraic mysteries, each with a symbolic name: *corax* (raven), *nymphus* (bridegroom), *miles* (soldier), *leo* (lion), *Perses* (Persian), *heliodromus* (courier to the sun), *pater* (father). The raven wore a raven's mask, the lion a lion's mask, the Persian a Persian cap, and so on. Literary records state that the initiate into the Mithraic mysteries had to submit to corporal punishment, that he was bound and then released. The initiation signified a ritually symbolic regeneration. The person being initiated as a 'soldier' had to undergo a test of courage. He had to force his way,

apparently by means of a duel, to a wreath. This done, an officiant came up to him and put the wreath on his head, but the candidate had to reject the wreath and say that Mithras was his wreath. For the rest of his life he was not permitted to wear a wreath, as this honour was due only to the god.

There were various initiation ceremonies, such as baptism, the common meal, obligation through shaking hands (in this ceremony we can recognize the old Persian god of contract). Those being initiated wandered through the underground passages; at some points passwords were demanded. On one fresco at Ostia, in Italy, the mystic is dressed as a 'bridegroom'. In Rome beneath St Prisca the fresco depicts a procession of 'lions'. At Capua, Italy, the initiate is being led towards the initiation point with his eyes bound. He then kneels down before the mystagogue (teacher or leader) who wears a Persian cap, and finally lies stretched out, humbly on the ground.

On some occasions lighting effects were used: there were reliefs which could be illuminated from the rear revealing a crescent or the head of Mithras or Sol (the sun) surrounded by a halo. There were also statues of Cronos, the god of time who swallows everything, which were hollow at the back and able to spit fire. At some shrines the relief showing the sacrifice of the bull, at the end of the grotto, could be turned round, revealing on the other side, for example, the common repast of Mithras and Helios. Either side could be shown, according to the demands of the liturgy.

Some verses from hymns of the Mithraic mysteries have been found as wall inscriptions under the church of St Prisca in Rome. There are also frescoes testifying to a syncretism of the Persian with old Roman ceremonies. The Mithraic sacrifice of the bull is connected with the old Roman feast of *Suovetaurilia* (the sacrifice of a boar, a ram and a bull); this sacrifice was offered up on the day of *Palilia*, another old Roman festival, when the founding of the city of Rome was celebrated. *Suovetaurilia* and *Palilia* were Roman national festivals, which were celebrated under the patronage

and with the participation of the emperor. The Mithraeum under St Prisca, where these representations may be seen, lay in a large complex of buildings which were imperial property. The Persian religion was thus set completely into an 'old Roman' framework, with the approval and even the encouragement of the emperor; in particular the Emperors Commodus, Septimius Severus and Caracalla probably favoured the Mithraic mysteries, for an exceptionally large number of dated Mithraic inscriptions originate from their period. Also characteristic of the blend of Persian and Roman ideas is a representation found in a Mithraeum at Ostia of the Roman god Silvanus, and instead of *pater* in the inscriptions we sometimes read *Pater patratus*. This is an old Roman title for a priest whose task it was to form alliances. Thus, in the service of the Persian god of contract, there was the renewal of a priest's title which had been in use in ancient Rome for the negotiation of contracts.

The sacrifice of the bull had been the great holy deed of Mithraism. The sun god, through his messenger, the raven, had commanded Mithras to sacrifice the bull; on some reliefs the raven flies to Mithras on a sunbeam. The god carried out the sacrifice with great reluctance: in many represen-

tations he is sadly averting his gaze, he is innocent of the animal's suffering. But when the bull died, a great miracle occurred – the world began: the cloak of Mithras was changed into a celestial globe on which planets, the zodiac and fixed stars were shining; the white bull, now a crescent, was moved into the heavens. (Luna, the moon goddess, is seen in the reliefs frequently averting her eyes from the sacrifice). From the tail and from the blood of the bull arose ears of corn and the vine. Then came all the trees and plants, the four elements, the winds and the seasons; from the seed which issued from the bull there arose the good animals and all living things. This Mithraic deed was a blessing: 'Thou hast saved us also by pouring out the blood eternal', according to one of the few verses we have obtained from a Mithraic hymn. The power of evil wanted to prevent the creation; the scorpion, snake and lion try to drink the seed of the bull. Evil will not be destroyed until the end of time; as long as he is on earth man must always struggle for good and against evil.

Particularly instructive is a relief in London on which Mithras is sacrificing the bull not in the cavern but in the celestial sphere, which is indicated by the zodiac: the heavens arose following the

Above Zoroaster struggled against Mithraism, which he regarded as deplorable. He took the story of Adam and Eve from the Bible, and in this Islamic miniature Ahriman is depicted as an old man who offers the fatal fruit to the first human beings in the Garden of Eden *Opposite* The gods Ohrmazd and Mithras, flanking the Persian King Ardeshir II: the Persian Mithras was a god of contract, a mediator between gods and man, and was closely connected with both the sun and the kingship, the principle of law and order in society

sacrifice of the bull. Each sunrise signifies a repetition of this cosmogony. The stars began to revolve in the sky, and this was the birth of time. The sun circling around the earth caused the day, the orbit of the moon the months, and the path of the sun through the zodiac (the ecliptic) the years.

There are numerous other Mithraic myths to be seen in the reliefs, often in the small pictures near the main scene: the birth of Mithras from a tree; Mithras shooting at the cloud with an arrow (bringing the rain), or at the rock (causing a spring to gush forth); cutting the corn; taming the bull; his contract with the sun god; the holy meal; the ascent to heaven on the chariot of the sun god. The myth of the birth of Mithras from the rock has the same significance as the sun rising over the mountains on the horizon and the cosmogony in the sacrifice of the bull. The birth of Mithras from an egg depicted on the relief

at Newcastle-upon-Tyne shows the egg turning into a celestial globe, represented by the zodiac; here Mithras is equated with the Orphic primeval god Phanes (Eros) who arose out of the egg.

The beautiful Mithraic statues of Venus, Mercury and Jupiter show that, as well as Mithras and Cronos, the god of time, the gods of the planets were worshipped.

The Mithraic myths have been interpreted into a complete theology, in accordance with the Platonic myths. The cavern of the mysteries was the world, as in the cave allegory of the Platonic state. The mystic had to try to free himself from the shackles of materialism and ascend to the true sun, like Mithras on the chariot of the sun god. The way up led through the spheres of the seven planets, a progress already anticipated on earth in the Mithraic initiations, when the mystics ascended through the seven grades of initiation, each of which was related to a planet. This ascent was symbolized by the seven-runged ladder at Ostia; at each initiation the mystic passed through a new gate. On the reliefs at Capua and Rome there is the Platonic Eros, or the Orphic Phanes (Mithras), guiding the psyche of the mystic. The ascent of Mithras has been compared with the ascent of the soul to the firmament in Plato's *Phaedrus*.

The cosmogony of the mysteries was interpreted from the cosmogony in Plato's *Timaeus*. Mithras was named 'father and creator of the universe', in words reminiscent of the *Timaeus* and the attack by the evil

animals, shown on the reliefs, corresponds with the attack of the elements on the new-born babe in the *Timaeus*. Above all, however, the dualistic outlook of Persian religion found its philosophical interpretation in the two rotations of the heavens seen on the Mithraic reliefs: the constant rotation of the vault of heaven with the fixed stars to the right and the variable orbit of the planets through the zodiac to the left. From the combination of these revolutions arose inconstant time. But man must strive for the eternal and, by-passing the gods of the planets, ascend to the one true eternal.

This Platonizing interpretation of the Mithraic myths is secondary in relation to the old Persian religion; but the Roman mysteries were probably first established on the basis of this allegorical interpretation. The founder or founders of the religion must have been Platonists. They rendered the philosophical teachings into the myths and rites of the Persian god and thus created an entirely new religion.

The Mithraic mysteries were therefore completely Hellenized and Romanized. The Persian god could be accepted as a traditional god of the Romans. There is a characteristic inscription from Carnuntum, near Vienna, from the year 307: the old Emperor Diocletian had consulted with the reigning emperors in order to settle disputes; together they restored a Mithraic sanctuary and dedicated it 'to the patrons of their empire'. The cult was to thrive as long as the emperors supported it.

Islam

Islam (properly called al-Islam), a word which indicates submission to God, is the name given to the religiously-based system resulting from the mission of the prophet Mohammed in Arabia in the 7th century AD. One who submits is a Moslem, a title including nominal adherents. A distinction is made in the Koran between submission and belief, or faith; belief is not mere acceptance of doctrine; it involves a pattern of behaviour.

At about the age of 40 Mohammed began to receive revelations in Mecca, but he had much opposition to face, and his movement was not really established until after his migration to Medina about 12 years later, in 622. There he found a larger number of followers and gradually built up a community of Moslems, a kind of theocracy in which he, as God's representative, must receive obedience. Islam does not distinguish between the sacred and the secular; it regards all aspects of life as coming under God's control.

There are divisions within Islam, but the vast majority of Moslems belong to the main body commonly called Sunnites, who developed a system with four bases. First, the Koran, God's eternal and uncreated word, revealed to Mohammed from time to time during the Meccan and Medinan periods, is regarded as infallible. It gives guidance on many subjects, summoning man to submit to God and to do God's will, threatening severe punishment in the hereafter, or promising delights in the garden of paradise, commending those who observe worship and pay legal alms, and at times expressing mystical thought in language of great beauty. But as Islam expanded many problems arose with which the Koran did not deal, so another authority was sought.

This was eventually provided in Tradition, traced to Mohammed, or at least to his Companions. During the first two centuries much energy was expended in collecting such material, but only in the 3rd century of Islam were the collections of Tradition which became canonical written down.

In the collections each tradition is preceded by a chain of transmitters, and remarks are commonly added about the quality of its reliability. An elaborate science developed regarding the transmitters, types of traditions, methods of receiving and transmitting. The chain, while an important element in deciding reliability, was not the only one.

The third basis is agreement of recognized authorities, even perhaps of the general community, for a tradition represents Mohammed as saying, 'My people will never agree on an error'. This basis has an element of vagueness, for Islam has had no councils for formulating doctrines or reaching decisions. But with the passage of time matters of agreement were recognized.

The fourth basis is deduction by analogy (qiyas). In earlier times some authorities gave decisions on the basis of their own opinion, or held that a certain procedure was for the good of the community. This was too subjective, so eventually qiyas prevailed; so qualified authorities form decisions by seeking an analogy in the other three bases.

According to Sunnite theory these bases provide guidance on all subjects. Schools of thought developed in Sunnite Islam, four of which survived. The Hanafi is traced to Abu Hanafa of Kufa who died in 767, but the real founders of the school were two of his pupils. It became the school of the

Opposite Allah is the only God according to the Islamic faith: design using the letters of his name in a mosque in Istanbul; pictorial representations of Allah are forbidden *Below* Devout Moslems perform formal acts of worship five times each day: muezzin calling the faithful to prayer

Turkish Empire and the Indian sub-continent. The Maliki school is traced to Malik ibn Anas of Medina (d. 795) who compiled a law-book, and whose ideas were developed by followers. It is now mainly found in North Africa.

The Shafii school goes back to Mohammed ibn Idria al-Shafii (d. 820), an outstanding authority whose writings exerted great influence. He studied with Malik and spent some time in other centres, eventually settling in Egypt. This school has been predominant in southern Arabia, Indonesia, Upper Egypt and East Africa. The Hanbali school is traced to Ahmad ibn Hanbal (d. 855) who had been a pupil of Shafii. In some respects it is stricter than others. It is now found in central Arabia, and has had some influence on certain reformers in Egypt.

These schools are not sects, for there is no serious difference on matters of theology; but their views differ regarding a number of details of legal practice. The law, called *sharia* (path), is a divine law, given by God and developed from this in matters of detail under divine control. It deals with all subjects, for God's law applies in every sphere.

In modern times adaptations have been made to the teaching of the schools. Some modern states have made selections from the teaching of different schools, but in some aspects of the law, states have separated from the sharia. In subjects such as family law and inheritance they follow the sharia, but other matters are dealt with in civil courts. To Algeria and the Indian sub-continent this is nothing new. In Turkey the ancient Moslem system has been completely replaced. Egypt and Tunisia have abolished sharia courts; the sharia family law is now administered in civil courts. Tunisia has enacted a law enforcing monogamy. There is a growing tendency for states to change the administration of the law without interfering with the conduct of purely religious practices.

There are five pillars of practical religion. The first is the recitation of the attestation of belief: 'God is the only God; Mohammed is God's messenger.' This stresses God's uniqueness and Mohammed's mission as the final prophet. It is whispered in the ear of the newly born child; it is continually repeated throughout life; it should be the last utterance of the dying; and mourners chant it as they carry the bier to the grave.

The second pillar is worship. The formal worship *(salat)* is performed five times daily, preceded by ceremonial ablution and an expression of one's intention. The times are before sunrise, after midday, in mid-afternoon, soon after sunset, and when the night has closed in. Worship is performed facing Mecca, the focal point towards which all prayer is directed being the *Kaaba*, God's House, in Mecca. Various postures are adopted, standing, bowing, kneeling, prostrating, and sitting back on one's heels. Koran verses, expressions of adoration, and some petitions are recited. Worship is

essentially adoration, which may be followed by private supplications.

A certain number of sections *(rakas)* are prescribed for each period, and some supererogatory prayers are recommended in addition. These are said individually without a leader; but the prayers said in company with others in a mosque or elsewhere must have a leader *(imam)* who is followed by the company in words and postures. One need not pray in a mosque, or even in company, but if a group worship together one member must stand in front as imam. Mosques have their regular imam, but he is not to be compared with a clergyman; Islam allows no priest between man and God. Attendance at the mosque is customary at midday worship on Friday, when a sermon is preached; afterwards people are allowed to resume their business, for Friday is not a sabbath.

Legal almsgiving *(zakat)*, the third pillar of religious duty, is now largely neglected because of other methods of taxation, but there are many who still pay it gladly. It is a tax on property possessed for one year, provided it exceeds a prescribed minimum. Assessments vary according to the nature of the land and whether the agricultural land is irrigated or depends on rain (the latter has a higher tax). Other criteria for the tax are animals, money and general possessions. It may be paid to a collector or directly to one of the classes entitled to benefit. In paying the intention must be expressed, otherwise it is just voluntary charity.

The fourth pillar, fasting, applies mainly to Ramadan, the ninth month of the Moslem lunar year, when one must abstain from food, drink and bodily satisfactions from early morning when one can distinguish a black from a white thread till after sunset. Travellers and invalids are exempt, but when the journey or the illness is over they should make up for the days of abstention missed. The lunar year is 11 days shorter than the solar, so the months go round the seasons in 33 years, which means that the observance is severe in hot countries when Ramadan occurs in summer.

A sincere Moslem carefully observes the fast, the only modification being in a country of high latitude with long days in summer and short in winter, when he may calculate an average length of day. Some, however, are content to fast at the beginning and end of the month, and others pay little heed. Fasting on a festival is forbidden. The two main festivals are the day of sacrifice during the Pilgrimage and the day following Ramadan, when the holiday often lasts four days. Ascetics have observed additional fasts, but Tradition states that three days at a time are the limit. Some misdemeanours or sins of omission are expiated by fasting.

Pilgrimage is the fifth pillar of practical religion. In the pre-Islamic period rites were observed at the Kaaba at different times, and at some places within about 12 miles from Mecca in the twelfth month of the lunar year. The purely Meccan rite is

Paul Watkins

called *umra* and the other *hajj*. The umra may be performed at any time; the hajj, which has specified days in the twelfth month, is a duty which should be performed once in a lifetime by adults who are sane and have sufficient means. Women must be accompanied by a relative. If a person has the means to observe the hajj, but is incapacitated, he may pay the expenses of a deputy acquiring no merit for himself however, thereby.

Pilgrims must halt at a station outside the sacred area and don the pilgrim garb *(ihram)*. Men wear two garments, one thrown over the left shoulder and tied at the right side, the other tied round the waist and reaching below the knees. Women wear a long robe and commonly, though not necessarily, cover the face. In donning the ihram one must express the intention. If careful about the wording, a person entering Mecca some time before the hajj may remove the pilgrim garment after the umra and resume it later in time for the hajj.

The umra consists of going round the Kaaba seven times, kissing, or at least saluting, the Black Stone fixed in the wall, praying at certain holy spots, and running seven times between two hillocks, al-Safa and al-Marwa; a rite connected with Hagar's search for water when Abraham sent her away with Ishmael.

A sermon giving instructions about the hajj is preached on the seventh day of the twelfth month, the eighth day being the first day of the hajj proper. The people go out to Mina, but some go straight on to Arafat where, from after midday till sunset on the ninth day the people stand on or round a sacred hill, this being the high point of the hajj. The pilgrims next stampede to Muzdalifa and go on the following day to Mina where there are three pillars, at which they throw stones. They are said to be stoning Satan, but the origin of the practice is not clear. Animals are sacrificed, a rite observed that day throughout the Moslem world.

This is the great festival. The head should be shaved, or the hair cut, after which ordinary clothing is assumed. For three days the pilgrims throw stones at the three pillars in the valley of Mina, at one on the first day, and at all three on the others, then go to Tanim where they put on the pilgrim dress before performing a farewell umra, after which they may leave. Many come to Mecca hoping to die there, bringing their shrouds which they dip in the sacred well Zem Zem; pilgrims commonly take some of the water home with them. Many visit Mohammed's tomb at Medina, a natural act of piety, but not a religious duty.

Islam has had its theological differences. The Koran is not a theological treatise, for Mohammed was primarily a preacher, and like many preachers he was inclined to overemphasize the point he was making. This is clear in references to God's omnipotence at one moment and to man's responsibility at another. If one chooses one's texts from the Koran, ignoring those which contradict them, it is possible to argue that man is responsible for his actions and able to do right, or that God is the only agent with man somewhat of an automaton.

Mohammed obviously did not believe the latter, for if so it would have been useless to urge men to obey God. But some who felt that he did, turned the argument against him by saying, 'Had God so willed we should not have served anything apart from him' (sura 16.37), to which Mohammed's only reply was that their fathers had spoken similarly. Discussions soon took place and parties arose.

Out of the discussions an important movement developed which made use of rational arguments to uphold its views. It was called Mutazilitism, coming from a root meaning 'to withdraw'. The conventional explanation speaks of someone seceding from the community, but there is reason to question this. The Mutazilites called themselves the people of unity and justice, indicating two important doctrines. They believed so strongly in God's unity that they rejected the doctrine of the eternity of the Koran, as this suggested an eternal being alongside God. For the same reason they denied that God has attributes, for this seemed to indicate multiplicity; and when it was said that God's attributes were in his essence, this appeared even worse than the Christian Trinity. They held the attributes were God's essence. The insistence on justice means they held that God does what is best for his creatures, and this involves man's free will.

Some earlier Western scholars thought the Mutazilites were free-thinkers, but further knowledge has discredited this. They were sincere Moslems, and although some of them indulged in speculation, insistence on God's unity – the fundamental Islamic doctrine – coloured all their thinking. It was unfortunate that the Caliph al-Mamun issued a decree in 827 stating that the Koran is created. There was violent opposition, and an inquisition started, but so persistent was the opposition that some 20 years later the Caliph al-Mutawakkil declared official the doctrine of the eternity of the Koran, and instituted persecution of the Mutazilites.

The doctrine of al-Ashari (d. 935) who had been brought up in Mutazilite teaching but eventually abandoned it, and of others like him, was argued by rational methods learned from them. The Sunnite theology

Sonia Halliday

hardened under the scholastic theologians, among their chief doctrines being the eternity of the Koran, God's decrees, an acceptance of Koranic anthropomorphic phrases without asking how they could be used of God, and acceptance of items of eschatology, such as the bridge over hell.

An attempt at mitigation was made regarding the decrees by a doctrine called *kasb* (acquisition), meaning that while God

is the only agent, man can acquire his actions. It has been said this means little more than that man is the place where they occur. 'God will not burden any soul beyond its power. It will be credited with the good

The Blue Mosque in Istanbul: it is customary for Moslems to attend a mosque for midday worship on Friday, but apart from this it is not considered necessary even to pray in company; although worship is led by an imam, who

stands in front of a group of worshippers, he cannot be compared with the Western clergyman as Islam allows no priest between man and God and indeed the element of priestly sacrifice is totally absent

Sonia Halliday

it has acquired and debited with the evil it has acquired' is claimed as a basis for the doctrine. Some may argue that if God is the only agent it matters little where his actions occur, and man's being credited or debited with actions cannot be called just.

The famous mystic and theologian, al-Ghazali (d. 1111), argued that tyranny can occur only when one interferes with another's property. As all property is God's, what he does cannot be called tyranny. This may do justice to God's omnipotence, but it suggests a low conception of man. One must not, however, assume that because of theological doctrines all Moslems are fatalists. There is an element of fatalism, especially among the common people, but no one can be a practical fatalist. Many stoutly uphold man's free will.

There were ascetic trends in early Islam, connected with which a significant movement developed. This was that of the Sufis, a name derived from *suf* (wool) referring to the coarse woollen garments of ascetics. Sufis have similarities to mysticism in other religions, but their beliefs are closely related to the Koran and Mohammed. Those who wished to join the Sufis normally attached themselves to a spiritual director who demanded implicit obedience as he guided them in following the Path and controlled their excitable tendencies.

From the 12th century Sufi orders developed, tracing themselves to some great Sufi. In addition to the prescribed prayers they have their own rituals observed by those who spend their lives in worship and by others who visit their centres to share worship. A typical practice is the *dhikr*, which may consist of repeating the name Allah, or some sacred phrase, and is often associated with music which has no place in mosque worship.

Many Moslems have held that there is something evil in music, especially stringed and wind instruments, which have been called the Devil's pipes. A dance may also be associated with the dhikr, the Mevlevi dervishes being specially noted for this particular practice. The dhikr may lead to a state of trance, novices being under the supervision of a spiritual director.

The Sufi Path has for its goal union with God, and some Sufis have uttered what orthodox Moslems consider as blasphemy. A notable example is the saying of al-Hallaj, 'I am the Truth', for which he was crucified in 922. There are sometimes suggestions of pantheism, especially connected with the doctrine of the Oneness of Being which teaches that God is the only absolute reality. But Sufism found a place within Islam, thanks largely to the influence of al-Ghazali, the great teacher who resigned his chair in Baghdad and devoted himself to solitude for 11 years.

Belief in the virtue of saints developed, and still has a firm hold on the common people. There are different categories of saints, in descending scale from those who sustain the world to saints connected with Sufi orders and local saints. They have the virtue of conveying blessing *(baraka)*, so their tombs are often visited and their prayers are sought. Each saint has also a special season when people gather at the tomb for the annual visit *ziyara*, when a fair is held.

In North Africa *marabouts* (hermits and monks) exert great influence, both alive

The founder of Islam, Mohammed first began to receive revelations from God in about 610 AD, but the movement was not established until some 12 years later; even then there was strong opposition to the teachings of the Prophet, and fierce battles were fought with the unbelievers: 17th century miniatures in the Topkapi Museum in Istanbul show *(above left)* Mohammed being greeted by one of his followers, taming a lion *(above)* and *(opposite)* the enemies of the Prophet, mounted on elephants, preparing to battle with him

and dead, and are consulted in time of need. In Shiite Islam visits are paid to the shrines of the *imams* (hereditary semi-divine rulers) at Meshed, Karbala, Najaf and Kazimayn; and so important are the imams that many feel such visits are equivalent to the hajj.

In the early period the caliphate's role was also important although at no time had the caliph the right to determine matters of faith, however some might have liked to do so. He is not to be compared with the pope, as was sometimes done in the past. He was simply the defender of the faith and head of the community.

There is, however, within Islam a party which considers a leader of paramount importance. This is Shiite Islam, the official religion of Persia and the religion of important communities in Iraq, India, Pakistan and elsewhere. The Shiites speak of an imam whose function as a leader is more comprehensive than that of a caliph. The movement, with political origins as is characteristic of Islam, developed among supporters of Ali, Mohammed's cousin who, they felt, should have been first caliph.

In course of time specific doctrines, different from those of the Sunnites, began to develop. The Imamites, the main body of the Shia, believe in 12 imams, the first being Ali, the next two his sons al-Hasan and al-Husayn, and the remainder in direct line of descent from al-Husayn who, with his followers, was killed at Karbala, an event which is remembered annually. The imams are held to be sinless, and it is believed that a divine light passed from one to another. The 12th imam, Mohammed al-Muntazar, withdrew from human affairs in 878, but is still ruling the world. At its opening early this century the first parliament in Persia was said to be held under the auspices of the hidden imam.

The imams are invested with an almost divine aura, not conveying any idea of incarnation, but rather that they are endowed with divine qualities. The 12th imam, who is to return at the end of the age, is believed to have absolute rule. Love of the imams is necessary for salvation. It is believed that on the bridge which all the dead must attempt to cross, one of the barriers is love of the imams. No one lacking this can cross.

Shiites have their own collections of traditions, transmitted through imams, but there is no place for the analogical deduction and consensus of recognized authorities of the Sunnites. Instead there are *mujtahids,* 'men who exert effort', agents of the imam, who have complete knowledge of the Koran and traditions and guide the people.

In doctrine Shiites teach free will, and they differ from Sunnites in minor details of ritual, as well as adding a phrase to the call to prayer. A temporary marriage with a specific date for its termination is allowed. A Shiite may dissemble his beliefs when in danger because of them.

The Ismailites are a smaller branch of Shiites, but came into prominence earlier than the Imamites. They believe in seven imams. A dynasty was established in Tunisia in 910 headed by Ubaydallah, called the Mahdi, a reputed descendant of Mohammed's daughter Fatima. This was the Fatimid Caliphate which conquered Egypt and ruled there till overthrown by Saladin in 1171. During its ascendancy Egypt was a centre of culture, and many Fatimid buildings and works of art remain.

There have been splits among the Ismailites. The Aga Khan, head of one section, is invested with an element of divinity. The Nusayrites in north Syria broke off from the main stream, a notable feature of their doctrine being belief in Ali's divinity.

Another early split in Islam was that of the Kharijites who had fought on Ali's side against Muawiya, but objected to the dispute being put to arbitration. They were originally warlike and puritanical, some more so than others, and for long were a thorn in the side of the caliphate through their beliefs.

They taught free will, insisted that faith must be proved by works, held that serious sin is apostasy, and felt they were the only true Moslems. They admitted no superior class or hereditary claim, holding that anyone, no matter what his origin, was eligible to become caliph, provided he was a sincere Moslem and possessed the requisite qualities. If a caliph proved unworthy he could be deposed. For them fighting to spread the faith was a missionary task.

Today they are represented by the Ibadites in Oman, East Africa, and parts of North Africa, but are not uncompromising like their ancestors. They are prepared to intermarry with other Moslems, making no excessive claims for themselves. They do not believe the Koran is uncreated, they allegorize Koranic anthropomorphisms, and hold that serious sinners will go to hell for ever, contrary to the common Sunnite view that Mohammed will intercede for his people and that all who have had a grain of faith will eventually be taken from hell and set in heaven.

Early Islam saw much fighting, first in Arabia, then farther afield. The word *jihad* (striving) has been used for what is called the holy war, but it has a much wider connotation. The Koran rebukes men who failed to go out to fight, but Mohammed was fighting against Arab pagans.

Mohammed

Born in Mecca about 570 AD, Mohammed (more correctly Muhammad) was a citizen of an important commercial city, for Meccan caravans travelled annually to south Arabia, the Mediterranean and the Persian Gulf. Mecca was also a religious centre, with the Kaaba to which pilgrimage was made from many regions. Other sacred sites in the neighbourhood were also visited by pilgrims. So Mecca derived profit from both its commerce and its sanctity.

Tradition says that Mohammed belonged to an influential family, but though he had some influential connections, he lived in obscurity and even poverty in his early days. The Koran (sura 93) says, 'Did he (God) not find you an orphan and give you shelter? Did he not find you erring and guide you? Did he not find you poor and enrich you?' Before Mohammed's birth his father died, and when he was five his mother died. He came under the care of his grandfather Abd al-Muttalib and, when he died, of his uncle Abu Talib. Mohammed is said to have been employed as a shepherd and he is also said to have travelled with traders into Syria. Such a journey would bring him in contact with Jews and Christians, whose religions had made little impression on Arabs, though Arabia had Jewish and Christian communities. Yet there was an indirect effect, for some Arabs, called haneefs, had abandoned idolatry for the worship of one God.

When Mohammed was about 25, a prosperous Meccan widow named Khadeeja, employed him as her agent in a caravan to Syria, and was so pleased with his success that they married. While Mohammed probably continued to conduct business, he now had time for leisure, part of which he occupied visiting a cave on Mount Hira, near Mecca, for meditation.

Eventually, about the age of 40, he had a vision. Tradition says that an apparition appeared before him and commanded him to read (or recite) in God's name. He protested that he could not do so, and the command was repeated twice more. Then he recited the words at the beginning of sura 96 of the Koran, 'Read (recite) in the name of your Lord who created, created man from congealed blood . . .' Mohammed doubted the divine origin of the message, fearing that some devil had taken possession of him, but due to Khadeeja's encouragement he became convinced that he was divinely inspired.

Sura 3 speaks of two visitations. In the first the visitant is said to have given his

Right An angel reveals the Koran, the sacred book of Islam, to the Prophet, who is shown encircled by flames: Shiite doctrine speaks of the light of Mohammed, which was created in time immemorial and passed to his successors
Opposite Interior of the Blue Mosque: engraving by Thomas Allom of the scene when crowds gathered there in 1839 to see the Sacred Standard of the Prophet, which was being displayed in the mosque

servant (Mohammed) the inspiration he conveyed. Sura 81 says, 'Your comrade is not jinn-possessed; he saw him on the plain horizon, nor does he grudge to communicate the unseen.' Dr Bell has argued (in his *Introduction to the Qu'ran*) that Mohammed first thought he had seen God, but later interpreted the visitant as Gabriel. But whatever development Mohammed required in understanding, once he was assured that the message had a divine source he no longer doubted that he was called by God to be a prophet.

A period of depression followed, without inspiration, but messages later began to come regularly. Mohammed started to preach publicly and was ridiculed. But when the Meccans began to fear that his denunciation of idols might deprive them of the income from pilgrims, persecution followed. Mohammed had the protection of Abu Talib's clan, but most of his followers were poor, some being slaves, so he advised those without protectors to go to Abyssinia where they

could live in safety under its Christian king.

The Koran depicts a lively controversy with the Meccans. The salient points of Mohammed's teaching were that there is only one God, who has appointed him as his prophet, that the rich must treat the poor justly and be honest in their business dealings, and that judgement follows death, when mankind will be rewarded or punished. Though the Meccans acknowledged a supreme God, Allah (from *al-ilah* 'the god'), local objects of worship meant more to them, and they refused to abandon polytheism or to accept Mohammed as a prophet. Some called him jinn-possessed and a poet, an accusation he vehemently rejected, because poets were believed to be inspired by a familiar spirit.

Mohammed insisted that he was inspired by God. He recounted stories of former prophets who had been rejected, ending with an account of the terrible fate of the unbelievers. The Meccans replied that he rehashed stories at second-hand.

They also ridiculed his teaching about a bodily resurrection, arguing that everyone knew the body decayed after burial. To this Mohammed had the reply that God who had created the body in the first place surely had power to bring it back to life if the divine will was such.

Mohammed lost both his encourager and his protector when Khadeeja died in December 619 and Abu Talib died the following month. At the pilgrimage season, he met 12 people from Yathrib (later Medina), a town about 180 miles north of Mecca, who were willing to accept his teaching, and he sent back a missionary with them. The following year, 70 people from Yathrib met Mohammed and agreed to protect him if he came to Yathrib. With this assurance he decided on emigration.

This emigration (the Hegira) in 622 AD was a turning-point in Mohammed's career. Many difficulties remained, but the change improved his fortunes and Islam became established as a separate religion. The earlier preaching suggests that Mohammed considered himself in the line of the prophets, proclaiming the monotheism of Abraham; but circumstances made him realize that Jews and Christians did not accept all his teaching. The importance of the emigration was early recognized, for when the calendar was fixed in the time of the second caliph, 622 became the year 1 of the Hegira.

Times were still hard, and not all the people of Yathrib welcomed Mohammed. Those who did were called Helpers and those who did not declare themselves were called Hypocrites. The phrase 'the Emigrants and the Helpers' became a technical term for the Medina Moslem community as it evolved subsequently.

Hostility towards the Meccans led to fighting. Meccan caravans passing to the west of Medina were sometimes raided by men who owed allegiance to Mohammed, and in the second year of the Hegira he himself led out a number of followers to attack a rich caravan. The caravan escaped, but Mohammed with 305 men met a Meccan supporting force three times as large and defeated it. The booty brought some relief but the knowledge that they could win gave the battle even greater significance. Mohammed declared that squadrons of angels had come to assist the Moslems, marking the victory with God's approval.

Mohammed gradually strengthened his position, engaging in many expeditions against Arab tribes, resulting in an oath of allegiance being sworn to him by tribes which recognized his strength. At the beginning of 630, in a practically bloodless victory, he conquered Mecca, clearing it of its idols and sacred stones, leaving only the Black Stone in the Kaaba, which is venerated, but not worshipped, by Moslems to the present day. Henceforth Mecca was the most sacred town to Moslems, but Mohammed returned to stay in Medina which he made his headquarters.

He had early drawn up a constitution recognizing him as leader in all matters and making provision for peaceful relations with the Jews. But he soon realized that the Jews were unwilling to welcome him, for they disputed his prophetic claims and questioned the accuracy of his knowledge of earlier revelation. He first showed his disapproval by changing the direction of prayer from Jerusalem to the Kaaba in Mecca, and substituting the fast of Ramadan for the Atonement previously observed, and the summons to prayer by the human voice for the Jewish trumpet and the Christian bell.

Soon Mohammed had good reason to suspect the Jews of dealings with his enemies and he expelled them, a tribe at a time, from Medina. Some rich Jewish settlements to the north were also conquered in this campaign against them.

Mohammed died in 632 AD. Starting as a prophet with an unpopular message, he ended as leader of a large community. From beginning to end his driving motive was to bring men to belief in God's unity, and to abandonment of idolatry. Something of the nature of a totalitarian state resulted, and was implicit in his doctrine, for if God is universal king, every sphere of life is subject to his control.

Mohammed rose from obscurity and poverty to become the prophet of a great religion, and legends naturally gathered about him *Left* His mother is told that she will give birth to a son who will change the world *Above* Mohammed's vision of the ascent into heaven

Gerald Cubitt

Gerald Cubitt

Buddhism

Buddhism denies that there is a personal world-creator, yet it affirms men's capacity to meet and become superhuman saints, saviours endowed with vast wisdom and compassion. It denies that there is an immortal soul, but affirms that there is personal continuity from life to life through many rebirths until liberation is attained. Permitting wide liberties of thought and practice to individuals and groups, Buddhism exhibits sharp sectarian differences. Yet all kinds of Buddhists are agreed that the supreme goal is Enlightenment, and that in this world-age the way and the goal were discovered and proclaimed by Siddhartha Gautama, the Sage of the Sakya tribe.

Gautama, the Buddha or 'enlightened one', preached his first sermon near Benares in c 530 BC. When he died 45 years later, he left a flourishing community of hundreds of monks and thousands of lay followers. As his successor he nominated, not a disciple but the *Dharma,* his 'truth' or 'doctrine'. These teachings were transmitted orally and were not written down until the 2nd

Buddhism grew up originally in India, though few traces of it remained there after c 1200 AD, but it still has a powerful influence in the Far East. The temple of the Emerald Buddha at Bangkok, Thailand (above left) is one of the great shrines in Southeast Asia. Buddhists believe in demons and spirits, like this guardian spirit (above right) in the same temple

century BC. By this time the teachings had been edited and amplified but the marvellous memories of the professional reciters, and the zeal of the various Buddhist sects to prevent each other from adulterating the scriptures, kept changes within bounds.

Buddhism's essential aim is to achieve enlightenment or liberation, Nirvana, which is liberation from the remorseless round of birth, death and rebirth. Unless a man achieves liberation, he is reborn over and over again, 'transmigrating' from one existence to another. Faced with this prospect of never-ending reincarnation, a man might react by pursuing worldly pleasures or, at the other extreme, by asceticism and the attempt to set himself apart from all worldly things.

Gautama in his first sermon proclaimed a Middle Way between vulgar pleasure-seeking and futile self-denial. This Way, leading to enlightenment and Nirvana, is the Holy Eightfold Path: right views, intention, speech, action, livelihood, effort, mindfulness and concentration. He declared the Four Holy Truths: that life is fraught with suffering; that the source of suffering is craving for sensual pleasure, for afterlife and for annihilation; that there is an end of suffering when craving ceases; and that there is a path which leads to this ending, the Holy Eightfold Path.

The five mendicants who heard this sermon experienced a spiritual awakening.

That the words themselves were not the sole cause of this is plain, for readers usually do not attain the first degree of sainthood upon perusing them. The early account mentions the Buddha's tremendous personal charisma, the thorough readiness of his listeners, and the solemn way in which he imparted this gnosis.

Meditation on suffering is not recommended out of any penchant for melancholy, but because it kills lust and arouses compassion, quells wishful illusions and liberates energy. Transmigration, the round of birth and death, is fraught with suffering because living beings constantly re-condemn themselves to this predicament by their worldly desires. In early India it was axiomatic that you become what you desire. Cessation, the ending of suffering, is Nirvana. It is a happy state in this life, consequent upon the extinction of ignorance and craving, and an indescribable state after the death of the liberated saint, the *arhant.*

Another formula for the Path is the 'three trainings' of morality, concentration and wisdom. Morality here means abstention from specific wrong acts. The five basic precepts observed by Buddhist laymen and monks alike are: not taking life, not taking what is not given, not engaging in sexual misconduct, not telling untruths, and not drinking liquor. The monk also undertakes to observe a code of over 200 rules of restraint. Particular importance attaches to. not harming human or animal life, and most of the other precepts serve that objective.

The chief roads to concentration are the four 'abodes of mindfulness': contemplating the body, the feelings, mental states and dharmas (doctrines). You watch your breath go in and out; you are mindful of your actions, whether walking, standing, sitting or lying down; you reflect on the body as consisting of 32 parts and of the four elements of earth, water, fire and wind; and you imagine the successive stages of the body's decomposition after death. As for feelings, you note pleasure, pain and neutral feeling, whether of body or of mind. States of mind are to be watched, noting lust, hate, folly, concentration or distraction. The meditator on dharmas notes what hindrances are present in him. He is aware of the presence or absence of the factors of enlightenment, namely mindfulness, dharma-investigation, vigour, rapture, tranquility, concentration and equanimity. He contemplates the Four Holy Truths until he really understands them.

Concentration is characterized by single-mindedness. After passing through the preliminary stages, the meditator attains the first trance, which is filled with rapture and happiness. In the second trance rapture gives place to serenity and clear awareness. By the time the fourth trance is reached, the meditator is beyond pleasure and pain, beyond joy and grief; he dwells in equanimity and pure awareness.

Three grades of wisdom are distinguished, the lowest based on hearing the doctrine, the next on thinking about what has been heard, and the highest on meditative trances. Morality provides a base for concentration, which in turn supports wisdom, and through wisdom the mind is freed from the 'outflows' – sensual desire, becoming (living again and again) and wrong views. Extinguishing the outflows, one becomes a saint (arhant), attains Nirvana, and is freed from further births.

Prominent among the fruits of meditation are the six super-knowledges: magic powers (such as flying, walking on water, changing one's form and projecting a mind-made body), clairaudience (the ability to hear sounds not actually present), mind-reading, memory of former lives, clairvoyance, and extinction of the outflows. The first five are mundane. They are reached through concentration, and may be attained by non-Buddhists. The sixth is supramundane, reached through insight, and attained only by arhants.

The early tradition regarded the mundane super-knowledges with ambivalence. The great saints, including the Buddha himself, went on shaman-style journeys to the paradises and hells, received communications from spirits through clairaudience and clairvoyance, read the minds of their students in order to select the the appropriate teaching or meditative practice for them, and remembered their own and others' former lives. They also foretold the future, 'saw' human events that were going on at a great distance, and subdued demons.

On the other hand, monks were forbidden to exhibit their psychic powers to ordinary people, because this cheapened the spiritual attainments. They were to refrain from reciting spells and from interpreting dreams, omens and the stars. Similarly, the super-knowledges were not to be used for worldly purposes, because this would conduce to worldly greed. Yet the literature of Indian Buddhism is full of tales in which a saint used his paranormal powers to rescue someone from worldly distress. This tension between worldly engagement and Nirvana-oriented disengagement characterizes the entire history of Buddhism.

So far it appears that the early Buddhist ethic was merely one of abstention, and that the goals of the religious life were entirely ascetic and unworldly. This is not the case. Donation was a cardinal virtue for both laity and monks. The laymen earned merit by giving material requisites to monks and nuns, and by helping the sick and the needy.

Merit is a sort of spiritual currency, that can be spent on a happy next life in a paradise, or turned over to the benefit of a deceased relative, or invested in further spiritual progress. The monk was not rich in material goods but he was supposed to be rich in Dharma (Doctrine), which he donated by teaching it. He also earned merit just by living the monastic life, and like the layman he often devoted his merit to the well-being of deceased relations.

Another merit-earning activity is worship (puja). In the household life, puja means honouring your parents, guests, teachers and other worthy persons. In a sacred context, it means making the same ritual gestures of reverence and hospitality: bowing with palms pressed together, kowtowing, touching the honoured one's feet, circumambulation, chanting salutations and verses of praise, and offering food, water, lights, incense, flowers, cloth and precious substances. Today in the Theravada countries of Sri Lanka and Southeast Asia, foot-washing is performed for holy guests, images are bathed, and monks and other worthy persons are splashed with water on New Year's Day.

Most worshipful entities are the Buddha, the Dharma (Doctrine) and the Sangha (Community). These are the three Jewels or Treasures. The Sangha has four divisions: monks, nuns, laymen and laywomen. But in common use the word means chiefly the community of monks. You become a Buddhist by declaring, 'I go to the Buddha-refuge, I go to the Dharma-refuge, I go to the Sangha-refuge.' Here the third refuge is the community of holy persons, not all of whom are monks, just as not all monks are saints.

The early teaching sets forth a simple series of stages on the path. The primary division is between worldlings and saints. The worldling who has taken the refuges is a faith-follower, one who pursues the truth and accepts the doctrine on the authority of another. There are four grades of holy person or saint. The stream-winner is certain not to fall into a bad rebirth and not to relapse until he attains enlightenment. This stage is attainable through morality and perfect faith in Buddha, Dharma and Sangha. In no more than seven births the stream-winner will attain sainthood. The once-returner, free from the fetters of lust and ill-will, will attain sainthood in his next human rebirth. The non-returner gets rid of all his fetters in this life, and then is reborn in a high heaven where he reaches Nirvana. The arhant extinguishes all the outflows and in this very life realizes liberation of mind through wisdom.

In the earlier layers of the early scriptures, Buddha is little more than the first arhant among equals. His uniqueness consists of having reached full enlightenment without having a master in this life. In later parts of the early canon, the Buddha is exalted far above his holy disciples. Whereas the earlier texts ascribe to him only the three great cognitions (memory of his former lives, cosmic vision and knowledge that his outflows were extinguished), later Pali texts claim he was omniscient.

Gautama was probably never considered to be the only Buddha. The Pali texts speak of a series of six former Buddhas, whom Gautama remembers through his own super-knowledge, and of the future Buddha, Maitreya, who is now a Bodhisattva (Buddha-to-be).

Is Nirvana annihilation or eternal existence, the cessation of all thought and feeling or perfect beatitude? The early texts give enigmatic answers. They say that there is an unborn, unbecome, unmade, unconditioned; and then they define the unconditioned as destruction of lust, hatred and folly. Whether the Buddha exists after death ranks as an undeclared point, along with whether the world is eternal, whether the world is infinite, and whether the soul and the body are the same. The Buddha refused to admit that the Buddha exists after death, or does not exist, or both exists and does not exist, or neither exists nor does not exist. To each of these statements he answered, 'This does not fit the case.' Then he likened the Buddha after death to a fire which has gone out; it has not gone north, south, east or west. The Buddha, he says, is deep and immeasurable like the great ocean. Since the Nirvana-realm is unique, analogies are inadequate, and the prudent teacher guards against treating them as descriptions. The only adequate indication of Nirvana is instruction on how to experience it.

Early Buddhism rejected the Upanishadic concept of a world-soul (brahman, atman), the material and efficient cause of all things

in existence. Nirvana is not a stuff out of which the world is made, and its attainment is not a reversion of the soul to its unmanifested state. The Buddha denied that there is an atman or self, in the sense of an unchanging substance which serves as host to changing and transient properties. He treated all phenomena as processes and declared a Middle Path between the eternalist extreme of being ('what is, always is') and the annihilationist extreme of non-being ('then it was real, now it is extinct'). The action of cause and effect is not a modification of substances, but dependent co-arising: 'When A exists, then B comes into being; when A does not exist, B does not come into being.' Relations are real, substances are not.

Transmigration is not the re-embodiment of a soul, but the passing over of a consciousness, consisting of the seeds of good and evil deeds *(karma)* committed during this life and previous lives. It is likened to the flame passing from one candle to another, or a poem passing from the teacher's mind to the pupil's. The transmigrant consciousness finds a species and a family in conformity with its moral legacy.

The world of transmigration *(samsara)* consists of three realms: the *desire-realm* (comprising the subterranean hells, the animal world, the ghost world. the human world, the demon world and the lower god worlds); the *form-realm* (the higher god worlds); and the *formless realm,* inhabited by beings who as contemplatives in this life achieved the trance-planes of endless space, endless consciousness, nothing-at-all, and neither-perception-nor-non-perception.

Buddhist cult practice implements the conviction that all living beings are members of one cosmic family. Merit is transferred to the account of beings in hell, to alleviate their

sufferings and hasten their release. Animals are given sanctuary in temple precincts, hunting and butchering are considered immoral, and veterinary treatment is provided as a pious act. Offerings of merit, rice-cakes and water are made to the ghosts of departed relatives on the anniversaries of their deaths, and to all the ghosts on the 15th day of the seventh month. Offerings are made to numerous gods, godlings and demons. In return, the gods grant worldly blessings such as children, riches and freedom from danger and disease. The two great Indo-Aryan gods of the 6th century BC entered early Buddhism, Indra as protector and Brahma as inspirer of the Dharma. Rebirth in Brahma's heaven is obtained through the four contemplations known as 'Brahma-dwellings': friendly love, compassion, sympathetic joy and equanimity. In general, the early Buddhist approach to spirits was to subdue them through Dharma, then treat them with friendly respect rather than with terror or aversion.

During the second century AN (after the Nirvana of Gautama in or about 483 BC), the Buddhist monastic order split into two sects, the Sthaviras (Elders) and the Mahasanghikas (members of the Great Assembly). The former restricted their assembly to arhants, and denied that a layman could become an arhant, thus excluding laymen from their councils. The latter admitted laymen and non-arhants to their meetings, which consequently were called 'great'. The Elders were an ecclesiastical establishment, enhancing the status of the cleric and the arhant. The Mahasanghikas made less of arhantship, and exalted Buddha even more than the Elders did. They maintained that he is supermundane, does not reside among men, has an infinite body, has boundless power, and is endowed with endless life. He

sends out apparition-bodies throughout the whole cosmos, and through them works ceaselessly for the salvation of all living beings.

In or about 274 BC Asoka came to the throne of the Maura Empire. After consolidating his power and expanding his territory, he was stricken with remorse at the bloodshed and destruction he had wrought in the course of conquest, and became a Buddhist convert. He went on pilgrimages, gave up hunting, frequented the company of monks, and spent some time in retreat. Then he proclaimed a policy of Dharma-conquest rather than military conquest, and appointed special Dharma-commissioners to oversee the execution of his policy. He commended tolerance between sects and urged all to concentrate on the common essence of Dharma. But he promoted the growth of Buddhism and other ascetic sects, and by sending missionary monks to foreign countries he gave Buddhism tremendous impetus.

During Asoka's reign, the sect of Vibhajyavadins (Distinctionists) split off from the school of the Elders. The Vibhajyavadins themselves soon split into several sects. Their strongholds were in western India (present-day Madhya Pradesh and Maharashtra). An archaic Vibhajyavadin sect which called itself simply Theravada (the Doctrine of the Elders) passed through the south of India to Sri Lanka in the late 3rd century BC. After many vicissitudes and recurrent encroachment by Hinduism, other Buddhist sects and Christianity, it is still there.

In the 5th and 6th centuries AD, there were Theravada centres on the Madras coast, from which the sect spread to Burma. Today it prevails in Burma, Thailand, Laos and Cambodia as well as Sri Lanka.

About four centuries AN there arose a movement calling itself the Bodhisattvayana or Mahayana (great course or vehicle), in contrast to the Hinayana − inferior course or vehicle. Initially it was probably not a separate sect but just a new way of stating some typical Mahasanghika doctrines: that the phenomena of the world are illusory and empty, that the true Buddha is transworldly, that the Buddhas who appear in the world are his phantom-bodies, that they exist simultaneously in many world-realms, and that the saving activity of the Buddhas never ceases.

The idea of the Bodhisattva − the one who is on the path of becoming Buddha − was acknowledged by all the Hinayana sects, but most used the term only to designate Gautama before he attained enlightenment. Mahayana proclaimed that the Bodhisattvayana is the course which all devotees should follow. It taught a path along which even the humblest could set out, and it assured him of help from an array of celestial Bodhisattvas and Buddhas.

We know from stone reliefs that stories of the Buddha's former lives were popular by the 2nd century BC. These tales celebrate a

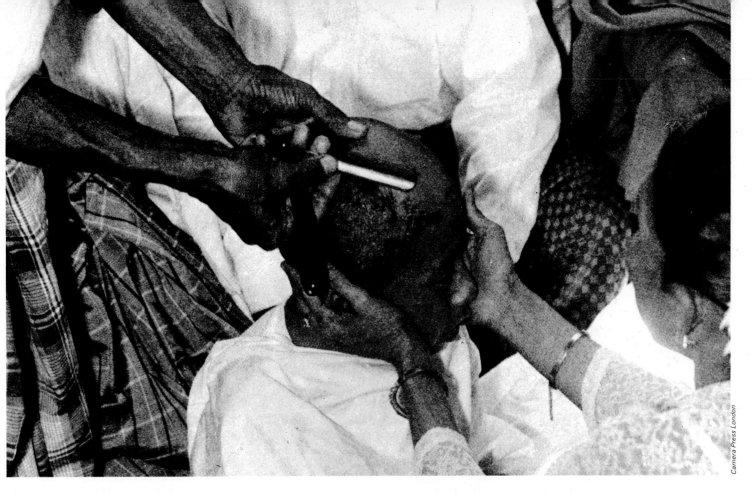

series of virtues called 'perfections'. The idea of the perfections was developed by the Elder sects, and Mahayana adopted the idea and made it the heart of the Bodhisattva path, which it recommended not just for admiration but for practice by all devotees, whether male or female, monastic or lay.

The Bodhisattva path begins with the awakening of the aspiration for supreme, perfect enlightenment. This momentous act requires the accumulation of much merit and wisdom, and the aid of good spiritual friends. It also has great results. It cancels bad karma, prevents bad rebirths and leads to good ones.

Having awakened his aspiration, the Bodhisattva cultivates good qualities, does good to others, and meditates on the aims of his career. In due course he makes a set of vows, resolving to save living beings and often specifying that when he becomes a Buddha his Buddha-land will have such-and-such amenities and advantages.

Then the Bodhisattva proceeds to practise six virtues until they become perfections. *Donation* means giving one's goods, the Dharma, and even one's life and body, to those who have need of them. It is a perfection when the giver has no thought of reward, and is spontaneous and unselfconscious about the act. *Morality* consists of observing the precepts, transferring the resultant merit to the account of others, and encouraging others to do the same. *Patience* means enduring hardship and injury from others, and accepting difficult and unpalatable doctrines. *Vigour* is unflagging energy and zeal in overcoming vice and cultivating virtue. *Meditation* consists of practising the trances, concentrations and attainments without accepting the worldly advantages these can procure. *Wisdom* is the queen of the perfections, since it consists in the direct

You become a Buddhist by saying, 'I go to the Buddha-refuge, I go to the Dharma-refuge, I go to the Sangha-refuge': the Dharma being the true doctrine and the Sangha the community of holy persons, including monks and laymen. The monks vow to observe a code of more than 200 rules but the five basic rules are not to take human or animal life, not to take what is not given, not to engage in sexual misconduct, not to tell lies, and not to drink intoxicants

Opposite A young boy, regally dressed, sits with the women of his family before taking the vows which will make him a Buddhist monk *Above* The boy's head is shaved. This is a mark of the renunciation of the worldly life in many different societies: Christian monks, for instance, have 'tonsures' or shaved patches on their heads *Below* Later the boy takes the saffron-yellow robe of a monk and vows to keep it holy as long as he breathes

Gerald Cubitt

realization of the truth of emptiness and isolation, which quells all fictions and 'thought-constructions' and thus renders the other five virtues perfect.

When the Bodhisattva masters the six perfections, he achieves the non-relapsing state and is not bound to rebirths by his karma, but chooses at will where he is going to be reborn in order to benefit living beings. Eventually he becomes a Buddha, unless he has vowed to remain a Bodhisattva until all living beings attain enlightenment.

The celestial Bodhisattvas in the Mahayana pantheon are Great Beings who have achieved the non-relapsing stage and sovereignty over the realms of transmigration. Most of them are probably descended from the deities of North Indian popular religion in the last five centuries BC, and they have taken over the attributes and functions of the great gods Indra and Brahma. They occupy subordinate positions in the early Mahayana Sutras, but become more and more prominent after 200 AD, until they surpass the Buddhas themselves.

Devotion to Maitreya, the coming Buddha, is common to Hinayana and Mahayana. He will be born at Benares in the distant future when human virtue and prosperity have increased immensely. Meanwhile he is staying in the Tusita Heaven, where the devout may be reborn if they earnestly pray for it, particularly at the moment of death. There they will pass the interlude in celestial bliss, listening to Maitreya's discourses. And when he comes to earth again, they will accompany him. As a high god Maitreya is powerful, and as a Bodhisattva he is compassionate, so worshippers can expect a response to their prayers. He is the

inspirer of Buddhist teachers, appearing to them in dreams or trances, consoling them when they are in doubt or frustration. He also saves people from danger, receives confessions of sins, and comes to the dying to lead them to his paradise.

Manjusri is said to have become a non-relapsing Bodhisattva 64 myriads of aeons ago. Because he vowed not to hurry to enlightenment but to remain in samsara as long as a single living being is unsaved, his Buddhahood is not imminent. He was born in Gautama's time as a Brahmin and lived 450 years. Merely hearing his name deducts many ages from one's time in transmigration and worshipping him guarantees good rebirth. If you recite a certain Sutra and chant his name, he will appear to you in seven days, in a dream if you have bad karma, otherwise in a waking vision. He is the embodiment of Wisdom, and in art is shown riding a lion, holding a sword in his hand.

Another Great Being is Avalokitesvara who appears in multifarious forms in order to help and save living beings – as a Buddha, as a Bodhisattva, as an arhant, or as a Hindu god. The merit from devotion to him is equal to that from worshipping a vast number of Buddhas. He grants boons to those who call him to mind and recite his name. He saves them from evil passions, grants a son or daughter (as she chooses) to a supplicant woman, and saves those who think of him from fire, shipwreck, robbers, execution, prison, witchcraft, demons, wild beasts, snakes and thunderbolts. His cult burgeoned during the 4th century AD, and by the 7th he was the most popular divinity in the Indian Buddhist pantheon.

We have seen how the Mahasanghikas idealized the Buddha, and treated the historical Gautama as one of numerous apparitions projected by the eternal, supermundane Buddha. They also believed, as against the Elders, that many Buddhas exist in the universe at the same time, each reigning over a Buddha-field or Buddha-land.

From the beginning, there was an apparent contradiction between Gautama's various roles. The Lotus Sutra, completed c 200 AD, declares that he did not really enter Nirvana at the end of his 80 years on earth, but only gave the appearance of doing so, to shock and invigorate people who would otherwise have taken his presence for granted. In reality, he is always active, teaching and helping all living beings in this and all other worlds. The Buddha of the Lotus Sutra is a marvellous and ever-present teacher, but he does not relieve the pupils of the necessity to make an effort, gain merit and accumulate wisdom. In India, Gautama always remained the most popular of the celestial Buddhas.

Vairocana, 'Descendant of the Sun', began as an epithet of Gautama but became one of the chief Buddhas in the Avatamsaka Sutra (c 300 AD). Aksobhya, 'the Unshakable', was popular in the first two centuries AD. He presides over a Buddha-field in the Eastern Direction where people who do good deeds or hear his name can attain birth. Amitabha, 'Unlimited Light', (also called Amitayus, 'Unlimited Lifespan' and in addition the Amida of Japan) presides over a paradise in the Western Direction called 'the Happy Land'. All beings who go to Amitabha's land unfailingly attain enlightenment. To obtain rebirth in the Happy Land one must have a minimum of good conduct, must hear the name of Amitabha, and must fix one's intent on going there. There are no hells, animals, ghosts or women in that land. All material requisites come just by wishing for them. Fragrant jewel-flowers shower down from jewel-trees, and the clouds play continual sweet music. And the beings there hear whatever Dharma-discourse they wish to hear. The cult of Amitabha was never as popular in India as that of Sakyamuni, but it enjoyed tremendous fortune in China.

Tantric Buddhism, or Vajrayana, 'the Thunderbolt Vehicle', arose c 600 AD,

Above Serenity in stone: faces of Bodhisattvas, saints who are on the path to becoming Buddhas, at the Bayon Temple in Angkor Thom, Cambodia, built in the 12th century by the Emperor Jayavarman VII, a supporter of Buddhism in an area where Hinduism and Buddhism co-existed and influenced each other, as they had earlier done in India **Opposite** Buddhist worshippers put flowers in the hats of these statues, burn incense to them and periodically give them new clothes. Worship earns merit, which can be spent in a happy next life in a paradise before another rebirth on earth, or which can be used to alleviate the sufferings of a dead relative in one of the numerous hells

after a long period of incubation. The Tantric centuries equalled in glory any other period in Indian Buddhist history. They produced great art and architecture, profound scholarship, and a remarkable line of holy men. Just as Mahayana revitalized a tradition that was falling prey to academic hair-splitting and complacency, so Vajrayana revived spiritual zeal and accomplishment at a time when the Bodhisattva ideal was more celebrated in academic analyses than realized in practice.

From the 7th to the 12th centuries, Vajrayana flourished in Bihar and Bengal. The great monastic universities of Nalanda and Vikramasila taught the whole range of Buddhist, Hindu and secular learning to thousands of students, including Chinese, Tibetans and Southeast Asians. But Moslem invaders destroyed organized Buddhism in the Ganges valley, sacking Nalanda in 1198 and again several times over the next decades. It survived as a folk cult for two or three centuries, then subsequently vanished from the Ganges area.

Vajrayana also prospered in the sub-Himalayan valleys, in Swat, Gilgit, Kashmir, Katmandu. It was exterminated by Moslem rulers only in the 15th century. It survives to this day in the Katmandu Valley.

It is doubtful whether Buddhism ever had much strength in the Tamil country in southern India, except in a few towns such as Conjeeveram, a great centre of learning where there was still a Theravada community even in the 15th century. West India and the Deccan were Buddhist strongholds to the end of the 7th century but the last Buddhist monuments in Maharashtra date from the 5th century, and thereafter Hinduism dominated the whole region. Probably Brahmin advisers at the courts were more skilful at winning the princes' favour than were the Buddhist monks. Buddhism flourishes best in strong nation-states (as in Sri Lanka, Burma and China in the T'ang period). The loosely structured feudal society of the Rajput period favoured the almost equally loosely organized faith that became Hinduism.

While it is not true that Hinduism absorbed all the best from Buddhism, it still assimilated and perpetuated a great deal. The strong emphasis on compassion in devotional Hinduism owes much to Buddhist inspiration. The later Vedanta schools are indebted to Buddhism. Samkara's Vedanta supplanted Buddhism by borrowing not only philosophy but monasticism from it.

Modern India has rediscovered its Buddhist heritage with pride. A few caste Hindus and millions of former untouchables have been converted to Buddhism and for every convert, there are many more Indians who study Buddhist doctrine with approval, go on pilgrimage to the Buddhist holy places, and see the religious universalism of the Buddha as a forerunner of the egalitarian democracy India is now striving to develop. Asoka's ideal of Dharma-victory still lives, and its symbol, the Wheel of the Dharma, stands in the centre of India's flag.

Zen

Zen is a Chinese-Japanese branch of Mahayana Buddhism. Although nowhere within the boundaries of its special teachings is there demanded faith in a God external to the universe who has created the cosmos and man, nor is there any single sacrosanct collection of revealed scriptures to be venerated like the Christian Bible or Hinduism's *Vedas*, Zen followers and teachers nevertheless consider Zen a religion. In their view, Zen's form of Buddhism is a natural, indeed inevitable development from such challenging and iconoclastic statements by the founder of this major world faith as 'Look within, *thou* art the Buddha'. Zen is concerned with teaching that all men, with disciplined individual effort, are capable of attaining the Buddha's Enlightenment, known as *satori* in the Zen vocabulary.

Zen's emphasis, in the present as well as the past, falls on specific meditative practices designed to 'see into one's nature', a descriptive phrase attributed to one of the most important figures in the annals of early Zen, the Chinese master of the 7th century, Hui-Neng (638-713; in Japanese, Eno). The late author and scholarly authority on Zen Buddhism, D. T. Suzuki, called Hui-Neng's statement 'the most significant phrase ever coined in the development of Zen'. Some 13 centuries have passed since Hui-Neng uttered these words but they remain as basic to Zen teaching as they were when he spoke them, and it is this phrase, and others similar to it, that have turned a number of Western psychoanalysts and psychiatrists – including Carl Jung, Erich Fromm and Karen Horney – to a serious study of Zen methods in relation to their own interests in the attainment of self-knowledge. Existentialists, also, of the stature of Martin Heidegger, have claimed to find in ancient Zen writings some of the very ideas they have been developing in modern times.

The recent phenomenon of a steadily growing interest in Zen teachings in Europe and the United States arises, it has been suggested, in part because Zen's emphasis on 'finding out for oneself' appeals to modern people who have difficulty accepting fixed dogma or traditional religious authority in a world now in scientific and philosophic flux. It is not only Japanese *roshis* (venerable spiritual teachers) but Westerners as well who, after training in Japanese monasteries, are today carrying to the West Zen's interpretation and extension of original Buddhist teachings. Through body-mind techniques of 'quiet sitting' as well as through the challenge of the dynamic conundrum known as the *koan*, Zen aims to establish unshaken personal faith in life's 'Is-ness', the universe seen as an indissoluble unity, a single totality of which man is but a part.

In Buddhism's slow but irresistible spread over all Asia the Mahayana branch of teaching reached China around 525 AD. From China in time it moved on to Korea and to Japan acquiring, in the usual flexible Mahayana style, certain colourations from the cultures encountered in its passage. The Indian mystic root, with strong pragmatic and humanistic influences from China, the land of Confucius and Lao-Tze, are so clearly traceable in Zen's development that Zen as known today might be fairly described as a unique blend of Indian mysticism and Chinese naturalism sieved through the special mesh of the Japanese character. The very origins of its name indicate its historical genesis. Zen is the Japanese way of writing and speaking the Chinese word *ch'an*, which is a transliteration of the Sanskrit word *dhyana,* meaning meditation or, more fully, 'contemplation leading to a higher state of Consciousness' or 'union with Reality'.

It was in the 12th century that the special development of Buddhist philosophy known in China as ch'an was definitely established in Japan under the name of Zen. Prior to this date, however, there had been a significant exchange of Buddhist monks and teachers between the two countries; a traffic of inestimable importance not only to Japanese culture but to the history of Zen philosophy and the world's art. These religious emissaries acted, in effect, as disseminators and preservers of Chinese civilization at its brilliant height in the great Sung Dynasty. When the Sung idyll was brought to its end by an invasion of Mongols, Japan escaped the invaders and thus became the sanctuary not only for the scriptures and teachings of a new-old, India-born, Chinese-influenced philosophy but for its intimately related arts as well.

So allied with Zen philosophy is its unique aesthetic that one cannot separate the two and still have a profound comprehension of Zen's underlying precepts. This is true in particular of those swiftly-executed 'spontaneous' ink paintings which manage to express with consummate subtlety both a passionate love of Nature and a singular harmony with it. Waterfalls, mountain peaks, birds, stones, flowers, bamboo, pines in mist all speak of a hidden Unity, of the belief that the Buddha nature is immanent not alone in man but in everything that exists, animate or inanimate. The traditional culture of Japan is grounded in Zen perceptions which have been preserved, encouraged and practised in an amazingly pure stream of transmission right up to modern times. Qualities such as naturalness, simplicity, tranquillity, asymmetry, emptiness are expressed in Japanese plays and poetry, in flower arrangement (a highly regarded art in Japan), in *sumi* ink painting and calligraphy, in the subject matter and performances of the traditional theatre, in the design of gardens and house interiors. The room in which the tea ceremony is held, for example, is known as 'the abode of vacancy' and taking tea might be fairly described as a Zen practice in unfaltering awareness and joy in simple objects. The precise disciplines of judo, archery and ceremonial swordsmanship are also rooted deep in Zen. Most importantly the stripped, evocative 17-syllable Japanese verse form known as *haiku* affords special clues to the Zen state of mind:

> The water-fowl
> Lays its beak in its breast
> And sleeps as it floats.

> An old pine tree preaches wisdom
> And a wild bird is crying truth.

> How marvellous, how miraculous
> I draw water,
> I gather fuel.

What is being said in lines like these is that one should come to rest in the great Emptiness, that in every moment of life there is chance for enlightenment and that in the very seeming commonplaceness of existence one may discover the deepest mystery and wonder.

Zen claims to be the direct inheritor of principles of thought and behaviour first promulgated by the historic Buddha. In the 6th century BC he preached a doctrine of a Middle Way of Understanding. He taught that certain methods of thought and behaviour could lead a follower to freedom from attachment to objects and to the eventual release from that cramping and illusory sense of a special self or ego which, cutting off man from his fellows and from all other forms of life, gave human existence its tragic tone.

The Buddha's illuminating perception that he was, in a strictly personal sense, 'no-thing' and 'no-body', his profound realization of the indescribable, existential indivisibility or One-ness of all life, freed him forever from the fetters of *maya* (illusion) and from the necessity for rebirth or participation in the ceaseless round of 'becoming'. At this point in the spiritual history of Buddhism it is assumed that the Enlightened One might of his own volition have left the physical plane. Instead, after a period of doubt and uncertainty he accepted the sacrifice and responsibility of going forth to try to teach the unteachable; a truth that could not be described in words, that must instead be individually experienced as he had experienced it in his own moment of

Intuitive understanding of that which 'goes beyond the Word' is basic to Zen; one of the criteria by which Noh drama, rooted in Zen, is judged is whether a performance expresses that which is 'ineffable, indescribable yet communicable and capable of being intuitively experienced': child actor in Noh drama

Picturepoint London

life after death and similar insoluble mysteries. To this typical sophist the Buddha remarked that his demands were comparable to those of a man who refuses to leave his burning house until he has found out who set the house on fire; or like a man who, shot with a poisoned arrow, will not remove it until he has ascertained all the facts about the arrow's source. In other words, speculation can only lead to further speculation with no possibility of any final solution; individual penetration to the heart of life's meaning cannot be brought about by the mind alone.

The second story in this general style describes the Buddha's so-called Silent Sermon, to a Zennist perhaps the most eloquent of all the Buddha's discourses. On one occasion before a great gathering of followers and disciples, the Buddha sat without speaking, turning a flower quietly in his hand. Some of the versions relate that he regarded the flower with joy, that he even broke into laughter. As he, without words, turned the flower in his hand he also looked into the faces of his followers waiting for a flash of understanding. At last it came. One disciple, Kasyapa, smiled, a serene inward-turning smile of awareness which told the Buddha that he had really *seen* the flower, had grasped that 'which goes beyond the Word'. It is significant that this perceptive disciple was subsequently chosen by the Buddha as his successor in the role of teacher. It is also worth mention in passing that to this day a canon of judgment brought to bear on Japan's ancient Zen-rooted Noh drama, is whether a performance does or does not possess 'the true flower', in other words express that which is ineffable, indescribable yet communicable and capable of being intuitively experienced. This basic Zen emphasis on an understanding that lies outside verbalism has been put succinctly in a famous four-line statement:

A special transmission outside the
  Scriptures;
No dependence upon words and letters;
Direct pointing to the soul of man;
Seeing into one's own nature and thereby
  attaining Buddhahood.

These four lines, expressive of the very essence of Zen, might be said to find their original embodiment in a semi-legendary missionary monk from India known as Bodhidharma (in Japanese, Daruma). The date of his first appearance in Zen annals is uncertain but we are told that

supreme clarity while seated under the Tree of Wisdom.

It is this act of profound selflessness on the part of the historic Buddha which has led to the development in Mahayana Buddhism of the theory of Bodhisattvas, enlightened beings who have taken the vow to postpone their own release in order to assist all other creatures in the attainment of Nirvana, a state of total inner Peace and Freedom; in other words, Buddhahood itself is arrived at. Although this profoundly mystical and, in a sense, paradoxical concept of Bodhisattvas as personifications of the highest wisdom and compassion did not originate in Zen, they preside in spirit over Zen halls of instruction and meditation, and the chanting of a Bodhisattva's four vows of dedication to the Buddha's Way are a part of each day's routine in teaching centres and monasteries. Sculptured or painted forms of such great Bodhisattvas as Kuan-Yin (Japanese Kwannon), Manjusri,

Maitreya (Miroku) and others, are found in the priceless art collections of Zen monasteries, and are numbered among Japan's greatest national treasures. In old Chinese and Japanese art one can even find the Buddha himself depicted as a Bodhisattva, notably in such a moving masterpiece as the 12th century Chinese painter Liang K'ai's picture of the Great Teacher leaving the mountain top of his Enlightenment preparing to descend again into the world. Shown as a worn, weary, shabby ascetic, he stares down with an expression of profound questioning into the valley below, where he must now go on his self-determined mission to carry a light into the 'darkness of the world'.

From the annals of early Indian Buddhism, Zennists pluck certain stories which to them represent the very crux and significance of Buddhist teaching. One is the Buddha's rebuke to a disciple who kept demanding intellectual answers to such questions as the nature of the First Cause,

Above Flower arranging, a highly regarded art in Japan, reflects the Zen philosophy of joy in simplicity, and unfaltering awareness *Opposite* The Zen belief that the Buddha nature is immanent not only in man, but in everything that exists, animate or inanimate, is reflected in the traditional culture of Japan; qualities such as tranquility and emptiness are expressed in the design of gardens and house interiors, in plays and poetry: sand garden in Kyoto, symbolizing the sea

Buddhism was already established in China when he arrived. It is related that he came all the way from India, a journey of incredible hardship, with the purpose of restoring to Buddhism its original directness and meaningful simplicity; to teach Buddhist followers enlightenment.

One of Zen's outstanding characteristics is a zany sense of humour which has found expression not only in its literature but in a coexisting art of sharp and subtle commentary. The famous roshi Hakuin (1685-1768), known in his time as 'the greatest sage in 500 years' was not only a master teacher but also a great artist in the spontaneous free style favoured by Zen painters and calligraphers. Among his astringent masterpieces there is a cartoon-like drawing of a one-eyed monster in company with a simple blind man. The grotesque creature, depicted with a single fierce headlight-eye in the centre of his forehead, is glaring at the unconcerned blind man as he exclaims, 'Hey! I am a one-eyed monster. Aren't you afraid of me?' 'I have no eyes,' replied the blind man, 'Why should I be afraid of you? You should be scared of me'. A comical sketch, by another painter-monk, shows a neophyte warming his backside at a burning statue of a Bodhisattva. The accompanying anecdote tells that when caught in this irreverent act the culprit innocently replied that since there had appeared in the ashes no sign of *sarira* (a special substance found only in the remains of cremated saints) he concluded it was only a wooden statue – and it was a very cold day.

This kind of rough humour and seeming irreverence has in no way prevented Zen temples and monasteries from remaining repositories of great religious art, nor has it stopped Buddhists from prostrating themselves before Buddha images as an act which 'horizontalizes the ego-mast' as one interpreter has put it. Zen's countless humorous anecdotes spring from the wish to avoid self-conscious religiosity or pompous smugness about spiritual attainment. Satori, in Zen annals, is often accompanied by a kind of transcendental laughter, as in the story of the monk who came to his roshi for help with one of the classic questions assigned to neophytes: 'What is the meaning of Bodhidharma's coming from India?' The master, to whom the question was put, suggested that before proceeding with the problem the inquiring monk should make him a low salaam. As he was dutifully prostrating himself the teacher administered a good swift kick. At this unexpected impact the disciple's murky irresolution was instantly resolved. Afterwards he told everyone he met, 'Since I received that kick from Ma Tsu, I haven't been able to stop laughing.'

A number of modern students of Zen feel that the koan exercise has been over-stressed in Western literature about Zen, and that too much has been made of practices followed in certain Zen training centres: the swift thwack on the drowsy or irresolute student's shoulders by an attendant with a special stick (invariably accompanied, however, by low bows on the part of both the dealer of the blow and its recipient) or the loud rude shouts of disapproval and dismissal from an impatient roshi to whom a student has brought an obviously thought-out answer. There are also critics who are disturbed by the West's over-emphasis on the idea of the suddenness of the breakthrough into satori which tends to give the impression of 'instant Zen' when in truth illumination, though it may be sudden in its impact, is experienced only after prolonged effort and a number of satori-like experiences (*kensho*) prior to the Great Enlightenment in all its stunning finality.

Something of the nature of Zen may be discovered from the words of an old poem:

> When one looks at it, one cannot see it;
> When one listens for it, one cannot hear it;
> However, when one uses it, it is
>   inexhaustible.

Zen claims to point a paradoxical Way, at once abstract and personal, that is markedly different from the practices of more conventional religions.

Alan Irvine

Hinduism

'Hindu' is a Persian word and it means simply 'Indian'. Thus for the Moslem invaders of India the 'Hindu' religion was identified with the Indian people. It was the national religion of India, just as Judaism is the national religion of the Jews. The Indians themselves, however, never refer to their religion as the 'Indian' religion: rather they call it the *Sanatana Dharma*, the 'eternal *dharma*', distinguishing it thereby from all other religions, which have known founders and are therefore rooted in history. Hinduism is 'eternal and ageless' (*Sanatana*): it has no known founder and is considered to have existed for all time. But this does not mean that its forms do not change in the course of time: the essence is changeless but the forms in which it expresses itself are ever-changing. It is the religious expression of the very stuff of Nature and the Divine as the Hindus see them — perpetual change seen against a changeless and timeless background.

Hinduism is also a dharma, a word which has a great variety of meanings. It is derived from the root *dhr* which means 'to hold together' — something, therefore, that gives coherence to what appears to have none. Etymologically it is connected with Latin *firmus*, 'firm', and *forma*, 'form', the abiding form of things that makes them as they are and not otherwise. In this sense it is 'law', both the eternal law that governs Nature and the moral law that rules or should rule among men: it is law, religion and righteousness, the norm by which men live in the wider context of Nature and the universe. It is not something man-made but the principle that governs all things and to which the gods themselves are subject.

'The gods' because Hinduism is a polytheistic religion, but a polytheism that is also in some sense a monotheism. This sounds paradoxical but it is not really so, for even in the earliest times the gods are only manifestations of an immanent and unitary principle which is the ground of the universe — a principle that is at first regarded as being an impassive absolute but which may also appear as a personal God.

Although Hinduism has no founder it has, like all the 'higher' religions, a body of sacred literature. This is called the *Veda*, a word meaning 'wisdom' or 'knowledge'. The Veda is a vast collection of sacred texts containing material that seems to have little coherence, for its earliest strata which are frankly polytheist seem to be quite different from the later which are frankly pantheist (holding that God is in everything). It is the latter period, however, that is important, for it set the tone once for all for the later development of this highly complex religion.

There are three strata within the Vedic canon: the *Samhitas*, the *Brahmanas* and the *Upanishads*, succeeding each other in time and each expressing a different point of view. In the *Samhitas* we meet with a polytheism that is recognizably related to that of the Latins and Greeks, but more clearly so to the religion of India's neighbours the Iranians, who share many of the Indians' gods. The *Samhitas*, usually called simply the 'Veda', were originally three in number, and they are composed of hymns extolling one or other of the gods who make up the Vedic pantheon. These hymns were the accompaniment of the all-important sacrifice, the function of which was to mediate the good things of this world to man. The gods were real and powerful, and the sacrifice was the means by which contact was established between them and man to the mutual advantage of each. Through the sacrifice man gave gifts to the gods so that the gods might give man gifts in return — prosperity, abundance of sons, victory in war, and so on: 'for sustained by sacrifice the gods will give you the food of your desire. Whoso enjoys their gift yet gives nothing in return is a thief, no more nor less,' as the *Bhagavad Gita* says. By sacrifice too man enters into communion and fellowship with the gods: he partakes of their nature and thereby of their immortality.

In the second stratum of the Vedic canon, the *Brahmanas*, sacrifice becomes all-important. It is the reflection of the world-process itself, and its correct performance assures the regular working of the cosmic process. In a sense it *is* the cosmic process, and since the gods themselves are dependent on this process, the sacrifice now takes precedence over the gods who *must* therefore do what the sacrifice demands of them. The gods are thereby demoted and become little more than the servants of the sacrifice and of man who manipulates it. The stage is now set for the third stage in the Vedic development, the stage represented by the *Upanishads*.

In the course of time the supreme efficacy of the sacrifice came to be demoted: the supposedly infallible magic no longer seemed to work, for whatever the sacrifice might bring about, it could not satisfy Indian man's deepest desire, his desire to transcend the world of flux and to win for himself immortality. The old religion of the gods had already passed away in favour of an all-pervasive and all-powerful sacrifice. And now, in its turn, the sacrifice too must pass away. External religion has proved a broken reed: man must turn his glance within himself, for it is only there that he can discover the immortal principle which at the same time sustains the whole dharma of the universe.

This is the crucial turning-point in Indian religion. The ancient polytheistic heritage which the Indians had shared with their sister Indo-European peoples is now definitely put behind them, the gods surviving only as superior beings, differing from men in length of days and power but subject, like men, to the relentless wheel of birth and death, re-birth and re-death. The early Indians did not believe in reincarnation but believed that men lived only once, being rewarded at death by a life of bliss in heaven with the gods, if they had lived a good life, or by punishment in hell if they had done evil. This uncomplicated belief they had shared with the Iranians. But now all this was to change.

We can only assume that the original inhabitants of India, whom the invading Aryans conquered, held religious beliefs totally different from those of their conquerors; and, as is so often the case, the religion of the conquered utterly transformed or replaced the religion of the victors. So it must have been in India; for it seems clear that the Dravidians, as the native inhabitants are called, must have believed in reincarnation with a total belief; for, from the time of the *Upanishads* on this belief becomes ineradicably ingrained not only among what we may now call the orthodox Hindus, but also among the Buddhists and Jains who split away from them. So strong was this belief that it would be wrong to call it a dogma. It is much more than this; it is accepted as a self-evident fact of existence that no sensible person would query. And it is this that in part accounts for the totally new perspective of the *Upanishads*.

But in part only: for throughout the earlier Vedic literature a tendency had developed which tended to identify everything with an all-embracing Whole: the plurality of gods were seen to reflect one single reality and the sacrifice was thought of as identical with the world-process or at least as a reflection of it. One thing was generally agreed and that was that life in its endless repetitions was a burden too grievous to be borne and that the one thing needful was somehow or other to put a stop to it forever, to break away from it and so to become free. But how?

The Buddha who appeared in the 6th century BC claimed to have found the definitive answer. The world of flux in which we live, to which we return and from which, apparently, we cannot escape, is by its very impermanence synonymous with suffering. The cause of suffering is desire. Find a way of life which eliminates desire, and you will have won salvation. But salvation is not at all what Christians understand by that word, but rather total liberation from the shackles of earthly life which tie us remorselessly to impermanence and pain. The way of life which leads to the transcendence of earthly life as we know it the Buddha claimed to have found: he called it

The army of the Kauravas clashes with the forces commanded by Abhimanyu, the son of Arjuna; the heroic wars between the Kauravas and their cousins the Pandavas form the subject of the immense Indian epic, the *Mahabharata*

the Noble Eightfold Path, and it led one to a type of existence totally distinct from the life we know, a state called Nirvana, which means the extinction of desire and therewith of all becoming, of all coming-to-be and passing away. Nirvana is pure impassivity and impassibility, a timeless citadel to which the seeming pleasures and real sufferings that bedevil our life in time have no access. Between the two there is a gulf fixed and man's goal is to pass, by dint of much religious effort, to the stable and inviolate state of Nirvana.

This was the Buddhist solution but it was not the way of the *Upanishads*. The Buddhists were not interested in any Absolute on which the world of relativity might depend: they were interested only in escaping from the relative world altogether. The Hindus were more metaphysically minded; above all they wanted to know what was the changeless principle that held the changing world together and gave it coherence.

'What is it on which the worlds are woven, warp and woof?' 'Who is it, abiding in the earth, who is other than the earth, whom the earth does not know, whose body is the earth, who controls the earth from within?' These were the kind of questions they were asking. This unknown Something they called Brahman (which originally meant 'sacred utterance' or 'sacred action') or Atman (originally meaning perhaps 'breath' but very soon settling down in the meaning 'self'). Their answers were at first perhaps rather naive: it was food, or it was breath, mind, understanding, space or joy. None of these answers, however, seemed satisfactory; for when all was said and done, this eternal

Something could indeed by experienced, but it could not be described. 'This Self – what can you say of it but "No, no!" It is impalpable, for it cannot be grasped; indestructible, for it cannot be destroyed; free from attachment, for it is not attached to anything, not bound. It does not quaver, nor can it be hurt.' Whatever it is, it is the timeless and spaceless principle of eternal Being which indwells the heart of man and which envelops and exceeds the whole physical universe.

The account of Brahman in the *Upanishads* is a brave attempt to put into words an essentially mystical experience which transcends verbalization. It is what is sometimes called 'cosmic consciousness' which, in the words of a modern Canadian author who had the experience himself, shows 'the cosmos as entirely immaterial, entirely spiritual and entirely alive, it shows that death is an absurdity, that everyone and everything has eternal life; it shows that the universe is God and that God is the universe, and that no evil ever did or ever will enter into it.' This is absolutely true of the dominant thought-pattern of the *Upanishads*: the man who has realized himself as Brahman has passed beyond good and evil. Being the All and at one with the principle that keeps the All in being, he is invulnerable because he is outside time and cannot be affected by what takes place in time.

> Those who see all beings in the Self
> And the Self in all beings
> Will never shrink from it.
>
> When once one understands that in oneself
> The Self's become all beings,
> When once one's seen the unity

> What room is there for sorrow?
> What room for perplexity?

These passages are typical of the pantheism of the *Upanishads*. In the state they describe, all dualities, all seeming discords, disappear into a perfect harmony grounded in the One of which all so-called created things are only imperfect appearances. This is and remains the essence of Hinduism: what is divine and eternal in the heart of man is the same as the divine and eternal which pervades all Nature. If the essence of God is pure Being, then this is equally true of the essence of man. Since both are Brahman, it is possible to say that both are God. 'This finest essence – the whole universe has it as its Self: that is the Real: that is the Self: that *you* are.'

Here there is no attempt to separate the eternal from the temporal, the relative from the Absolute, for the 'All' – the universe – is at the same time the One, and by realizing the One Brahman in himself man realizes himself as God. This is the main tenor of the *Upanishads*, but since the Hindus were and are born metaphysicians, they were not prepared to let this pantheistic mystery be; and so in the later *Upanishads* two divergent trends develop, one 'monistic' and the other 'theistic'. The monistic tendency is represented by the *Mandukya Upanishad*, the 'theistic' by the *Svetasvatara*.

Following up earlier Upanishadic ideas, the *Mandukya* speaks of a 'fourth state' in which all is *absolutely* One, static and eternal. This is 'conscious of neither within nor without, nor of both together . . . one with whom there is no commerce, impalpable, devoid of distinguishing mark, unthinkable, indescribable, its essence the firm conviction of the oneness of itself, bringing all development to an end, tranquil and mild, devoid of duality, such do they deem this fourth to be. That is the Self: that is what should be known.'

This is the classical text on which the philosophy of absolute monism of Sankara and his school was to be based. It is a radical departure from the dominant Upanishadic position in which Brahman is seen as the One manifesting itself in the many: here the many are simply eliminated as being purely illusory. Only the One remains, and that is the *real* man and the divinity beyond God – God seen as creator and sustainer of the universe being, in the last analysis, as unreal as the universe he sustains. This absolute monism has dominated Indian philosophy from Sankara, who lived in the 9th century, up to the present time; but it has not dominated Indian religion, as indeed it could not, since it abolishes God as being ultimately unreal.

On the other hand, through the *Upanishads* a theistic movement was developing which tended to make a distinction between the 'highest' Brahman, now called the 'Lord', and the individual 'selves' who had realized themselves as immortal and eternal. The 'Lord' who is at the same time the highest 'Self' of all things is now seen to transcend and comprise not only the universe but also all individual selves. The totality of existence is compared to a wheel, and of this wheel the Lord is both the hub and the rim whereas individual 'selves' are the spokes that connect the two: they are inseparable from God but they are not identical with him.

Brahman in the *Upanishads* was the 'Real of the real', transcending and indwelling both the eternal and the temporal. In the *Svetasvatara Upanishad* this supreme position is assigned to a personal God – the ancient Vedic god Rudra, who is now also referred to as Shiva (or Siva), the 'Mild'.

In the *Upanishads* Brahman is usually thought of as an impersonal Absolute, but sometimes he appears as a personal God. In the *Svetasvatara Upanishad* he or it is identified with the Vedic god Rudra. This *Upanishad* and the *Bhagavad Gita* complement each other, for in both a highly personal God is raised to a supreme eminence, higher than Brahman, the principle of eternity itself. In the *Svetasvatara* the God is Rudra-Shiva, in the *Gita* it is Vishnu incarnate as Krishna. Neither god was prominent in the earlier literature, and it still remains rather a mystery how these two gods finally emerged as God with a capital G. Each has his own characteristic mythology, but each is for his own devotees the supreme Being, both Brahman as eternal Being and the God from whom the universe emanates, by whom it is sustained and into whom it dissolves. Though Brahman may be both the eternal and the temporal, the great God Shiva rules over both these aspects of it.

> In the imperishable, infinite city of Brahman
> Two things there are –
> Wisdom and unwisdom, hidden, established there:
> Perishable is unwisdom, but wisdom is immortal:
> Who over wisdom and unwisdom rules, he is Another.

The *Svetasvatara Upanishad* is important because it exalts the personal God Shiva over both the perishable and imperishable aspects of existence. The destiny of the individual self which is a 'part' of God in some sense, however, still remains isolation or entry into Brahman (that is, eternity), not union with the personal God. As yet there is no idea of a real mystical *union* in and through love which is the core of the experience of the Christian mystics. All that will change in the *Bhagavad Gita*.

In the *Bhagavad Gita* the supreme God is Vishnu, incarnate as Krishna. The *Gita*, unlike the *Upanishads*, does not form part of the Veda, and theoretically it does not enjoy canonical authority. Its supreme importance was, however, acknowledged from very early times and not only has it been commented on by all philosophers of note, it has also been and remains a popular classic, which the more abstruse *Upanishads* have not. The reason is that it introduces an entirely new element into Hinduism, the element of love. For Vishnu, in his incarnation as Krishna, is above all a God of love, and the ideal becomes intimate union and communion with the incarnate God, both in his timeless essence and in his ceaseless beneficent activity in the world.

C. M. Dixon

As in the *Svetasvatara Upanishad* God is Lord of the perishable and imperishable alike. The 'perishable' is identical with matter, and matter, though controlled by God, nevertheless does act as a barrier and a veil. Hence it is first of all necessary to divest oneself of matter and to realize one's own eternity, if one is to commune with God who is the source of both eternity and time. To 'see oneself in all beings and all beings in the self' is then only a preliminary to seeing all beings in God and God in all beings, and to realizing that this cosmic vision is to see everything with God's eyes, not with one's own. This makes the immortal timeless 'self' realize that he is not an independent unit but wholly dependent on God. This gives rise to a deep love of God and intimate communion with him, for the self or soul now realizes that this personal God, Vishnu-Krishna, is 'the base supporting Brahman – immortal Brahman which knows no change – supporting too the eternal law of righteousness and absolute beatitude'. By realizing one's own timeless immortality one becomes Brahman, and 'once a man has become Brahman, with self serene he neither grieves nor desires; the same to all contingent beings he gains the highest love and loyalty to me (Krishna is speaking). By love and loyalty to me he comes to know me as I really am, how great I am and who; and once he knows me as I am, he enters me forthwith.' And just as the liberated soul enters into God in an ecstasy of love, so does God love him in return.

This is the significance of the *Bhagavad Gita:* it exalts the personal God above Brahman seen as principle of eternity, and

it shows that God is a God of love, identical with you in so far as you have Being, but separate from you in so far as he is the object and subject of love. After the *Bhagavad Gita* popular Hinduism becomes predominantly a religion of love.

In the canon of the Veda, the gods Vishnu and Shiva (Rudra) played a very minor part. Just how and when they rose to supreme eminence we do not know, but each of them appears as the Supreme Deity by the time of the *Mahabharata* (? 300 BC – 300 AD). At first there is rivalry between them, but later, as is usual in Hinduism, they coalesce, each being regarded as the 'personal' form of the Absolute. Thus Hindus tend to be worshippers of Vishnu or Shiva.

As the supreme God, Vishnu becomes incarnate from time to time, 'for whenever the law of righteousness withers away and lawlessness arises, then do I generate myself on earth. For the protection of the good, for the destruction of evil-doers, for the setting up of the law of righteousness I come into being age after age.' In fact Vishnu is worshipped not so much in himself as in his two principal incarnations, Rama and Krishna. Rama is the hero of a great epic, the *Ramayana*, and he is the model of ethical and chivalrous man – obedient to his parents, devoted to his wife, affectionate to his family, impatient of evil, brave, chivalrous and courteous. He is God incarnate as morality.

The Krishna of popular religion is not the Krishna of the *Bhagavad Gita* but the Krishna who develops in the later literature, notably in the *Bhagavata Purana* dating from about the 9th century AD. Much more

Shiva and Vishnu each appears as supreme God in Hinduism *Left* Shiva with his wife Parvati and sons Ganesha and Karttikeya, the elephant-headed god and the six-faced god of war; Shiva and Ganesha are stringing together the skulls of the dead, for Shiva in one of his aspects presided over cremation grounds *Above* Vishnu and his wife Lakshmi riding Garuda; besides acting as the chariot of Vishnu, Garuda, half man and half bird, was king of the birds and the enemy of serpents *Opposite* Vishnu is worshipped particularly in his eighth reincarnation as the handsome, dark-skinned Krishna, who inspired passionate desires by the sweet music of his flute; the love of Krishna and the milk-girl Radha, celebrated in hundreds of poems and paintings, is sometimes taken to represent the union of the soul with its God

than Rama he is the object of the devotee's passionate love. Pre-eminently he is worshipped as a ravishingly handsome young cowherd who seduces the wives and daughters of the local cowherds with the sweet tones of his flute. He arouses passionate love in them and incites it the more in that from time to time he hides from them only to give himself more fully to them later. Sexual union is here used to represent the union of the soul with God.

This has sometimes shocked Protestant missionaries, but we find precisely the same phenomenon in the Christian mystical tradition, in which the Song of Songs, a clearly erotic poem which somehow or other found its way into the canon of the Old Testament, serves as a text on which to hang the most exalted conceptions of God's love for man. This does not, however, prevent the Krishna cult from degenerating at times

R. K. Singh

into pure emotionalism, a frenzied ecstasy for its own sake. Then the devotee imagines that he or she is Radha, Krishna's beloved concubine, and gives himself or herself up to him in total self-immolation; for in its relationship to the Deity the soul is always female, God the male.

Shiva is an altogether more austere deity. He is an extraordinarily complex figure, for he is both the model of all Yogins and ascetics and the ithyphallic God who delights in the worship of his erect phallus. As ascetic he is eternally at rest (the static 'Imperishable' of the *Upanishads*), 'isolated' and rapt in the contemplation of his own unfathomable Being, while in his phallic capacity he is eternally productive of forms. In him the infinite (the male principle) and the finite (the female) meet, and in him all the opposites are reconciled. In mythology Shiva has a consort variously called Uma, Parvati, Durga or Shakti (Sakti). In theology this consort, appearing in the form of Shakti, represents the divine creative power, very like the Christian Logos, that 'through which all things are made'. And so it is said that 'Shiva begets Shakti and Shakti gives birth to Shiva. Both in their happy union produce the worlds and souls. Still Shiva is ever chaste and the sweet-speeched Shakti remains ever a virgin. Only sages can comprehend this secret.' The soul in its relationship to Shiva through Shakti must again play the part of the female, abandoning itself wholly to the divine lover just as the individual 'self' is merged in the personal God in the *Bhagavad Gita*.

Sometimes, however, the divine Shakti is worshipped to the exclusion of Shiva; for in this scheme of things Shiva is forever immersed in Yogic trance and is therefore deaf to the prayers of men and unaware of their needs. Shakti, on the other hand, is creative force and destructive power, an intensely living Goddess and in her destructive aspect very much to be feared. In Bengal bloody sacrifices of goats are still offered to her in her terrible form of Durga, but this does not prevent her from being the object of intense and passionate devotion, for she is above all things the Mother and, despite all appearances to the contrary, really devoted to her children. The worship of Shakti in its so-called Tantric form (known as Tantrism) has always offended the puritanism of Anglo-Saxon missionaries; for her devotees of a later time would re-enact physically the ideal union of Shiva and Shakti, of the male and female principles in the One, by combining the strictest control of the senses with the sexual act itself. In this close embrace the cosmic unity is realized; the distinction between liberation and creativity, between eternity and time is transcended; and controlled sexuality is seen to reflect the Unity in diversity of cosmic existence.

Such practices, however, were aberrations from the norm of *Bhakti*, as the cult of loving devotion to a personal God was called. More typical are the hymns of the devotees of both Shiva and Vishnu in South India which not only breathe a spirit of total self-abnegation but also a sense of deep unworthiness that is truly reminiscent of Christianity at its best. Two examples must suffice: both are addressed to Shiva.

Thou gav'st thyself, thou gained'st me;
    Which did the better bargain drive?

Bliss found I in infinity;
    But what didst thou from me derive?
O Shiva, Perundurai's God,
    My mind thou tookest for thy shrine:
My very body's thine abode;
    What can I give thee, Lord, of mine?

Or again we find a sense of deep guilt and inadequacy in the face of the divine majesty:

Evil, all evil my race, evil my qualities all,
Great am I only in sin, evil is even my good.
Evil my innermost self, foolish, avoiding the pure:
Beast am I not, yet the ways of the beast I can never forsake.
I can exhort with strong words, telling men what they should hate,
Yet I can never give gifts, only to beg them I know.
Ah! wretched man that I am, whereunto came I to birth?

So far we have been dealing with Hinduism as a religion of mystical salvation; and this is right, for the goal of life is *moksha*, 'liberation' from the bonds of earthly life though not necessarily from earthly life itself. This 'liberation' can be experienced either as 'cosmic consciousness' or as a personal God in an act of pure love. In any case 'liberation' is the consummation of the four legitimate aspirations of man. The other three are, in ascending scale: *Kama*, 'pleasure', *Artha*, 'the acquisition of wealth' and *Dharma*, 'righteousness'.

In Hindiusm there is room for all – for the sexual adept described in the *Kama-sutras* as much as for the fiercest ascetic. There are endless discussions on the relative merit of *Kama, Artha* and *Dharma*; and although it is generally agreed that

British Museum

William MacQuitty

The lofty metaphysics of the Vedas has been overlaid by the worship of countless idols, though these may be explained as different manifestations of the divine unity *Opposite left* Jewelled image of Hanuman *Opposite right* Guardian deity from Nepal *Above* Surya the sun god, who with the weather god Indra and the fire god Agni formed a triad of ancient Vedic gods *Right* Many-armed image of Shiva, garlanded with flowers and riding a tiger; an extremely complex deity, Shiva was a god of both asceticism and sexuality

dharma, or the quest for righteousness, is the highest of the three, since it alone can create a condition of soul that fits it for 'liberation', the other two are nonetheless legitimate activities and should not be shunned by people who have a natural bent that draws them either to the satisfaction of their desires or to the amassing of a fortune. Indeed from the earliest times Hindu society was divided up into four main classes which roughly correspond to the four legitimate aspirations of man; hence caste. Thus, men are not born equal, and this for the obvious reason that one's class or caste in this life depends on one's *Karma* in previous lives – on the good and evil deeds that have piled up to one's profit or loss throughout millennia of successive incarnations.

What you have sown in other lives you reap in this one. This is the automatic way of the world and there is no injustice in it.

No doubt the four great classes existed in all their purity in ancient times but very soon a full caste-system developed, each caste being governed by its own rules, particularly as regards marriage and diet. In addition to the ideal four-class system,

which very soon ceased to have any relation to the social reality, the law-books laid down a fourfold way of life which members of the three 'twice-born' classes were theoretically supposed to follow. On attaining the age of reason and being invested with the sacred thread (a rite symbolizing his second birth), the now 'twice-born' youth was supposed to leave his home to study the scriptures with a Guru (spiritual director). To this Guru he owed absolute obedience and he had, moreover, to lead a life of complete chastity. Once he had become proficient in the scriptures he was to return home, take a wife, raise a family and, if possible, make a fortune. To his wife and family he would then be as a god and his wife in particular would owe him absolute obedience. The man was entitled to as many as four wives, but no woman could have more than one husband. There was no question of equality between the sexes.

This second stage of life is called that of a householder. It comes to an end when the householder 'sees that wrinkles are beginning to appear and that his hair is growing grey and when his sons are themselves fathers of sons'. At this point he should enter the third stage, that of a 'forest-dweller'. With or without his wife he retires to the forest where he lives on fruit and roots, wearing only a skin or tattered garment. He spends his time meditating on the *Upanishads* and chastising his body in preparation for the fourth and last stage, that of a fully-fledged Sannyasin (one who has finally renounced this world). He has now discharged his three 'debts'; he has absorbed the teaching of the Veda, has reared up sons to continue his line, and has

offered sacrifice according to his ability. Still in the world though not of it, he is now ready to put aside for ever the fetters that bind him to death and re-birth.

The four classes of society and the four stages of life were supposed to be the framework within which society functioned. In practice the classes split up into and absorbed a vast variety of castes and sub-castes, each forming a self-contained social unit. The religious ideal for all remained 'liberation' but for the masses this always remained an infinitely distant ideal, for 'among thousands of men but one, maybe, will strive for self-perfection, and even among these Yogins who have won perfection but one, maybe, will come to know God as he really is.' This is not for the common run of men, who must pile up good Karma or 'merit' by the strict performance of their caste-duty, by performing the daily domestic rites, by frequenting the local temple, by pilgrimage to holy places, by being lavish in their gifts to Brahmins. Then at the end of countless incarnations they will have acquired sufficient merit to be reborn in the 'family of men well advanced in Yoga, possessed of insight.' But even so 'such a birth as this on earth is exceedingly hard to obtain.'

The rise of the *bhakti* sects added a new dimension to Hindu spirituality but it did not threaten in any way the rigid social structure based on caste. Successive Moslem invasions from the 7th century on were quite another matter. Islam is of its nature a proselytizing religion, and with the conversion of the Central Asian Turks it became aggressively so. Conversions were effected *en masse* both by force and, more

often, by consent, for conversion could only mean social improvement and emancipation for the lower castes and above all for the outcastes who were regarded as little better than animals. Hinduism's reaction to this stranger in its midst was to turn in upon itself; for Hinduism has always been mystical to its core, since it has always taught that by Yogic techniques man can realize here and now the eternal and divine within himself. So immanent is the Deity that to claim to be God is quite natural since, in some sense or other, everything is God. Hence the utterly transcendent Allah of Moslem orthodoxy held out no appeal for the Hindu. On the whole the new Moslem rulers did not interfere with his customs nor were they given to righteous indignation.

With the advent of the British and the Protestant missionaries who came in their wake things were very different. The missionaries were nothing if not stern moralists. To them the burning of widows, child marriages, and the treatment of the outcastes were an intolerable scandal, and they did not mince their words. However tactless they may have been, they did at least succeed in arousing a social consciousness among the Hindus which had been noticeably lacking before. In the first flush of their optimism the missionaries had hoped that the conversion of India might be in sight. They reckoned without the Hindus' endless capacity to adapt and absorb alien ideas. Conversions were few, largely because conversion meant a complete break with the family and the caste into which the family was compactly built, and so with the whole fabric of Hindu society.

Christianity entered India as the religion of a conquering and technically vastly superior race. The missionaries were well aware of this and regarded Hinduism as a hideous hotch-potch of idolatry and superstition, making no effort to penetrate to its inner core, let alone to assess its spiritual value. Among the educated Hindus some were indeed converted to Christianity. Others who realized that the strength of the British· lay in their superior technocracy and perhaps also in the democratic principles they practised at home, not in their Christianity, abandoned religion altogether, while yet others sought to absorb the Christian ethic as preached in the Sermon on the Mount into Hinduism itself.

The various reformist Hindu sects of the 19th century and after oscillated between a policy of absorption and of reaction. The first of them, the Brahmo Samaj founded by Ram Mohan Roy, was as iconoclastic as its Protestant mentors. It turned its back on all the specifically Hindu rites and modelled its ritual on Protestant services. Though it had a certain success among the elite, it did not succeed in striking any deep roots and was in any case riddled with schism from the beginning.

Quite different was Dayananda's Arya Samaj; for while being quite as inimical to the corruptions of the Hinduism of its day, it did not look to Christianity for inspiration but to the most ancient stratum of the Veda as interpreted by Dayananda himself. With the Arya Samaj, Hinduism for the first time took the offensive against the imported creeds, Islam and Christianity. Its aim was both to reconvert those who had embraced Christianity and Islam, and to integrate the untouchables into its own form of Hinduism if not into orthodoxy itself.

Of more importance was the movement started by Ramakrishna Paramahamsa, and continued by Swami Vivekananda. The purely religious impetus was supplied by the first, the drive and organizing ability by the second. Ramakrishna was a charismatic personality and a visionary. He studied under every kind of Guru and even joined in the religious life of the Moslems and Christians. He continually had visions of the Divine Mother, to whom he remained passionately devoted; or again, imagining himself to be Radha, he would experience the presence of Krishna too. When among Moslem mystics he had a vision of Mohammed and study of the Christian Gospels duly induced a vision of Christ. The great variety of his religious experiences convinced him that all religions must be true, all being but different paths leading to the one goal which is to realize the absolute oneness of all things in the One Brahman. Hence, after he had himself realized his own oneness with Brahman, his aim was to induce this state in others too. He was not interested in good works as such. 'By these philanthropic activities,' he said, 'you are really doing good to yourself. If you can do them disinterestedly, your mind will become pure and you will develop love of God. As soon as you have that love you will realize him.'

Ramakrishna above all had the gift of spontaneity: he had no talent for organization nor did he see himself as the head of a movement. Vivekananda, whom he made his spiritual heir, not only had a most incisive personality but had also great administrative gifts. At the first session of the World Parliament of Religions at Chicago in 1893 he spoke of himself as belonging to the 'most ancient order of monks in the world' and of his own religion as the 'mother of religions'. Although he said, 'We accept all religions as true,' and although he condemned proselytism of any kind, this did not prevent him from founding Ramakrishna centres in America and Europe, many of which have been extremely successful; for it is the Ramakrishna Mission which has spread the 'gospel' of Hindu monism ('all things are one') in the West and which has made such distinguished converts as Aldous Huxley, Gerald Heard and Christopher Isherwood.

In the West the Ramakrishna Mission has concentrated on disseminating its own inward spirituality, thereby challenging conventional Christianity on its home ground. In India itself, however, it has concentrated on doing in a Hindu spirit what the Christian missions had done before to the shame of Hindu orthodoxy: it has sought to clothe the naked, feed the poor and instruct the ignorant. Both in India and the West it is still very much alive.

The Ramakrishna mission gave back to Hinduism that confidence which in its first confrontation with Christianity it had so grievously lost. There were to follow many other individual propagandists of this new form of Hinduism, men like Rabindranath Tagore, Sri Aurobindo and India's distinguished ex-president Sir Sarvepalli Radhakrishnan, but without any doubt the greatest and the most influential of them all was Mahatma Gandhi.

Seeing himself always as an orthodox Hindu (for none exceeded him in his reverence for the cow) Gandhi nonetheless attacked orthodoxy in some of its most firmly entrenched positions. Unlike Tagore and Radhakrishnan he was not primarily interested in Hindu mysticism, for intellectually he was quite as dependent on the Sermon on the Mount and on Tolstoy as he was on his own beloved *Bhagavad Gita*. Rather, he was interested in putting into practice what he conceived to be the true Hindu dharma here on earth. If his own interpretation of the dharma conflicted with Scripture so much the worse for Scripture. 'My belief,' he said, 'in the Hindu Scriptures does not require me to accept every word

Above left Rabindranath Tagore, poet author and mystic, and winner of the Nobel prize for literature in 1913, helped to make Indian thought better known in the West **Above right** Krishnamurti was hailed as a new messiah by Annie Besant; occult movements like the Theosophical Society found much that was congenial in Indian mysticism **Opposite** Eroticism has an accepted place in Hindu religion and many temples contain a lingam, or phallic symbol, or are covered with frankly erotic carvings such as these

and every verse as divinely inspired . . . I decline to be bound by any interpretation however learned it may be, if it is repugnant to reason and common sense.' His God is not the impersonal Brahman of the philosophers. God, rather, 'is Truth and Love; God is ethics and morality; God is fearlessness; God is the source of Light and Life, and yet he is above and beyond all these. God is conscience.' God is, in fact, Gandhi's own Inner Light, and the weapons he will choose against evil will therefore be truthfulness, non-violence, courtesy and love. The supreme evil in Hinduism was, he thought, untouchability, and against this he

directed all his moral force; and so great was his prestige that for the first time in history the orthodox were forced to open their temples to these 'people of God', as Gandhi in his deep compassion named them.

Gandhi saw himself as a Sannyasin and lived as one; but it was not the world that he renounced, but the evil that is endemic in the world – desire, anger, avarice and sloth – and it was his fervent desire that India should renounce them too, so that she might be liberated not only from the British but also from all the petty egoism that is inseparable from fallen man. He wished to be all things to all men and did not hesitate

to absorb into his own religion what he considered to be best in Christianity and Islam for, like Ramakrishna, he believed that all religions are true. The resulting fusion he offered back to the Indian people as their true dharma, changed it is true, but the eternal dharma still.

If Hinduism in all its manifold forms has a single message it is this: since all things are permeated by the Divine, renounce all that prevents you seeing this, renounce all egoism and all sense of separateness, so that you may return to what you have renounced but with a benevolent detachment.

THE PROBLEM OF EVIL

Dualism

In the history of religions, dualism means the belief that there is a radical opposition between two great principles which underlie the existence of what, in one way or another, is found in the world. In Zoroastrianism, for example, the two opposing principles are Ohrmazd, the creator and champion of the good, and Ahriman, the champion of evil. Ahriman and his army of evil beings harass the good creation of Ohrmazd, into which they have penetrated from outside, until at the end, far in the future, they are expelled and deprived of all their destructive power.

In Zoroastrianism, the theory of opposite principles takes various different forms. In the *Gathas* or 'Songs' of Zoroaster there is the opposition between the beings belonging to the good god's creation and the demonic beings who try to annihilate it. The *daivas* or demons joined the side of evil by their own choice. But an earlier choice had been made by the two 'spirits', the Holy Spirit and the Evil Spirit. They are described as twin brothers, which can be interpreted as indicating the symmetry between them. They are equal and contrary, the inspiring agencies and at the same time the opposite terms of the 'choice' to which all reasonable beings are committed.

Zoroastrianism soon became a clearly dualistic system in which Ohrmazd was opposed directly and from all eternity to Ahriman. Some non-Iranian sources testify to the existence in Iran of a myth recounting how Zurvan (Time or Destiny) gave birth to the twins Ohrmazd and Ahriman. This seems to have been an attempt to 'bridge' the dualism of Ohrmazd and Ahriman, with Zurvan as the impersonal principle of Time or Time-Fate, the sphere in which the actual agencies of the cosmic drama exist and operate. But the myth was finally rejected by the Zoroastrians themselves.

Another example is the 'anticosmic' dualism of Gnostic teachers and sects, like Valen-tinus, Basilides, the Manicheans and the Mandeans (or much later the Bogomils and Cathars). Here, this world itself is evil, made of a dark and essentially negative substance, and created not by the supreme God but by an inferior supernatural power, the Demiurge. Man's body and the lower level of his soul were created by the Demiurge but contain, imprisoned in them, the divine spark, the spirit which comes from God and which can only be freed from its prison by the *gnosis*, the liberating knowledge of God.

In the doctrine of some Gnostics, including Valentinus (2nd century AD), evil manifests itself only at a late stage in the creation of the universe. There is a succession of emanations from the divine world. The last of these is Sophia (Wisdom) and her 'fall' brings matter into existence. The dualism of the Manicheans and the Iranian Gnostics was more radical, for Light and Darkness were in opposition from all eternity.

According to the Bogomils in the Balkans, the evil principle, Satanael, who corresponds to the Demiurge of the Gnostics, derived from God but created an earth and a heaven for himself. He also created the body of man, which he treacherously caused to be animated by a spirit, sent by God.

A dualism partially analogous to that of the Bogomils can be found in a number of legends from eastern Europe; among some sects of western Asia, including the Yezidi of Iraq, the 'worshippers of the Devil' who venerate the Angel Peacock, a demiurge who is a rival of God but is later reconciled with him satisfactorily; and among a number of peoples of central and north-western Asia, including the Tartars and eastern Finns. An example is the story of Erlik, a rival who co-operates with the Supreme Being in the work of creation: he digs up for him a particle of earth from the bottom of the primordial sea and tries, with little success, to create a heaven of his own.

These stories imply a feeling of some

Michael Holford

Above Over the sacred tiger hang the interlocked symbols of Yin and Yang, encircled by eight trigrams *Opposite* According to Hindu belief Vena, the wicked king of the world, dies as punishment for his haughtiness. From his lifeless body spring two spirits, a dark evil one who goes off to lurk in the desert, and the resplendent Prithu, who is the saviour of men

inadequacy on the part of the Creator. Generally, the adversary is conquered in the end but the nature of his malignant deeds brings them into the fold of dualism proper. He breathes his own bad spirit into man or he soils man's person, and this is not because of any fault on man's part, especially as the intrusion of evil is described as occurring during the creation of man.

Something very similar occurs in a number of primitive mythologies from northeastern Asia and from North America, where we have the tales of Coyote, a typical trickster-demiurge who is an unhappy but not ineffective competitor of the Creator during the work of creation. Stories detected among the Dogon in Mali imply that reality has resulted from the opposing actions of a Creator and a competitor, the Pale Fox. The wide diffusion of dualistic myths warns us against always attributing dualism to Iranian or Manichean or Bogomil influence.

Another strand of dualism appears in the Orphics, in Empedocles and other early Greek philosophers, and in Plato. The world is thought to consist of two principles, which are seen as complementary to each other but usually unequal in value. In Plato there is the dualism of Matter on the one hand and the Ideas (with the supreme one, the Idea of Good) on the other. In Empe-

docles there is the dualism of the two opposite principles of Love and Discord, which prevail in turn in the universe. In Pythagorean doctrine there is the dualism of the Monad (Unity, perfection, eternity, infinity) and the Dyad (Duality, imperfection, limitation in time and space).

Gnostic dualism has something in common with this type of speculation, especially in the variety of Gnosticism which is called 'ophitism', in which the serpent (*ophis* in Greek) symbolizes the descent of the superior spiritual element (*pneuma*, literally 'breath') into the inferior world of matter, and its subsequent ascent again, or reintegration into the divine, heavenly realm. This concept of descent and ascent is related not only to the theory of the salvation of the human spirit, escaping from its imprisonment in this world, but also to the nature and creation of the universe. The spiritual

element is conceived of as animating matter and giving it life, form and movement, even if only precariously and provisionally.

The term dualistic can also be applied to certain Indian doctrines, found in the *Upanishads* and the Vedanta tradition, which are 'monistic' in that they reduce all that exists, in its manifestations in the realm of multiplicity and appearance, to a first principle, the ultimate ground and substance of the universe (*Atman, Brahman, Purusha*), which is immanent (pervading all things in this world) but also transcendent (surpassing, going beyond them). But these Indian systems are also dualistic, in the sense that they oppose the visible and illusory world with its limited and imperfect gods to the transcendent substance of Atman and Brahman.

Or there is the Chinese theory of Yin and Yang, the two ultimate principles of the universe, whose opposites – day and night, male and female, celestial and terrestrial, and the rest – underlie all manifestations of being. Again, in Taoist doctrine, these two principles are transcended by one first principle, the Tao itself, which is inexpressible, not reducible to a mere expedient to 'bridge' the Yin-Yang couple.

Sometimes the opposition between the two principles of a dualist system seems to reach into the very interior of Godhead, or whatever is substituted for it, as in some Iranian or heretical Islamic speculations. Peculiar developments of classical dualism, with its tendency to split soul or society or reality into opposing segments, can be detected in some forms of modern existentialism, of Freudian psychoanalysis and of Marxism.

But it is important to distinguish between dualism in the true sense of the term and so-called 'psychological' and 'ethical' dualism. A duality of ethical and psychological possibilities, the good ones and the bad, is to be found in every form of human thinking and behaviour. For example, it would be misleading to assimilate to true dualism the Jewish concept of the two 'spirits' which act in the soul of man, the good inclination and the evil inclination. For these do not detract from the biblical idea of a supreme Creator and Lord of the universe. The Dead Sea Scrolls expressly state that these two spirits were appointed by God to give man a choice.

Similarly, the Jewish and Christian concepts of Satan are not truly dualist, for Satan is a creature of God and creates nothing himself. Nor are the Jewish and the somewhat different Christian ideas of original sin, which are very different from the dualist Orphic, Platonic and Gnostic notion.

Fra Angelico's painting of the *Last Judgement*; the souls of the righteous, on God's right, go to heaven and the souls of the wicked, on his left, are subjected to the tortures of hell. Christian concepts of God and Satan, of good and evil, are not truly dualist for God remains the supreme Creator and Lord; Satan is a creature of God and creates nothing

Zoroastrianism

Zoroastrianism is the name that is given to the religion founded by the Iranian prophet Zoroaster, probably in the 6th–7th centuries BC. Modern scholarship tends to accept the traditional date of the prophet, '258 years before Alexander'. For the Iranians, 'before Alexander' could only mean the final extinction of the First Persian Empire at the sack of Persepolis by Alexander the Great in 330 BC. Hence Zoroaster's 'date' would be 588 BC. But what period in his life would this refer to? It might refer to his birth, to his first revelation at the age of 30, to his conversion of the local king Vishtaspa at

the age of 40, or to his death at the age of 77. Whichever date we accept, Zoroaster's life will have spanned the 7th and 6th centuries BC. This, however, like so much in Zoroastrian studies, cannot be regarded as at all certain. So too with the place in which he operated. The later tradition placed him in western Iran, in what is today Azerbaijan; but this is almost certainly not true, for the internal evidence – the dialect and the place names mentioned in the early Zoroastrian texts – points to the east, the country near the Oxus River, now in Soviet Central Asia. Modern scholarship would have it that

Zoroaster's field of activity was in ancient Chorasmia, corresponding roughly to what is today the Turkmen Republic of the Soviet Union. This again is highly probable but not certain.

Above Symbol of Ahura Mazdah **Opposite** Head of a Persian king: in the Teheran Museum: like other religions, Zoroastrianism developed and changed, and in its strictly dualist form as the official state religion of the Sassanian kings from the 3rd century BC to the 7th century AD, its doctrine of the great opposing principles in the universe influenced Judaism, Christianity and Islam

It must be emphasized at the outset that in practically every aspect of Zoroastrian studies uncertainty prevails, and this for a variety of reasons. The principal reason is that our main sources do not agree. The sacred text, the *Avesta*, itself only a fraction of the original scripture and handed down orally for at least 1000 years, is (as is the way of sacred scriptures) not consistent with itself, nor is it consistent with the contemporary sources – the inscriptions of the Achaemenian kings and the Greek accounts of Iranian religion from Herodotus onwards. The same is true of the second period of Zoroastrian supremacy during the Second Persian Empire, the so-called Sassanian Empire, which lasted from 226–651 AD. It cannot be claimed, then, that all that will be said in this brief survey is authoritative; for Zoroastrian scholars have disagreed with a vehemence of acerbity rare even among academics.

Zoroaster, or Zarathustra, as he is called in the *Avesta*, was born some time in the 7th century BC, fled from his native land because he preached a doctrine which his fellow-countrymen refused to accept, and found asylum with a certain King Vishtaspa in eastern Iran who finally accepted his teaching. That his teaching was at variance with the traditional religion is clear. Just what that earlier religion was is less clear. One thing is certain, however: that the Aryans, the common ancestors of the 'Aryan' invaders of India (who were responsible for the earliest sacred book of the Hindus, the *Veda*) and the Iranians who inhabited the Iranian plateau, had a common religion which was polytheistic in form. The original Aryan pantheon was, it seems, divided into two distinct groups of deities, the *asuras* (or *ahuras*) on the one hand and the *daivas* on the other. The asuras seem to have been remote gods who dwelt in the sky, while the daivas were nearer to men and more intimately associated with them. From the beginning there seems to have been tension between the two groups. In India the asuras, because they were held to possess magic powers which they were prone to use against men, finished up by becoming demons. In Iran precisely the opposite happened. The ahuras (the Iranian form of the Indian asuras) retained their divine status whereas the daivas were reduced to the status of demons. This probably happened before the appearance of Zoroaster, as the terms *ahuro-tkaesha* ('the religion of the ahuras') and *daevo-data* ('the law of the daivas') would seem to show. Already, it would appear, the ahuras were considered to be beneficent powers, the daivas maleficent.

Zoroastrianism has been described both as an ethical monotheism and as a classical form of dualism, which implies evil. How can one one religion be described in two such contradictory ways? The answer is that Zoroastrianism, like any other religion, developed and changed, now emphasizing one aspect of the prophet's message, now another. In any case the Zoroastrianism of the prophet himself was very different from the Zoroastrianism which became prevalent in the later stages of the First (Achaemenian) Persian Empire (550–330 BC), and this again differed considerably from the official Zoroastrianism of the Second (Sassanian) Empire (226–651 AD). The first could be called monotheism, the second modified monotheism, and the third dualism.

Zoroaster was born into a priestly family but he saw himself as a prophet, the bringer of a new message from a god called Ahura Mazdah, the 'Wise Lord', who revealed himself as the true God. This message is preserved in the oldest part of the *Avesta*, the *Gathas* or 'Songs' of Zoroaster himself. Zoroaster was a prophet every bit as much as were the Hebrew prophets who prophesied at much the same time. He was convinced that he was inspired by God and that he was charged with a message from him to man. He claimed to 'see' him and to hear his voice. Indeed, his relationship is so close that he can speak of it as one of 'friend to friend'.

The essence of Zoroaster's message is that God is One, holy, righteous, the Creator of all things, both material and spiritual, through his Holy Spirit, the living and the giver of life. He is good because he is productive and gives increase. His 'oneness', however, is a unity in diversity, for he manifests himself under various aspects: the Holy Spirit, as and through whom God creates; the Good Mind, as and through which he inspires the prophet and sanctifies man; Truth, Righteousness, or Cosmic Order (*Asha*), as and through which he shows man how to conform himself to the cosmos in accordance with righteousness; Sovereignty, as and through which he rules creation; Wholeness, which is the plenitude of his being; and Immortality, as and through which he will annihilate death.

These aspects of the Wise Lord were later to be called the 'Bounteous Immortals', and in the later periods of Zoroastrianism were to be associated with various material elements: they appear as God's creatures and are thus assimilated to the archangels of other traditions. Two of them demand special notice: Truth and the Holy Spirit. Like the other Bounteous Immortals these have acknowledged opposites or 'adversaries' which conspire to thwart and restrict them.

Ahura Mazdah, as Supreme Deity, has no opposite but, in so far as he is associated with Truth and the Holy Spirit, he is indirectly at variance with the 'Lie' and the 'Destructive Spirit', the later Ahriman, just as the Hebrew God is opposed to Satan in the later Judaeo-Christian scriptures. Hence it is not wholly illogical to describe the Zoroastrianism of the prophet himself as both a 'monotheism' and a 'dualism'; and in so far as Ahura Mazdah reveals himself under different aspects, it is not wholly absurd to describe it as a modified 'polytheism'.

In the *Gathas* the basic dualism is between Truth and the Lie — Asha and Druj — which can also mean the established cosmic order and what disrupts it. This dualism remains throughout all phases of Zoroastrianism. The Lie also means the disruption of the established political order (Darius described the rebels against his authority as 'liars'), and the disruption of the truthfully spoken word, or what we normally understand by a lie. As God, Ahura Mazdah is beyond both Truth and the Lie, but as and through Truth he is inexorably opposed to its opposite, which is also the spirit of disruption.

Similarly in the case of the Holy Spirit. The Holy Spirit is irreconcilably opposed to the Destructive Spirit or Ahriman: and this opposition was later to be regarded as characteristic of Zoroastrian dualism. Of these two Spirits it is written:

In the beginning those two Spirits who are the well-endowed(?) twins were known as the one good and the other evil in thought, word and deed. . . And when these Spirits met they established in the beginning life and death that in the end the followers of the Lie should meet with the worst existence, but the followers of Truth with the Best Mind. Of these two Spirits he who was of the Lie chose to do the worst things; but the most Holy Spirit, clothed in rugged heaven, (chose) Truth as did (all) who sought with zeal to do the pleasure of the Wise Lord by (doing) good works.

Opposite **Ruins of a fire temple at Naqsh-i-Rustam, near Persepolis: fire was called the 'son' of Ahura Mazdah, and the rite of sacrificing the plant haoma centred round the sacred fire** *Right* **The Parsees, the Indian Zoroastrians, chose high places as the most suitable sites for their mortuary towers, since they do not allow any corpse to polute the earth. For the same reason they do not burn corpses either**

Although the two Spirits choose to do good and evil, the Holy Spirit can nevertheless say to 'him who is Evil: "Neither our thoughts, nor our teachings, nor our wills, nor our choices, nor our words, nor our deeds, nor our consciences, nor yet our souls agree."'

Ahura Mazdah, the Wise Lord, is himself described as being the 'father' of the Holy Spirit (as he is of several other Bounteous Immortals), but he is also in a sense identical with him. As and through the Holy Spirit, then, he is as irreconcilably opposed to the Evil or Destructive Spirit, the author of death, as he is to the Lie, for he is both Life and Truth. But if he is the father of the Holy Spirit, and the Holy Spirit is the Destructive Spirit's twin, does it not follow that he is the father of the Destructive Spirit too? In the later literature, the Wise Lord is roundly identified with the Holy Spirit, and once this has happened Zoroastrianism becomes a classically dualist religion.

A minority, however, remembering that the two Spirits had been spoken of as twins insisted that they have a common father.

Heaven and hell are states rather than places — the best existence and the worst existence or, more graphically, the House of the Good Mind and the House of the Worst Mind, the House of Song and the House of the Lie. In the one there is 'ease and benefit', in the other discomfort and

torment, 'a long age of darkness, foul food, and cries of woe'.

In addition there is a final reckoning 'at the last turning-point of existence', when there will be a Last Judgement in the form of an ordeal by fire and molten metal which will allot to the righteous and the unrighteous their final destiny of weal or woe. The Last Judgement then, merely confirms the individual judgement at death: salvation and damnation are fixed for all eternity. This 'black and white' doctrine was to enter Judaism and, through Judaism, Christianity and Islam. The Zoroastrians, however, were later to modify it themselves, for in the later texts the Last Judgement (which seems unnecessary anyhow) becomes not a judgement at all but a purgation by molten metal in which the wicked are finally purged of their sins and the just suffer nothing since the molten metal has no terrors for them: they experience it as if it were warm milk.

These, then, are the basic doctrines preached by the prophet Zoroaster himself: there is one supreme God, Creator of all things, spiritual and material; aside from him there are two irreconcilable principles — Truth and the Lie, the Holy Spirit and the Destructive Spirit. Alongside these there are 'aspects' of God and also, though less markedly, 'aspects' of the Lie and the Destructive Spirit. Man must choose between the two, and in

accordance with his choice he will either be blessed with eternal bliss or chastized with everlasting torment. By 'good' is meant Truth, the proper ordering of things, life, and prosperity: by evil, the Lie, disorder, death, and misery. The dualism is not one of spirit and matter but one of spirit and spirit, matter being in itself good because created by God, though later corrupted by the Devil.

From the Achaemenian inscriptions, from proper names like Mithridates, from rock reliefs of much later date, and from the extraordinary diffusion of the cult of Mithras throughout almost the whole of the Roman Empire shortly after the rise of Christianity, it is clear that the most important of these ancient deities was Mithra — like Ahura Mazdah himself originally a god of the sky and later identified with the sun.

As with everything connected with Zoroastrianism, there has been furious debate as to whether or not the Achaemenid kings were Zoroastrians. About the religion of the earliest of them, Cyrus and Cambyses, there is no evidence, but about Darius the Great (521–485 BC) there is plenty.

With the collapse of the Achaemenian Empire, Zoroastrianism disappears as an organized religion until it becomes once more the state religion of the Second (Sassanian) Empire from 226 to 651 AD. To judge from rock reliefs during this period, it would appear that Mithra and Anahita still enjoyed considerable favour both with the royal house and among the people. It was, however, the policy of the new dynasty to seek to establish religious conformity throughout the empire. Now for the first time one can speak of religious orthodoxy; and this, to judge from the Pahlavi books which draw their material from this period, was a rigid dualism in which the Bounteous Immortals and the ancient gods resuscitated in the late Achaemenian period were reduced to the status of angels. The scene was now dominated by two eternal principles, Ohrmazd (Ahura Mazdah) and Ahriman, Ohrmazd being identified with all goodness and light and dwelling in the Endless Light above, Ahriman being equated with all evil and darkness and dwelling in the Endless Darkness below. The two kingdoms are totally separate and independent, but the time comes when Ahriman becomes conscious of the light of Ohrmazd, envies it, attacks it, and invades the material world which Ohrmazd had created as a bulwark against him. For 3000 years the issue of the battle is in doubt, but in the last 3000 years of the existence of this world the power of evil is slowly but relentlessly ground down until the Saviour, the Saoshyans, appears to make all things new. The souls of men, whether they be in heaven or in hell, are reunited with their bodies and are purged in a sea of molten metal. When this is done, Ahriman is expelled back into his native darkness and rendered unconscious for ever. Then the whole creation enjoys eternal bliss in the presence of Ohrmazd, the Lord.

This dualist orthodoxy, however, was questioned by a theological deviation called 'Zurvanism' which subordinated both Ohrmazd and Ahriman to a higher principle, Infinite Time or Zurvan. However, no matter what the main theological trend may have been at the time, Sassanian Zoroastrianism was so wedded to the Sassanian state that, when the latter was overthrown by the forces of the new religion, Islam, which had arisen in the Arabian desert in the 7th century AD, the Zoroastrian Church, no longer being the 'established' Church, rapidly and irreversibly declined. Iran, once the centre of two great empires of which Zoroastrianism had been the official religion, now became a Moslem country; and the Zoroastrian community, having steadily lost ground throughout the centuries, has now been reduced to a mere 10,000 souls living mainly in Yazd and Kerman in the southeast, while another 100,000 or so, descendants of refugees from persecution, survive as the rich and enlightened community of the Parsees in Bombay and other Indian cities. Such has been the fate of a religion that once ruled proudly throughout the Iranian lands.

Manicheans

Manicheism was essentially a gnostic, dualistic religion, founded by a Babylonian prince of Persian origin named Mani, who was born in 216 AD. According to the *Fihrist* of the Arabic author An Nadim, when Mani was 12 years old God sent an angel called at-Taum (twin) to him, ordering him to leave the ascetic sect to which his father belonged. When Mani was 24, this same angel appeared to him and told him that now the time had come to appear in public and proclaim his own doctrine. From Manichean sources, partly written by Mani himself, we hear more about this twin or familiar. He is said to accompany Mani and protect him. Even at the hour of death, Mani was gazing at this familiar, the one who waited for him always and opened before him the gate unto the height.

So Manicheism is based upon a special revelation, a personal experience of the founder. The 'higher Self' of Mani revealed himself to him, inspired him with the doctrine he had to proclaim to the world, protected him during his missionary journeys and awaited him at his death to bring him to the eternal realm of Light. Sometimes this Self is described in Christian terms: then it is designated Christ or the Holy Spirit. This is the case in Western sources, especially in the Coptic Psalms discovered at Medinet-Madi in Egypt, in 1931. The problem is whether we should interpret the experience of Mani in a Christian or in an Iranian perspective (as is supposed by G. Widengren and L. J. R. Ort).

The concept that man has a spiritual double or twin appears in the Greek author Lucian's *Dialogues of the Dead* (2nd century AD); according to him the 'shadow' *(eidolon)* of Heracles was his exact image and counterpart, his twin. In other sources it is stated that the 'daimon' or attendant spirit of a man is his image. This influenced the Jewish religion of the time, according to which the guardian angel was the *iqonin*, the image of the man to whom he belonged.

Through Judaism the concept was integrated into Christianity, where we find it at a very early date, allegedly already in the community of Jerusalem (Acts 12.15). From there it seems to have spread in many directions, especially to the Syriac Christianity of Edessa in Mesopotamia. In the *Gospel of Thomas,* written there about 140 AD, the guardian angel is called ikon, image, the eternal counterpart of man. In the *Song of the Pearl*, contained in the *Acts of Thomas,* also originating from Edessa (c 225 AD), the encounter with the Self is described as the encounter with the eternal Garment, which is the mirror of its owner: 'for we were two in distinction, and yet again one in one likeness.' In the same *Acts of Thomas* the apostle Thomas is called the twin of Christ.

Mani seems to have known Christianity mainly in its Syriac form. He knew the *Gospel of Thomas* and he may very well have known the *Acts of Thomas*. From Syriac Christianity, which was strongly encratitic (prohibiting marriage, wine and meat) he may have taken his severe asceticism, according to which the fall of Adam was his intercourse with Eve, and marriage as such is sinful. So Mani's religious experience, the revelation of the twin, which is the Holy Spirit, can be understood in a Christian perspective.

Christianity in Edessa, however, was not exclusively encratitic. Before the sect of Encratites, Jewish Christianity had come to the city, possibly from Jerusalem via the Ebionites. These Jewish Christians called themselves Nazorees or Nazarenes, as the Syrian Christians did later on. The Manichean *Kephalaia* preserves a debate of Mani with a Nazoree about the problem of whether God, as judge, is not necessarily bound to use evil when he punishes. The implication seems to be that, according to this Nazoree, God was the origin of both good and evil.

Mani's abhorrence of the doctrine that God creates evil was one of the sources, and possibly the main source, of his absolute dualism. According to Mani, evil was Satan

Opposite Born during the 7th century BC, Zoroaster saw himself as a prophet, the bringer of a new message from a god called Ahura Mazdah, the 'Wise Lord', who was the true God: *Zoroaster in his study*, a 15th century Flemish miniature *Right* A miniature which illustrates an incident in the life of Mani, a Babylonian prince of Persian origin and the founder of Manicheism. The glass cover over a water-tank was continually being broken by the women who came to draw water, so Mani drew attention to the glass by painting a picture of a dead dog on it

or Matter, not a god, as in Persian religion as Ahriman. This did not prevent Mani from taking over certain views of the Jewish Christians. During his trial, which ended with his death, he proclaimed solemnly that he had received his doctrine from God through the intermediary of an angel. So according to him, his twin and familiar, the Paraclete ('Counsellor') or Holy Spirit, was an angel. This of course is in disagreement with orthodox Christianity, but can be found in the very archaic *Ascension of Isaiah*. Similarly, in the *Manual of Discipline*, one of the Dead Sea Scrolls, the Angel of Light (possibly Michael) is called Holy Spirit and Spirit of Truth. On the other hand, Mani called Christ 'the right hand': this he must have taken from Jewish Christians, who used the same terminology. Of course, Mani took the designation Paraclete from St John's gospel (14.16) but the fact that he considers this Paraclete to be an angel seems to hint at familiarity with Jewish Christians in Mesopotamia.

Mani considered Buddha, Zoroaster and Jesus as his predecessors. He visited northwestern India and during his missionary trips in the Persian Empire, favoured by King Shapur I, he must have become thoroughly familiar with the Iranian religion. If he died in prison (possibly in 274 AD) owing to the hostility of the official magians (fire-priests) who influenced King Bahram I, this does not mean that he did not integrate Iranian religious concepts into his system.

It is not quite clear which elements in Mani's religion are Iranian or Buddhist, mainly because it is not clear what these religions taught at that period. Later Buddhism of north-western India, mother of Tibetan and Zen Buddhism, had very little in common with original Buddhism and may have been influenced by western Gnosticism. But Mani was probably inspired by Buddhism to respect the suffering life of the particles of light mixed up with matter (see below), and perhaps drew the idea of reincarnation from this source. From Iranian religion he may have taken his absolute dualism, the opposition of light and darkness; this he combined with the gnostic dualism of spirit and matter, and equated with the opposition of God and Satan.

Yet all these influences do not explain the unmistakably gnostic character of Manicheism. It has been established that Mani was familiar with the views of the Mandeans, a baptist sect still existing in Iraq, most probably originating from Palestine and possibly already then living in southern Babylonia. It seems plausible that the sect of the Mughtasila (Baptists), to which Mani's father belonged, was a sort of Mandean or Proto-Mandean sect.

The difficulty is that the Mughtasila are said to have been strongly encratitic, whereas the Mandeans are not, and never seem to have been. Moreover it is not certain that the Mandeans, now a gnostic sect, were already then gnostic to the same extent as they are now. And Manicheism has certain gnostic elements which seem to be absent from Mandeism. The god of this world, the demiurge, is called in Manichean sources Saklon or Saklas. This goes back to Saklas (Aramaic for 'fool'), which is the name for the Jewish god and creator of the world in the gnostic *Apocryphon of John* (early 2nd century), but has no parallel in Mandean sources.

This Saklas, the ruler of darkness, together with his subjects, creates Adam after the image of the primal man, created by God. In the same way, in the Apocryphon of John, Saklas and his powers fashion Adam after the idea of God, his image, also called first man, who revealed his reflected image in the water of chaos. It is even said, in Manichean sources and in the Apocryphon of John, that Saklas made Adam after the image of God and after the image of himself and his fellows, so that man is a microcosm of everything: 'Come! Let us make a man according to the image of God and according to our likeness.' This, of course, ultimately goes back to the *Timaeus* of Plato, where God contributes only the divine part of man, the soul, and leaves it to lower gods to fashion the mortal part of man. But the concept must have reached Mani through gnostic channels.

There must be some relationship between Mani and the various gnostic schools and currents of the 2nd century, quite apart from Mandeism. But at the moment we cannot be more specific, because the history of these sects in eastern Syria and Mesopotamia is almost completely obscure. This problem may come nearer to a solution when all the gnostic manuscripts found at Nag Hammadi in Upper Egypt have been published.

There is no doubt that Manicheism is a gnostic religion. It has a gnostic conception of man (as a divine spark), of the world (as a product of failure) and of God (as the suffering God), which is expressed in a systematic and consistent myth. Because this myth is so extremely complicated, even in the abridged form which we offer here, it is perhaps right to remember that according to Franz Cumont and Henri-Charles Puech the myth reflects and expresses the 'Self-experience' of Mani himself.

From the very beginning, the myth says, before heaven and earth and everything contained therein came into being, there were two principles, a good one and an evil one, the realm of light and the realm of darkness. In the realm of light dwells God, 'the father of greatness'. In Eastern sources he is called the 'four-faced God', because with his light, his power and his wisdom he forms a sort of quaternity.

In the realm of the dark dwells the king of the dark. He arose from his domain to invade the realm of light. Then God decided to go out and fight the battle against the invading forces. Thereupon 'the father of greatness evoked the mother of life and the mother of life evoked the primal man.' When God sends out the primal man, he is really going himself. The primal man and all the other light-figures of Manicheism are qualifications and manifestations of God himself. When the lost part of primal man, called Jesus patibilis (suffering Jesus), is said to hang on every tree, we should understand that it is God himself who is crucified in the world of darkness.

We have here a conception of God akin to, but not identical with, that of Christian theology. It is essentially gnostic. In the recently discovered *Gospel of Philip* it is said that the heavenly Christ saved his own soul, which he had lost since the beginning of the world. The idea of this Valentinian author is that the fall of divine wisdom (Sophia), through which this world came into being, is essentially a split within the godhead itself. The divine element is dispersed in matter and God, when saving man, is saving himself. This astonishing conception of the suffering God is not to be found in India, Iran or Israel. It seems to have its prototype in the Greek myth of Zagreus-Dionysus, who was torn in pieces by the Titans.

It is this gnostic and ultimately hellenistic concept of God suffering in the world and in man which the Manichean myth tries to expound, in the following way. The primal man, in his glorious armour of the 'five bright elements', went forth to repel the forces of darkness. But this fight ended in defeat and the primal man was left in the darkness in a state of unconsciousness. On the other hand, it was a sort of divine sacrifice, for in this way the primal man could also serve as bait to catch the forces of darkness, so as to assuage them and to prevent their attack upon the realm of light. When the primal man recovered from his swoon, he entreated the father of greatness to come to his support. From above he received 'the call', conceived as a spiritual being. To this he gave 'the answer', also a spiritual being. Thereupon the primal man returned to the realm of light, but had to leave his armour behind.

The adventures of the primal man are described in great detail in the Coptic Manichean Psalms, which show us how this myth reflected the situation of every Manichean. They too were living in the darkness of unconsciousness and matter, until the saving message of the doctrine appealed to them, revealed to them their real identity and so enabled them to return to the realm of light. A similar conception of salvation, and a similar myth, is found in 2nd century Gnosticism, especially in the documents from the school of Valentinus.

Here, the perfect man is Jesus. He leaves his 'members' behind in the world, to be formed by their life in history and to discover their own identity. The end of the world-process is achieved when all spiritual elements have returned to their origin above. In the same way, the Manichean primal man returns to the realm of light, but leaves behind his armour, or his soul.

Though the Manicheans regarded all sexual relations as inherently sinful, women were not discriminated against but were eligible to join the highest ranks of the movement. Mani appears on the left of this 18th century Persian miniature

This shows that scholars (including G. Widengren and R. Bultmann) who interpreted Manicheism as a myth of 'the saved saviour' were right. They were wrong when they supposed that Mani took this idea directly from Iranian religion. Before him the Valentinian Gnostic had a similar conception, which seems inspired by St Paul's view that the Church is the body of Christ, and by a Jewish myth that Adam regained Paradise.

The elements of light which had been absorbed by darkness had still to be delivered. To this end, the world was created as a mixture of spirit and matter. The myth here becomes very obscure and obscene. By a strange mixture of generation and cannibalism Adam and Eve were brought forth by Saklon (the Jewish god). 'Jesus Splendour' aroused Adam from his sleep, so that Adam became conscious of himself.

This process was continued during the whole history of mankind. Ever and again, messengers were sent to remind men of the divine spark in them. Such apostles were Sethel (Seth, the son of Adam), Enosh, Enoch, Shem, the son of Noah; Buddha in the East, Zoroaster in Persia, Jesus in the West. But their doctrines were not complete and soon after their death were corrupted by their pupils.

Mani admitted that Jesus revealed himself in Palestine at the beginning of our era to reveal the gnosis to man, though the body of Jesus was not held to be material. He admired St Paul but he held the Church to have disappeared completely ('a tree without fruits') in his own lifetime. Therefore the Paraclete, the Spirit of Truth promised by Jesus, had been sent to Mani, who was called to reveal the definite and consummate gnosis. For that reason Mani styled himself 'the apostle of Jesus Christ' and 'the seal of the prophets'. He must have thought that he lived in the last generation of mankind, before the final separation of light and darkness. Then the 'earth of light', the abode of God and all the saved, would be healed of the wound inflicted upon it by the attack of darkness. The earth would be destroyed by fire, the powers of evil would be confined within their original domain, and unrepentant sinners would be compacted together in a great round clod, known as the *globus*.

At last the realm of light would enjoy an eternal peace, no longer endangered by any attack of darkness. Dualism in the end will be permanent.

In order to realize the duality of man and his higher Self, Mani had to postulate a highly dualistic philosophy. And this is understandable, because the unity of the innermost man with his heavenly Self, according to Mani, is only possible when man is ready to reject everything material.

Manicheism spread in the West, where the young St Augustine was attracted to the sect, until it was completely suppressed by the combined forces of Church and State in c 600 AD. In the East, especially outside the Roman Empire, it flourished in spite of persecutions and remained for a thousand years one of the main religions of Asia. The medieval sects of the Bogomils and Cathars had much in common with Manicheism in their concern with evil. The Cathars owed much to the Bogomils of Bulgaria, who in turn originated from the Armenian Paulicians and perhaps the Syrian Messalians. Neither Paulicians nor Messalians were Manichees and we have no evidence that Manichees were active in the Byzantine Empire at the time the Bogomils entered history. But the 'medieval Manichees' were so similar to the 'classic Manichees', that perhaps in the future some missing link will be discovered.

(Since this article was written a Greek papyrus has been discovered, which tells us explicitly that to the age of 25 Mani was a member of the Jewish Christian sect of the Elchesaites in the south of Babylonia.)

Parsees

Concentrated mainly in several towns of western India, where they number about 100,000, and Pakistan, where they total about 5,000, Parsees consider themselves to be descendants of small groups of people who emigrated from Persia in the 8th century AD in order to avoid forceful conversion to Islam, and to retain Zoroastrianism. The precise details of their escape from Persia and perilous sea voyage to India are largely legendary. It is believed that they first landed on the island of Diu off the south coast of Kathiawar, and that from there they sailed to Gujarat and obtained the local ruler's permission to settle at a place near Sanjan on the Gujarat coast. The first group of refugees was later joined by others who fled from the increasing oppression and religious intolerance of the first caliphs of the Abbasid family.

From Sanjan, Parsees spread subsequently as settlers and merchants both northwards to places such as Navsari, and southwards to the region of the present Bombay. Wherever they settled they established fire temples and by about 1300 AD there were Parsee colonies in various parts of western India. In the early 14th century Moslem invaders defeated the Hindu overlords of the Parsee of Sanjan, and the latter had to flee once more. After various vicissitudes they settled at Bansda.

It is believed that in the 15th century the Parsee community in India was strengthened by further emigrants from Persia, and that these new arrivals brought about a revival of religious practices abandoned in the Indian environment. At that time there were also conversions of Hindus to the Zoroastrian faith, but in later times such proselytizing activities ceased and the Parsees did not admit any new converts to their community. The first references to Parsees by Europeans are contained in accounts by Portuguese writers of the 16th century, who mention a class of merchants and shopkeepers of Persian origin living in the towns of western India.

A great opportunity for the Parsee traders came with the establishment of European business enterprises. Some of them entered the service of foreign companies, and others developed trade in Western goods on their own account. Parsees had begun to settle in Bombay under the Portuguese (1530–1666) and several Parsee families attained high positions in the town which ever since, and throughout the period of British rule, has been their main stronghold. The Parsees, more than any other community of Indian traders, were responsible for the development of the trade of Bombay, and particularly the trade connections with China, which Parsee merchants visited as early as 1756. Next to Bombay the port of Surat became an important Parsee centre, and early in the 18th century they also spread along the Malabar coast and some families established themselves in Madras. Less inhibited than Hindus by social and ritual restrictions, the Parsees found it easy to make contact with Europeans.

A minor threat to that cohesion had appeared in the 18th century over the matter of calculating the calendar. Because of the long separation between the Parsees of India and the small Zoroastrian community remaining in Persia, a discrepancy had developed in their calendars, and the Parsees were one month behind their co-religionists in Persia in commencing their New Year. For a long time little notice was taken of this fact, but in 1746 a Persian came to Surat and together with a group of Parsee priests introduced the calendar as observed by the Persian Zoroastrians. The members of this group called themselves *Kadmis*, 'ancient', whereas the bulk of the Parsees, who became known as *Shehenshais*, 'royal', stuck to their old dates. A division into two sects arose from this schism over the calendars and at times they engaged in angry disputes and discouraged intermarriage between their members. Later amicable relations were restored, but the main annual festivities are still observed on different dates. The Shehenshai sect greatly outnumbers the Kadmis, but some very prominent families belong to the latter.

When the ancestors of the Parsees first settled in India they spoke Persian, but being a small community they gradually adopted the language of their host country and became speakers of Gujarati. Pahlavi, the language of the Sassanian period of Persia (3rd to 6th centuries AD), was retained as a ritual language but the Pahlavi texts, which the priests had to learn by heart, were no longer fully understood. There are also Zoroastrian texts written in modern Persian and in Gujarati.

The influence of the Indian environment also affected the social organization of the Parsee community. Little is known of its internal government during the centuries following the arrival in India, but by the beginning of the 18th century it was – on the model of a Hindu caste – controlled by a *panchayat*, an assembly of a certain number of leading men. It is believed that a properly constituted panchayat was first formed in Bombay after the islands passed into British hands, when the number of Parsees had begun to increase greatly. The panchayat exercised considerable influence, not only in Bombay but also in several towns of Gujarat where Parsees had settled. As Bombay grew in importance under British rule this city became the Parsee headquarters, and whenever any dissensions or differences of opinion arose the advice of the panchayat was asked for and followed. In religious matters, however, the priests of the small town of Navsari held their own as the supreme authority.

Towards the end of the 18th century, the panchayat sought and received confirmation of its power from the British authorities, and in the course of the 19th century it initiated a number of reforms.

With the gradual extension of the British legal system to all aspects of Indian life the panchayat became obsolete as a legislative body. In order to codify Parsee customary law relating to marriage and succession, a Parsee Law Commission was instituted, and its findings were incorporated in a number of Acts which were passed by the Legislative Council of India in 1865. With this, the Parsees' status as a separate community with its own family law, distinct from that of Hindus and Moslems, was formally acknowledged.

Although the Parsees have adjusted themselves to some extent to Hindu ways of living, they retained until recent times certain items of dress which set them apart from other communities. Only those who were entirely Westernized abandoned their traditional style of clothing. They conformed to Hindu dietary habits in that they ate neither beef nor pork, but there was no prejudice against the drinking of alcoholic

Opposite **Mani expounding his theories: he considered Buddha, Zoroaster and Jesus as his predecessors, calling himself 'the apostle of Jesus Christ' and 'seal of the prophets'; gnostic influence is also evident in his teachings** *Right* **Decendants of small groups of Persians who travelled to India in the 8th century AD to avoid conversion to Islam, the Parsees still retain their own traditions and religious customs, and their own family law which is distinct from that of Hindus and Moslems: a saffron mark symbolizing happiness and the goodwill of the household is placed on the brow of a visitor to a Parsee home**

beverages. Like Hindus they regard eating as a religious act, during which the orthodox do not engage in conversation.

The early roots of Zoroastrianism lie in a cultural environment similar to that of Vedic Hinduism, but the character which it assumed in its formative period bears the imprint of its prophet and founder Zarathustra (whom the Greeks called Zoroaster), a priest who lived in eastern Iran sometime between 1000 BC and 600 BC. The Parsees refer to him as Zartusht. He was a reformer who attacked the old Indo-Iranian religion, particularly the practice of cruel animal sacrifices, and advocated a break with the worship of the old gods. Legend tells of his retreat into the mountain fastnesses of Iran, where he strove for enlightenment in a state of ecstatic trance, and saw in a vision Ahura Mazdah, the supreme spirit of good, who is diametrically opposed to Ahriman, the spirit of evil.

A belief in the opposing powers of good and evil, who fight for domination over human beings, reflects the dualistic trend in Zoroastrianism, but already there were certain contradictions in Zarathustra's teaching, and Ahura Mazdah appeared standing in one sense above the contrast between good and evil. The modern Parsees refute the characterization of their religion as dualism and describe their faith as pure monotheism. They are certain of the final victory of good over evil, but each man has to decide where he stands in the struggle between Ahura Mazdah and Ahriman.

The sacred scriptures of the Zoroastrians are known as the *Avesta*, parts of which stem from different times. The original texts were written in Avestan, an extinct language understood by only a few Parsee scholars, while the commentaries were written in Pahlavi. Belief in the existence of the one supreme deity Ahura Mazdah, now usually referred to as Ohrmazd (or Ormuzd) and credited with the creation of the spiritual and material worlds, is a basic element in Parsee doctrine as we know it. He is the source of all blessings and good things and Parsees address themselves to him in all their prayers.

Ohrmazd stands at the pinnacle of a hierarchy of celestial beings which consists of seven *Amesha spentas*, 'holy immortals', and 30 *Yazatas*, 'adorable ones'. These divine beings have been compared to archangels and angels, but their status is higher and they are more independent than the angels of Christianity. They are the rulers, fashioners, protectors and preservers of the creation of Ohrmazd, and Parsees make offerings to them and invite them to visit their houses. The 30 Yazatas preside over natural objects and give their names to the days of the month; Zarathustra, alone among human beings, is now regarded as one of them. These celestial beings interact with mankind and it is through their aid that man learns to know Ohrmazd, to dispel demons and to prosper in this world.

The most prominent among them are Mihr (the ancient Iranian god Mithra – or Mithras), Srosh and Rashu. They are the judges of the dead, each with a specific function. Mihr administers justice at the heavenly court, and exposes those guilty of having broken a promise. He saves the souls of truthful persons when they come to the Bridge of Judgement, where he and Srosh await the departed. Rashu holds in his hand the golden balance on which he weighs the good and evil deeds of the souls.

Distinct from these prominent celestial figures are the hosts of unnamed *fravashis*, guardian spirits who have left the heavenly sphere and chosen to move to the world of humans where they assist men in the fight against evil. The Parsees believe that each man has a guardian spirit, who leaves him at death to return to the company of the fravashis; but he remains a link between living and dead, and is begged to convey offerings to the departed.

Parsees have often been referred to as 'fire worshippers', but they resent this description and point out that though fire is an important element in their cult, it is a symbol of the deity and not an object of worship. As among the Vedic Hindus, fire occupied a central position in all rituals of the ancient Zoroastrians, and it was not always easy to distinguish between the concepts of the fire as such and the divinity presiding over it.

Among the Parsees today fire is held to be sacred, and the so-called 'fire temples' are buildings for the preservation of the sacred fire. In Gujarat they do not differ greatly from the dwelling houses of the wealthier families. Inside they have an outer and an inner hall. In the centre of the latter is a solid stone stool and on this stands an urn of copper, brass or silver, in which burns the sacred fire fed with sandalwood and other kinds of wood.

There are three types of sacred fires. The lowest grade is consecrated fire in a dwelling house or small family temple; this is the hearth fire which a Parsee never allows to die. If he changes his place of residence he carries his fire with him to his new abode. Fires of greater sacredness burn in temples which should be built wherever numbers of Parsee families are living. They are made of fires taken from a priest's house and the houses of three families of other classes, a process of consecration accompanied by the recitation of sacred texts.

The fire of the highest grade burns only in the most important temples, of which there are less than a dozen. At least 16 different fires are needed to prepare this fire, and ceremonies and rites of consecration are complicated and expensive. A sword and maces hang on the wall of the temple, and there is a brass bell which the priest rings at each watch when he performs a ceremony near the sacred fire.

Only priests may enter the sanctuary where the fire is burning, but many devout laymen pay frequent visits to a fire temple, particularly on the four days in the month which are sacred to fire. The worshippers, both men and women, bring offerings of sandalwood and money. In return the priest gives them ashes from the sacred fire, and these they apply to their forehead and eyelashes. Many of the smaller Parsee communities have no temples, but assemble for prayers in the open.

The most famous sacred buildings of the Parsees are the so-called 'towers of silence'; large structures of stone or brick situated on hills and usually surrounded by gardens. In these the bodies of the dead are exposed to the sun and to flesh-eating vultures, for according to Parsee belief corpses should not defile either earth or fire. These roofless towers consist of an outer wall some 300 feet in circumference and a deep pit lined with masonry. Dead bodies are laid on a stone platform which is divided into three rows, the outermost for men, the next for women, and the innermost for children. The construction of a tower of silence is accompanied by elaborate ceremonies, and after the first dead body has been deposited, the tower is closed to all, including Parsee priests, with the exception of the corpse-bearers who enter it through a high iron door. When a body has been placed on the appropriate stone slab, the bearers leave and the vultures soon descend upon the corpse and tear the flesh from the bones. Whatever remains is thrown into a central pit filled with sand and charcoal.

Parsees living in small rural communities which lack such funeral towers, and all those living in East Africa and other countries overseas, bury their dead in coffins. Wherever there are funeral towers a special ceremony in honour of the departed is performed on a day comparable to the All Souls' Day of Christianity. Parsees go there to offer prayers for dead relatives and friends, and those who have lost a relative during the year spread carpets and hold a feast in the yard or garden round the tower.

There are several festivals which are celebrated on specific dates. One of these is the Sun Festival, which is traceable to the Persian worship of the sun, now personified by Mihr. During another of these feasts, held in honour of the water spirit, Parsees go to the seashore or to a riverbank, and throw coconuts, sugar and flowers into the water. Women, who have made a vow to do so if their affairs prosper, make sweet cakes, some of which they send to friends, and throw the rest into the sea or into a river. On a festival known as the Fire Feast Parsees go to a fire temple, with offerings of sandalwood, and pray before the fire. The rich distribute money to the priests and to poor Parsees who gather there. The so-called Animal Festival is the culmination of a month in which Parsees show special kindness to animals, feeding stray dogs with milk, and cattle with grass. During this time the very devout abstain altogether from animal food, while others observe this type of abstinence on four specific days. Besides these principal feasts there are six seasonal festivals, each of which lasts five days, during which all members of the local community meet on terms of equality.

Towers of silence are the most famous sacred buildings of the Parsees; believing that corpses should not defile either earth or fire, they place the bodies of their dead in these structures, where they are exposed to the sun and to flesh-eating vultures

Every religious rite has to be conducted by a priest, and there is a hereditary priesthood that is completely distinct from the laity. All Parsee priests in India are believed to be descended from a priest who is supposed to have been among the original settlers in Sanjan. Different branches of the original family have been allocated to districts in each of the Parsee settlements, in which members of one branch alone may serve as priests. In each of these districts there is a high priest whose office is hereditary and passes from father to eldest son. He does not leave his headquarters to

visit the priests under his charge, but hears and settles any complaints against his priests that are brought before him.

While members of the class of priests may engage in secular business, no one born into a family of laymen can become a priest and officiate at religious rites. Until recently it was not customary for the daughters of priests to marry laymen, but the sons of priests were free to take wives of lay status. Members of the priestly class who are full-time priests are supposed to have beards and to dress entirely in white. Those who engage in secular work, shave their beards and wear colours, are disqualified from performing the higher priestly offices.

The functions of a priest include reciting prayers in the temples, and in the houses of laymen, performing the rites for the dead, and conducting ceremonies such as weddings and initiations. There are two orders of

priests, known respectively as *Herbad* and *Mobed*. Among the modern Parsees these represent two stages in a ranking system, the Herbad being junior and inferior to the Mobed. But in the Sassanian period of Iran there was a distinction in kind and function between the two classes of priests. The Mobed were the magicians, who had specific functions at animal sacrifices, and the Herbad were the fire priests, found mainly in south-western Iran. In the 3rd century the two classes became fused, and the Parsees have no trace of the original distinction between Herbad and Mobed.

The son of any Parsee priest can become a Herbad if he has learnt by heart a large number of chapters of the *Avesta*, and various parts of other scriptures. He must then undergo a ceremony of purification. Two priests and several male friends and relatives take the novice to the purifying

place, which is an open enclosure strewn with sand. A dog, cow's urine, holy ashes, pomegranate leaves, sticks of a special kind and some bathing vessels are required for the elaborate rite which is to be performed there. A confession of sins, and lengthy prayers for purity of mind and deeds are part of the ceremony. Afterwards the novice is taken to a fire temple where he spends nine days and nights in retreat. He then returns to his home, but after a short time undergoes a second purification. At the end of this he is clothed in pure white garments and presented with flowers. The final ordination, which must be conducted by a high priest, then follows.

When a youth has been a Herbad for two or three years, and has learnt additional parts of the scriptures, he may be ordained as a Mobed or full priest. This includes undergoing further purification rites as well as reciting sacred texts. When the ordination has been completed the new priest is fully qualified to perform all sacerdotal functions. From then on he must never be bareheaded and never shave his head or face. He is supposed to retain his state of purity and eat no food cooked by a person who is not of priestly class.

All the main phases in a Parsee's life are marked by rites and ceremonies. Between the ages of seven and nine boys and girls are initiated into the Zoroastrian faith. The ceremony consists of investing the child with a sacred shirt and a sacred cord, and this is followed by a ritual bath and offering of prayers by a priest. Both betrothal and marriage are the occasion of elaborate ceremonies. At least two priests are required for the wedding rite, and they pronounce the marriage blessings in Old Persian and in Sanskrit. The questions addressed to bride and bridegroom are in Persian and so are their answers. Parsees have not permitted polygamy since 1865, but a widowed or divorced person may remarry.

Parsee funeral rites are relatively simple. The basic principle is to dispose of the dead body with the least possible risk of harm to the living. As a precaution all deaths are held to be caused by infection, and care is taken that people should come into as little contact as possible with the dead bodies as a result of this belief.

When death is approaching, a prayer of repentance should be said by the dying person or, if he is unable to do so, by a priest or a relative on his behalf. A short time after death the corpse is washed, and dressed in a clean set of clothes which are destroyed afterwards.

Three days after the funeral a ceremony of prayers is held in the house of mourning and the following morning white clothes, drinking vessels, fruit and wheatcakes are consecrated to the dead in the local fire temple. There is a belief that for three days after death the soul of the departed remains within the precincts of this world, and that at dawn after the third night following death it reaches the Bridge of Judgement which connects this earth with the unseen world. There the soul's fate is decided, and the relatives of the deceased try to influence this decision by the recitation of prayers addressed to the celestial judges. The righteous are believed to enter into a state of bliss in a heaven peopled by divine beings, and those whose deeds have been evil are confined to a place of darkness and suffering.

According to Zoroastrian belief punishment in hell does not last for all eternity; there will be a final renewing of the world, when evil will be overcome and the entire creation assume the quality of Ohrmazd, the source of all goodness and happiness. The dualism of good and evil is considered capable of ultimate resolution, and the world view of the Parsees is basically optimistic.

Unlike Hinduism, which extols asceticism and favours a pessimistic attitude to life, the ideology of the Parsees is basically life-affirming, and its dualistic trends do not imply a confrontation of mind against matter. The flesh is not regarded as evil, celibacy is abhorred, and there is more equality between men and women than in either Hinduism or Islam. The life-affirming element in Zoroastrianism is consistent with the role of the Parsees as the most progressive ethnic element, economically and materially, in the whole of India. Their contribution to the development of commerce and modern industry, scholarship and art is out of all proportion to their numbers.

Above The Parsee priesthood is hereditary, and all its members are said to be descended from a priest who was one of the original settlers in India; full-time priests are supposed to have beards and dress entirely in white: initiation of a Parsee youth. All the main phases in a Parsee's life are marked by rites and ceremonies *Far left* A young girl initiate: she has been invested with a sacred shirt and a sacred cord woven from lamb's wool by women of the priestly class *Left* Parsee wedding: at least two priests officiate at the ceremony, and the blessings are pronounced in Old Persian and Sanskrit; grains of rice, symbols of abundance, are scattered over the couple *Opposite* Gnosticism was a religion initially, but some of its ideas lent themselves readily to magic

Popperfoto

Popperfoto

Gnosticism

Some early Christian writers, including Irenaeus, Hippolytus and Epiphanius, tell us that there existed in their time certain sectarians or heretics who called themselves Gnostics ('those who know') because they claimed to possess *gnosis*, 'knowledge'. In modern times the label has been applied to a whole set of Christian heretics, from the early centuries AD onwards, who had some characteristics in common and of whom Valentinus in the 2nd century was the most important.

The fragments of Gnostic teachings transmitted to us by their early Christian opponents have been thoroughly studied, especially by German scholars. The gnosis that the Gnostics claimed was not scientific or philosophical knowledge, acquired by the use of reason, but knowledge acquired through a revelation given by the grace of God, a 'knowledge of the heart' as one Gnostic writing (the Gospel of Truth) calls it. It consisted of intuitive knowledge and esoteric lore, which was believed to carry with it the salvation of its possessor.

It has also been established that Gnosticism was not specifically Christian. It has its counterparts in pagan Hellenism (in the collection of Greek-Egyptian occult writings called the *Corpus Hermeticum* — or Hermetica) and even in Judaism. Professor Gershom Scholem has discovered a Jewish form of esoteric and ecstatic mysticism which he calls 'Jewish Gnosticism', though it lacks one of the beliefs generally characteristic of Gnostics: the distinction between the unknown supreme God and the demiurge, the lower spiritual power that created the world.

These findings led some scholars to consider Gnosticism as a religion of its own with its own characteristic features, by contrast with earlier views of it as a system of Greek religious philosophy, or as a Christian heresy, or as the descendant of Babylonian, Persian and Indian concepts. According to Hans Jonas (*Gnosis und Spätantiker Geist*, 1933) Gnosticism was neither Greek and philosophical nor a survival of oriental ideas but a new and revolutionary movement, rebelling against the structures of this world, which the Greeks venerated as a harmony and the Jews believed to have been created by God. Gnosis was an awareness of being a stranger in the world, of having been thrown into an absurd universe. The systems of the Gnostics should be read as an expression of such basic experiences as fear, anxiety, disgust and despair.

This picture is correct but one-sided. In *Gnosis als Weltreligion* (1951) it is suggested that Gnosticism expressed a specific religious experience, which was frequently turned into a myth. An example is the story that when Mani, the founder of the Manichean religion, was 12 years old God sent an angel to him, to inspire him. When he was 24, the angel came to him again and said, 'The time has now come to make your public appearance and to proclaim your own doctrine.' The name of the angel means 'twin' and he is the twin-brother or 'divine self' of Mani.

This Manichean myth expresses the encounter between the I, the ego, and the divine self. In the system of Valentinus we find the similar concept of the guardian angel, who accompanies a man throughout his life, who reveals the gnosis to him, forms a couple with him and is not allowed to enter eternal bliss without him.

The discovery in the 1940s of texts written in Coptic, at Nag Hammadi in Egypt has greatly enlarged our knowledge of Gnostic beliefs. These manuscripts also threw new light on the origins of Gnosticism. They show that Gnosticism had its roots, or some of its roots, in Judaism, at least in its later manifestations.

This new solution of an old problem was stubbornly opposed as long as Judaism was identified with the Pharisees and was regarded as a monolithic, monotheistic religion. After all, the early Gnostics rejected the Jewish god who created the world, relegating him to the position of demiurge, and rejecting the Old Testament. But at the beginning of our era Judaism embraced various different groups.

There were the adherents of Wisdom, of which the book of Proverbs speaks. According to their literature, Wisdom was a companion of God. She created the world, became the paramour of the wise man and, according to certain versions, left the earth and returned to her heavenly abode. It is in this perspective that we must see the doctrine of Simon Magus of Samaria, according to which the Idea of God, called Wisdom or Helen, springing forth from God and knowing his will, descended to the lower regions and brought forth the angels and powers (the rulers of the heavens) by whom

British Museum

this world was made. This is a gnostic development of the Samaritan and Jewish concepts that Wisdom was instrumental in creating the world.

There were also the Essenes near the Dead Sea, who taught a dualism of light and darkness, and stressed the importance of knowledge of God. Much remains uncertain here, because the relationships between the Essenes, John the Baptist and Gnosticism are obscure.

The Fathers of the Church considered the Samaritans Dositheus, Simon Magus and Menander to be the first Gnostics. The books of the Samaritans, who were heterodox Jews, reveal a mythological imagery which could easily lead to Gnosticism, and it is probable that Gnosticism did begin in Samaria, that is, on Palestinian soil.

It would be unwise to be too specific, however. In many cases we can find in Gnosticism certain elements derived from Judaism without being able to identify the exact channels through which these concepts were transmitted.

But how could the Gnostics, who distinguished between the high unknown God and an inferior creator, the Jewish god or demiurge, to whom they were violently hostile, be Jews or in sympathy with Jews? Some find here traces of antisemitism, which was by no means absent in Antioch and Alexandria, centres of early Gnosticism. Others point out that the Gnostics usually regarded the demiurge as an angel, and that there was a sect among the Jews who held a similar opinion. This was the pre-Christian sect of Magharians, who distinguished between God and an angel who is the creator of the world and is responsible for all the anthropomorphic descriptions of God in the Old Testament.

So it would seem that the Gnostic concept of the world-creator as an inferior angel was derived from Jewish sources, though from rebellious and heterodox ones. This is important for Gnostic origins in general. Some scholars distinguish between absolute dualism and relative dualism. The first is called 'Iranian', implying that it must be of Iranian origin, because Iranian religion is an absolute dualism of light and darkness, and also of good and evil. But the concept of the demiurge as an angel reflects a relative dualism, which seems to be the original concept. Absolute dualism is Gnosticism in a secondary and later development.

The Gnosticism of the 2nd century sects involved a coherent series of characteristics that can be summarized in the idea of a divine spark in man, deriving from the divine realm, fallen into this world of fate, birth and death, and needing to be awakened by the divine counterpart of the self in order to be finally reintegrated. This idea is based on the concept of a downward movement of the divine whose periphery (often called Sophia or Ennoia) had to submit to the fate of entering into a crisis and producing – even if only indirectly – this world, upon which it cannot turn its back, since it is necessary for it to recover the *pneuma* (literally 'breath', the fallen divine element).

Valentinus expressed these ideas in a myth which is not transmitted by any author of antiquity but which can be reconstructed. His followers split into an Occidental school led by Ptolomaeus and Heracleon who introduced some innovations and alterations, and an Oriental school which remained more faithful to its master. So the myth of Valentinus can be hypothetically reconstructed in the following way (and it may be added that the recently discovered Valentinian treatises of the Jung Codex have confirmed this hypothesis).

In invisible and ineffable heights Depth was pre-existent. With him was Silence. Together they generate the Pleroma (fullness of the spiritual world), consisting of 30 aeons (patterns of thought or archetypes). The very youngest of these, Wisdom (Sophia), led astray by pretended love, which was actually *hubris* (overweening pride), desired to understand the unfathomable depth of God and is expelled from the Pleroma. (The underlying idea is that philosophical reason cannot penetrate the mysteries of God and is the origin of the fall.)

In the empty space devoid of knowledge which she had created by her trespass, Sophia brought forth Jesus in remembrance of the higher world, but with a kind of shadow. And he purged the shadow of deficiency from himself and returned to the spiritual universe above. Left outside, alone, Sophia was subject to every sort of passion, sorrow, fear, despair, ignorance. (From these passions the elements of the world together with the world-soul and the demiurge were to be derived.)

At her request, Jesus asked the aeons to help Sophia. After the Holy Spirit had revealed the gnosis of God to them, the aeons together formed the Saviour, Christ, who is the perfect expression of the spiritual

world. He was sent with his angels to Sophia, the world-spirit in exile, and delivered her from her passions, which became the world.

There are three layers of reality in this universe: the sublunar, material world, dominated by the Devil; the celestial, psychic world, dominated by the demiurge or Yahweh, who tends to be hostile; and the world above the planets, where Sophia and the spiritual beings are. Correspondingly, in man there is a material part, the body; a soul, the seat of ethical awareness and the power of reason; and a spirit, which dreams unconsciously in man and is the divine spark, of the same substance as Sophia and even God.

Not all men are spiritual. Some are materialistic, the pagans. Others, called 'psychics', have a soul and believe in the demiurge but have no awareness of the spiritual world above: these are the Jews and the ordinary Christian churchgoers. So history is a progress from materialism and paganism, by way of religion and ethics, to spiritual freedom and gnosis. All this is a necessary process. The world-spirit in exile must go through the Inferno of matter and the Purgatory of morals to arrive at the spiritual Paradise. The spirit in man is united with the soul so that it may be formed and educated in practical life, for it needs psychic and sense training.

In this system it is Christ who brings the decisive revelation of gnosis. He assumed or 'put on' Jesus at baptism, and thereby the whole of spiritual mankind, and saved it through the Resurrection. Since Christ, man can become aware of his spiritual self and can return to his origin above. When every spiritual being has received gnosis and has become aware of his divine being, the final consummation of the world-process will take place. Christ and Sophia, who have been waiting for the spiritual man at the entrance of the Pleroma, enter the bridal chamber to achieve their union.

They are followed by the Gnostics and their guardian angels as higher Selves, who are bride and bridegroom also. In the Pleroma they perform 'the spiritual and eternal mystery of sacred marriage', which is the complete union of the I and the Self.

This doctrine of Valentinus should be compared with the Apocryphon of John, of which three copies were found at Nag Hammadi. In antiquity Irenaeus said that the doctrine of Valentinus was based on an earlier and more primitive system. This could be a system like that of the Apocryphon of John. There too we find an impressive description of the unknown God and his female counterpart, who together bring forth a spiritual world of aeons. The last of these, Sophia, falls through lust, brings forth a hostile demiurge and brings about the world-process, in which the spirit fights against evil and is delivered through gnosis. But in this system Christ has no part as Saviour. It would seem that this system (dating from c 100 AD) is non-Christian in origin.

The Christian influence on Valentinus now becomes clear. According to him, it is Christ who brings gnosis, or 'self-consciousness', to mankind. The philosophy of history which saw the delivery through Christ as the surpassing of paganism and Judaism, and as the central event in the evolution of the universe, appears as a new idea. Valentinus has hellenized and Christianized an existing gnostic myth which was essentially non-Christian.

His followers of the Occidental school went further. Valentinus taught that God was two, Depth and Silence: an adherent of the Occidental school, quoted by Irenaeus, declared that God is one. Valentinus des-cribed the demiurge as generally hostile: according to the Occidental school, the demiurge, though ignorant, was friendly and helpful. Valentinus thought that Christ had only a spiritual body. Ptolemaeus said that Christ also had a soul and a psychic body. This implied that not only the spiritual men but also the psychic men, if they behaved well, could be saved and would live eternally in the spiritual world at the entrance of the Pleroma.

These clumsy innovations, which made the Valentinian position so confused and bewildering, reveal the desire to compromise with the Church, which taught that God was one, that Christ was a real man, that the simple true believer would inherit eternal life. But these concessions could not disguise the fact that Gnosticism was a different religion from Christianity. Even if the demiurge is friendly, he is not the creator of heaven and earth who is the Father of Christ in Christianity. Even if Christ has a psychic body as well as a spiritual body, he is not a real man. Even if the ordinary churchgoer as well as the Gnostic could become spiritually immortal, this is far from the doctrine of the Church, which taught a bodily resurrection and a final ending of the material universe.

The Gnostic doctrine of the inferior demiurge, and their denial of the real body of Christ and of bodily resurrection, remained the principal targets of Christian authors like Irenaeus and Origen in the 2nd and 3rd centuries. But though Origen opposed Gnosticism, he accepted many Valentinian ideas and in a way continued the Christianizing process which Valentinus had begun and been carried further by Heracleon.

It seems probable that the Tractatus Tripartitus, one of the treatises of the Jung Codex, is due to Heracleon. In it we find several doctrines which come very near to the concepts of Origen. For example, the Tractatus Tripartitus stresses the freedom of the will, which is responsible for the fall of Sophia. Sophia fell through her free will.

According to Origen, the fall is due to the free decision of the spirits who lived in the spiritual world before our world was created. This emphasis on freedom is the main contention of his system, for he uses the belief in free will to attack the Gnostic view that only a few men will be saved.

It is more difficult to measure the influence of the Gnostics on the philosopher Plotinus: on the contrary. He was a friend of Gnostics (Valentinians, as it transpires) and tolerated them for years in his school before he wrote a famous treatise against them. His system has much in common with Valentinus and Heracleon, and so Gnosticism served as a fertilizer of the two main streams of thought which were to dominate the future of the West, Christian theology and Neoplatonist philosophy.

Gnosticism did not disappear. Gnostic schools persisted in the Roman Empire for many centuries but they were no longer a deadly threat to the Christian Church and they do not have the historical importance of the schools of the 2nd century. Outside the Roman Empire, Gnosticism deeply influenced Mani and it was in the religion which he founded that Gnosticism became a world religion. Obscure eastern sects which were probably influenced by Gnosticism in turn influenced the medieval Bogomils and Cathars. The theosophical movement of this century has much in common with Gnosticism and rightly lists the Gnostics among its spiritual ancestors.

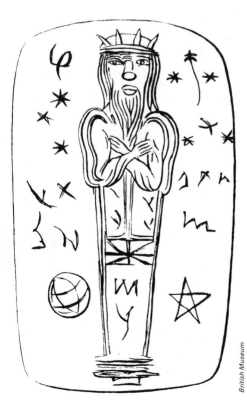

Neoplatonism

The religious philosophy which modern scholars call Neoplatonism is the final stage in the long development of the revived Platonism of the Roman Imperial period. It was a very long development. After a period of scepticism, Antiochus of Ascalon revived dogmatic, positive philosophical teaching in Plato's school at Athens, the Academy, in the 1st century BC. Later Platonism continued as a distinct philosophy, taught by its own pagan professors, till well after the official closing of the pagan schools at Athens by Justinian in 529 AD and therefore had a history of over 600 years, a period as long as that which separates philosophers of our own time from 14th century scholastics.

In the 3rd century AD, perhaps the most decisive phase in the transition from the classical to the Byzantine and medieval world, later Platonism was re-thought and given a new coherence, strength and vitality by a great philosophical and religious genius, Plotinus (205–270 AD). It is the philosophy of Plotinus and his successors which is nowadays called Neoplatonism. But no one at the time was conscious of any break in the development of Platonic philosophy, and Plotinus was by no means regarded as a second founder of the school. Nor would he, or any of the philosophers who came after him, have been at all pleased to be called Neoplatonists. They claimed to be expounding the authentic teaching of Plato, and to say that their philosophy was in any sense 'new' would have seemed to them an insult. The more ancient a doctrine was, to men of that period, the more likely it was to be true.

The Platonism which Plotinus took over and transformed was already a strongly religious philosophy. Most Greek philosophers (though not all, for there were sceptics, agnostics and materialists of quite a modern type among them) were much concerned with religion and morality. An essential task of philosophy was to lead and help men to live as well as possible on the basis of a knowledge of the truth about the gods, the universe and their own natures. And this is particularly true of the great majority of philosophers of the Roman Imperial period, Stoics, Epicureans and Platonists alike. A strong religious and moral concern is already apparent in the works of Plato. But the Platonism of the Roman Empire, when its main outlines begin to become clear to us in the 1st century AD, is more obviously and exclusively a religious and moral philosophy, and its religious concepts are closer to those we have ourselves inherited, and less ambiguous and baffling to our minds than those of Plato himself. There is now unmistakeably one God at the head of the system (as there is not in Plato), a divine Intelligence of perfect wisdom and goodness. The Platonic Ideas or Forms (the eternal objects of true knowledge and patterns according to which material things are made) are generally held by the later Platonists to be the thoughts of this supreme God, existing eternally in his mind. He makes the material world (directly or through an intermediary) on their pattern, generally from an eternally pre-existing matter. Sometimes this is thought of as evil and the cause of evil, sometimes there is an evil, disorderly soul which opposes and tries to thwart the efforts of the Maker to keep the universe in order. A hierarchy of gods and spirits depends on the supreme God.

In some systems the distinction between the First God or intelligence and a second God or intelligence, the active cause of the universe, becomes important and is linked with a stressing of the absolute transcendence and mysteriousness of the supreme God, and sometimes with the assertion that he is unknowable because he is infinite: he is not a 'this' or 'that' and has no definable nature which we can comprehend. This is something new in Greek philosophy. The idea of God as infinite and so unknowable is already to be found in Philo the Jew of Alexandria, an older contemporary of St Paul who was the first to use Greek philosophy in an attempt to give a reasonable account of a revealed religion: it appears in the Gnosticism of Basilides in the 2nd century AD. But its presence in later Platonism is unlikely to be simply due to the influence of Philo or the Gnostics. There are reasons in earlier Greek philosophy which could have led to this development.

An important feature of later Platonic religion, as of most religion in later antiquity, is that the physical universe as a whole is alive and divine (as it was for Plato) and so are its most important parts, the earth, and above all the sun, moon and stars, the visible, embodied divinities in the visible heaven. Man's soul too is divine in a very subordinate degree, a being quite distinct from and greatly superior to the body which it temporarily inhabits, and the object of the good and wise man is to escape, by the study of philosophy and the practice of an austere morality, from incarnation in an earthly body and either to become a star or to leave the visible universe altogether.

This 'Middle' Platonism, as it is generally called by modern scholars, was developed into what we call Neoplatonism, as far as we know, by Plotinus. He had been the pupil in Alexandria of a mysterious, self-taught and entirely unofficial philosopher called Ammonius, who also taught the great Christian thinker Origen. But Ammonius wrote nothing, and we really know next to nothing about his thought, so his contribution to the development of Neoplatonism must remain problematical. The first and greatest collection of Neoplatonic writings is the set of treatises written by Plotinus in his later life when he was teaching at Rome. These were arranged by his pupil and editor Porphyry (died c 305) into six volumes, each containing nine treatises, the *Enneads*. It is impossible here to give more than the barest outline of the rich, profound and many-sided philosophy which is expressed in them in very difficult, but sometimes magnificent Greek. The first thing which it is necessary to understand is that philosophy is for Plotinus, even more than for the Middle Platonists, a religious way of life demanding total commitment and the most intense effort not only to think well but to live well. It is not the detached observation, dispassionately and from outside, of a reality distinct from ourselves, or the construction of a coherent theory, but a process of waking ourselves up and discovering who we really are. What we discover is that we are souls who have an eternal existence, different from and higher than that of which we are aware in ordinary experience, in a divine world of living intelligence. If we are prepared to make the tremendous effort required we can be aware of that world and live our lives in it even when we are still in the body and necessarily to some extent preoccupied with its affairs. Our higher soul never 'comes down', is not really united with body nor integrated into the life of the sensible world. Animation of the body, sense-perception, desire and emotion belong to lower phases of soul.

When we have become aware of the higher self and are living its life on the level of divine intellect, we can share, occasionally, in the eternal mystical union by which this divine intellect is united to its source, the One or Good. Plotinus distinguishes much more sharply than any of his predecessors (as far as we know) between the first real being, the divine intellect which is also the Platonic World of Forms, and its transcendent and mysterious source. The One or Good is beyond being; it or he (Plotinus generally uses neuter substantives and masculine pronouns in speaking of this supreme origin of all things – occasionally he calls it God) is not any one definite particular thing which can be named or described. We cannot really talk about him except in an inadequate way, pointing towards him, not saying that he is anything. He is beyond intelligence: he is so perfectly one, so utterly himself that he does not need to take possession of himself in thought. And he does not need anything below himself: he is in his infinite goodness sufficient for himself and everything else. He eternally brings into being, spontaneously but also inevitably, without deliberation or desire to do so, by a free giving which cannot be otherwise and leaves him unchanged and undiminished, the Divine Intellect. This is the world of the Platonic Forms, which in Plotinus is a world in which each of the Forms is a living intelligence, which knows and so in a sense is the whole; all are transparent to each other and interpenetrate, and so form the most perfect unity possible below the One.

Divine Intellect in its turn produces, with

the same inevitable spontaneity, the great world of Soul, extending down from the universal soul which inhabits the world of Intellect, and forms and orders the material world on the model of the Forms (without planning or choosing to do so or sinking into it and becoming involved) to the life-principle in the earth and in plants. The material world, as the work of divine Soul, is good in its degree; but the matter which underlies it is evil, though inevitably produced by Soul, a principle of negation and corruption.

We are souls, and can live on any level of Soul we choose, and the whole object of the philosophical religion of Plotinus is to bring us to live on the highest, in the world of Intellect in which we can return to union with the One. This for Plotinus is not a matter of theoretical aspiration but of experience. He seems to have had not only the experience of mystical union with the One but the other experience, an indispensable preliminary to it in his way of thinking, of finding himself a part of the divine All, the world of Intellect which he describes in some wonderful passages of the *Enneads* as a world eternal but 'boiling with life', full of movement, light and colour, in which everything is one with everything else. Of the ultimate union with the One he says little, but he seems to have experienced it as more like a union of lovers than as realization of a pre-existing identity or as absorption into something blank and impersonal.

Plato's Academy, a Roman mosaic: the philosopher is pointing to a globe. A myth in *The Statesman* tells how in one cosmic period God spins the universe one way and in the next it spins the other way, so that everything reverses. The neoplatonists claimed to be expounding the authentic teaching of Plato, and to suggest that their philosophy was 'new' would have seemed an insult

MAN & HIS DESTINY

The Human Situation

All the major religions are based upon distinctive evaluations of human nature and destiny. In some religions, such as Christianity, this evaluation is consciously formulated into a doctrine of Man; in others it finds expression in ideas and terminologies that are never precisely defined, but clearly incorporate basic assumptions about life. Indeed, on the final analysis, religion itself stems from mankind's endeavour to understand its own reason for existence relative to the universe in which it finds itself placed.

That man, from the very dawn of culture, was able to abstract himself from the business of living and ponder the enigma of human destiny is attested by his burial customs. For the very fact that man has so concerned himself about his dead symbolizes the difference of his attitude to death from that of the other animals, which show no care for their dead.

The earliest known writings certainly show that men must have reflected on human nature and destiny long before they could record their opinions in writing. For these writings, of Egyptian and Sumerian origin and dating from the third millennium BC, reveal a maturity of expression indicative of long established traditions of belief. They also show that the two peoples concerned held very different views about human life in this world and the next.

The Egyptian view of man's nature and destiny, despite its great antiquity, is one of the most complex that was ever recorded. One of its most notable characteristics is the preoccupation with death that seems to characterize ancient Egyptian civilization. This preoccupation was indeed a fact; yet it was not inspired by any innate morbidity of

temperament. On the contrary, the Egyptians had a fierce love of life, and it was this love that made them so concerned about death. They were basically optimistic, for despite their profound abhorrence of death, they believed that they had the means, if properly employed, to secure resurrection from death and a happy afterlife.

The Egyptians planned for the life after death in a practical manner, as they did for their life in this world. They had a lively apprehension of the perils that faced them after death, particularly of the judgement before Osiris, but these were really incidental, and the wise and prudent would so arrange their affairs that they might safely surmount all obstacles. However, despite this great concern about their eternal destiny, the ancient Egyptians remained curiously unconcerned about the purpose of their existence. Their creation myths almost completely ignore the creation of mankind. In contrast to their Mesopotamian neighbours, they never seem to have asked why their creator gods had made men and women like themselves.

The peoples of ancient Mesopotamia took a very different view of human nature and destiny. In one way it was a more thoughtful view, in that they were interested in the purpose of mankind's existence. The explanation given in their mythology was that the gods originally had to labour to provide their own food. Tiring of this obligation, they had created mankind to serve them by building temples and providing sacrifices. However, although the Mesopotamians were concerned to find a divine purpose for the human race, they came to form a most pessimistic estimate of human destiny.

They believed that the gods had intentionally made mankind mortal, so that when they ceased to have any further use for an individual, he died. Death effected an awful change in those who died. For while living, a human being was a kind of psycho-physical

organism, being compounded of a material body and an animating principle, called in Akkadian *napistu*. At death this organic whole was irrevocably shattered. What survived, known as the *edim* or *etimmu*, was a horrible daemonic entity that could terribly plague the living, especially if its body were not properly buried. Its everlasting abode was *kur-nu-gi-a*, 'the land of no-return', located far below the earth, where all the dead dwelt, in dust and darkness, with no differentiation between the good and the wicked. There they were ruled by the terrible god Nergal and his grim wife Ereshkigal.

The pessimism of this Mesopotamian view of man's destiny calls for explanation and its likely cause has a great significance for the study of religion. It would seem, on the one hand, to have been based on a realistic estimate of the phenomenon of death as the complete disintegration of the living person. On the other hand, it was inspired by the inability of the unsophisticated mind to conceive of complete personal extinction. Hence the grim belief that something did survive of the former living person, though horribly transformed and so doomed to an existence of unending misery.

This Mesopotamian view of man was not unique in the ancient world; parallels to it are found in ancient Israel and in Greece. The Hebrew estimate is graphically presented in the story of the Fall of Adam. Yahweh, the god of Israel, makes Adam out of clay, and then animates him by breathing 'the breath of life' into his nostrils. Adam thus becomes 'a living soul' (*nephesh*, which is akin to the Babylonian *napistu*). The animals are also described as 'living souls', and are similarly fashioned from clay. After Adam commits his fatal act of disobedience, Yahweh pronounces his doom: 'clay thou art, and unto clay shalt thou return.' Since Adam was the progenitor of mankind, this fate was inherited by all his descendants.

The official Hebrew doctrine of Man was, accordingly, very similar to the Mesopotamian view. The living person was regarded as a psycho-physical organism, compounded of material body and an animating principle, *nephesh*. Death irretrievably shattered this composite entity, and the consequences are vividly described in 2 Samuel (14.14): 'We must all die, we are like water spilt on the ground, which cannot be gathered up again.' What survived this disintegration departed to Sheol, an awful subterranean deep, like the Mesopotamian 'land of no-return'.

This pessimistic view of human destiny was changed in the 2nd century BC by the acceptance of the idea of a resurrection and judgement of the dead. What caused the change is not clear but it had significant repercussions for the Hebrew doctrine of Man. Human destiny was now extended with positive significance beyond death. However, because the traditional conception of human nature, as a compound of physical and psychical elements, was retained a resurrected life meant a reconstitution of the physical body. On this point, Hebrew eschatology became similar to that of Egypt, for both were based on the conviction that a body was essential to personal existence. But where the Egyptians sought to preserve the body by mummification, the Jews looked to its miraculous reconstitution by Yahweh.

What may be described as the classical Greek evaluation of human nature and destiny was as pessimistic as the Mesopotamian and early Hebrew views. It first finds expression in the Homeric poems. The most dramatic presentation occurs in the *Odyssey* (book 11), which describes how Odysseus descended into Hades to learn the cause of the misfortunes that prevented his return home after the fall of Troy. In Hades he meets the shade of his dead mother. He tries vainly to embrace her shadowy image, and cries out in frustration and grief. His mother's shade replies: 'this is the way decreed for mortals when they die. The sinews cease to hold the flesh and bones together; for they are destroyed by the power of the blazing fire, as soon as the (conscious) life (*thymos*) leaves the white bones, and the shade (*psyche*), hovers about and then flits away.'

This passage mentions the three constituents of human nature, according to Homer: the body, which was cremated at death; the *thymos*, which was the conscious or rational self; the *psyche,* the life-principle. Death disintegrated the union of these constituent elements: the body was destroyed, the *thymos* ceased to exist, and the *psyche* descended to Hades. The *psyche* was imagined as a shadowy replica (called an *eidolon*) of the living person, but it had no consciousness. In Hades the shades of the dead are portrayed as being capable only of making chirping noises like birds. However, as this episode in the *Odyssey* shows, they could acquire a momentary consciousness by tasting the blood of a sacrificed animal – an idea derived from the primitive belief that blood is the 'life-substance', and therefore very potent.

Several attempts are made in the *Iliad* to account for human fate. In one place Zeus is pictured as arbitrarily handing out mixtures of good and bad lots to individuals from two urns that stood on the floor of Olympus. Other imagery is used elsewhere: that the gods 'bind' men's fates upon them; that 'mighty Fate' spins 'her thread' of destiny at a person's birth; that Zeus weighs the fates of heroes in his golden scales. The fluidity of this imagery suggests that, at this early stage in Greek thought, the problem was gradually emerging of relating human destiny to the divine government of the universe. But it was a problem that was never satisfactorily solved, for the Greek concept of deity was essentially based on experience of cosmic power, which is indifferent to human aspirations and values. This is clearly evident in Stoicism, which represented the most sustained effort made in the Graeco-Roman world to produce a philosophy of life in terms of a realistic appraisal of the human situation.

According to Stoic doctrine, the superiority of man over the animals lay in his possession of a rational mind *(nous)*, which enabled him to grasp the scheme of the universe. This implied that man could consciously will 'to live according to Nature', which in practice meant conforming one's desires and conduct to the limitations of human existence imposed by the physics of the universe. It was an austere creed, which offered the individual no hope beyond the personal satisfaction of having the strength of steeling himself to accept ultimate personal extinction. For death, as the Stoic philosopher Epictetus explains, is necessary, 'so that the revolution of the universe may be accomplished; for it has a need of the things that are now coming into being, and the things that shall be, and the things that have been accomplished.'

Stoicism was a product of the innate rationalism of the Greek mind, which could assess life objectively, uninfluenced by a religious tradition that claimed the authority of divine revelation. As such it appealed to minds sufficiently educated to appreciate its logic and resolute enough to live according to its austere counsel. But there is an abundance of evidence that, apart from professed Stoics, many ordinary people also resigned themselves to the fate that Homer first describes, and which finds expression in subsequent literature of all kinds. The many surviving funerary monuments, carved with scenes of the last farewell of the deceased, express a quiet but infinitely sad acceptance of the inevitable. Occasionally a note of defiance is heard, as in the following epitaph: 'I was not; I became; I am not; I care not.'

This pessimistic estimate of man's nature and destiny, which can be traced throughout classical culture, from Homeric Greece to Graeco-Roman society, was not accepted by all. Despite its obvious realism, many sought for a more comforting creed.' The ancient Eleusinian Mysteries and Orphism promised their respective initiates deliverance from death and a blessed afterlife.

Orphism was the more sophisticated cult and it involved the idea of the transmigration of souls, an idea which implied a very different conception of human nature from that of the classical tradition. It presupposed that in each person an immortal ethereal soul *(psyche)* was imprisoned in a material body. Orphic mythology explained that this situation was due to an ancient crime, and that the soul's true destiny was to return to its original divine source. This destiny could be achieved only by the soul's realization of its true nature, and by following a discipline designed to emancipate it from attachment to the world of material things. A favourite Orphic saying was *soma, sema*, 'the body, a tomb'.

Orphic ideas seem to have influenced the philosophy of Plato, in which the immortality of the soul is a major theme. He represents his master Socrates as exhorting his fellow-countrymen 'to take care of the soul'. He accepts the idea of the transmigration of the soul through many incarnations in both human and animal bodies, from contact with which it is contaminated and must make atonement. He proclaims it to be the task of the philosopher, through his superior knowledge, to free his soul from bondage to the body and assist it to regain its original state of blessedness.

This dualistic conception of human nature, of an immortal soul dwelling in a mortal body, became a firmly established tradition in the Graeco-Roman world. It was the basic concept of Gnosticism, Hermeticism, Neo-Pythagoreanism and Neoplatonism. These religio-philosophical cults were concerned to explain how the ethereal soul came to be incarcerated in a physical body, living in a world of material things. Each offered a way, usually involving esoteric knowledge and discipline, by which the soul might be delivered from its bondage and return to the divine source from which it had fallen. These ideas profoundly affected the Christian doctrine of Man.

Since Christianity began in Judaea and the first Christians were Jews, Jewish ideas about human nature and destiny inevitably formed the basis of the primitive Christian view. As the New Testament shows, belief in the resurrection and judgement of the dead were fundamental tenets of the new faith. The conception of the resurrection reflected the Jewish view of human nature as a psycho-physical organism in a very literal sense. This is most notably seen in the description of the resurrected Jesus. According to St Luke (chapter 24), when the disciples saw Jesus in his resurrected state, they were terrified, supposing 'that they saw a spirit'. But Jesus assured them of his physical reality: 'See my hands and my feet, that it is I myself: handle me, and see; for a spirit has not flesh and bones as you see that I have.' When some disciples still remained doubtful, he proposed a further test: 'Have you anything here to eat?' They gave him a piece of a broiled fish, which he proceeded to eat before them.

This amazing emphasis upon the concrete

reality of the resurrected body of Jesus reflects the belief of the early Christians about the essentiality of the physical body. But as the writings of St Paul show, when this Jewish idea was presented to Gentiles who held the dualistic view of human nature that derived from Plato and Orphism, offence was given. In consequence, adjustments were made to accommodate belief that the soul was immortal by nature and able to exist independently of the body. However, the Jewish concept of a physical resurrection was too integral a part of the original Christian message to be abandoned. It was retained, together with the idea of a Last Judgement.

The Christian doctrine of Man thus taught that God created human souls to be immortal, but placed them in physical bodies with which they became essentially connected. At death, the soul left the body and was immediately judged. For the majority of mankind this judgement resulted in the soul's consignment to purgatory, to expiate its sins. At the Second Coming of Christ, the decomposed bodies of the dead would be reconstituted and their souls would re-enter them for the Final Judgement.

The Christian doctrine of Man involved the doctrine of original sin. It was taught that Adam had implicated all his descendants in his original act of disobedience to his Creator. Consequently, all subsequent generations were deserving of God's wrath from the moment of birth, quite apart from the guilt they later acquired by their own actual sins. Being thus a Fallen Race, mankind was predisposed to evil. This meant, according to Christian theologians, that man was not only unable to save himself from the state of perdition into which he was born, but he could not even desire to repent without God's grace. The means by which God provided salvation for mankind is expounded in the doctrine of the Atonement, and constitutes an essential part of the foundational teaching of Christianity. Through the Atonement, those who repented of their sins and accepted Christ as their Saviour could hope that, after enduring the cleansing fires of purgatory, they would be reunited with their bodies, and, justified at the Last Judgement, would pass on to the eternal bliss of the Beatific Vision of God.

The doctrine of Man in Islam has some affinity to those of Judaism and Christianity; the fact constitutes part of the problem of the relation of the Arabian religion to Judaism and Christianity, which predated it. The affinity is especially marked in the eschatology of the Koran. Mohammed regarded himself as sent by Allah to warn his countrymen of the coming of divine judgement. This 'Last Judgement' would involve the resurrection of the dead, and would result in the vindication of the faithful and their reward in paradise, and the eternal damnation of the wicked to the torments of hell.

Man was, by implication, created to serve Allah and repudiate all other gods. According to the Koran, man is made of fire-clay which was transformed into flesh.

Within the body was a vital principle or soul *(nafs),* and the two united to form the living person – hence the stress laid on a physical resurrection at the Last Day. The theme of human predestination figures much in Islam, owing to the supreme emphasis put on the omnipotence and omniscience of Allah. It leads to such uncompromising statements as that of sura 25 of the Koran: 'Allah leadeth astray whom He willeth and guideth whom He willeth.' However, the very word 'Islam' is derived from an Arabic verb signifying the idea of submission to a supreme will. As such, it presupposes that the individual has the freedom of will to submit himself absolutely to the commands of Allah.

The meagre references in the Koran to the nature of man led to much later speculation about the soul. The belief became generally established that human souls were created by Allah and kept in a shrine beneath his throne until required for their respective incarnations. The immortality of the soul was also accepted. The Sufi mystics held that the soul was of divine origin and craved for reunion with its Creator, and that this reunion could be achieved by mystical trance. However, despite these developments, Islam has remained essentially a simple faith founded on the revelation, made to Mohammed, of Allah's purpose for man, and formulated in a few practical precepts of conduct.

While these various evaluations of human nature and destiny were being worked out in the ancient Near East and Europe, in India another estimate was gradually established

Gayomart, the first man of Zoroastrian legend, reclines on a tiger skin: his seed fell into the earth and became a rhubarb plant which turned into the first human couple; 15th century Persian manuscript

which was destined to affect most of the peoples of eastern Asia. This estimate was similar to that of Orphism in as far as it was based on the idea of the transmigration of souls. But the Indian interpretation dates from about 600 BC, and is undoubtedly older than the Orphic view. Whether the latter derived from India has been much debated, without any agreed conclusion. The idea of the rebirth or transmigration of souls is not necessarily a sophisticated concept, and it occurs among many primitive peoples.

The Indian view of Man is certainly a sophisticated estimate. It maintains that the individual self, or *atman,* is really identical with Brahman, the source or principle of existence. But owing to *avidya,* or ignorance, the atman believes itself to be an individual self-conscious person. In turn it takes the phenomenal world for reality, and involves itself in it. Consequently, it becomes subject to the process of Time, which is manifested in unceasing cycles of creation and destruction. For the atman or self this means *samsara,* or rebirth, which is likewise a ceaseless process of dying and being reborn, with all the attendant suffering. Together with samsara operates the law of karma, which causes the atman to work out in each incarnation the consequences of its actions in past incarnate lives. This process conditions the form of

Camera Press

each of the several periods of rebirth.

Thus, according to this Indian doctrine, at any given moment every living being is in that state of fortune, be it good or ill, which his past karma has entailed. However, this situation is not hopeless and Hinduism, in its various forms, offers a way of deliverance. Basically this involves the effective apprehension of its own true nature by the atman. Such apprehension implies the recognition, as the *Chandogya Upanishad* tersely puts it, that 'the self of mine within

the heart, this is Brahman'. But this recognition is not just a mental act; if it is to be effective, it involves an effort to abstract the self from its fatal attachment to existence in this world, which it has taken for reality.

Such abstraction is difficult and can be achieved only by a hard discipline. When *moksa,* 'salvation', is finally achieved, individual existence in this world ceases, and the atman is absorbed into Brahman as a drop of rain merges into the sea.

This Indian interpretation of existence, in its early Upanishadic form, seems to have provided both the basis and point of departure for the Buddhist doctrine of Man. Buddhism concentrated particularly on the miseries of human existence by way of introduction to its own gospel of salvation. It accepted the doctrines of samsara and karma; but it rejected the Hindu concept of a self (atman) that was continuously reborn to new forms of incarnated life. Instead, it maintained that the idea of the empirical self stems from a conglomeration of various mental and physical factors *(skandhas),* which produce the sensation of individual existence in a material world. Since this illusory self cherishes its sense of personal being, it takes the world apprehended by its senses for reality and attaches itself to it. Hence, as in Hindu thought, the individual becomes subject to the process of continuous death and rebirth, with all their concomitant suffering.

According to the Buddhist analysis of the human situation, this universal illusion of personal existence is due to a kind of primordial ignorance (avidya), which it is the task of the Buddhist teacher to expose. To gain deliverance from samsara and karma, the disciple has to pursue an austere discipline of mind and body. The final suppression of all desire for personal existence achieves Nirvana. Owing to the essential subtlety of Buddhist metaphysics, it is very difficult to be certain what this term means. Literally it implies personal extinction; but as used in Buddhist texts it seems to denote a positive state of being, yet one that is so wholly other from empirical existence that it negates all known forms of being.

The spread of Buddhism throughout eastern and south-eastern Asia has meant that the Buddhist view of human nature and destiny has influenced a large part of mankind. It was accepted into China, where it tended to intermingle with or affect the native faiths of Confucianism and Taoism. The native Chinese evaluation of man, however, had certain distinctive features.

The interpretations of man so far described, although they have varied much in their estimates, have had one feature in common. They all set mankind, as a unique species, over against the rest of creation. Instinctively they assume that man should have a special destiny in the scheme of things. The Chinese estimate has notably lacked this assumption. On the contrary, it has stressed man's integration with his natural environment. This approach finds characteristic expression in the idea of Yin and Yang. The terms denote two alternating principles which the Chinese, from at least the 5th century BC, discerned as operative in all forms of being throughout the universe. Man was not excepted from their operation, and a Yin-Yang anthropology was elaborated which explained human nature in these terms. The following passage from the *Lu-shih Ch'un Ch'ui* succinctly states this view: 'Heaven, Earth and all things are like the body of one man, and this is what is called the Great Unity *(ta t'ung).'* And it goes on to define the duty of the Sage as that of showing 'how the *yin* and *yang* form the essence of things, and how people, birds and beasts are in a state of peace'.

The original teaching of Zoroaster on the subject of Man is obscure. He uses two

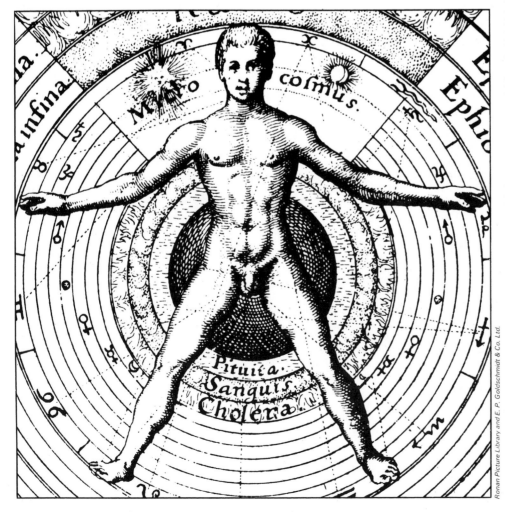
Ronan Picture Library and E. P. Goldschmidt & Co. Ltd.

Above Holy man from a cave fresco at Ajanta in India **Left** Man as microcosm, illustrating the theory that man is the universe in miniature, that he contains 'in himself all that is contained in the greater world': drawing from *Utriusque Cosmi Historia*, a work by the 17th century mystical philosopher Robert Fludd **Opposite** The Tree of Life, equated in this 18th century drawing with the cross on which Christ died to rescue human nature from the predicament to which the sin of Eden had condemned it. In the foreground 'this present evil world' is contrasted with the heavenly New Jerusalem in the background

terms, *urvan* and *daena,* signifying the non-physical components of human nature that survive death. The urvan seems to approximate to the 'soul', and the daena to denote something akin to 'conscience'. In later Zoroastrianism five constituents of human nature were distinguished and the idea of the daena was also curiously elaborated. The dead were described as meeting their daena after death: to the righteous it appeared as a beauteous maiden; to the wicked as a hideous hag. Zoroastrian eschatology involved a corporeal resurrection, with adults restored to a physical state of 40 years of age, and those who had died as children to the form of 15 years. There was also an Immediate and a Final Judgement of the dead.

'What is man that thou art mindful of him? . . . Yet thou hast made him little less than God' (Psalm 8). These opposite feelings, of man's humble insignificance and yet of his overwhelming importance, were expressed for hundreds of years in the West, in the theory of macrocosm and microcosm, that man is the universe, and perhaps God, in miniature, a toy copy of a great original. 'Man,' Agrippa said, 'hath in himself all that is contained in the greater world, so that there remaineth nothing which is not found even really and truly in man himself,' and man 'also doth receive and contain even God himself . . . Therefore man is the most express Image of God, seeing man containeth in himself all things which are in God'.

Since the universe, or macrocosm, is conceived of as a gigantic human organism it has naturally sometimes been pictured as the body of man, the universal or primal or heavenly man. In the Cabala this is Adam Kadmon, whose body is formed by the sefiroth of the Tree of Life. In the Lurianic Cabala, when the divine light of the godhead flowed out into space, the first being which came into existence, the first and highest manifestation of the godhead, was Adam Kadmon. It was from his eyes, ears, nose and mouth that the splendid lights of the sefiroth so brilliantly shone forth.

Adam Kadmon is not the same as the godhead, which is beyond human comprehending, but he is God the Creator, God manifested in the universe, and he is the God who can be known by man, for earthly man is a miniature image of him. Adam Kadmon is the whole universe as we know it, the sum total of all the possibilities open to man, and it has been pointed out that his mind, which is the 'universal mind', resembles Jung's collective unconscious.

In Manicheism, the primal man was a manifestation of God, clothed in the armour of light and sent out to do battle with the invading forces of darkness. It was his defeat which allowed particles of divine light to be captured by the evil powers and imprisoned in matter. In the Lurianic Cabala, the divine light emanating from Adam Kadmon broke the vessels which should have contained it, and so particles of light were scattered, a catastrophe paralleled by the Fall of Adam in Eden. The biblical Adam, according to

this theory, was at first a spiritual man, not a physical one, a 'great soul' whose body was made not of matter but of light. He was created to restore the fallen sparks of light to their proper place but he failed. His 'great soul', in which the entire soul-stuff of humanity was concentrated, shattered and its divine sparks became exiled in the world of human matter and earthly human nature.

In Gnosticism, again, man contains the divine spark, the inner seed of heavenly light imprisoned in the darkness of the material world and the physical body, a spark which can escape from its prison to

be reunited with its source in the godhead. The liberation comes when it realizes its identity (paralleled in Hinduism by the self's 'effective apprehension of its own true nature' – see above). 'The Gnostic is a Gnostic because he knows, by revelation, who his true self is.' Similarly, the Manicheans believed that their doctrines 're-vealed to them their real identity', and so freed them from the grip of evil and matter.

Gnosticism and Manicheism seem to have been based originally on a religious experience, the discovery of the true and divine self in a man's innermost being,

Brompton Studio

described as the higher Self, the twin or familiar, or the guardian angel. The discovery and liberation of the true self remains the great aim of Western occultism and magic. It is this divine element in his nature which in magical theory gives man his potentially limitless power. 'The proper study of mankind is man', with a vengeance, for man is both the measure and the master of all things.

According to the gnostic 'Secret Book of John', for example, man was created by the god of the Jews, an evil supernatural being named Ialdabaoth (probably a corruption of Jehovah Sabaoth). He seduced Eve after the expulsion from Eden and fathered on her the two sons men call Cain and Abel, but whose real names are Jehovah and Elohim. The one has a face like a bear and the other like a cat. (Elohim, like Jehovah, is one of the names of God that are found in the Old Testament.)

In Manichean theory, Adam was created by an evil power, begotten of the coupling of two great demons as a receptacle for certain particles of heavenly light, which had been captured by the forces of darkness. The Adam the demons produced was blind, deaf, fast asleep and unconscious of the divine light within him but the sowers of light sent a redeemer – called Ohrmazd or the Son of God or brilliant Jesus or Jesus the brilliant light – to rescue him. From his demon ancestors man has inherited his physical body and its desires but he also contains the divine light.

The Manichean Adam was spawned by evil as a copy of the heavenly 'primeval man', who had earlier been created by the powers of light. The two different creation stories in Genesis encouraged some Jewish and Gnostic writers to suggest that the first story describes the making of the ideal 'heavenly man', the image of God, a spiritual, non-material being who combined both sexes in himself; and that the second story describes the making of actual earthly man, a being who is part spirit and part matter (his body, made of earth) and who is divided into two sexes. Here again is the constantly recurring theme of the dual, and in some ways contradictory nature of man, material and spiritual, animal and divine.

The idea survived in Jacob Boehme's theory (which powerfully influenced William

Blake) that there were two Falls. The original Adam was an angelic spiritual being, immortal, bisexual and virgin. He fell for the first time in acquiring a physical body and dividing into male and female. This was followed by the second Fall when the serpent successfully tempted Eve, bringing death and the necessity for reproduction of the species because man was no longer immortal.

The belief that the original Adam was the perfect pattern of humanity, which man had lost but might regain, inspired various medieval heretics to maintain that men and women should go about naked and refrain entirely from work, which would restore them to the state of perfection of Adam and Eve in Eden before the Fall. In 1925 a group of Adamites were discovered living in California.

Their leader was Eve recreated, her husband was Adam and their farm was the Garden of Eden. They used to dance naked in the farmyard round a bonfire and a lamb was burnt alive on at least one occasion. It is a far cry from the beauty and far-reaching significance of the Old Testament story but the Adamite heresy may perhaps have contributed to the notion that nudism is physically and psychologically healthy.

What is Man?

O Lord, our Lord,
how majestic is thy name in all the earth! . . .
When I look at thy heavens, the work of thy
 fingers,
the moon and the stars which thou hast
 established;
what is man that thou art mindful of him,
and the son of man that thou dost care for him?
Yet thou hast made him little less than God,
and dost crown him with glory and honour.
Thou hast given him dominion over the works
 of thy hands;
thou hast put all things under his feet . . .

Psalm 8

Hamlet . . . indeed it goes so heavily with my disposition that this goodly frame, the earth, seems to me a sterile promontory, this most excellent canopy, the air, look you, this brave o'erhanging firmament, this majestical roof fretted with golden fire, why, it appears no other thing to me than a foul and pestilent congregation of vapours. What a piece of work is a man! how noble in reason! how infinite in faculty! in form and moving how express and admirable! in action how like an angel! in apprehension how like a god! the beauty of the world! the paragon of animals! And yet, to me, what is this quintessence of dust? man delights not me.

Shakespeare *Hamlet*

Opposite As Mahan journeyed through the Wilderness of Ghouls he met an army of evil monsters, whereupon his horse turned into a seven-headed dragon. Ghouls were demons of the Mohammedan world who inhabited lonely places and fed on human bodies; they seem to have personified the terrors of the desert: according to Babylonian legend, the appearance of demons was so dreadful that they fled in horror when shown reflections of themselves in giant mirrors: from a manuscript in the British Museum **Right** Anubis **(left)**, the jackal-headed god, conducted the souls of the dead to the other world and presided over funerals. The ibis-headed god Thoth **(right)** was the wise and benevolent scribe of the gods

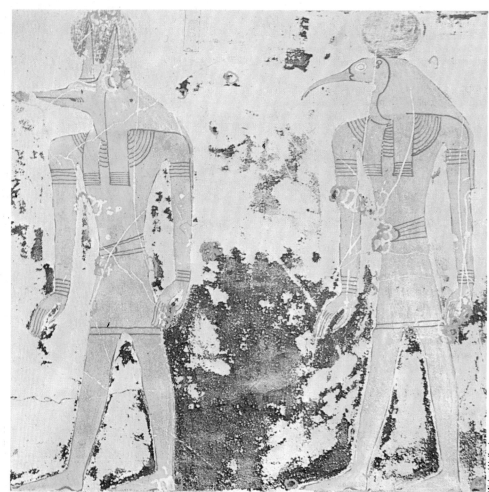

Michael Holford

Evil

Two things have been regarded by mankind down the ages as fundamentally evil: pain and death. Naturally these experiences have been seen in different ways. In some of the more sophisticated interpretations a deeper spiritual evil has been assumed behind the physical realities of pain and death: for example, Christian theology has followed St Paul's pronouncement that 'the sting of death is sin' (1 Corinthians 15.56). However, it is invariably found, on the last analysis, that the concept of evil is essentially inspired by man's experience of pain and his fear of death. The significance given to sin ultimately depends upon the evaluation of death in the pattern of human destiny.

Most religions, consequently, have sought to explain the origin of evil in terms of the cause of pain and death. And they have generally tried to find this cause in the action of some supernatural being or some primordial happening involving the supernatural. Very rarely have pain and death been regarded as natural features of biological life. The most notable exceptions to this general view have been Buddhism and Stoic philosophy. Buddhism, which accounts for the individual person as a temporary combination of various physical and psychical entities, the *skandhas*, explains death as an inevitable disintegration of this combination. Stoicism, a school of thought which originated in Athens, explained death as physical change occasioned by the physics of the universe, and counselled men to live 'according to Nature', in other words, to accept and endure the fact that they were part of a cosmic process that was not designed to accommodate their personal likes and dislikes.

The various explanations of the origin of evil advanced by the chief religions can be reasonably grouped under three headings: as attributable to divine action; as resulting from cosmic dualism; and as due to sin or ignorance on the part of human beings.

The most notable example of the first view— that evil is the result of divine action - is provided by the religion of ancient Mesopotamia. The three peoples who lived in this area and shared in a common cultural tradition, namely, the Sumerians, Babylonians and Assyrians, viewed life very pessimistically. They believed that the gods had created mankind to serve them, but that they had withheld immortality from their human servants. One Sumerian myth told how the god Enki and the goddess Ninmah, after creating mankind, in their sport made various human freaks such as eunuchs and barren women or diseased and decrepit persons, whom they set on the earth. In other words, the evils of disease, malformation, decay and death were due to the gods. The most that the Mesopotamians could hope from their gods by faithful service to them was a long and prosperous life, and defence

from demonic attack. Although they believed that their gods had arbitrarily imposed pain and death upon them, the Mesopotamians never seem to have questioned the justice of this.

A similar acceptance of the basic ills of life as being of divine origin occurs in some other religions, although it does not find such vivid mythical presentation: ancient

Hebrew and Greek literature and the Koran provide examples. This interpretation of the origin of evil inevitably results when a religion assigns the creation of the world and mankind to divine agency alone, without suggesting the existence of an evil power that rivals that of God or the gods. The problem here is inherent in any monotheistic interpretation of the universe, and it finds

expression in varying forms in the great monotheisms of Judaism, Christianity and Islam.

What are called dualistic interpretations of the origin of evil are based upon a more realistic estimate of man's experience of life than are those of the monotheistic faiths. Such experience seems to show that the world is a battleground between a good creative force and an evil destructive force, and that mankind is involved in the struggle both actively and passively.

The most notable example of a dualistic religion is Zoroastrianism, which originated in Iran from the teaching of Zoroaster (or Zarathustra) who was born about 570 BC, and which became a distinctly presented dualism between Ohrmazd (identified with Ahura Mazdah) and Ahriman (Angra Mainyu). All that is good in the world was attributed to Ohrmazd, with Ahriman responsible for all that is evil, including death, disease, demons and noxious animals.

Dualistic interpretations of life have been propounded in some other religions, though not so consistently as in Zoroastrianism. The Hindu gods Vishnu and Shiva were conceived of as being both creators and destroyers of life; in China all existence was explained in terms of the two alternating principles of Yin and Yang.

Judaism had come, by the 1st century AD, to account for evil in terms of a modified dualism. This view represented a change from the earlier conception of Yahweh (Jehovah) who, as the sole omnipotent deity, was regarded as the source of both good and evil: 'Shall we receive good at the hand of God, and shall we not receive evil?' asks the pious Job (Job 2.10).

However, probably due to Iranian influences during the Exile in Babylonia in the 6th century BC, the Jews developed a demonology which held that God's good purpose in this world was thwarted by the Devil and his demonic forces. Both the Dead Sea Scrolls and the Christian gospels show the prevalence of this dualistic outlook. In the latter, physical and mental disease are attributed to demons, and Jesus is tempted and afflicted by the Devil as the 'Prince of this world'. St Paul called death 'the last enemy' that Christ would destroy, and in early Christian thought death was often identified with the Devil.

A dualistic explanation of the origin of evil of a very different type arose out of the conception of man as an immortal soul incarnated in a physical body, and doomed to inhabit a material world. Where the body was regarded as a corrupting prison of the soul, the origin of evil had to be sought in whatever put the soul in such a direful situation. One of the earliest explanations is Greek, given in the Orphic myth of the devouring of Dionysus-Zagreus, the son of Zeus, by the wicked Titans. From the ashes of these Titans, blasted by Zeus for their crime, mankind arose, having a dual nature, for they were compounded of the evil Titans and the divine Dionysus whom they had eaten. Each human being had, therefore, within his Titanic body a soul, divine of origin and longing to return to heaven.

The Orphic mystery cult was designed to free the soul from its contaminating prison and the misery of existence in a material world, and enable it to ascend to the ethereal realm to which it rightly belonged.

Gnosticism, which flourished in the 2nd century AD, in a somewhat similar myth accounted for the present unhappy lot of mankind as being due to the incorporation of a divine soul, fallen from heaven, within a physical body derived of material Nature. Likewise Manicheism, which had a great vogue in Graeco-Roman society, explained the suffering of human existence as resulting from a primeval fall whereby the two contrary principles of the universe became intermixed; these principles were variously designated Spirit and Matter, Good and Evil, Light and Darkness.

The third way in which the origin of evil has been explained is in terms of some primordial sin or ignorance on the part of man. The best known and most influential version of the former view is the account of the Fall of Adam as recorded in the book of Genesis (2.4–3.24); it was composed about 900 BC. The writer was concerned to show that death and the miseries of human life were due to the sin of the first parents of mankind. Accordingly he represents Adam and Eve, after their creation by Yahweh, as living an idyllic existence in the garden of Eden. They are immortal; but Yahweh warns them not to eat of the mysterious Tree of the Knowledge of Good and Evil in the midst of the garden, for if they do they will surely die.

Prodnose Studio

Demons took an immense variety of shapes, as shown by these illustrations from Collin de Plancy's *Dictionnaire Infernal*: from left to right, Amduscias, who gave concerts on the trumpet; Lucifer; Ronwe, who gave knowledge of languages; Orobas, grand prince of hell; Ukobach, inventor of frying foods; Xaphan, who fanned the furnaces of hell; and Eurynome, prince of death

There has been much discussion among scholars about the meaning of this forbidden Tree. For if 'Knowledge of Good and Evil' should mean moral or ethical knowledge, it would be strange that Yahweh should prohibit the first man and woman from acquiring such knowledge, and also threaten them that, if they did acquire such knowledge, they would die. The serpent, however, in tempting Eve, declares that 'God knows that when you eat of it your eyes will be opened, and you will be like God, knowing good and evil.' When they do eat the forbidden fruit, they do not immediately die; instead, they become conscious of their nudity. Their act of disobedience nevertheless has fatal consequences. For when God discovers that they have broken his command, he pronounces Adam's doom: 'In the sweat of your face you shall eat bread till you return to the ground, for out of it you were taken; you are dust, and to dust you shall return.' In other words, by disobeying his Creator Adam becomes subject to death.

There has been much speculation about how this penalty was connected in the mind of the Yahwist writer with eating of the Tree

of Knowledge. The most likely interpretation seems to be that to this ancient Hebrew writer 'Knowledge of Good and Evil' meant knowledge of how to reproduce human life. This seems to be implied by the fact that the immediate consequence of eating the forbidden fruit was that Adam and Eve became conscious of their nudity, which meant their sexual potency; it is only after acquiring this knowledge that 'Adam knew Eve his wife, and she conceived' (Genesis 4.1). But such knowledge was fatal; for the first human pair thus created those who must inevitably replace them.

Whether that was indeed the idea of the Yahwist writer in connecting the Fall of Adam with the mysterious Tree of the Knowledge of Good and Evil, must necessarily remain uncertain. What is certain is that he traced the origin of death to Adam's disobedience to his Maker's command. With death, as the penalty of that original sin, the Yahwist writer also associated the hard toil of agriculture and the pain of childbirth.

The part of the serpent in bringing these evils upon Adam and Eve must be noticed. In the Genesis story, the serpent is described as 'more subtle than any other wild creature that the Lord God had made' and it is represented as having the ability to speak. However, it is not identified with the Devil, as it was in later Hebrew and Christian thought; for instance, in the Wisdom of Solomon: 'By envy of the devil death entered into the world.' The part played by the serpent in the fall of Adam was possibly

inspired by the serpent in the Mesopotamian *Epic of Gilgamesh*. In this celebrated poem the hero is robbed of his opportunity of immortality by a serpent, an idea doubtless derived from a primitive belief that the serpent, by sloughing off its old skin, rejuvenated itself.

The Genesis story of the Fall of Adam exercised a profound influence on Christian thought about the origin of evil. It inspired St Paul to formulate the concept of original sin, which became one of the basic tenets of the Christian doctrine of salvation. He writes in his Epistle to the Romans (5.12-13): 'Sin came into the world through one man and death through sin, and so death spread to all men because all men sinned.'

Christianity, accordingly, came to teach that death and all the other ills which afflict men and women are due, primarily, to their partaking in the original sin of Adam. Furthermore, it taught that mankind add to this inherited penalty by their own actual sins, making themselves even more deserving of the wrath of God. Accordingly, Christianity accounts for the origin of evil in terms of human sin, both original and actual. However, since Christianity inherited the demonology of 1st century Judaism, it has also associated the origin of evil very closely with the Devil, sometimes tracing evil back to the Devil as a fallen angel named Lucifer, who revolted against God before the creation of the world.

Judaism and Christianity, therefore, both find the origin of evil in human sin, but with some dualistic suggestion of a pre-cosmic

159

revolt of an angel or angels against God. Other religions have also traced evil back to man; however, they assign it to his ignorance or error, not to his disobedience to his Maker's command. Hinduism and Buddhism are the two great religions that account for evil in this way.

According to a view that first finds expres-

sion about 600 BC in Hindu compositions known as *Upanishads*, through a primeval ignorance *(avidya)* human beings have made two fatal mistakes: they have taken the phenomenal world, that is, the world apprehended by the senses, as reality; and they cling to existence in this world, believing that they are individual persons or selves *(atman)*.

Opposite The Devil dragging away a sinner to Hell by means of a rope fastened around the hair; 15th century German illustration *Below* The Persian hero Rustem was a great enemy of demons; his most famous exploit was his rescue of the King of Persia by slaying the White Demon within his cavern in the mountains of Tabaristan

Hell

'Oh, you knotty, rugged, proud piece of flesh! You stony, rocky, flinty hard-heart, what wilt thou do when thou art roaring amongst the damned?' Bellowed by a hellfire preacher of the 17th century, the question frightened a ten-year-old boy named John Rogers half out of his wits, and he went to sleep every night with his hands in an anxiously prayerful attitude in case the demons came to fetch him. Ola Elizabeth Winslow quotes the story in her life of John Bunyan, who as a boy was so haunted by nightmares of hell that he wished he was a devil himself, on the principle that it would be better to be a torturer than one of the tortured. Another famous preacher of the day, Vavasor Powell, traced his conversion to a bout of toothache which caused him to wonder, if the temporary pain of toothache was so hard to bear, what would the eternal agony of hell be like?

At this period the established doctrine of hell was beginning to be challenged, though rarely in public because those who disbelieved in it considered the threat of hell the supreme deterrent to atheism, immorality and crime. But hell kept its hold on most Christians, though with steadily weakening force in succeeding generations, into this century. In 1916 James Joyce published, in *A Portrait of the Artist as a Young Man*, one of the most powerful descriptions of the horrors of hell ever written, based on what he had been taught at a Roman Catholic school in Ireland. And on the Protestant front, fundamentalist hellfire preaching is by no means extinct.

Hell retained its long grip on the Christian mind because its existence is stated in the New Testament, because of its supposed value as a deterrent, and because of the common human observation that in this life the wicked flourish while the good suffer, with the consequent demand for rewards and punishments to right the balance in the life to come. In descriptions of hell, much ingenuity was frequently devoted to making the punishment fit the crime.

In addition, though to explain belief in hell solely in terms of sado-masochism is to oversimplify, there is no mistaking the lip-licking avidity with which its torments were relished. For hundreds of years the 'dooms', horribly imaginative pictures of the tortures to come, were carved and painted on the walls of churches to warn unbelievers and sinners. The *Apocalypse of Peter* of the early 2nd century, which ranked second in popularity among Christians only to the beauties and terrors of the Book of Revelation itself, described the 'place of punishment':

And some were there hanging by their tongues; and these were they that blasphemed the way of righteousness, and under them was laid fire flaming and tormenting them . . . And there were also others, women hanged by their hair above that mire which boiled up; and these were they that adorned themselves for adultery . . . And in another place were gravel-stones sharper than swords or any spit, heated with fire, and men and women clad in filthy rags rolled upon them in torment. And these were they that were rich and trusted in their riches . . . Beside them shall be girls clad in darkness for a garment, and they shall be sore chastised and their flesh shall be torn in pieces. These are they that kept not their virginity until they were given in marriage . . .

The medieval picture of hell, a gigantic concentration camp of appalling fiery heat far underground, with its entrances through volcanoes like Etna (or through the gaping mouth of Leviathan, the terrible dragon of the Old Testament) hit on something very close to geological truth, as Jacquetta Hawkes has pointed out (in *A Land*) for beneath the earth's surface the rock substance is molten with heat. 'Only a score of miles below the surface on which we walk the crust is molten . . . we do in fact maintain our fragile lives on a wafer balanced between a hellish morass and unlimited space.' It also hit on a psychological truth, for accounts of hell closely resemble some visionary experiences, and some states of mind induced by drugs or by mental illness.

Prehistoric burials suggest that the earliest human beings were believers in some sort of existence after death; and the custom of burying the remains in the earth suggests the belief that the dead lived on underground.

Headless figures, if they represent the spirits of people who had been beheaded in life, may contain the glimmerings of the idea that what happened to a man while he was alive would affect him after he was dead. The headless figures attacked by huge black vultures at Catal Hüyük may even, at a guess, represent the wicked being punished.

The earliest people who definitely believed in a judgement after death, with rewards and punishments, were the Egyptians. They concentrated on rewards and said little of the punishments. There is one reference to the wicked being tortured in pits of fire but generally the Egyptians thought that those who were weighed and found wanting after death would be eternally annihilated.

In Mesopotamian literature there is no punishment after death, and no reward either. All the dead, good and bad, rich and poor, powerful and humble alike, go to the 'land of no return', the house of darkness which was like a gigantic communal grave, surrounded by walls and barred by gates, where the ghosts flew about like spectral birds and gnawed miserably on clay and dust.

Homer's underworld is also not a hell but a place of dreary darkness to which all, or nearly all, the dead go. This was the house of Hades, the god of death, whose name means 'the unseen' and who ruled what the *Iliad* calls 'the hateful Chambers of Decay that fill the gods themselves with horror.' Some vengeful lines of Sappho emphasize the hopeless condition of the dead:

When you are dead you will lie in your grave, forgotten for ever,
Because you despise the flowers of the Muse; in Hades — as here —
Dimly your shadow will flit with the rest, unnoticed, obscure.

The Greeks feared death so intensely that they did not like to name it, saying as many people still do that someone who died had 'departed'. In the *Odyssey* the ghost of Achilles says that he would sooner be alive as the servant of a landless peasant than be king of all the dead.

Hades became a name for the underworld itself, and later a name for the Christian hell. It was either far in the west, where the sun died in the evening, or deep underground with the entrances at many places on the earth's surface. These entrances may be the legacy of an earlier belief that the dead stayed in the places where they were buried. The Styx, a stream in Arcadia, which disappeared underground, became the principal river of the underworld, across which the dead had to be ferried by Charon in his boat. What later became the most famous entrance of all ('easy is the descent to Avernus') was at the lake of Avernus, not far from Naples in Italy, which Virgil described in the *Aeneid*. 'There was a deep and rugged cave, stupendous and yawning wide, protected by a lake of black water and the glooming forest . . . poisonous the breath which streamed up from those black jaws and rose to the vault of sky.'

An intense love of, and concentration on, this life naturally tends to reduce the next world to a faint shadow-play. But although the Homeric picture of the dead remained extremely influential, there were other views. Some of the more important dead lived on their tombs, where they were venerated and consulted by mortals. Belief in different treatment for different people in the next world was stimulated by the mystery religions which promised a blessed afterlife to those who were initiated.

Punishment in the underworld appears even in Homer. In the *Iliad* the Furies 'make men pay for perjury in the world below' and even the deposed god Cronus and his allies are found imprisoned in the 'the bottomless pit' of Tartarus, 'where the deepest of all caverns yawns below the world, where the Iron Gates are, and the Brazen Theshold, as far below Hades as the earth is under heaven.' In the *Odyssey* (book 11) a fortunate few go to a happy afterlife in Elysium and a few who have personally insulted Zeus are tormented in Tartarus.

In Plato's time (4th century BC) there were stories about punishment after death. A character in the *Republic* mentions them and says that when a man grows old he cannot help uneasily wondering whether the stories are true. In the last book of the *Republic* the 'myth of Er' describes how the dead are judged and how the unjust are sent down under the earth. For every wrong they have done they will suffer tenfold and after a journey of 1000 years under the earth they will be purged. Er saw tyrants and other peculiarly evil men at the mouth of a cavern. When any of them who had not been sufficiently purged tried to emerge from it, the mouth 'gave a roar' and 'wild men of fiery aspect' seized them, flayed them with scourges and took them away to plunge them into Tartarus.

The descent of Aeneas to the underworld influenced the medieval picture of hell, and especially as shown in Dante's *Inferno* which was so graphic that simple-minded people assumed that the poet had really visited hell. In the *Aeneid* (book 6) Aeneas sees the great battlements of Tartarus and the burning Phlegethon. The entrance is guarded by a Fury and from inside comes the sound of savage flogging, the clanking of iron chains and a terrible lamentation.

The picture of life after death as a powerless obscurity in darkness, found in the literature of Homeric Greece, Mesopotamia and early Palestine, conflicts with the archeological evidence from the same areas that the dead were buried with grave goods, implying an active life in the otherworld. Evidently the literature does not adequately reflect the full range of beliefs, and in Palestine it seems clear that the adherents of Yahweh as the one supreme god deliberately discouraged belief in an active life after death, to prevent people from trafficking with any other supernatural beings.

In the older passages in the Old Testament all the dead, good and bad alike, go to Sheol where they live in dust and darkness (like the Mesopotamian dead) and where they know nothing, so that it is no use trying to consult them. Sheol is a great pit or a walled city, 'the land of forgetfulness', 'the land of silence'. Maggots are the bed beneath you there and worms are your covering. No god rules in Sheol and the dead are forgotten by Yahweh. But as the story of the witch of Endor (I Samuel, chapter 28) shows, they were not entirely forgotten by men and some tried to enlist their help.

Jewish hatred of foreign oppressors, with the desire to see them punished in the next world if not in this, was partly responsible for a change of attitude. So was the old problem of the unfairness of life, vividly expressed in the book of Job (chapter 21): 'One dies in full prosperity, being wholly at ease and secure, his body full of fat and the marrow of his bones moist. Another dies in bitterness of soul, never having tasted of

Above Pluto, the king of the Greek underworld enthroned in the 'hateful Chambers of Decay' with his wife Persephone. At their feet lies the monstrous dog Cerberus, guardian of the entrance: from a French MS *Opposite* Hell, final resting place of the damned, is the demonic counterpart of Heaven, home of the righteous. The Devil rules in the nether regions, while Christ sits enthroned on high: medieval manuscript illustration. So vivid was the medieval imagination, many thought that Hell really did look like this

good. They lie down alike in the dust, and the worms cover them.'

Considerations of this kind led to a growing belief that the lot of all men after death was not the same. In the 2nd century BC the Jewish leader Judas Maccabaeus made an offering of money at Jerusalem on behalf of some of his dead soldiers, on whose bodies had been found objects consecrated to idols. This was 'a reconciliation for the dead that they might be delivered from sin' and implies the belief that they would otherwise

suffer in the afterworld (2 Maccabees, chapter 12). The book of Daniel predicts the 'many of those who sleep in the dust of the earth shall awake, some to everlasting life, and some to shame and everlasting contempt.'

There is no mention of physical torture here, but there is in another work of the same period, *1 Enoch*, which includes a vision of 'a place chaotic and horrible' with 'seven stars of the heaven bound together in it, like great mountains and burning

Giraudon

with fire.' It was here that the angels who mistakenly lusted after human women would be punished, an early trace of the belief that the fallen angels, or demons, live in hell. Then Enoch sees Sheol itself, a mountain in the west with hollow compartments in it where the souls of the dead are to wait for the day of judgement. One is for the righteous and one is for the sinners, who wait there 'in great pain' (chapters 17–22). In a later passage there is 'a deep valley with burning fire. And they brought the kings and the mighty, and began to cast them into the deep valley' (chapter 54).

This valley of fire was Gehenna where, it came to be believed, the wicked would writhe tormented in the flames. Some of the Jewish rabbis said that the punishment there would not last more than 12 months. Some said that the righteous would go straight to paradise, the wicked to eternal pain in Gehenna, and the in-between would suffer for a year in Gehenna and then be annihilated. Gehenna has three entrances, one in the wilderness, one in the sea, and one in Jerusalem. It was next door to paradise, with the implication that part of the misery of the condemned was to see the bliss they had lost, an idea that passed into Christian theology.

The development of a Jewish hell may

have been influenced by Persian Zoroastrianism in which the 'followers of the lie' are punished after death. Hell is in the far north, deep down beneath the earth, dark and stinking, the home of demons and lies, a place of stench, filth, pain and misery. There the damned soul must remain until Ahriman himself is defeated and destroyed, by which time it will at last have come to understand reality and the wickedness of Ahriman, and will be ready for its release.

A holy man named Artay Viraf saw hell in a vision induced by hashish. It was like the inside of a grave. He experienced 'cold and an icy wind, dryness and stench', and he saw a narrow and fearful pit, thick with darkness. Noxious beasts tore and worried at the damned. And this hell had also the horror of the grave's solitariness, for each soul thought 'I am alone'.

From Gehenna Christian hell developed. Jesus said that when the Son of Man comes in glory, he will separate the good from the wicked like sheep from goats. The goats will be driven away 'into eternal punishment' in the fire prepared for the Devil and his angels (Matthew, chapter 25).

The association of fire with hell, sometimes taken as a symbol of purging, seems to have originated in the idea of burning up rubbish. Gehenna took its name from

the valley of Hinnom where the rubbish of Jerusalem was burned. There is the same notion in Malachi (4.1): 'all evildoers will be stubble; the day that comes shall burn them up.' Again in Matthew (chapter 13) Jesus tells a parable about the burning of weeds and explains it with: 'The Son of Man will send his angels, and they will gather out of his kingdom all causes of sin and all evildoers, and throw them into the furnace of fire; there men will weep and gnash their teeth.'

Many of St Paul's references to the fate of the wicked suggest that they will be annihilated, though in Romans (chapter 2) dealing with 'the day of wrath', he says that for every human being who does evil 'there will be tribulation and distress'. In the book of Revelation (chapter 21) 'the lake that burns with fire and brimstone, which is the second death' is the final destination of the cowardly, the faithless, the polluted, murderers, fornicators, sorcerers, idolaters and all liars. The brimstone is sulphur ('burning stone') and the reference is to Isaiah (30.33): 'For a burning place has long been prepared . . . the breath of the Lord, like a stream of brimstone, kindles it.'

Only one passage in the New Testament (Matthew 25.46) says that the punishment in hell will last for all eternity and in the

3rd century the great theologian Origen suggested that the torment in hell would not last for ever, that the wicked and even the Devil himself would eventually be redeemed and evil totally annihilated, and that the 'fire' of hell might not be a real fire but the pangs of guilty conscience. Even he was worried that by questioning the eternity of punishment he might weaken the chief deterrent to immorality, but in fact his views were rejected by the majority of Christians and condemned as heretical by the church.

In the medieval hell the damned suffered 'the pain of loss' the agony of being cut off from God, and 'the pain of sense' the physical tortures inflicted by demons. Most of the dead did not go to hell, or to heaven, but to purgatory where they were purified of sin and could be helped by the prayers of the faithful on earth, but in most descriptions of purgatory the agonies are almost as frightful as those of hell itself. Many modern Christians have returned to the outlook of Origen, seeing hell as a place where the guilty are purged of evil and unbelief, but not by physical torture. Others reject hell entirely, believing that God's infinite mercy will extend to everyone, or alternatively, that the irredeemable are not tormented and tortured but are simply annihilated.

Christ was crucified on the first Good Friday and, as the Apostles' Creed says, 'descended into hell'. He rose from the dead on Easter Sunday.

The word 'hell' itself comes from an Anglo-Saxon root meaning 'to cover' or 'to conceal' with an obvious application to a grave. The Scandinavian goddess Hel ruled those who died of old age or disease (those who fell in battle went to a happy afterlife in Valhalla). She was fierce and pitiless and her underworld of Nifelheim was freezing cold, like the lowest circle of hell in Dante's *Inferno*.

The Islamic picture of hell resembles the Jewish and Christian ones, by which it was influenced. In India the idea of punishment of the wicked after death is very old but in both Buddhism and Hinduism the numerous hells are not places of eternal torture but stages in the chain of birth, death and rebirth which the self must undergo unless it can escape from the cycle altogether. At each death the self goes to a paradise or a hell corresponding to the way it has behaved in each life.

The Tibetan Book of the Dead says that after death each person goes before Yama, the King of the Dead, who holds up to him a mirror in which his deeds are reflected. 'The mirror in which Yama seems to read your past is your own memory, and also his judgement is your own. It is you yourself who pronounce your own judgement, which in its turn determines your next rebirth.' The terrible god and the frightening monsters which are seen are 'an illusion'. But popular belief in India, China and Japan imagines tortures and torturers as real, as vindictive and as ingenious as any in the western traditions. The history of hell is a descent into the infernal pit of the human mind.

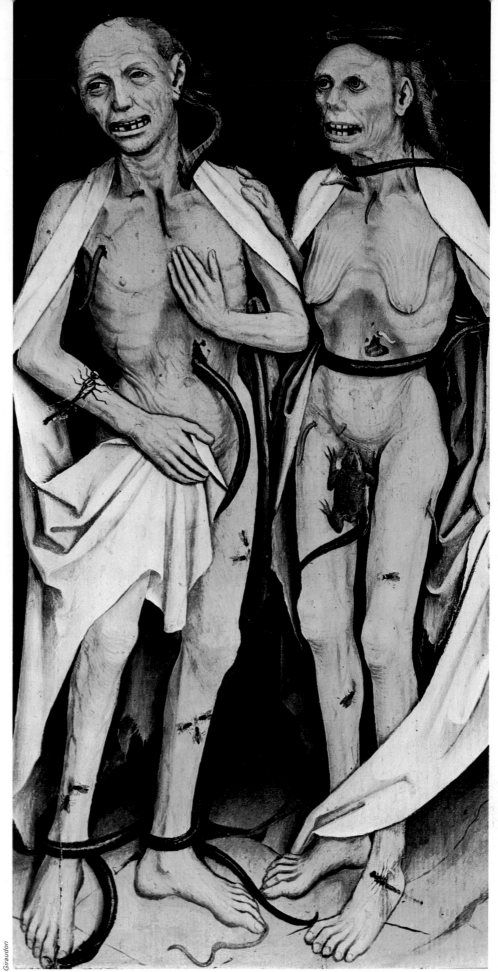

Giraudon

Opposite After his crucifixion, Christ was believed to have descended into hell, broken open the gates and released the dead from the chains binding them: *The Harrowing of Hell* by a 15th century painter of the School of Savoy, where hell is a vast mouth

Above In this painting entitled the *Damnation of Lovers* by the 16th century German artist Mathias Grünewald, the flesh in whose joys the sinners have luxuriated is aged and withered and is pierced by noxious beasts, representing the poison and corruption of lust

The Judgement of the Dead

That the fate of the dead is decided at a post-mortem judgement is an idea which is very ancient and widespread. It naturally involves belief that the dead survive death, that they remember their past lives and are conscious that they are now dead, and that they can experience the pain of punishment and the joy of reward. Where death is regarded as the virtual extinction of personality, as it was for example in ancient Mesopotamian and Homeric religion, there is no basis for belief in a post-mortem judgement – the shades of the dead, good and bad, are doomed to virtual non-existence.

The earliest known evidence of belief that the dead would be judged for their conduct in this life occurs in Egyptian records dating c 2400 BC. The belief was obviously already well established by that date, and its origins doubtless lie back in a more remote past. In the Pyramid Texts inscribed on the interior walls of certain pyramids at Sakkara two different conceptions of this judgement were apparently current. One is of an unsophisticated kind, and it was probably inspired by contemporary juridical practice. It finds expression in a series of anticipatory declarations of innocence made by the deceased in respect of various crimes. The

idea behind these declarations seems to be that in the next life complaints might be brought against the dead as they were brought against the living in this world. As, in the primitive courts of Egypt, the accused would vehemently reject the charges and protest his innocence, so it was apparently thought well to anticipate such charges in the afterlife by prior solemn declarations of guiltlessness. In these passages, however, no reference is made to a judge of the dead.

The other conception was of a much more involved kind. In one Text it is said of the dead pharaoh: 'He desires that he may be justified *(maa kheru)* through that which he has done'. The words *maa kheru* meant literally 'true of voice', and they acquired a specific significance through the legend of the god Osiris. The ancient Egyptians believed that the case of the divine hero Osiris, after his resurrection from death, had been brought before a tribunal of the gods of Heliopolis. Osiris was there adjudged *maa kheru*, 'justified', and his murderer Seth was condemned. Since the dead king, in the Pyramid Texts, was ritually identified with Osiris in order to participate in his resurrection, this identification also caused him to acquire Osiris's title in the state after

death of *maa kheru*. The Pyramid Texts thus reveal the origin of an idea which later came to dominate the Egyptian conception of the judgement of the dead.

Certain tomb inscriptions of about the same period, or slightly later, reveal an important development in this idea of a posthumous judgement. At that time the royal government of Egypt was weakening, with much resultant social disorder. Tombs were being either robbed of their funerary equipment or taken over by others for their own mortuary use. To the law-abiding, such happenings were most terrible, for they threatened their hopes of a blissful afterlife. Some Egyptians sought to meet the danger by threatening inscriptions on their tombs. Thus Herkhuf, an Aswan

Above Virgil's account of the underworld as a place of retribution, where demons and writhing snakes plague sinners, greatly influenced the medieval concept of hell: in Orcagna's *Inferno*, the wicked are their own tormentors *Opposite* In this painting by St John of Climax, judgement takes place on a ladder, symbolizing the link between heaven and earth: the blessed mount towards God and his angels, while the wicked are dragged off to their doom below

noble, warns any would-be robber: 'As for any man who shall enter into this tomb as his mortuary possession, I will seize him like a wild fowl; he shall be judged for it by the Great God.'

The 'Great God' whom Herkhuf here invokes was doubtless the sun god Re, who was regarded as the upholder of *maat*, the principle of cosmic order. In other words, Herkhuf not only claims that, though dead, he was able to attack any who might rob his tomb; he confidently asserts that Re himself would punish so vile a crime. But the thought of the divine judgement that would fall on the robber apparently led Herkhuf to think about his own situation. For he goes on in his inscription to declare: 'I was one saying good things and repeating what was loved. Never did I say aught evil, to a powerful one against any people, for I desired that it might be well with me in the Great God's presence.'

In other words, this ancient Egyptian not only threatened any would-be violator of his tomb with divine judgement; he was mindful that he had himself to undergo such judgement.

No hint is given in this earliest evidence of how the judgement after death was imagined. Some kind of tribunal was evidently envisaged. Herkhuf seems to imply that Re was the judge, but he makes no reference to the way in which the verdict was reached. A clearer picture emerges

from the next document that mentions the post-mortem judgement. It is known as the Instruction for King Meri-ka-re, and dates from c 2100 BC. The dead are depicted as being tried by a panel of judges with Thoth, the god of wisdom, acting as prosecutor. Their deeds are set before them in two heaps, presumably of the good and the bad. This imagery, however, did not establish itself and the Coffin Texts of the Middle Kingdom period (c 2160–1580 BC) reveal a fluidity of concept about the judgement.

During this period, however, a new idea emerged that was to dominate the later conception of the judgement. References occur in the Coffin Texts to weighing on balances as the mode of assessment. How this weighing was done is obscure: in one passage the balance is actually personified as 'this god of mysterious form, whose two eyebrows are the two arms of the balance, who casts his lasso over the wicked (to hale them to) his block, who annihilates the souls, in that day when evil is assessed, in the presence of the Master of all.'

The motive that inspired the idea that the dead would be assessed by weighing is an interesting subject for speculation. On the available evidence, it would seem that the ancient Egyptians sought for an image that would express the absolute impartiality of the judgement after death. Doubtless their experience of legal chicanery caused them to avoid the imagery of earthly

tribunals. The earlier idea of assessing the dead by the witness of their good and evil deeds set out in heaps had invoked the practice of the market place; but, though a vivid image, it was evidently found inadequate. The process of weighing must obviously have been deemed a better conception, and by the New Kingdom (c 1580–1090 BC) it was developed into one of the most impressive scenes in the religious iconography of the ancient world.

The best picture of the scene, beautifully drawn and coloured, is in the Papyrus of Ani, now in the British Museum. The scene depicts the dead scribe Ani and his wife watching apprehensively the weighing of Ani's heart in the Hall of the Two Truths. The great balance occupies the centre of the scene. In one scale-pan the hieroglyph symbol of the heart is represented, and in the other the feather symbol of *Maat*, truth. The heart of Ani is being weighed against truth. In ancient Egyptian psychology the heart was regarded as a kind of independent censor or witness within each person and in most copies of the Book of the Dead the heart is implored not to witness against the deceased at this decisively critical moment.

The fateful balance is attended by the jackal-headed mortuary god Anubis, who adjusts its plummet, while the text above him exhorts him to be exact. To the right of the balance stands Thoth, the ibis-headed

Mary Evans Picture Library

Medieval representations of the judgement emphasize the horrors of hell. Dante's *Inferno* describes ten divisions of hell in all *Above* Detail from a 12th century mosaic in Torcello Cathedral: angels thrust the damned into the flames while the Devil sits with Antichrist in his lap *Opposite left* Dante is shown a frozen lake where icy figures symbolize the extinction of all feeling *Opposite right* Tyrants boil in a river of blood

god of wisdom, who records the verdict of the weighing on his scribe's tablet. The adjacent text gives the report which Thoth makes to the divine assessors seated above. Ani is acquitted: 'His soul *(ba)* has stood in witness thereof. His case is exact on the Great Balance. No crime has been found in what he has done.' In turn, the divine tribunal is represented as replying to Thoth: 'Confirmed is that which comes forth from your mouth. Just *(maa)* and righteous is Osiris (namely) the scribe Ani. He is justified . . . Entrance into the presence of Osiris shall be granted to him.'

The scene ominously indicates the fate which awaited the guilty. Behind Thoth is depicted the fantastic monster Am-mut, the 'eater of the dead'.

This judgement scene is followed by another representing the god Horus who is seen leading the justified Ani into the presence of Osiris, who sits enthroned and attended by the goddesses Isis and Nephthys. Subsequent vignettes in the Papyrus show Ani and his wife enjoying the delights of the otherworld, over which Osiris ruled. In most other depictions of the judgement scene Osiris is represented as presiding in person over the transaction.

The presentation of the judgement in the Book of the Dead is complicated by chapter 125, which is entitled: 'Words spoken when one enters the Hall of the Two Truths. To separate N from his sins, and to see the face of all the gods.' Then follow two lists of what are often called 'negative confessions', but which are more correctly designated 'declarations of innocence'. The first, and shorter, is addressed to Osiris; the second to 42 other deities. The sins, of which the deceased declares that he is innocent, range widely and include moral offences, such as murder and unnatural sexual relations, and ritual offences like hindering the procession of a god. The conception of the judgement implied in this chapter is quite different from that presented by the weighing of the heart. The discrepancy is probably to be explained by the conservatism of the Egyptian mind. For these 'declarations of innocence' doubtless derive from the primitive asseverations of guiltlessness from specific sins that appear in the Pyramid Texts. Never willing to discard ancient traditions, the Egyptians retained this one even when the idea of the weighing of the heart had become the dominant theme of the judgement. They apparently reconciled the differing conceptions by representing the 'Declarations' as being made first by the deceased on arrival at the Hall of the Two Truths. The subsequent weighing of his heart against the symbol of truth proved whether his protestation of innocence was just.

This Egyptian conception of the judgement after death is unique in the ancient world. It remained an effective belief in Egypt until the Christian era; it is only in Christianity that the idea achieved a like importance and such dramatic presentation.

Until the 2nd century BC Hebrew religion did not provide the necessary basis for belief in a judgement after death. According to its view of human nature, man was a psycho-physical organism which death irreparably shattered. The shade that survived this dissolution descended to Sheol, conceived as a deep pit far below the foundations of the world, where all the shades of the dead dwelt in dust and gloom, with no distinction between the just and the unjust. However, about the time of the Maccabaean Wars, a change took place. Belief in a resurrection of the dead suddenly made its appearance, together with the idea of a judgement of the dead. The earliest evidence is the following brief statement in the book of Daniel (12.2): 'And many of those who sleep in the dust of the earth shall awake . . . some to everlasting life, and some to shame and everlasting contempt.' The statement is admittedly obscure, particularly in its limitation of resurrection to an undefined 'many'. However, this first problematic evidence of the belief is soon supported in Jewish literature by an abundance of references to, and descriptions of, a future judgement of the dead. In turn, the conception of Sheol changes from the place where all the dead dwell, undifferentiated by their moral character, to a place of punishment for the wicked.

The Jewish conception of the judgement of the dead was essentially conditioned by the strong nationalist factor in Judaism. It had long been believed that there would be a 'Day of Yahweh' when the god of Israel would signally punish the oppressors of his people. In later Jewish apocalyptic literature, owing to the deterioration of

Israel's political position, this belief was gradually changed into an intense conviction that Yahweh would soon intervene dramatically in the existing world situation. The 'Day of Yahweh' was, in consequence, transformed into a Last Judgement, coincident with the catastrophic end of the world. The following passage from the apocalyptic writing known as II(IV) *Esdras* (chapter 6) vividly presents this Last Judgement at which the god of Israel would pronounce the doom of the Gentile Nations, who had afflicted his people:

And the earth shall restore those that are asleep in her, and so shall the dust those that dwell in silence, and the secret places shall deliver those souls that are committed unto them. And the Most High shall be revealed on the seat of judgement, and compassion shall pass away, and longsuffering shall be withdrawn: but judgement only shall remain. . . And the pit of torment shall appear, and over against it shall be the place of rest: and the furnace of hell shall be shewed, and over against it the paradise of delight. And then shall the Most High say to the nations that are raised from the dead, see and understand whom ye have denied, or whom ye have not served, or whose commandment ye have despised. Look on this side and that: here is delight and rest, and there fire and torments. Thus shall he speak unto them in the day of judgement.

In Jewish apocalyptic belief the Last Judgement was primarily an 'Assize of Nations', at which the Gentiles would be punished for their oppression of Israel. It was to be preceded by a general resurrection of the dead, and accompanied by cosmic cataclysm. In some versions of the belief the Messiah, instead of God (Yahweh), would be the judge. This idea of a Last Judgement was taken over by Christianity, and profoundly influenced its doctrine concerning the 'last things'.

Neither the Greek nor the Roman religion offered hope of a significant afterlife, and therefore no ground existed for belief in a post-mortem judgement. The description of the dead given in Homer's *Odyssey* (book 11) set the pattern for what might be called the classical view of human destiny. At death the *psyche,* a wraith-like image of the living person, descended to the gloomy realm of Hades. There it joined the other dead, who dwelt there bereft of consciousness. The logic of this situation negated belief in a judgement after death.

The idea of Hades as a place of retribution, thus implying a judgement, gradually developed, chiefly through the influence of Orphism (connected with Orpheus) and Neo-Pythagoreanism. The fate of the dead turned on whether they had been initiated or not into the Mystery cults concerned. But the post-mortem judgement gradually came to be thought of as a moral test. A vivid description of Hades as a place of retributive punishment for sins is given by Virgil in the *Aeneid* (book 6). In the underworld, his hero Aeneas comes to a parting of ways:

one leads to Elysium; the other to Dis, a great fortress-like place, encircled by a flaming river. Here Rhadamanthys 'holds his iron sway; he chastises, and hears the tale of guilt, exacting confessions of crimes, whenever in the world above any man rejoicing in vain deceit, has put off atonement for sin until death's late hour'. Awful demons, with writhing snakes, torment these sinners. This horrific depiction greatly influenced Dante as his *Inferno* shows, and it is reflected in many medieval descriptions of hell.

Christianity began in Judaea as a Jewish messianic movement. Its outlook was thus conditioned by current apocalyptic belief. Jesus was identified with the Messiah and, after his crucifixion, it was believed that he would soon return with supernatural power to complete his messianic task. This belief finds dramatic expression in the gospel of Matthew (25.31–33), where he presides at the Last Judgement: 'when the Son of man shall come in his glory, and all the angels with him, then shall he sit on the throne of his glory: and before him shall be gathered all the nations, and he will separate them one from another as a shepherd separates the sheep from the goats, and he will place the sheep at his right hand, but the goats at the left.' Although the passage at this point suddenly changes from envisaging an Assize of Nations, according to Jewish apocalyptic, into a trial of individual persons, the judgement is the traditional Last Judgement at the end of the world. The most graphic presentation of this Judgement in the New Testament is given in the Revelation of John (20.11–13).

The first Christians believed that the return of Christ and the Last Judgement would happen within their own lifetime. But the non-fulfilment of this expectation gradually caused a change of outlook. Although belief in an apocalyptic Last Judgement was never abandoned, subsequent generations of Christians had to adapt their faith to the fact that they would doubtless die before Christ returned. The question inevitably arose, therefore, of the situation of the dead until the Last Judgement determined their eternal fate. A solution was found in the idea of a judgement immediately after death, which was implied by Christ's parable of Dives and Lazarus (Luke, chapter 16). Hence emerged the concept of two post-mortem judgements in Christianity: an immediate or particular judgement and a final judgement. And with it developed the doctrine of purgatory. It was taught that immediately after death the soul would be judged and sent to purgatory, unless its sins were such that it was already damned beyond redemption. In purgatory expiation was made for past sins, in the hope of ultimate acquittal at the Last Judgement, when the purified soul would be admitted to the beatific vision.

A distinction was drawn between the torments of purgatory and those of hell. In purgatory the souls of the dead were disembodied; hence their sufferings were not physical as they would be in hell, where the damned suffered in their resurrected bodies. Further, the souls in purgatory suffered in the hope of ultimate deliverance; but the pains of hell were eternal. However, despite these theological distinctions, it would appear from medieval art and literature that the torments of purgatory were imagined just as realistically as those of hell.

The prospect of immediate judgement and purgatory did not lessen concern about the judgement to come. From about the 12th century the representation of the Last Judgement became a major theme of Christian art in both the Eastern and Western Church. These medieval depictions are generally composed of three registers of scenes. At the top Christ appears as the awful Judge; he shows the wounds of Crucifixion, and attendant angels bear the symbols of his Passion. On either side the Virgin Mary and St John kneel, supplicating the stern Christ to spare sinful humanity. In the bottom register the dead rise from their graves at the sound of the Last Trump. It is in the central register, however, that the crucial drama is enacted. Generally, the Archangel Michael is represented weighing the souls of men, and repelling the attempts of the Devil to interfere with the verdict. This *psychostasia* or weighing of souls was derived from ancient Egypt, by way of Coptic Christianity; its adoption into the medieval Doom constitutes a fascinating instance of the transference of ideas.

In the Doom (the name by which representations of the Last Judgement are known in England, where they often appear on the chancel arch of a church), the weighing of souls divided the two groups of the redeemed and the damned; the division was obviously intended to denote its decisive nature. The redeemed are usually represented as being carried by angels to Abraham's bosom (Luke 16.22). Abraham is quaintly depicted as seated, with a crowd of diminutive souls looking complacently out from the bosom of his robe. The damned, on the other side, are herded by demons, horrible and relentless, towards the mouth of hell or cast into the cauldron of hell. The medieval Doom vividly testifies to the importance of the idea of the Last Judgement in medieval Christianity. Although the depiction of it virtually ceased after the Reformation, the idea continued to haunt Christians and it was a basic theme of both Catholic and Protestant teaching until the 19th century.

In Islam the final judgement was a foremost topic of Mohammed's teaching, and reflects Judaeo-Christian concepts. The idea of a post-mortem judgement occurs also in popular Buddhism, where it has been adapted to the idea of the transmigration of the soul and the doctrine of *karma.*

The ruler and supreme judge of the dead in Japanese Buddhism is Emma-O: the sinner is weighed and his sins are reflected in a mirror; he is then condemned to a particular hell according to the sins he has committed

C. M. Dixon

Purgatory

The fact that the sanctions for unjust and immoral conduct which can be imposed in this life are inadequate might occur to any thinking man. What form the penalties of another life might take would be a matter for guesswork, but that there should be some penalty seems reasonable to many who believe in the immortality of the soul and who in consequence accept purgatory as a condition or place of spiritual cleansing for the dead. That there should be a restoration of the human soul to a lost integrity, where that is possible, also seems reasonable. In the *Aeneid* Virgil pictured a threefold purgation of souls that were too earthy, the elements of fire, water and air being called upon to do the work; some were seared with fire, others hung out as on a clothes-line to suffer the action of the air,

and a third sort churned in a vast whirlpool. Virgil was governed by the Stoic idea that this process lasted for 1000 years and that then the life of the world began anew.

The Pythagoreans, with whose views Virgil was not unfamiliar, held that the soul at death passed upwards through the air, then through the waters above the air and finally through the atmosphere warmed by the sun, until it was deposited in the Isles of the Blest. This passage through air, water and solar radiation was looked upon as the purgation of the soul. Once in the Isles of the Blest it might be left for a time and then escorted to a still higher Elysium, or alternatively it might be sent down to join another body on earth from whence it had come. The Isles of the Blest were located in the moon and disembar-

kation there was considered to be endangered by certain 'customs officers' who might rob the soul of its assets. Ritual acts performed while on earth might be a guarantee that the soul would escape harm from these searchers.

Towards the end of Old Testament times, Jewish belief was centred on prayer and sacrifice for the dead in such cases where hope for the remission of their sins might be entertained. The famous incident of Judas Maccabaeus set the pattern; after a victory he had found that some of his dead warriors had pagan amulets under their tunics. They had died nobly for the liberty of their Jewish faith, but they had also offended God by superstition or else by greed. Judas directed that sacrifice should be offered for them at Jerusalem that they might be set free from their sins (2 Maccabees, chapter 12). The book of Enoch (22.12) holds out a prospect that sinners who are themselves sinned against will not stay for ever in Gehenna with those sinners who have no such asset.

The coming of Christianity meant that the two books of Maccabees were taken over as part of the scriptures of the Church and the incident there reported was valued as precedent. Prayer for the dead (as distinct from prayer to those who had died by martyrdom) was a Christian practice from the beginning. The mention of 'the house of Onesiphorus' (2 Timothy, chapter 1) in a context where the past good works of its head are commemorated, implies that this Onesiphorus was already dead and is being commended to mercy. Inscriptions of the 2nd century ask the passer-by to intercede for the soul of the dead person who is named.

St Paul himself once indicated that he held the same belief. In 1 Corinthians (chapter 3) he speaks of the varying work of evangelists; some are good builders, others run up a shack with anything that is to hand. When a fire sweeps through the town, the good building of stone will stand, but the shack will burn, and its occupant may only just manage to get out, 'being saved as it were through the fire'. The careful evangelist is rewarded; the careless one is saved, but only just. This is an allegory of heaven and purgatory, though not a direct formal pronouncement of belief. The saying in the gospel of St Luke (12.59) about the officer of the law putting in ward the evil-doer and keeping him there till he pay the last farthing was likewise taken as an indirect way of describing the fate after death of the soul whose sin was not irremediable.

While urging prayer for the dead, the Church was also teaching that there were certain capital sins which, if they were not forgiven in this world, could never be pardoned. Thus the category of what came to be called venial sins (those which could be pardoned) was established, and the conclusion was reached that it was these which the living by their prayers could cause to be remitted for their dead

Above **The souls of those who were not already damned beyond redemption went to purgatory; there expiation was made for past sins in the hope of acquittal at the Last Judgement: 12th century relief of the Last Judgement from Autun Cathedral** *Opposite* **There are traces in pre-Christian pagan belief of 'a condition or place of spiritual cleansing for the dead'; at the Roman Catholic Xaghra Shrine, Malta, a statue flanked by torches over the archway symbolizes purgatory**

friends. Not without a purpose did the Church at Rome substitute a feast of the *Cathedra* of St Peter for the pagan festival of the *cara cognatio* on 22 February. On that day pagan Roman families celebrated the memory of their departed relatives by setting out food for their spirits. Christians were reminded by the Petrine feast that the keys of pardon had been assumed by St Peter when he was set to guard the gates of heaven.

Infiltrations of pagan practice troubled the Christian Church from time to time, and a Gallican Church council at Tours in 567 had to forbid the practice of putting out food for the spirits of the dead on this feast. Origen included in his writings the figures of the evil 'customs officials' who wait on the boundary of the world to despoil the dead of their hard-won merits. Origen also pictured Christ as standing like another John the Baptist by the side of a river of fire, baptizing in fire those who came forward to cross the river. In a Christian poem by Commodian (c 250 AD) the myth is introduced of the lost tribes of Israel living in tranquillity across the river of Persia, with toil and death but with no disease

and no sin, awaiting the end of the world.

One notable difference between Christian practice and other religions was that monarchs and other famous men sought to be buried within Christian churches, so that they might benefit after death from their being remembered by the priests praying at the altars. The Emperor Constantine set this fashion in 337, soon after the building of the first great basilicas; and the tombs in Westminster Abbey are originally due to the same motive. The prayers in the liturgy, as witnessed by the oldest of the Sacramentaries, correspond with this idea, asking for 'purgation after death' for the departed faithful. The nature of this purgation was much debated.

The institution of a system of public penance by the Church was more exactly carried out in the West, with its juridical background of Roman law, than in the East. The Western belief that a penitent who was admitted to Communion on his death-bed could work off the remainder of his public penance in purgatory was not so clearly understood in the East. At the Council of Florence (1439) the Greeks readily accepted the lawfulness of praying for the dead. After discussion they also agreed on a formulation of the expiatory character of purgatory for penitents who had not carried out their full penance. Soon after this the Western mystic St Catherine of Genoa (1447–1510) gave a new direction to theological thought by her account of her mystic experiences. She claimed that those in purgatory rejoiced at their growing awareness of the removal of all obstacles to their future union with God. Having passed beyond their period of free will they

could no longer sin, and hence could not grudge the happiness of those who departed from purgatory before themselves; neither could they gloat over the thought of leaving before others, as in an earthly prison.

The *Purgatorio* of Dante Alighieri is a seven-storey mountain where the expiation goes on of what was due to the seven capital sins which a man may have repented of before death. Dante uses purgatory to read a lesson to those still alive who incline to the capital vices, very much as Chaucer's Wife of Bath said of her dead husband: 'On earth, I was his Purgatory'. St Patrick's Purgatory, the Irish penitential sanctuary on Lough Derg, became famous before Dante's time and indeed certainly influenced him.

The short and sharp penance done there was held to mitigate enormously what might await the sinner in the next life. The other great work of literature inspired by purgatory, Cardinal Newman's *Dream of Gerontius,* has through Elgar's music brought the idea of purgatory once more into the awareness of the English-speaking world from which it had so largely faded at the Reformation. The medieval painting of a weighing of souls, still to be seen in the church at Catherington in Hampshire, may owe its form to the classical picture of Hermes weighing Achilles against Memnon, but here the hand of the Virgin Mary has adjusted the arm of the balance to the advantage of the soul that is being weighed against his sins. There is a mildness about Christianity which paganism did not dare to envisage and which, indeed, it was virtually incapable of coming to terms with, without succumbing to it.

Paradise

Happiness was associated with enclosures rather than open spaces in the ancient Middle East, for deserts and hills, the wind and the sun, were generally too harsh to man. When he thought of a pleasant place, he thought of an oasis or garden, where he could relax in the shade with ample water and fruit. Given the resources, he might create such a place for himself.

The word 'paradise' is of Old Persian origin. It means an enclosure, and especially a royal park or hunting ground, a piece of land made more agreeable than its surroundings by cultivation. The Greek translators of the Old Testament, about the middle of the 3rd century BC, employed the word once or twice in that sense, for example in Ecclesiastes 2.5: 'I made myself gardens and parks, and I planted in them all kinds of fruit trees.' But their most momentous use of it was in referring to the garden of Eden, the divinely appointed home of Adam.

This appears in Genesis, chapter 2. After creating the world, God plants the garden 'in Eden, in the east'. He places Adam in it and creates the first woman, Eve. The name 'Eden' may be Babylonian. Among the luscious vegetation, God's garden contains the Tree of Life, and the Tree of the Knowledge of Good and Evil. A river flows through it and splits up into four streams.

Life in this earthly paradise is instinctively innocent, with the Lord as a close companion. It is no lazy idyll: Adam must till and keep the garden, with Eve's aid. God forbids them to eat of the Tree of Knowledge. When they disobey, they are expelled. The reason given (Genesis, chapter 3) is that if they stayed, they might eat the fruit of the Tree of Life also, and live for ever. This would have been permissible before; now it is not. Henceforth men must drudge to live. Women must be subject to male dominance and bear children in pain. Meanwhile the garden goes on existing but an armed angel at the gate keeps fallen humanity out.

While the Judaeo-Christian Fall of Man in the garden is in some ways unique, the garden has partial parallels in non-Hebrew mythologies. Two motifs, in particular, connect other 'paradises' with this one. First, Genesis gives the Hebrew version of a widespread idea – the idea of a definite place, an 'otherwhere' or even an 'otherworld', which is part of the universe we know, yet different in quality from the part we live in: a good place, blessed and happy.

Second, Genesis directs attention to the many legends of a lost Golden Age. Long ago, human beings were carefree and guiltless. They were immortal, or at any rate felt no reason to fear death. They lived without sickness in a kindly climate, and never had to work hard. Gods dwelt familiarly among them. For whatever reason, the Golden Age is no more. The gods have withdrawn. Death and disease and wickedness have poisoned life.

But in some mythologies the two themes converge; the paradisal good place not only exists, it is a fragment of the golden world that remains inviolate. If we could reach it we could still find there the delights and divine companionship of the Golden Age.

In classical myth, the Golden Age was the epoch when the Titan Cronus, or Saturn, was supreme god, at least initially. After his son Zeus ousted him, the world declined. But Cronus went on reigning in exile, in the regions of sunset. There, for the Greeks, was the 'good place', out over the Atlantic behind a barrier of water. There lay the Isles of the Blest where, in Hesiod's words, 'the bounteous earth beareth honey-sweet fruit fresh thrice a year'. There lay the plain of Elysium 'at the world's end' where, according to Homer, 'living is made easiest for mankind, no snow falls, no strong winds blow and there is never any rain'.

Celtic myth looked in the same direction. The Isle of Avalon (before its re-location at Glastonbury) was a warm western Elysium, sometimes described in language borrowed from classical literature. Irish seafaring romances, such as *The Voyage of Bran* tell of an enchanted archipelago beyond the horizon, including an Island of the Blest which is larger in extent than Erin itself, a place 'without grief, without sorrow, without death'.

Medieval Irish legend drew the pagan and Christian paradises together. The usual Christian belief was that the earthly paradise of Genesis was in a remote part of Asia. Some Irish Christians, however, located it in one of their own legendary lands beyond the Atlantic, and gave it a Celtic atmosphere. The greatest of all their voyage-romances tells how St Brendan sailed in quest of it, and finally arrived on its borders. The author of *St Brendan's Voyage* probably knew that the world is round, and he may have harmonized his fancies with orthodoxy by imagining that Brendan reached Asia by sailing west.

Adam's lost abode remains, humanly speaking, empty. Other paradises are variously peopled. The Golden Age dream of freedom from the curse of death is recurrent. The citizens of paradise are, as a rule, immortals. In the Babylonian epic of Gilgamesh, the hero, grief-stricken at human evanescence, goes to an island-otherworld expressly for the secret of immortality. He meets Utnapishtim, the chief survivor of the flood, who is indeed exempt from death. But Gilgamesh achieves nothing by his visit.

In more familiar mythologies, such places as Elysium are likely to be the homes of gods, demigods or fairy-folk, all undying. When human beings do enter, we hear (in the oldest stories) of only a chosen few transported there while alive, and endowed with immortality as a special gift. Homer names Menelaus, husband of Helen of Troy. A better known instance is King Arthur who is said

to have gone to Avalon after his last battle, and to be still living there.

Classical Greece carried the idea a step farther. Pindar describes the Isles of the Blest as inhabited by a select few of the noble dead, with Cronus as their king. Here the Blest have actually died; the Golden Age motif, though still present in the person of Cronus, has receded somewhat; the Elysian realm is becoming a sort of heaven.

Within the mainstream of Greek religion, this idea remained tentative. But farther afield, similar beliefs are asserted with more conviction. Sometimes the good place, the 'otherwhere', has little or no explicit Golden Age aura and is more essentially a home of the dead. Where admission is a reward of virtue we approach the concept of heaven in its full Judaeo-Christian meaning: the eternal, blissful abode of all those among the dead whose lives have earned such a reward and of no others; the final beatitude; the ultimate goal.

The approach, however, is by degrees. At the more naive mythical levels, the good place may be simply the place of the dead in general. Everybody goes there, to an improved version of earthly life. The spirit realm of the Tumbuka, in Malawi, is an underworld where the departed are always young and never hungry or sad. Such beliefs occur also in New Guinea and New Caledonia. Some American Indians, the Ojibways and Choctaws for example, have kindred hopes about the region of sunset, or a happy hunting-ground in some secret country. These places are paradises and the homes of the dead, but scarcely heavens, because they are not selective. The goodness of the good place is not a reward.

When selectivity does come in, it may still not take an ethical form. Admission may depend upon social rank. In the Leeward Islands in the Caribbean, aristocratic spirits go to 'sweet-scented Rohutu' and commoners go to 'foul-scented Rohutu'. In Peru, the mansions of the sun were reserved for the Incas and their nobles. Even when conduct is a passport, and the good place has to be earned, the demands are not always moral. Entry may depend on having performed a ritual, or gone through an initiation.

The motif of achieving the good place for one's afterlife through merit appears crudely in the Norse Valhalla, which was reached by martial prowess. Further refinement of selectivity accompanies the development of imaginative power, which tends to locate the good place in the sky rather than on earth. Celestial dwellings for the dead are nearly always selective; the wicked and ignoble seldom go upward. In Egypt during the 3rd millennium BC, the pharaohs hoped to join the sun god and attend him on his journeys through space. While this is another instance of privilege through rank, early texts show that the god's attitude to a deceased ruler could depend partly on his virtues. Later,

world of strange brightness, a happy resting-place for pure spirits. But besides this – in Orphism apparently and in later Mystery cults undoubtedly – there was also a disposition to look upward. Gradually the good place was transferred to the sky, as in Asia.

The 'heavens' which the teachers of mystical doctrines drew into their systems were at first simply the upper regions. The prevailing astronomy made them concentric spheres, the spheres of the sun, moon, planets and fixed stars, rotating around the earth. Now, by becoming involved with notions about the soul's ascent, 'heaven' acquired a paradisal and more-than-paradisal sense as well as an astronomical one. The Mysteries (with Egyptian influence from the cult of Osiris) and the gnostic schools of the early Christian era envisaged purified souls as rising. Instructed in the right passwords, the adept eluded the planetary demons of middle space. He soared (by grace of his chosen saviour, such as Mithras) to a superior heaven outside the visible system. Here he lived blissfully with the gods and fellow-initiates, for ever.

Meanwhile, in the contemporary Hebrew world of ideas, two trends had emerged. When most of the Old Testament was composed, Israel's religion had no clear notion of personal immortality. Its only paradise was the lost garden. Heaven, as elsewhere, meant the sky, with the added concept of a pre-eminent heaven beyond, where God sat enthroned among his angels.

Judaism, as it grew after the exile in Babylon, slowly came to adopt a more cheerful outlook. Probably under Zoroastrian influence, it spoke of a future resurrection of the dead, a last judgement, a world to come. No unanimity on these matters was reached, not has it ever been. Rabbinic tradition, however, has usually resisted world-spurning metaphysical speculations. It has its own place, Gan Eden, where the righteous will dwell after the resurrection. Gan Eden is, in effect, Adam's paradise restored. It will be revealed and opened on earth. Its citizens will go there as living people, rather than in the form of shades.

The Greek doctrine of a disembodied existence for souls, between now and the resurrection, never fitted entirely easily into Judaism, which is vague about any celestial heaven; though its teachers and mystics have sometimes spoken of heaven as a vast celestial extension of Gan Eden already in existence. The uncanonical book of Enoch includes a vision of 'resting-places of the righteous' in a realm of angels above the sky. Judaism, today, does teach the soul's immortality. But it has always shown a tendency to keep its feet on the ground, and hope for a future paradise on earth.

In the time of Jesus, such hopes were bound up with apocalyptic and Messianic dreams. The Lord's Anointed would appear, life would be transfigured, the dead would be raised, the earthly Kingdom of God would bring paradise regained . . . for the righteous. Jesus employed apocalyptic language himself, but to convey a message of spiritual

The motifs of celestial city and paradise-garden are combined in this painting from a Bulgarian monastery, illustrating Jesus's saying that many will join Abraham, Isaac and Jacob in heaven (Matthew 8. 11): St Peter unlocks the gate with a golden key *Following pages* **The garden of Eden, the earthly paradise of Adam and Eve, is partly paralleled in non-Hebrew mythologies; the belief in some kind of definite 'otherwhere' or 'otherworld', and legends of a time when human beings were carefree and innocent both connect other paradises with this one: garden of Eden, by Jan Breughel; in the Victoria & Albert Museum**

when similar hopes were extended to lesser men, this idea of judgement became more prominent.

In the ancient Vedic religion of India the monarch of the dead was called Yama, and he reigned in the outer sky, a realm of light, over all the worthy departed. Their life was an enhancement of earthly life (as in most paradises of myth) with music, sexual fulfilment, and many more pleasures of the same type, and with no pain or care.

Hinduism allots regions above the clouds to Indra, Shiva and other deities. Each is a place of beauty and sensual joy, to be gained by a combination of correct ritual and correct morality. Buddhism inherited such schemes from Hinduism. In its advanced Mahayana form it has a graded series of paradises in a vague, non-astronomical sky. Ecstasies become more spiritual as earth is left farther below. The ascent is by way of virtue and holy meditation.

It is important to grasp that these quasi-heavens of Hinduism and Buddhism still belong to a mythological order of ideas. They are not ultimate, nor are they central to

the philosophy of either religion. The goal of the highest quest is not personal happiness, but total release from the bondage of personality – in other words Nirvana. The celestial realms, therefore, are mere consolation prizes. They appeal to those whose minds are not ready to transcend personal desire and descriptions of them are poetic, not doctrinal. They are also temporary. The soul may dwell in them for aeons, but if it goes there at all, it has not completed its pilgrimage and must eventually leave. The sole exception is in a popular form of Chinese and Japanese Buddhism, the Pure Land sect.

Only in the Mediterranean world does the good place acquire dogmatic status as the final reward of all mankind's spiritual strivings, with salvation consisting in its attainment, damnation in its loss. Heaven in this full sense is associated with Hebrew monotheism and ethical seriousness; with Hellenic firmness of outline and appetite for truth.

As long as Greece had no positive doctrine of immortality, and dismissed the dead as shades, Elysium could survive as a fantasy without raising major issues. But from the 6th century BC onward, the mystics of the Orphic cult (after Orpheus) were asserting such a doctrine and for those who accepted it, the island-paradise would no longer serve. An abode for the blest on the familiar earth was out of keeping with Orphic ideas, which proclaimed salvation as a release from matter as we know it, and from earthly bondage.

A more exotic home was offered to the right-living initiate. The Orphics adopted the word Elysium and altered its meaning, speaking of 'Elysian Fields' in an under-

revolution: the kingdom, he declared, is 'within you'. This teaching opened the way to a fusion of Hebrew and Hellenic motifs.

For the first Christians, the resurrection of Christ was proof of the coming resurrection of all the dead. When that happened, the Last Judgement would allot them their destinies according to their deserts. The book of Revelation looks ahead not only to the Judgement, but to a material New Jerusalem for the resurrected saints. This, like the Jewish Gan Eden, will be the second paradise; Christ is the second Adam.

But when the resurrection and judgement did not come quickly, a question arose as to what was happening to the dead meanwhile. Christ himself had promised the penitent thief, one of the two criminals who were put to death with him, an immediate paradise (Luke, chapter 23), which must therefore be in existence. In the Christian apocalypse there is already a heaven apart from earth. It is, as ever, the celestial dwelling place of God. The New Jerusalem, when it comes, will come 'down out of heaven'. Until then the souls of the blessed have their heavenly places near God, where, a perfect society, they await final reunion with their bodies.

Christianity compiled its heaven from both Hebraic and Hellenic sources. From Judaism it adopted the region of the sky where God and his angels dwelt. From Greece the Christians took the celestial machinery, the spheres outside one another, the spiritual journeyings. The idea of seven heavens, with the seventh as proverbially the most exalted, is also Greek. Dante's *Paradiso* portrays the souls of the saved appearing in the spheres appropriate to them – those of the sun, moon, planets and stars. The true home of them all, however, is heaven proper, above the cosmic system.

While it carried the concept of heaven to its loftiest heights, Christianity never resolved certain queries. If the souls of the saved went to heaven at once, what would be the point of the future Last Judgement? It could only confirm a destiny already fixed. St Augustine maintained that until the end of the world, spiritual life in heaven was an interim state, a foretaste, an answer which may have owed a debt to a tradition inherited via Judaism from Zoroastrianism.

Nor have Christians agreed about the qualifications for entry. Even baptism is not universally insisted upon, despite the words of Jesus that: '. . . unless one is born of water and the Spirit, he cannot enter the kingdom of God' (John 3.5). Luther dismissed salvation by works in favour of salvation by faith. Calvin (with a curious reversion to the pagan Elysium) taught salvation by arbitrary divine choice. Islam, in its own version of the Judaeo-Christian scheme, distinguished seven heavens and various hells, temporary or permanent; and it made everything depend on faith. Every Moslem, however wicked, would get to a paradise of some kind sooner or later, and no infidel would.

What happens in heaven? The paradises of mythology offer ardent, fairly civilized sensual delights, but Islam is the only major religion which does so. The Koran promises the faithful a reward suited to male Arab tastes. Their home will be a sort of splendid oasis – a true 'paradise' in the ancient sense – with gardens, rivers and trees. Men will wear silken robes and lie on couches; they will have unlimited fruit and wine, and access to virtually unlimited harems.

With increasing culture, however, Moslem thinkers have joined Jews and Christians in a more abstract opinion. Heaven is the place where God is; so the final happiness is the beatific vision of God, the source of all good, and this is therefore thought of as being completely satisfying.

There is no logical flaw in this conception of a Supreme Good from which the soul would never willingly turn away. But in practice it is hard to imagine a convincing heaven, because any perfection that we can specifically think of would pall. The German philosopher Schopenhauer observed that imaginative authors are more successful with hells than with heavens, because their own lives furnish materials for the former, but not the latter.

Copernican astronomy also raised difficulties. Heaven could no longer be simply a good place above the sky. However, its removal from the visible cosmos – from space and time as known to humans – turned out to bring certain advantages. Disengagement from time meant that such problems as tedium were less forbidding. Life in heaven need not be a monotonous going-on-for-ever. It might be something else, beyond present comprehension, but different.

Abstraction had already gone far in the time of William Blake, who denounced as barren the 'allegoric heaven' of the Churches. Progressive thought in and after the 19th century often dismissed it altogether ('pie in the sky' was the classic term of derision) and talked of building a heaven on earth. This, however, could only be conceived of in figurative terms.

Aldous Huxley has suggested that paradisal ideas arose from heightened states of consciousness, which can be induced by drugs. On this showing, the religious apparatus is valid, but not literally so. It symbolizes a genuine, transcendent experience, which human beings can rightly pursue.

Opposite Some souls are thought to spend many years in the otherworld between incarnations, while others return immediately to earth; Tibetans believe the Dalai Lama (shown here) to be an embodiment of Avalokitesvara, whose soul enters a child's body at the moment of a Dalai Lama's death Below A modern writer, A. J. Stewart, who believes herself to be a reincarnation of James IV of Scotland described her life as the King in a book called Falcon: portrait of James IV

Reincarnation

One of the more controversial religious beliefs, reincarnation has long been accepted by Hindus and Buddhists, and is today being increasingly adopted as an article of faith by a large number of people in other religious denominations. Reincarnation implies the state of being 'embodied anew'. That is, that the soul of a deceased person, after an interim period in the otherworld, is reborn in accordance with the merits acquired during its previous lifetime.

The human soul, it is believed, is a fragment of the divine, and will ultimately return to its divine source. But it is necessary for its own evolution that it should savour to the full the various experiences that life provides, and learn to distinguish the good from the bad, the eternal from the temporal. However, its ultimate destiny is far too great for this education to be completed in one brief sojourn on earth, and in the limited range of one lifetime and a single bodily form. For instance, the psycho-physical experience of a male is totally dissimilar to that of a female, and it is essential to have both if half of a fundamental experience is not to be missed. Obviously the soul must cover a wide range of knowledge and suffering in order to mature satisfactorily and only the soul that has been through tribulation can hope to be fit for the divine purpose for which it is intended.

Slowly, in the course of its successive rebirths the soul rids itself of its accumulated and inherited impurities, and evolves towards the goal of perfection. The novelist Sir Henry Rider Haggard, who was extremely interested in reincarnation, said: 'The Personality which animates each one of us is immeasurably ancient, having been forged in many fires.'

Belief in reincarnation is very old, and is found in widely scattered primitive and preliterate communities. Its postulates are basic to Hinduism and most schools of Buddhism. Roman writers said it was prevalent among the Gauls and Druids. Several Greek schools of thought, notably the Orphics and Pythagoreans, subscribed to it, and Plato mentions it in the concluding part of his *Republic*. In later times the doctrine was adopted by the Essenes, Pharisees, Karaites and other Jewish and semi-Jewish religious groups. The Neoplatonists and Gnostics also held the theory, and it formed part of the cabalistic theology of medieval Jewry.

St Jerome (340–420) said that reincarnation in a special sense was taught among the early Christians and was given an esoteric interpretation that was communicated to a select few. Origen (186–253) thought that only in the light of reincarnation could certain scriptural passages be explained. But it was condemned by the Second Council of Constantinople, convened by the Emperor Justinian in 553, and became for a time a heretical doctrine. 'If anyone assert the fabulous pre-existence of souls,' decreed the Council, 'and shall submit to the monstrous doctrine that follows from it, let him be anathema.' Some scholars nonetheless believe that they can detect traces of the teaching in the writings of St Augustine, St Gregory and even St Francis of Assisi. Among its modern exponents are Theosophists, Anthroposophists and certain Spiritualists.

Many people feel that the theory of reincarnation is in keeping with the idea of evolution and human progress and perfectibility. If man has shown a progressive advance from the lower animal forms to his present state of intellectual and moral development, it is clear that further progress is part of the plan for his future. The physical universe provides the environment for this advance to perfection, and it is here that he must work out his own destiny.

If the ultimate reasonableness of the cosmic purpose is accepted, a theory that can so logically account for the birth of congenital idiots, for those who die in childhood, and for others who have been given no chance to live out their lives, should clearly be given serious consideration. The orthodox Christian finds it hard to explain the existence of a child who dies in infancy, bringing nothing but heartbreak to his parents. What is the purpose of the infant's transient passage through this world? What is his final destiny? Does he go to heaven?

If he does, it would seem to be unfair to the adult who must face the vicissitudes and temptations of a long life, and in the end perhaps find himself condemned to be punished for having succumbed to the temptations to which he was inevitably exposed. By a stroke of good luck the child, who has never encountered such pitfalls, goes straight to the happy lands reserved for the blessed.

According to reincarnationists, the stillborn baby, the mongol, the child who dies in infancy, are all merely adjusting the balance sheet of their own previous lives by these temporary shifts and accommodations. Some are receiving their reward, some their punishment, for what they have done before. It will all work out equitably in the end. There is a mathematical precision about the way the law of destiny operates. No one can escape its clauses. The fate of mortals must be worked out in accordance with strict principles and all the apparent inconsistencies, injustices and contradictions will be sorted out in future lifetimes.

The doctrine of reincarnation, say the believers, therefore absolves God from any charge of injustice, favouritism, cruelty or caprice. Each person is ultimately responsible for his own destiny. Much that seems inexplicable in the situations that confront man in this life can be reviewed against this background, for they are the result of events that occurred in a past incarnation.

The pattern of our destiny is woven with the threads that we ourselves have spun.

In what form does the soul return to earth? Some schools of belief, particularly in Hinduism, hold that a man does not necessarily assume a human form in his next incarnation. Certain Hindu sects teach that the soul may be reborn as a plant, or an animal. Someone who has lived a life of vice or crime may be re-embodied as a cactus, a poison ivy, a lizard or a toad. According to the early Hindu law-giver Manu, the slayer of a Brahmin enters the womb of a sow or she-ass; a drunkard will be reborn as a bird that lives on dung; and other sinners and reprobates will become hyenas, rodents, insects and creatures of low and repulsive estate. Those who have done well will return as men and women.

Plant and animal transmigrations are not as a rule accepted by Western reincarnationists, who believe that once a soul has reached the human stage in its evolution it never returns to animal form. Human beings can only be reborn as men and women, and have the status and grade commensurate with their deserts, earned in their previous lives. One may be born a prince, a blind man or a leper.

Other questions are: how often does the soul return? Is the process indefinite? Considering that all men fall woefully short of the glory of God, what hope is there for anyone to attain the state of perfection required under the terms of this belief?

The number of chances each person has is said to range from three (once as a man, once as a woman, and once in the sex in which the soul fared better) to many thousands, some of which started at the beginning of Creation and may continue to the end of time. But it is generally believed that the cycle of birth-death-rebirth can be terminated by one or more of the various disciplines prescribed in the religious texts. Among them are renunciation, asceticism, good works, prayer, ritual and faith.

The length of time that the soul remains in the otherworld between incarnations is said to be determined by a number of factors. It seems to depend primarily on the condition of the soul concerned. In some cases it may return immediately, and in others after years, even centuries.

Certain advanced beings do not have to

return at all, but do so voluntarily in order to assist the efforts of other men in their evolution towards perfection. In Buddhism such evolved beings are called Bodhisattvas, and it is believed that some of them have reincarnated again and again, and will continue to do so until all men are saved.

The Tibetans believe that the Bodhisattva named Avalokitesvara became incarnate as their spiritual head, the Dalai Lama, and that each successive Dalai Lama is the embodiment of that august being. This idea determines the choice of successor to their deceased pontiff. When a Dalai Lama dies his soul does not wait in the otherworld as do the shades of lesser mortals, but immediately occupies the body of a child born at the precise moment of his death. It is the task of a special committee of senior lamas to find the child in question.

What the soul does while it awaits re-embodiment is again a matter of opinion among the various schools. Generally it is thought that in the next world it reaps its crop of rewards and punishments and learns its lessons before being despatched to earth again. Some dim vestige of memory survives this experience and is brought back to earth.

According to the Platonic theory the soul participates in the transcendental world of Ideas before it enters the earthly body at birth. These Ideas are Truth, Beauty and Goodness, of which the soul continues to receive intimations during its sojourn in bodily form. This recollection arouses in the individual a desire to regain the lost glory of his former estate. Man can, consequently, find true knowledge by remembering truths known to him before he took on a mortal frame. This idea is combined with another Platonic notion of what happens between incarnations. In his *Republic* Plato relates the legend of the warrior, Er the Pamphylian, son of Armenias, who was killed in battle and was found some days later, brought home for cremation, and suddenly came back to life. He described what occurred after death.

Each soul, he said, was given a chance to select the form of its next incarnation, but the choice was hampered by its own short-comings, for whether it chose wisely or foolishly now depended on the insight and wisdom acquired during its past life. The responsibility was entirely its own. Heaven was guiltless. It was a wonderful sight, he said, at once melancholy and ludicrous, to watch how everyone made their choices. After their selection they had to drink of the river situated in the Plain of Forgetfulness, so that they lost all remembrance of the past. They were then sent earthwards this way and 'that, like shooting stars.

Chinese Buddhism speaks of Meng P'o, the presiding goddess of the underworld, who makes all souls assigned to her dread domain between incarnations partake of a drink of broth before they go back to earth to live out another life. This broth is both bitter and sweet and causes all that happened before to be forgotten. It is because they have quaffed the drink of forgetfulness in Meng P'o's kitchen that men do not remember the acts

of their previous existence, or wish to return.

But there have been highly evolved souls who claimed to be able to recollect their past lives. The Greek philosopher Empedocles, who lived in the 5th century BC, is said to have remembered himself as a fish, a bird, a maid and a youth, and several other thinkers among the ancients made similar assertions.

Modern exponents of the doctrine of the transmigration of souls also claim to remember their past lives, some going back to Rome, Greece, ancient Egypt or prehistory. The important Theosophist Annie Besant believed that she had lived as the female Neoplatonist martyr Hypatia (d. 415 AD), and as the philosopher and martyr Giordano Bruno (d. 1600). Her colleague Colonel Olcott had been a prince in Atlantis, and then Odysseus, as well as other eminent people.

A fact that creates a certain suspicion in the minds of sceptics is that advocates of the rebirth philosophy generally claim to have been Egyptian pharaohs, Babylonian kings, Persian rulers, Chinese princesses and so on; few indeed believe that they lived humble lives as ordinary men and women. Among various explanations, this could be due to a subconscious wish in the minds of those bound down by the drudgery of the workaday world for the more spacious days of the past.

Critics of the theory of reincarnation also argue that if the soul is sent to earth in another body in order to progress in its spiritual evolution, it would seem reasonable that it should remember its past so that, knowing its shortcomings, it might benefit from its experience. However, they point out that, except for a handful of adepts, hardly anyone remembers what his past has been and where he has failed. How then do we know that we have had any previous identity, and what is there to link us with it?

Reincarnationists point out that forgetting a previous existence need not preclude the idea of one continuing personality, and the identifying of a man's present self with his earlier forgotten selves. Human beings spend about one-third of their lives in the mysterious phenomenon called sleep, about which they remember virtually nothing when they awake; yet no one can deny that he is the same person before and after sleeping.

The curious phenomenon of child prodigies may provide further evidence that people recapture flashes of their forgotten lives. In the 18th century, for instance, Jean Cardiac knew the alphabet when he was three months old, could converse in his mother tongue, French, when a year old, in Latin when three, in English when four, and in Greek and Hebrew at six, apart from various other languages. He also picked up a number of arts and skills before dying in 1726 at the age of seven. The famous 'Infant of Lübeck' in Germany, born in 1721, talked within a few hours of his birth, knew the chief events of the early parts of the Bible at the age of one, of the whole Bible at the age of two, and of world history at the age of three. At the same time he acquired a knowledge of Latin and French. He was sent for by the

King of Denmark and astounded the monarch who had refused to believe in his powers. The child predicted his own death, which occurred when he was four.

Cases of mathematical prodigies of astonishing ability are also well attested. Many of these children answered in a matter of seconds intricate mathematical problems involving astronomical numbers, their minds apparently working like computers. Musical prodigies are also well known. Mozart, for instance, could compose at the age of five. Another famous prodigy was Pascal who discovered a new geometrical system when he was 11 and wrote a treatise on acoustics the following year. According to the reincarnationists, all these children brought with them knowledge remembered from their past lives; they picked up their talents where they had left off.

There is also the curious, and not uncommon, phenomenon of *déjà vu* (French for 'already seen'), in which people claim to have seen something, or known certain people, or had an encounter, not in this life but at some period that can only have been in another existence. A person brought up in England who has never travelled abroad before may pay a first visit to Norway, for instance, and while touring a remote village in the interior he may be suddenly gripped with the conviction that he has been there before. His surroundings lose their strangeness, and take on a semblance of familiarity. He is certain that he has been here before, although he is just as sure that he has never been anywhere near the place in his present life. People in similar situations have been able to describe what they would see when they turned the corner and what lay over the crest of a hill, or behind a certain street.

Although this kind of experience can be explained as being a recollection of scenes viewed in a travel book or film travelogue or, more rarely, during an astral journey, reincarnationists tend to accept such instances as evidence of the person concerned having been there in a past life.

In Europe practical work has been conducted in what is called age-regression which, according to some reincarnationists, has provided further reinforcement of their claims.

Reincarnation may not be universal. The intensity of a man's faith may ultimately determine what happens to his soul in the next world. To the Christian the cycle of birth-death-rebirth, if indeed there is any such cycle, is broken by Christ's atoning sacrifice. Faith in its redemptive power not only dissolves the bonds of Satan but also releases the soul from the wheel of eternal return. In other words for the Christian the belief is superfluous; he does not need it.

In Hinduism gods are believed to appear in the world in bodily incarnations age after age: the god Vishnu, in his incarnation as the boar Varaha, raising the earth goddess from the primeval ocean; 12th century AD

The Four Horsemen of the Apocalypse, by G. F. Watts, now in the Walker Art Gallery, Liverpool: the first horseman rode a white horse and carried a bow, 'and he went out conquering and to conquer'; the second, on a red horse, carried a sword and brought war; the third rode a black horse and carried a balance; the fourth was Death, on a pale horse, 'and they were given power over a fourth of the earth'

THE ELEMENTS OF RELIGION

Divine Revelation

Religion, in all its forms, implies a relationship between human beings and superhuman powers which are believed to affect human affairs. The history of religions shows that man has rarely been content to acknowledge the existence of such powers as remote entities with which he can have no kind of personal contact. He has invariably personified them, ascribing to them purposes, and likes and dislikes in regard to himself. In turn, he has sought to know what were these purposes and sentiments, and has devised means of discovering them.

Most religions, both primitive and sophisticated, have traditional ways of learning the divine will, whether it be of a supreme god or of deities believed to control such important matters as the fertility of the land, the weather or disease. Shamans and witch-doctors claim to communicate with supernatural forces; oracles have been consulted, like the famous one of Apollo at Delphi; various forms of divination have been contrived, such as the inspection of the entrails of sacrificial victims or the flight of birds; and Chaldean astrologers sought to interpret the movement of the stars as the 'writing of the heavens'. In all such ways of acquiring supernatural knowledge the initiative has been taken by man. He has sought by special faculties such as clairvoyance, or by ecstatic trance or magical skills to elicit from gods or spirits information concerning human affairs and fortune. In many religions, however, it is claimed that supernatural knowledge has also come through divine initiative: in other words, that the deity has itself revealed its purpose or will, or truths about its nature and operations.

Such revelation has taken many forms. It may be claimed that the revelation was given without human mediation. An example of this occurs in the Egyptian Book of the Dead, which is referred to in the form of a rubric attached to chapter 30, which concerns the witness of a man's heart at the judgement after death. It states that the text of this chapter was found at Hermopolis under a statue of the god Thoth, in the reign of Menkaure (c 2600 BC), and that it was inscribed on stone 'in the writing of the god himself'. A somewhat similar claim is made in chapter 22 of 2 Kings, which describes the discovery of 'the book of the law' during repair work in the temple of Yahweh at Jerusalem in the reign of King Josiah.

Claims to divine revelation have not generally assumed this automatic form, but have involved human agents. Thus the pharaoh Akhenaten, who tried to change the religion of Egypt to his own design, claimed that his god, the Aten, had revealed his design to him. Gudea, the ruler of the Sumerian city state of Lagash c 2150 BC, records how in a dream three divine beings instructed him to build a temple, communicating to him what its ground plan should be. The book of Exodus (chapter 24) contains a graphic account of how Yahweh, the god of Israel, gave to Moses on Mount Sinai 'the tablets of stone, with the law and the commandment, which I have written for their (the Israelites') instruction'. The account goes on to describe how Yahweh also communicated on Mount Sinai long, detailed instructions for the making of the Ark and Tabernacle and their furnishings. A similar idea finds expression in the bas relief at the top of the stele on which the famous Code of King Hammurabi of Babylon is engraved. Hammurabi is depicted as receiving his commission to write the laws from the sun god Shamash, who was also the god of justice.

The theme of divine revelation permeates the whole of Hebrew religion. The idea is succinctly stated in the words of the prophet Amos: 'Surely the Lord God does nothing without revealing his secret to his servants the prophets' (Amos 3.7). Unfortunately, both the origin and nature of prophecy in ancient Israel are very problematic. Some indication of this basic obscurity is given in the following statement in 1 Samuel 9.9: 'Formerly in Israel, when a man went to inquire of God, he said, "Come, let us go to the seer (ro'eh)"; for he who is now called a prophet (nabhi) was formerly called a seer.' But the issue is even more complicated than this later editorial comment suggests. Generally it would seem that the seers were clairvoyants, attached to the cult of Yahweh, who were consulted about such things as the whereabouts of lost animals, as for example Samuel was; but Yahweh might also reveal his intentions to them about more important matters, as in 1 Samuel, chapter 9. Prophets, as 1 Samuel, chapter 10, shows, were originally regarded as persons subject to ecstatic trance, on whom 'the spirit of God came mightily', and who 'prophesied' in that state.

The great Hebrew prophets, however, were essentially men who felt themselves inspired by Yahweh to proclaim publicly what was his will concerning matters of current political and social concern. The accounts given of the revelations made to Isaiah and Amos provide significant information about the mode and content of such revelation. In the post-Exilic period (after 538 BC), prophetic revelation became progressively preoccupied with eschatological themes, such as the End of the World and the Last Judgement. The book of Daniel is an early example of this new kind of revelation, and the Christian writing known as the Revelation to John represents the continuation of the tradition into the 1st century AD. But these writings were carefully contrived compositions, purporting to foretell the coming of divine vengeance on the enemies of Israel or the persecutors of Christians.

Christian theologians have maintained that the whole history of Israel as recorded in the Bible, the career of Jesus, including his death and resurrection, and the founding of the Church, reveal the purpose of God manifested in history.

Prophecy

A word of Greek derivation, prophecy really means 'speaking before'. In modern English it usually implies foretelling the future. Originally, however, this was not a prophet's essential function. He was the human spokesman of a god (pre-eminently of Yahweh, the God of Israel) and therefore a transmitter of divine messages, which might concern the future or might not.

Even in English the idea of prediction has not always been present. When St Luke's gospel describes the beating and taunting of the blindfolded Christ, his assailants say, 'Prophesy! Who is it that struck you?' (Luke 22.64). What is demanded here is proof of such supernormal knowledge as a true messiah ought to possess.

The Old Testament sometimes employs the term 'prophet' very loosely. For instance, Abraham is a 'prophet' because he is the friend of God. Moses and his brother Aaron are called prophets, and their sister Miriam a prophetess, each for a different reason: Moses as the appointed mouthpiece of divine laws, Aaron as their translator into practice, Miriam as a leader of song and dance in God's praise. The common factor in these four instances is a special relationship with Yahweh.

Miriam's song of triumph over the Egyptians (Exodus 15.20–21) may be the oldest thing in the Bible, a kind of 'spiritual' made up on the spot. It proves the antiquity of 'prophecy' in some sense. However, the Hebrew prophesying that led up to the poetry of Isaiah and Jeremiah had a more specific character. It took place in a state of ecstasy. The prophet was a *nabhi*, a 'called' person. The Holy Spirit of Yahweh breathed upon him, and he leaped and sang and saw visions, and burst out into oracular sayings. Nabhi enthusiasm could be contagious, like the dancing mania of the Middle Ages, deplored often by the Church, attacking people not normally subject to it. It appears first in chapter 11 of the book of Numbers, where 70 Israelite elders undergo a temporary collective seizure in the presence of Moses. In 1 Samuel (chapter 19) the rapture engulfs its victims against their will.

Men or women could prophesy. But when prophets began to combine in guilds, membership was apparently confined to men. The full-time nabhi who had the gift was often a strolling player with a flute, harp or tambourine. He wore a skin mantle with a leather belt. In the early period when Samuel and Saul flourished (c 1050–1015 BC) the nabhi might appear to be hardly more than a fortune teller, offering 'inspired' messages in return for presents and hospitality. But a graver theme always underlay his vocation, even at its most debased. Ostensibly at least, he received the word of Yahweh.

When we search for parallels outside Israel, we should recognize a distinction. The nabhi might look like a soothsayer or medium, but in fact he was not. Saul knew the difference, and banished persons of the latter type while respecting prophets (1 Samuel 28.3). Soothsaying and mediumship in the ancient world were based on techniques. Diviners had their pseudo-sciences of dream interpretation and omen-reading. Even the priestesses of Delphi, who succumbed to possession by Apollo, put themselves into a drugged state which induced the prophetic process and brought the oracle.

The Hebrew nabhi, if true to his calling, did not seek answers to questions by any similar art. He might make himself receptive by prayer or fasting, but he could not compel the Lord. It was the Holy Spirit that came, or did not come, with an imperiousness beyond the prophet's control. The prophet might deceive others, and himself, into thinking the Spirit was upon him when it was not – as in the remarkable story of Ahab and the battle of Ramoth-Gilead (1 Kings, chapter 22) – but he never pretended that his message was extracted from God by some technique of his own.

The sounder parallels with the Israelite tradition are to be found in the realm of ecstatic religion. There is an account of a Canaanite fanatic becoming possessed by a god, about 1100 BC, chronologically between Moses and Saul. Closer still to the nabhi excitement, and better documented, is the frenzy accompanying the cult of Dionysus in Greece. But while the outward symptoms may have been much the same everywhere, Hebrew prophecy had a unique capacity for growth and enrichment. Yahweh was more than Dionysus. To faithful Israelites he was not merely a god but supreme, the only higher power that mattered, at least to them; and his cult had an ethical content, both for the community and for the individual. The nabhi experience could and did mature, over the centuries, into a solemn disclosure of the divine will through inspired speakers.

Its Greek counterpart passed from the fiery Dionysiac phase into Orphic mysticism eventually. Hebrew prophecy went on growing as a phenomenon in its own right, even after it transcended its nabhi origins. In the end it transformed Israel's religion without losing its identity.

So profound were its effects that some scholars have claimed what is certainly too much. They have contended that the later, literary prophets – Isaiah and the rest – actually invented Israel's religion, and that Old Testament history is largely fiction, concocted to give a pedigree to their teachings. This theory is now out of favour for several reasons, but chiefly because of what the history says, and the tone which the prophets take.

We get a picture, first, of a priestly cult of Yahweh as the God who rescued his people from Egyptian bondage and settled them in the Promised Land. The nabhi prophets have only a subsidiary role. Then, after many years, come the literary prophets. They do not speak like innovators founding a new religion; they appeal to a pure ancestral faith, which they say has been corrupted by monarchy, material wealth, a court priesthood and flirtation with paganism. The priestly-political tradition and the prophetic tradition are two aspects of the same religion. It is incredible that either party would have invented the other in just this way. But having recognized the fact, we should also recognize that it was the prophets, rather than the priests, who gave Israel's faith its eventual grandeur and permanency.

Between the nabhi and the authors of the later Old Testament books stands the transitional figure of Elijah. He denounced paganism and tyranny in the northern Israelite kingdom under Ahab (875–853 BC). A memorable event in this prophet's career is a visit to Mount Horeb in Sinai, where Moses had received Yahweh's commandments. Elijah witnesses much the same portents – wind, earthquake, fire – but 'the Lord was not in' them. The Lord speaks to him in a 'still small voice'. Here Israel's religion is moving toward a new spiritual level.

Elijah left no writings, apart from a doubtful fragment preserved in 2 Chronicles 21.12–15. About 760 BC, however, literary prophets began to be active, in a succession that went on for centuries and has had no parallel in any other religion. Even these were speakers rather than authors: they harangued crowds, recited verses and told stories in public, underlining them with symbolic gestures, such as smashing a pot in token of a city's ruin. But some of their doings and utterances were set down on sheets of papyrus, either by themselves or by their disciples. The sheets were glued side by side to form a continuous roll; these rolls are the books of the prophets, as we have them in the Bible after many transcriptions.

The literary prophets were still men on whom the Spirit breathed as it had on the nabhi. Habakkuk seems to have regarded himself as a nabhi still, and to have made himself receptive with conscious purpose (Habakkuk 2.1). But in both respects he was unusual. Generally, ideas and images surged unbidden into the prophet's mind; visions forced themselves on him, in sleep or waking; and now, instead of pouring them out in a raw state, he reflected on them

A prophet was the human spokesman of a god and this special relationship to the divine led to the association of miracles and supernormal abilities with prophecy, including the ability to see into the future: Elijah is miraculously fed by ravens, illustration from a 15th century manuscript

and gave them poetic form in his writings.

The most important literary prophets fall into two groups. The first quartet comprises Amos, Hosea, Isaiah and Micah. Amos was a shepherd and labourer. His book of divine messages is notable as the earliest known left-wing manifesto. It denounces the complacent nobles of Israel, and foretells a 'day of the Lord' which will bring retribution on an unjust society. Hosea attacks religious corruption. Isaiah and Micah scan a broader horizon, seeing the Lord as ruler over other nations besides Israel, and foreshadowing a world-wide peace when he will be worshipped by all mankind, if his chosen will only be faithful.

A second quartet of prophets arose in the late 7th century, after the northern Israelite kingdom had been destroyed by Assyria. These were Zephaniah, Nahum, Habakkuk and Jeremiah. Jeremiah, the most important, was a priest; there was no inevitable clash between the two callings. He speaks darkly of the sins of Jerusalem and its impending fall. However, he looks farther ahead to a restoration and a 'new covenant', which the Lord will write upon the hearts of his people.

Jeremiah, in fact, envisaged a future when the purified religion of Israel would develop into something greater and nobler. So did the unknown author of the mistakenly attached portion of the book of Isaiah which begins at the 40th chapter. This 'Second Isaiah' prophesied in Babylon during the Jews' captivity. He hails their deliverer in the person of Cyrus the Great, who will conquer Babylon and let the captives go home. He calls Cyrus the Lord's Anointed, or Messiah. By launching that momentous theme, and predicting a universal reign of righteousness under the One God of all mankind, the Second Isaiah takes a further step toward the expansion of Israel's faith into a world religion. So, in another way, does the book of Jonah, which depicts that prophet bearing God's word to the Gentiles of Nineveh.

Ezekiel, like the Second Isaiah, belongs to the Babylonian exile. He is the least spontaneous of the prophets, the nearest to being a composer of planned essays. His book closes with a description of a Utopia for the Jews. Afterwards come a few post-exilic prophets who add little. Judaism regards prophecy as ending with the Old Testament canon.

It will be noticed that while the prophets' main objects were to teach, warn and encourage, they did foreshadow future events: hence the notion of prophecy as prediction. But the divinely revealed hints at the future are never the whole message. Some, moreover, are conditional and not absolute: 'If you do this, such and such will happen,' not simply 'Such and such will happen.'

Yet with every allowance made, the predictions raise difficulties for their religious interpreters. If inspired, they must be right. But how should they be construed?

Above From the 8th century BC, the words of the Hebrew prophets began to be written down, and have come down to us in the Old Testament. Hosea *(left)* attacked religious corruption. Jeremiah *(centre)*, who was priest as well as prophet, envisaged a future when the religion of Israel would develop into something greater and nobler. Ezekiel *(right)* is 'the least spontaneous of the prophets'. Illustrations from a Byzantine manuscript, 13th or 14th century *Opposite* The angel Gabriel brings a message to Mohammed, who was said to have written the Koran at the angel's dictation. Mohammed's mission was to restate and perfect the teachings transmitted by God through five prophets before him, including Moses and Jesus *Left* Habakkuk receives the word of the Lord: from a 14th century manuscript. The Old Testament prophet was a man whom God inspired: he would keep himself in readiness to receive God's message, but did not attempt to obtain it by any art of divination and often suffered hardship as a result

On a literal reading, some have been fulfilled (the repeated promise of Israel's return to Palestine, very impressively indeed); but several of the more grandiose have not. There is, for instance, no sight of the prophets' Golden Age.

Here Christians and Jews part company. The orthodox Jewish view is that the Golden Age and similar consummations still lie ahead. They will come with the Messiah. Christians have sought to gather the prophetic loose ends together by applying them to Christ and the Church. Often the application is figurative, but not always. The gospel of Matthew insists on Jesus's literal fulfilment of various cryptic texts in the prophets, from his birth at Bethlehem onward.

Many of the Christian interpretations involve a species of hindsight. In the light of Christ the prophetic text may seem to make sense, and sometimes it manifestly does. Yet a person reading the text beforehand would seldom have been able to predict the fulfilment. The strongest argument for the Christian view is probably Isaiah, chapter 53, which describes a suffering 'servant of the Lord' in terms that fit no historical person but Jesus. An episode in the Acts of the Apostles (8.27–35) shows how strangely readers were driven to speculate about this passage in Jesus's time, and how quick the Christians were to apply it.

Christianity counts John the Baptist as the last prophet of the old dispensation. Christ himself assumes the prophetic role when he foretells the fall of Jerusalem and the Temple. His words raise the same problem as the other unfulfilled prophecies, because they suggest that the world will end when the Temple falls, or soon after, and that some of his contemporaries will live to witness both events. The Temple fell in 70 AD, but the world did not end. One explanation is that Jesus was simply wrong. Another is that he spoke of the nearer event as a type or symbol of the more distant, and his sayings on the two topics have not been clearly enough distinguished. Another is that the prophecy was conditional like Jonah's, and the condition, whatever it was, has been left out of the gospels.

Christianity pursues the prophetic theme in the story of Pentecost (Acts, chapter 2), when the Holy Spirit descended on the disciples. Official Christian prophecy ends with the Apocalypse, the last New Testament book.

Has valid prophecy occurred since? Jews deny this. Roman Catholicism asserts, as a matter of faith, that the Holy Spirit abides in the Church, preserving it from error but never adding to the content of revelation. The main Protestant bodies have taken the same stand, often more firmly.

Nevertheless, several extremists of the Reformation period claimed to be, in effect, prophets; and the term has since been applied occasionally to leaders of sects. The Mormon Church refers to its founder as 'the Prophet Joseph Smith', on the

Sonia Halliday

ground that he was a vessel of special revelations. Roman Catholic theologians have argued that such events as visions of the Blessed Virgin are Christian equivalents of the pre-Christian prophetic experience. Mary's appearances at Fatima in Portugal in 1917 are said to have been accompanied by predictions of future happenings.

Islam, the third great religion with Old Testament antecedents, places prophecy at the heart of its scheme. Mohammed, in Islamic belief, was and is *the* Prophet. Rejecting both Jewish legalism and the divinity of Christ, he declared that prophets were the only true teachers. His mission was to restate and perfect the teachings transmitted from Allah by five predecessors — Adam, Noah, Abraham, Moses and Jesus — all of whom had been misconstrued. The Koran, supposedly dictated to him by the angel Gabriel, is frequently spoken of as the

Islamic Bible; in fact it is more like a single prophetic book of the Old Testament. While no Moslem can ever supersede Mohammed, Islam has allowed a kind of prophecy to continue, in such cults as Sufism, for example. The predictive element has always been less conspicuous than in Judaism and Christianity.

In other religious contexts it is doubtful whether the word 'prophecy' should ever be used. There are no close parallels to the Jewish literary genre. As for the more primitive excitements that are reminiscent of the nabhi, these are better discussed in terms of 'ecstasy' or 'possession'.

Can any safe conclusion be drawn about the prophetic experience? Visions, voices and so on can doubtless be explained away, but does the explanation dispose of the message? Bertrand Russell once alleged that

we can draw no objective distinction between a man who eats too little and sees heaven, and a man who drinks too much and sees snakes. However, such dismissals cannot be final, because prophecy never took place in isolation. It was a factor in the life of Israel, or the Church, or the Moslem community. The depth and durability of the prophets' insights, the effects on history, are a matter of record. The alcoholic does nothing comparable with his delusions.

Nor does Russell refute the one modern genius who professed to be a prophet himself and, in some sense, demonstrably was: William Blake the mystic. It is thought that Blake's visions and revelations may have come to him in a hypnagogic state, between sleeping and waking. But the prophetic books which he based on them are not mere 'automatic writing'.

The final judgement should turn, perhaps, on the nature of the messages. Where they carry a spiritual or moral charge, it should seriously be considered whether something like Hebrew prophecy is occurring again. With Nostradamus that element is slight. Jeane Dixon, on the other hand, has made predictions about the future of religion, including the rise of a new messianic figure born in February 1962. It is noteworthy that although she is a devout Catholic, she concurs with two other Catholic seers in expecting an early end to the papacy as we know it. Such a forecast, against the forecaster's presumed beliefs, certainly suggests an idea forcing its way in from outside the conscious self.

Few attempts have been made to explain prophecy scientifically, except in the sense of explaining it away. The Holy Spirit's

Camera Press London

Above Cave dwellings in Cappadocia, Turkey, used by several generations of early Christian worshippers *Opposite, above* The book of Jonah reflects concern with the expansion of the Jewish faith, and depicts the prophet *(left)* carrying God's word to the Gentiles of Nineveh. Joel *(centre)*, one of the 'minor' prophets, wrote after the return from the Exile, as did Malachi *(right)*, the last of the Old Testament prophets *Opposite* Daniel's vision of the destruction of the Temple: detail from a 16th century Flemish tapestry

visitations are explained in psychological terms; the predictions are swept aside as guesswork, wishful thinking or, when correct, as forged after the event. Among rationalists who have admitted that knowledge, including knowledge of the future, may indeed come from 'beyond',

the best known is J. W. Dunne, author of *An Experiment with Time* (1927).

Dunne had noticed that stray images entering his mind — either in dreams or in passive receptivity — fitted into experiences which he underwent later, yet could not have foreseen. He persuaded 22 experimental subjects to write down their dreams immediately on waking, and watch for fulfilments within a limited time. Several produced images and motifs, some highly unlikely, which figured later in their waking experience. None was associated with any important message or meaning. Still it might fairly be urged that some features of biblical prophecy were being reproduced.

Dunne proposed a theory of multiple time. The human mind stretches away back from ordinary consciousness into an inner self that can observe other temporal

dimensions. This sometimes pushes through into the conscious ego with glimpses of what that ego may eventually see for itself, but has not seen yet, because it has not reached that point on its own time-track.

Possibly the main interest of Dunne is that while he sets up a kind of unconscious in place of God, he concedes that this unconscious must be more than psychoanalysts recognize. If it is to fill its ambitious role, it must have its own methods of cognition. Much the same view has been advanced, as the logical conclusion of Jung's system, by the Catholic psychologist Victor White. In any impartial study of prophecy, the most fruitful approach may well be to say: 'Yes, I agree with any Freudian or Jungian that these things come from the unconscious. But how did they get there in the first place?'

189

Priests

At most levels of civilization priests act as the socially recognized mediators between men and supernatural beings. They are the experts in the performance of rituals, and in pre-literate societies it is they who preserve, by oral tradition, the myths and the body of religious concepts and ideas which constitute a people's intellectual heritage. The functions, selection, training and social position of priests differ widely even within simpler societies, and the designation 'priest' has been applied to a large variety of religious practitioners, who may have little in common except for their alleged ability to establish contact with gods and spirits, or to manipulate supernatural forces.

In some societies there is a distinction between priests, who are the official religious leaders and representatives of the community, and magicians, shamans and prophets whose power derives from individual supernatural experiences or what is presumed to be direct inspiration by deities or spirits. In practice, the functions of these two types of religious practitioners often overlap, and the distinction is not universal.

At the lowest level of economic development, there is little scope for the emergence of ritual experts or any other form of occupational specialization. Most societies of nomadic food gatherers and hunters lack religious specialists comparable to the priests of more advanced peoples. All adults are considered capable of invoking gods or spirits and of soliciting their favour by way of prayers and offerings. Cult acts involving all the members of a group may be conducted by old men experienced in the performance of ritual, but no training or hereditary qualification is required for such activity, nor do those engaging in the organization of religious rites enjoy any special privileges.

Where larger and stable social groups have developed, increased economic efficiency enables man to divert some energies to the elaboration of religious practices. In most societies of some complexity the task of establishing contact with transcendental powers tends to be vested in individuals who act as the representatives of their clan or village. Such individuals need not possess outstanding intellectual gifts, but the ability and the right to perform priestly functions may be hereditary in certain families, lineages or clans. Another claim to priesthood is derived from psychological states interpreted as possession or selection by a divinity or spirit, who is supposed to invest the priest with powers and knowledge not accessible to other men. Priests who base their position on hereditary rights and priests called to their vocation by the gods may co-exist in the same society.

The Hill Reddis, an aboriginal tribe of southern India, for instance, depend on two classes of intermediaries in their relations with the supernatural world: the hereditary priest of the local group or village, and the magician who derives his powers from an intimate connection with a specific god or spirit. The hereditary priest is normally a descendant of the village-founder, and membership of the lineage of the man who first settled in the locality is sufficient qualification for his office. He is regarded as the head of the village, and as the appropriate mediator between man and the deities and spirits who dwell in the area.

As representative of the village he performs those rites and ceremonies that are believed to secure the prosperity of the community as a whole. And since this prosperity is intimately linked with the thriving of the crops, it is above all the agricultural rites that call for the intercession of the priest. He must inaugurate the sowing of the grain, propitiate the earth deity with sacrifices, and perform the rites at the great seasonal feasts. No special intuition or skill is required for these tasks.

Less simple are those that fall to the magician. While the hereditary spiritual head of the community follows the broad and well-trodden path of long established ritual, the magician must battle through the wilderness of the supernatural world to discover the cause of disease and threatening disaster, and must devise the means of placating the wrath of malignant spirits. The priest acts, so to speak, while all is well; his offerings are tendered to gods while their mood is benevolent, and his prayers are designed to solicit their favour for the welfare of the community, and their protection against dangers not yet arisen. It is only when misfortune is rife that the magician is called in to restore the disturbed relations with supernatural powers, to draw the sick from the jaws of death or to counteract the black magic of an enemy. This power, which he could not wield unless he himself possessed a thorough knowledge of magical practices, justifies his being called a 'magician'.

Every Reddi village must have a priest, but there may or may not be a magician in the community. Being a magician is an art, acquired by learning or bestowed by supernatural beings on an eager apprentice. It is an art and a power within reach only of those men and women who are predisposed towards it by particular mental qualities. Naturally these may occur in a priest as well as in any other man, and his frequent performance of ritual acts is bound to favour their development. Nothing debars a priest from learning the practices of a magician, and the combination of both functions is fairly common.

No Reddi is born a magician and aptitude for the work does not manifest itself in childhood. A magician frequently owes his knowledge to the instruction of his father or an older kinsman, but not every son of a famous magician has the talent or the desire to assimilate his parent's teaching. The co-operation of a deity is indispensable to the process of becoming a magician, and it is not only men who seek the gods; on occasion the gods themselves take the initiative. Reddi magicians agree that they receive their inspiration and knowledge from the gods, either while in a state of trance or through the medium of dreams. When a magician is called on to treat a sick person, it is usually his guardian deity who tells him what medicines to apply and what animals to sacrifice.

While the roles of priest and magician are clearly distinguished in some of the simpler societies, they overlap in others and a distinction between the functions of priests and magicians is hardly perceptible. Both deal with the control of supernatural forces and priests are generally expected to influence the gods through prayer and ritual performances, while magicians exert their power through spells and the manipulation of certain material objects possessed of mysterious efficacy. But as the principal duty of priests is to mediate between mankind and the higher powers, the faculty of communicating with gods and spirits is a primary qualification for the priesthood in many societies. This ability may be proved in different ways. When a person falls into a state of trance or ecstasy, people think that he or she is under the influence of a supernatural power, and therefore suitable for the role of mediator between men and gods. Or the supposed connection between priests and the spirit world may be that they have one or more tutelary deities of their own who assist them when required.

A striking example of this type of link between priests and supernatural beings occurs among the Saora tribe of Orissa in India. Among these primitive hill-farmers, placating the vast otherworld of invisible and often hostile beings occupies the energy of a small band of dedicated men and women. Armed with a few fragile implements, and devoting themselves to supplication of spirits and the sacrifice of animals, these people strive bravely to protect mankind.

There are two types of religious practitioner among the Saoras, the village priest and the shaman or magician. The priest's special function is to maintain the cult of the local shrines and to guard the village lands from the interference of hostile spirits and sorcerers. When a new priest is to be

There is frequently a close relationship between kingship and the priesthood, and in the ancient Near East the gods were served by official state priesthoods, with the implication that priestly authority was one aspect of the royal government. The king was himself the chief priest, though in practice he delegated most of his priestly functions to others: statue of an Egyptian priest; there was often rivalry between the priests of different gods

Picturepoint, London

appointed a shaman is called and, falling into a trance, he asks the gods and ancestors whether the proposed candidate is acceptable to them. If they agree that he is, the shaman summons the ghost of the last priest to hold office in the village. If he too approves, the shaman — possessed by, and representing, the dead man — puts his hands on the head of the new priest and tells him to do his work well. This selection and installation of a Saora village priest demonstrates the co-existence and friendly co-operation of two quite different types of ritual expert.

For practical purposes, however, the shaman, who may be male or female, is the most important religious figure in a Saora village. He has the power not only to diagnose the source of trouble or disease, but to cure it. He is doctor as well as priest, psychologist as well as magician, the repository of tradition, the source of sacred knowledge. His primary duty is that of divination; in case of sickness he seeks the cause in trance or dream. Every male shaman has a spirit-wife in the underworld and every female shaman has a spirit-husband, whom she visits in her dreams. These tutelary spouses are the strength and inspiration of Saora shamans. The marriages are absolutely real in their own minds, and they believe themselves to be chosen by the direct intervention of the guardian spirit, through whom they subsequently have immediate access to the world of spirits and deities. A female shaman may have to be wooed by a spirit for a long time before she consents to accept him as husband. Usually such calls from the spirit world come as hallucinations or dream-experiences, and a girl may appear to be deranged and ill until the 'marriage' to her suitor from the underworld has been performed, and then all will appear normal.

Left According to Christian doctrine, Christ gave priestly authority to the apostles, who passed their authority to the bishops who came after them. They in turn consecrated other bishops, and it is this authority, which stems from Christ himself, that is transmitted to priests of the Orthodox, Roman Catholic and Anglican Churches during the ceremony of ordination, the central rite of which is the laying on of hands by a bishop: an Orthodox priest, in Cyprus *Opposite* Although the basic function of the priest, to communicate between man and the divine, is the same at most levels of civilization, their selection and training differ widely in different societies; in the Christian Church, for instance, the priest's authority is bestowed on him at his ordination, while in more primitive cultures a shaman will be selected because of his ability to fall into a trance or ecstatic state which is thought to invest him with knowledge and powers inaccessible to ordinary men. The Brahmins of India inherited their ability to perform priestly functions, and have been worshipped as though they were gods themselves. *Left* A Coptic priest in Ethiopia; *right* a lama in Nepal; *above* a clergyman of the Church of England

After the marriage, the shaman's spirit-husband visits her regularly and lies with her till dawn. He may even take her away into the jungle for days at a time. In due course a spirit-child is born, and the ghostly father brings it every night to be nursed by the human wife. This imaginary marriage is no bar to marrying a human husband, but the dream-spouse seems as real to a Saora shaman as her husband of flesh and blood, and it is believed that she will become a spirit herself after death.

The term 'shaman', now widely current in anthropological literature, was first applied to the religious practitioners of central and northern Asia, where the magico-religious life of most of the indigenous population traditionally centres on the shaman. He is the dominating figure, though in many tribes there are also priests concerned with the performance of animal sacrifices, and every head of a family is also the head of the domestic cult. The ecstatic state is considered to be the supreme religious experience, and the shaman is the great master of ecstasy. Unlike persons possessed by spirits and temporarily in their power, the shaman controls spirits. He is able to communicate with the dead, or with demons and Nature spirits, without becoming their instrument.

Shamans are separated from the rest of society by the intensity of their religious experience, and in this sense they resemble

the mystics of historic religions. The mental disposition which qualifies a person for the functions of a shaman points to an important feature of early priesthood. Among many peoples, priests must display a certain excitability of temperament, which in modern Western society might be considered as bordering on a psychopathic condition. The ability to fall into trance may be an essential prerequisite for the performance of certain rites, in which case only those capable of such psychological states are suitable as priests.

The importance attached to ecstasy as a visible means of divine inspiration is shown in the numerous instances of priests obtaining their initiation by inducing a state of delirium or trance through the use of narcotics or fasting. The convulsive movements and seemingly irrational utterances of the inspired person suggest that his own controlling will is in abeyance, and that an external force or being has taken possession of his body. In many cases a god or spirit is supposed to speak through his mouth and determine his actions.

Not all priests need to undergo a formal course of training, or be initiated into the mystery of relations with supernatural powers by a specific ritual. Those who succeed to the priesthood through inheritance, for example, are usually believed to have powers acquired by birth into a family or clan. On the other hand, there are many

preliterate societies which require potential religious practitioners to be subjected to a rigorous training in self-control and in the sacred lore of the tribe. Among the Eskimo, for instance, the priests are trained in their profession from childhood.

Where priests receive formal instruction, their education often consists of two different phases. During the first period the novice is under the care of an experienced practitioner, who initiates him into the body of religious beliefs and teaches him how to perform various rites. A later phase is devoted mainly to self-training, in the course of which the novice seeks mystic experiences, and through them a direct relationship with supernatural powers. During this preparation for the priesthood he may have to live in seclusion or submit himself to austerities such as prolonged fasting or exposure to the elements.

In some primitive societies the period of instruction and training culminates in an elaborate initiation ceremony which confirms upon the candidate the full status of an ordained priest.

In many societies, however, priests are trained in a much more casual way. Among the Ifugao tribe of the Philippines, for instance, there is no institutionalized method of initiating priests into the labyrinth of an immensely rich and complicated mythology. There is no organized priesthood recruited from a special social class. Any Ifugao possessing intellectual ability and a good memory may attach himself to an experienced priest of his kin-group or locality as an apprentice; but in many cases sons follow in the footsteps of fathers enjoying a reputation as knowledgeable and successful priests. Ifugao priests also act as chroniclers and genealogists, for the frequently repeated incantations of ancestors give them an unrivalled knowledge of genealogies. The ministrations of priests

form an essential part of all the innumerable rituals by which Ifugaos mark social as well as religious occasions.

Some of these rituals may extend over a whole day or even over several days, and the demands they make on the memory can be prodigious. The priests are of supreme importance to the Ifugao, for only they are thought to be capable of manipulating the gods and coaxing them to aid human endeavour. The relation between man and deities is looked upon as one of bargaining and of give and take, and the priests must exert all their skill to get favourable terms for their clients. Ifugao gods are regarded as morally neutral and unconcerned with the ethical conduct of men, and the priests do not take any stand on moral questions. They do not feel any need to behave in an exemplary way in their private lives, nor do they attempt to influence the moral conduct of their clients and fellow-villagers.

Unlike Christian priests or other holy men who regard themselves as representatives of a moral order that derives its sanction from a supreme deity, most priests in primitive societies act simply as the agents of their fellow-men, and are intent only on obtaining material benefits for them. They have no interest in giving them any guidance in moral matters. Priests of this kind do not preach to men, but address themselves solely to the deities they seek to influence.

In addition, whatever the circumstances in which a priest acts as an intermediary between men and gods, the quality which makes his mediation effective often resides in his office rather than in himself as an individual. Consequently it may not greatly matter what sort of person he is, socially, psychologically, or morally.

Because of his usefulness and power a priest may enjoy considerable prestige and authority, but his position is so precarious and easily damaged that he tends to be surrounded with taboos to protect him against harmful contacts with forces that might render him ineffective. The social position of priests varies greatly from one society to another. The ability to experience states of trance and spirit-possession is usually not combined with great economic efficiency or political acumen, and priests who on ritual occasions will act as the mouthpieces of gods may be withdrawn and comparatively ineffective personalities in ordinary life. On the other hand, someone who holds the position of clan-priest by hereditary right, and functions as the sole mediator between a powerful clan and its protective deities, may derive considerable prestige and material advantages from his office.

In some societies, as among certain West African tribes for instance, priests tend to increase the respect in which they are held by enveloping their proceedings in mystery. They often create a sense of awe and fear among the laity, in order to enhance their power. The special and sometimes fantastic attire donned by some priests is intended

Above Medicine-man of the Turkana tribe in northern Kenya *Opposite* Medicine-men often receive their knowledge and inspiration from the gods, and exert their powers through spells and by manipulating objects that are believed to possess mysterious efficacy: dried monkeys' heads, an important ingredient in curing disease, for sale in a Nigerian market. Often it is simply the priest's fund of practical knowledge, in primitive societies, that sets him apart from other people, rather than any mystical powers

partly to distinguish them from the rest of the population, and partly to impress deities and spirits or avert malignant forces. Masks worn by priests have similar purposes, and occasionally signify a mystical connection between the priest and an ancestor spirit or deity whom he embodies.

In primitive societies priesthood is not exclusively a male occupation, and there are many instances of women functioning as priestesses and magicians. It is rare for them to be debarred from marriage, just as male priests are usually expected to marry and lead a life not basically different from that of other members of their society. Though their priestly status may provide them with certain privileges and material benefits, occupational specialization among primitive populations normally does not go far enough to free religious practitioners from the need to till the soil or herd cattle. At that level of material development priesthood is seldom an exclusive profession, and a priest does not diminish his spiritual status or prestige by engaging in normal secular occupations.

Restrictions on the sexual life of priests and priestesses are usually found in the more advanced civilizations. Primitive peoples rarely place any value on celibacy and chastity, and priests are expected to have normal family lives. They may be obliged to abstain from sexual activities during periods of training or at the time of major rituals, in the same way as fasting is regarded as a preparation for spiritual experiences; but in general primitive priests are not expected to lead a life basically different from that of laymen.

Specialist priesthoods also play an important role in more complex societies where, although priestly functions may be performed by people who are not priests – the head of the family may say grace at meals, for example – the community's dealings with

195

G. Tomsich/Spectrum

Camera Press London

God or the gods are mainly conducted by the 'clergy' who are distinguished from the 'laity', the non-specialists who are by implication incapable of, or at least less efficient at, communication with the divine. This implication has been resented on occasion, and some Protestant Christian groups insist that all believers are priests. Some refer to their functionaries as 'ministers' or 'elders' rather than 'priests' (the English word is derived from Greek *presbyteros*, 'elder') and deny them any unduly exalted status. At the other extreme, the members of some priesthoods have claimed to be gods themselves. This is true of the Brahmins in India, who belong to a hereditary caste, and some of the lamas of Tibet are regarded as divine.

In the ancient world the principal duty of priests was to offer sacrifices and conduct the major rituals of the gods. They also discerned the will of the gods: in Rome the augurs were priests, and the oracles were staffed by priests. Appealing to the gods for help, for individuals or for the community as a whole, curing the sick and battling against evil spirits were also priestly functions. A priest was usually attached to a particular holy place, the shrine or temple of his god (unlike Christian clergy, who are not tied to sacred sites in this way).

In the Near East the gods were served by official state priesthoods, with the implication that priestly authority was one aspect of the royal government. The king himself was a priest, the chief priest in fact, though in practice he delegated most of his actual sacerdotal duties to others. In Mesopotamia, for instance, there were various classes of priests, who performed the temple ceremonies, who took omens and interpreted dreams, who were called in to cure diseases and expel demons, and there were also priestesses, who acted as sacred prostitutes. A priest inherited his office and lived on the offerings made to the god, including the food which in theory the god ate.

Man's gods and goddesses have always required their priests and priestesses *Opposite left* Coatlicue, the Aztec goddess of the earth, mother of life, death and the gods *Opposite* The Brahmin or priestly caste were the highest ranking in ancient India and spiritual power was reserved to them. Brahmin outside a temple in southern India *Right* Priests and monks have sometimes claimed to be more directly inspired in the Christian church by Christ himself: 13th century miniature showing an abbot receiving a manuscript from a monk who is shown with two faces, indicating that his work was divinely inspired *Below left* The earliest disciples of Christ became missionaries, in particular Peter who was the chief missionary to the Jews, and Paul who preached mainly to the Gentiles. This tradition has been vigorously continued, giving Christianity a foothold in every corner of the globe. Christians have been working in Africa since the 15th century: a missionary with an African Christian woman who has whitened her face, apparently to make her more acceptable to a white god. *Below right* In the Maya civilization

G. Tomsich/Spectrum

of Central America, the high priest of a city ranked equally with the 'ruler of men', who

was educated in religious magic: this relief shows a masked figure with a ceremonial sword

Camera Press London

C. Reyes-Valerio

In the Old Testament, patriarchs including Noah, Abraham and Jacob are recorded offering sacrifices to Yahweh but later legislation prohibited all sacrificial offerings except those made in the Temple by qualified priests. The priesthood has almost entirely disappeared from Judaism, and Islam 'allows no priest between man and God'.

In the New Testament, St Paul mentions various Christian officials – apostles, prophets, teachers, workers of miracles, healers, helpers, administrators, speakers in tongues (I Corinthians 12.28). An organized Christian hierarchy gradually developed, founded on the doctrine that Christ had given priestly authority to the apostles, who in turn passed their authority to the bishops who succeeded them, who in their turn consecrated other bishops, so that through this 'apostolic succession' a properly ordained bishop has inherited, as it were, an authority originally stemming from Christ himself. In the Orthodox, Roman and Anglican Churches priests are ordained by a bishop in a ceremony whose central outward ritual is the laying on of hands, a sign of the transmission of apostolic authority and grace over the ages. The laying on of hands in the appointment of officials by the original apostles is mentioned in Acts (chapter 6).

Above Government by the Supreme Power of Chinese religion was carried out through a bureaucracy, and the high gods were generally approached through honourable men, priests or monks: figure of a monk, Sung Dynasty (980–1279 AD) *Right* Lamas, the priests of Tibet, at one time made up about 20 per cent of the population; many lamas, and nuns, were regarded by Tibetans as being reincarnations of saintly predecessors: 17th century painting *Opposite* The head of 'Tollund Man', with the rope with which he was strangled or hanged around his neck, discovered in a peatbog in Denmark; he was probably sacrificed to the goddess Nerthus, guardian of the fertility of the fields

In Greece and Rome where, in historical times at least, there were no kings, the political importance of priesthoods was minimal. Many priests served only for short periods and were not expected to put aside their ordinary secular activities. The most revered priest in Attica was the chief priest of the shrine at Eleusis, who was chosen from the priestly clan of the Eumolpidae. He served for life and because he revealed the secrets of the Mysteries to the initiates, it was important for him to have an impressive voice. On appointment he took the name of Hierophantes, and formally threw his old name into the sea.

In Rome the formal worship of the gods by the community as a whole and the rituals which it entailed, as distinct from the devotions of pious individuals, were conducted by various priests, presided over by the pontiffs (*pontifices*) who had originally been concerned with the rituals which accompanied bridge-building. Their chief was the Pontifex Maximus. Among other priests were the *flamines*, of whom the most important were the flamen Dialis, the flamen Martialis and the flamen Quirinalis. The flamen Dialis, the priest of Jupiter, and his wife were bound by all sorts of taboos and restrictions to protect them from pollution.

G. Tomsich/Spectrum

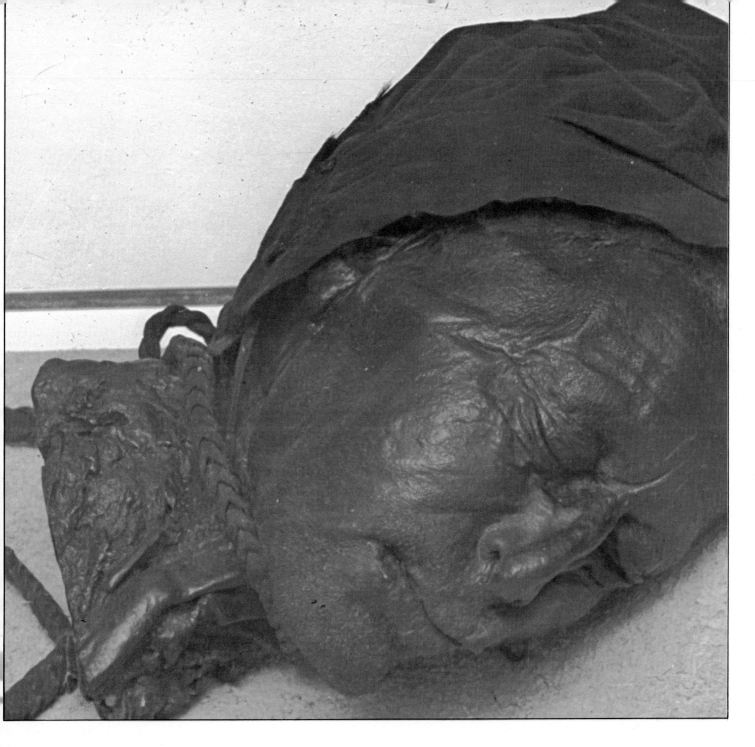

Sacrifices

In May 1950 a Danish archaeologist, Peter Glob, was called from his classes at Aarhus University to view a body. It had been discovered at a depth of almost seven feet in a peatbog in central Jutland. 'As dusk fell,' he later wrote, 'we saw in the fading light a man take shape before us. He was curled up, with legs drawn under him and arms bent, resting on his side as if asleep. His eyes were peacefully shut; his brows were furrowed and his mouth showed a slightly irritated quirk as if he were not overpleased by this unexpected disturbance of his rest.' Naked except for a leather belt and leather cap, the rope with which he had been strangled (or perhaps hanged) 2000 years ago was still around his neck.

'Tollund Man', as this discovery became known, may have been an executed criminal, but it is more likely that he had been sacrificed to the goddess Nerthus, the guardian of the fertility of the fields. Today he rests in a Danish museum, where the tourist can join the scholar in seeing a tangible piece of evidence of the nature of ancient religion.

Not all sacrifices were of human beings. But religion in the ancient world, and in parts of the modern world, involved so many forms of sacrifice that a full account of the history of this rite would be almost indistinguishable from the history of religion as such. It is this that modern man finds so hard to understand. To be sure, the word 'sacrifice' is still used: but in such a loose way as to obscure any original meaning it may have possessed.

It is first of all necessary to recognize that for most of history man has believed unquestioningly in the objective existence of a world parallel to his own, an unseen world peopled by gods, demons, ghosts, spirits, any one of which might influence his life in innumerable ways. Although for much of the time the workings of the unseen world were unpredictably mysterious, it was nevertheless believed that there were points of contact between the worlds, and that some degree of influence could be exerted at these points. In effect, the two worlds had to be kept in balance, and this involved man's acknowledgement of his proper position in the universe, and of his dependence on the unseen powers who controlled life, growth and death.

Sacrifice was the main means by which

he sought to make this acknowledgement. A wellnigh universal phenomenon in the history of religion, it should always be understood as a mode of communication between man and the unseen powers, and an expression of his intentions in relation to those powers. The word comes from the Latin *sacrificium*, denoting a victim killed and consumed on the altar, that is, an object or animal which has been made *sacer* (holy) by being devoted wholly to one or other of the gods. A sacrifice is therefore something consecrated to a deity, either with a view to bringing about a certain result or reciprocal act from the deity's side, or with a view to establishing fellowship between man and the god.

A sacrifice may be offered as a gift, as an act of atonement or as an act of fellowship and communion, but it is not always possible to distinguish sharply between these aspects. In the ancient world, for instance, the giving of a gift was in itself a means of establishing fellowship between giver and recipient, of restoring a broken relationship and of influencing the recipient. A king or emperor could not be approached at all unless gifts appropriate to the standing of the person concerned were offered, and there is a close connection between sacrifice and prayer, where a deity is approached in a similar way.

Clearly, a good deal depends on the worshipper's prior image of the deity, and on the degree to which the god is thought to be accessible to human approach. In many primitive societies the High Gods of the sky are the most remote of the gods and it is particularly interesting that in many cases no sacrifices are made to them. They may once have created the world, but are no longer concerned in its day-to-day running, which they have delegated to lesser entities; it is to these spiritual beings that the majority of sacrifices are offered. If they are believed to be dwelling in a celestial paradise, the offering will normally be made by fire, which acts as a mediator between the two worlds; in the case of gods and goddesses of the earth the sacrifice may be buried, poured upon the ground, hidden in a cave or – to return to Tollund Man – sunk in a peatbog. Offerings to spirits of the forest may be left on a tree trunk, offerings to household gods may be made on the doorstep or hearthstone. Whatever the means, the basic purpose of sacrifice remains constant: to acknowledge man's dependence on the supernaturals and so to ensure their continued benevolence.

The supernatural world, like the world of men, was believed to form a hierarchy, and it was therefore necessary for an individual to approach only those deities or spirits that occupied a position comparable to his own. In the ancient world, sacrifice to the greatest gods might be offered only by the king, acting on behalf of his people, and usually only once a year, as with the sacrifices offered by the Chinese emperors to Shang Ti (Imperial Heaven) at the Altar of Heaven in Peking. At other times, the king's prerogatives would be delegated to members of a college of priests, who would act as mediators between men and the gods, taking care that the sacrifices were performed correctly. The individual in his home might of course offer sacrifices to lesser deities without the need for mediation, just as he might approach the lesser officials of the secular state.

The places in which sacrifices were offered varied greatly. In primitive cultures, they were natural sites of peculiar sanctity (caves, hills, groves and the like), or tombs of the powerful dead. Such sanctuaries as these could strictly speaking be anywhere, consecrated for the purpose by the repetition of the appropriate sacred texts. However, with the advent of urban civilization, the necessity for a focus of sacred presence in the midst of the city led to the construction of temples as dwelling-places of the gods; and it was here, on the temple altar or altars, that sacrifice was mainly offered. The temple was often conceived on the analogy of a royal court, with the temple staff as the god-king's servants. Sacrifice was made to the god as an adjunct of personal and communal requests, and also as a regular feature of the daily life of the divine court. Thus the god would be given regular nourishment as well as being honoured by the worshippers' gifts. Today the Hindu temple in India corresponds most closely to this once universal form of sacred symbolism.

Sacrifice in a Hindu temple takes very innocuous forms. Except in a very few cases, what is sacrificed is food, drink, flowers and coloured powders (although at some temples of Kali, blood sacrifices still occur). The sacrificial altar has disappeared, and the offering is simply placed before the image, before being, in many cases, distributed among the worshippers. However, it must be recognized that this is the end product of a long development. In Vedic times (beginning in perhaps 1200 BC and reaching down into the Middle Ages) the practice of blood sacrifice was common in India, and the earliest Indian holy scriptures, the *Vedas* and *Brahmanas*, form in effect a sacrificial manual of great complexity. The entire Vedic religion centred on sacrifice. It was sacrifice that regulated relations between men and gods, that maintained the order of the universe and provided the only conditions on which man's life was believed to be possible.

An ancient Hindu text states that the gods exist by gifts from below, just as men exist by gifts from above. The idea may seem excessively naive, but there is evidence from a number of ancient religions that this was indeed believed to be the case. A well-known example is found in the ancient Babylonian *Epic of Gilgamesh*, which contains a story of a great flood. The gods were utterly famished when the flood cut off their supply of sacrificial food; and when the waters finally abated and Utnapishtim emerged from his Ark and offered a sacrifice, they gathered round the smoke 'like flies'. An echo of this is found in Genesis, chapter 8: 'Then Noah built an altar to the Lord . . . and offered burnt offerings on the altar. And when the Lord smelled the pleasing odour . . .'

A similar illustration is found in the writings of the *Bhagavad Gita*. The practice of cremating the dead had a great deal in common with the practice of offering sacrifice by fire: in each case the fire (the god Agni) acted as mediator between the two worlds, and the dead were transported to the heavenly regions, where they enjoyed the same conditions as the gods, and where the same kind of offerings could be made to them. At the opening of the *Gita*, Prince Arjuna is finding reasons why he ought not to engage in battle with his relatives in an opposing army, and observes that if one destroys a family (which he is about to do), then the rules of the family collapse; and since one of the rules has to do with the offering of sacrifices to the departed ancestors, the sacrifices will no longer be offered, and the ancestors will 'fall out of blessedness, cheated of their offerings of rice and water'.

The image of famished gods and ancestors toppling out of heaven is an intriguing one, but sacrifice was seldom conceived on this elementary level, or at least, the conception was soon outgrown. More important is the image of the temple as the court of the heavenly ruler, at which gifts were offered as a means of establishing a relationship with the deity, and as a necessary concomitant of petitionary prayer. The rule was never to go empty-handed to one's Lord – earthly or heavenly. In ancient Iran the word *yaz* means both 'prayer' and 'sacrifice', while in the Old Testament there occurs the text: 'O Lord, in the morning thou dost hear my voice; in the morning I prepare a sacrifice for thee, and watch' (Psalms 5.3).

With very few exceptions, sacrifice was offered in accordance with larger or smaller cycles of time. Like prayer, it might follow a daily cycle, dictated to some extent by the 'needs' of the god or goddess to whom it was offered. But the greater sacrifices were annual, falling at various points on the calendar (which was usually lunar) or at the solstices.

Over and above the annual or seasonal cycle, there was in some cases a multi-annual cycle. For instance, at the pre-Christian temple of Old Uppsala in Sweden, the greatest sacrifices of men, horses and other animals were offered every ninth year. 'It is customary,' wrote the 11th century historian and geographer Adam of Bremen, 'to solemnise at Uppsala, at nine-year intervals, a general feast of all the provinces of Sweden . . . The sacrifice is of this nature: of every living thing that is male, they offer nine heads, with the

The book of Genesis tells how God tested the strength of Abraham's faith by commanding him to sacrifice his son Isaac: 16th century Italian painting showing an angel preventing Abraham from offering up his son

William MacQuitty

burning the sacrificial beast as an offering.

Apart from its significance as an offering of life to the deity, the blood-sacrifice also served in some cultures to communicate new life to the fields at the beginning of a new season of growth. A particularly grisly example is known from the Pawnee Indians. A 15-year-old girl was taken and for six months treated royally; then she was led from hut to hut by the chiefs and warriors, at each one being given a gift. Her body was painted, after which she was killed. Finally her body was cut up and distributed among the cornfields. The spring ritual of the Aztecs contained similar elements, while at the Toxcatl Festival a young man was sacrificed to the sun god after having spent a year as a quasi-king. In the Americas, the link between sun worship and blood sacrifice is particularly noteworthy.

However, the sacrificial practices best known in the West (at least by repute) are those of the Old Testament. These are not isolated phenomena: their elements can easily be paralleled from many other cultures. But for at least as long as the Jerusalem Temple stood (that is, down to 70 AD), the sacrificial system was central to Israel's worship. Jewish sacrifices were of many kinds, carefully classified and regulated by the prescriptions and prohibitions of Leviticus. There was the burnt offering, no part of which was avail-

blood of which it is customary to placate gods of this sort. The bodies they hang in the sacred grove that adjoins the temple . . . Even dogs and horses hang there with men.'

This association of blood with the sacrifice is important. Blood was once thought (not unreasonably) to be the bearer of life, and special measures were taken to consecrate to the deity the blood of a sacrificial

animal or man. In the sacrifices of Viking times in the North, the main action was to take the blood and spread it on the altar and walls of the temple, and sprinkle it on the participants. One Old Norse expression meaning 'to offer sacrifice' is simply 'to redden with blood'. Similar practices are found in many other religions, including that of ancient Israel, where sprinkling blood on the altar was a preliminary to

able for human consumption, while in the peace offering, some parts of the animal were burned and others were consumed by priests and the worshippers.

The holiest of Jewish sacrifices were those known as sin offering and guilt offering (Leviticus 4.7), in which a broken relationship between man and God was symbolically restored. The entire action of these sacrifices was hedged about with the strictest taboos; for instance, the vessels in which any sacrificial offering had been contained had to be purified most carefully and even, in the case of earthenware vessels, broken.

This same theme – the restoration of the divine-human relationship – is also attested in one of the Jewish seasonal festivals, that of the Day of Atonement, *Yom Kippur*, which has been described as the summit of the Jewish sacrificial system. On this day, bullocks and goats were sacrificed, and their blood sprinkled within the Holy of Holies in the Temple – the only occasion in the year on which even the high priest was permitted to enter this innermost sanctuary. Subsequently the sins of the people were recited over a goat, the so-called 'scapegoat', which was then led away into the desert as an offering to a demon, Azazel. It happened that in later Jewish practice the animal was thrown over a cliff. However, practices such as these passed out of use early in the Christian era, and today even the solemn Day of Atonement is observed penitentially, rather than sacrificially.

In the ancient world the practice of sacrifice would often be accompanied by a banquet at which the worshippers would share table fellowship with the god concerned. Meat was eaten; wine or some other intoxicant was drunk. The Canaanites, according to the book of Judges, '. . . went out into the field, and gathered the grapes from their vineyards and trod them, and held festival, and went

Opposite above **Sacrifices and offerings have been one of man's traditional ways of showing honour and esteem to a human overlord, of denoting reverence to lords and to deities, and sacrifice itself still plays a significant part in Christian theology, especially in beliefs about the Eucharist or Mass. On New Year's Day, at the beginning of spring, a great festival was held at Persepolis under the auspices of Ahura Mazdah, supreme deity of Zoroastrianism, during which representatives of all the nations of the Persian Empire brought tributes to the king: relief at Persepolis showing a procession of Median nobles** *Opposite* **The blood shed by a sacrificial victim symbolized the offering of life to a deity; in some cultures it was also thought to communicate new life to the fields. Illustration from** *The Book of Life of the Ancient Mexicans:* **the Aztecs sacrificed human beings to the sun to ensure fertility in the coming year** *Above right* **Goats have been sacrificial animals in many cultures; the Greeks, for instance, sacrificed 500 in thanksgiving for their victory at Marathon: mosaic showing a goat being killed**

Sonia Halliday

into the house of their god, and ate and drank . . .' (9.27). 'Consider the practice of Israel,' wrote Paul, 'are not those who eat the sacrifice partners in the altar?' (1 Corinthians 10.18). He went on to stress that to partake of any type of sacrificial banquet was to establish a bond of fellowship with the deity concerned, even though it might be a demon: 'I do not want you to be partners with demons' (10.20).

In Scandinavia, the annual sacrifices to Thor, Odin and Freyr were accompanied by a banquet at which horns were drained to Odin on behalf of the king and to Freyr for a good year and for peace. Incidentally, drunkenness – the rule rather than the exception – might well have contributed to the sense of divinity which the worshippers undoubtedly felt on these occasions. In India, precisely this type of situation is reflected in the soma sacrifice. It is not

known for certain from which plant soma was extracted, although it has been suggested that it was the mushroom *Amanita muscaria*, but it is undeniably certain that it was the drink of the gods, that it was offered to the gods, and that it was at the same time shared by the worshippers.

Another type of table fellowship is seen in the Jewish celebration of the Passover, which is shared by the family in their home in remembrance of the release of the Israelites from Egypt. The Passover lamb was in later times sacrificed in the Temple, but the meal was an entirely separate concern; it is still the high point of the Jewish ritual year.

Early Christian teaching saw the Jewish sacrificial system (and particularly the sacrifices of purification and atonement) as having been summed up in the death of Jesus Christ. Jesus was the 'lamb without

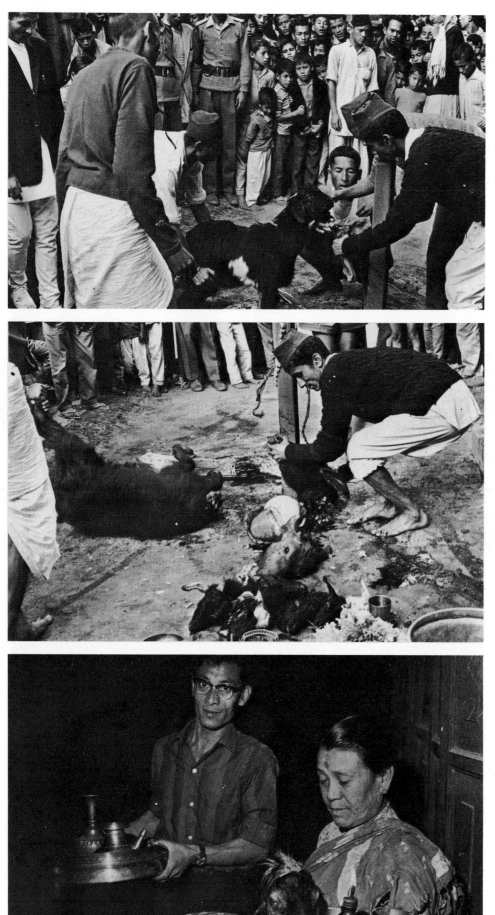

blemish or spot' (1 Peter 1.19) offered to take away the sin of the world. He fulfilled the role of the high priest on the Day of Atonement; 'he entered once for all into the Holy Place, taking not the blood of goats and calves but his own blood' (Hebrews 9.12). In the vision of John in the book of Revelation he was 'a Lamb standing, as though it had been slain' (5.6). In his death, therefore, the only possible offering for the sin of the world had been made, once and for all, and no further sacrifice need be made. Catholic teaching speaks of 'the Sacrifice of the Mass', and in this way incorporates much of the idea of table fellowship with the deity which accompanies sacrifice. However, there is no assertion that Christ is sacrificed afresh each time the Mass is celebrated: instead it is expressly stated that what is involved is a re-presentation, a continuation and a renewed application of Christ's death.

There have been, at least in the Indian and Western traditions, more or less elaborate protests from time to time against the view of deity which the sacrificial system implies. The Indian protest is made mainly in the interests of a metaphysical doctrine of God as pure Being, who cannot be adequately conceived in the form of an image before which sacrifices might be offered. In many areas of Hinduism, sacrifice is interpreted in a purely spiritual sense as meaning no more than an attitude of faith and devotion.

The Western protest might be said to have its roots in the Old Testament, and to rest its case on the priority of the ethical over the ritual in man's relationship to God. Hosea may serve as the spokesman of those Israelite prophets who condemned sacrifice in one form or another (though it may be suspected that they were in fact condemning less the sacrificial system as such than either the Canaanite form of it or a purely mechanical view of its efficacy). Hosea wrote – or said – on behalf of God: 'I desire steadfast love and not sacrifice, the knowledge of God, rather than burnt offerings' (6.6).

Most people today would probably agree with him. The process of secularization has meant many changes in man's view of the world, not least in his conception of the supernatural, and sacrifice can have little place in a world from which the supernatural is so firmly excluded. It must remain an open question whether 'modern man' is right in this. It is certain, however, that the symbolical links with the spirit world, which sacrifice regulated and normalized, have been broken.

Left A goat is ritually killed in modern Nepal and its head is carried on a tray; during the October festival of Bassain the Nepalese army sacrifices more than 30 bullocks and many goats to Durga, the Hindu goddess of victory **Opposite** St Maurice, a Theban Legion commander was killed by the Romans because he refused to attend a sacrifice. Painting by Mathias Grünewald

Sacraments

In seeking to possess himself of supernatural power or grace, man has instinctively felt the need to use forms of ritual action and manipulate material objects deemed appropriate to his purpose. There are some notable exceptions to this general tendency: for example, the mystic endeavours by mental or physical effort alone to achieve some desired spiritual state or virtue. However, since human nature is compounded of material and non-material elements, what has been called 'the sacramental principle' is both a necessary and intelligible pattern of behaviour. The sacramental principle is usefully and succinctly defined in the Catechism of the Anglican Book of Common Prayer as involving 'an outward and visible sign of an inward and spiritual grace'. This definition naturally expresses a Christian evaluation of what constitutes a sacrament, and it is related to the important place that sacraments have in most forms of Christian faith and practice. But the sacramental principle is to be found in many other religions,

The ancient Egyptian ceremony of the 'Opening of the Mouth' provides a particularly graphic instance. The rite was carried out shortly before the embalmed body of a dead person was lowered into the sepulchral chamber of the tomb. The process of mummification already carried out had ensured the preservation of the corpse from decay; but if the deceased person was to live in his tomb, as the Egyptians fervently hoped, it was necessary to restore to his embalmed body the ability to see and breathe, and to take nourishment.

The ritual 'Opening of the Mouth' was a curious compound of symbolic and practical action. It was symbolic in so far as the action was performed on the corpse, which was completely swathed in bandages, with a mummy-mask over its head and face. In other words, in the ritual actions of touching the mouth and eyes, to restore the use of these organs, actual contact was not made with them; it was enough to touch the appropriate parts of the mummy-mask as an 'outward and visible sign'. However, the action was not just ritual miming; certain other factors were involved for the achievement of the desired result, as the Egyptians conceived it. A peculiarly shaped implement of bronze called a *mshtiw* had to be used for 'opening' the mouth and eyes. The ritual action had to be accompanied by the reading of a prescribed text.

On analysis, therefore, to endow the dead person with supernatural power, the rite of the 'Opening of the Mouth' involved three elements: ritual action that required the use of a specified implement; a solemn statement of intent by an ordained minister; and the authority of a divine precedent.

In the famous Eleusinian Mysteries, the initiates, who had been fasting, partook of

Left 12th century stone carving from Old Sarum depicting Judas in the mouth of hell. *Above* The seven sacraments of Catholic Christianity are the Eucharist, baptism, confirmation, holy orders, penance, marriage and extreme unction, the first two being regarded as 'greater sacraments'. The Latin word *sacramentum* was used in the Western Church to

Michael Holford

a special drink called the *kykeon*. It was made of meal mixed with water and flavoured with soft-mint. The initiates drank this potion in memory of what the goddess Demeter had done at Eleusis during her search for her daughter Persephone. In sorrow, she had fasted, but finally had assented to drink a potion concocted as the kykeon. In the Homeric Hymn to Demeter, the authenticating occasion is described: 'And Metaneira mixed the draught and gave it to the goddess as she bade. So the great queen Deo received it to observe the sacrament.'

There has been much discussion among scholars about the significance of this ritual drinking of the kykeon. That it was commemorative of what Demeter was believed to have done is clear, as was also the abstention from food by the initiates. But there is much reason for thinking that the act was invested with a deeper meaning. In terms of the principle of the ritual perpetuation of the past, which operates in most

cultic acts, the solemn repetition of what Demeter had once done on a crucial occasion gave the initiates a sense of communion with the goddess.

These examples, selected from many, attest to the operation of the sacramental principle as a natural pattern of man's behaviour when in quest of supernatural power or grace. It is easy to describe the examples cited as magical transactions in a denigrating sense, but a more wisely sympathetic approach would evaluate them as significant expressions of the spiritual aspirations of mankind, of which the Christian sacraments are more sophisticated and refined examples.

The word 'sacrament' has acquired its distinctive theological meaning from Christian usage. The Latin word *sacramentum* meant originally the pledge of security deposited in public keeping by the parties engaged in a lawsuit, or the oath taken by Roman soldiers to the emperor. In the Western Church, the term was adopted to translate the Greek *mysterion*, which had long been used as a designation for the secret rites of the Mystery religions.

Catholic Christianity, both Eastern and Western, recognizes seven sacraments, of which two are distinguished as the greater sacraments. These are baptism and the Lord's Supper, the institution and ordering of which are clearly recorded in the New Testament. The origins of the five lesser sacraments are obscure, and their recognition throughout the Church was gradual. The interpretation of the sacraments has greatly occupied Christian theologians throughout the centuries, and many of their definitions, and the practices which have stemmed from them, have provoked great controversies. Rejection of certain medieval doctrines concerning the Lord's Supper or Mass characterized the Protestant reformers. Protestants generally recognize only baptism and the Lord's Supper as sacraments; but they disagree with aspects of the Catholic interpretation of them, and also differ from each other in their own interpretation and practice.

Catholic sacramental theology became very subtle in the terminology of its definitions, especially during the Middle Ages

Museum of Fine Art, Antwerp

translate the Greek word for the secret rites of the Mystery religions, and the Church of England has defined the sacramental principle as involving 'an outward and visible sign of an inward and spiritual grace'. Grace is conveyed by the enactment of the rite: Roger van der Weyden's painting, *The Seven Sacraments* **Top right** Nuns receiving Holy Communion

when it was influenced by Aristotelian metaphysics. A valid sacrament is defined as one having the proper 'matter' (for example, water in baptism); the proper 'form' (that is, the recitation of prescribed formulas: 'This is My Body; This is My Blood' in the Mass); and as being administered by a properly ordained priest or bishop, with the 'right intention' of doing what the Church ordains. If these requirements are satisfied, the faithful can confidently expect to receive the grace of the sacraments, irrespective of the worthiness of the minister. In other words, the grace is conveyed *ex opere operato*, by the enactment of the prescribed rite.

The seven sacraments of the Catholic Church are: baptism; the Mass, or the Lord's Supper; confirmation; holy orders; penance; matrimony; and lastly extreme unction. The supreme sacrament is that variously described as the Lord's Supper, Holy Communion, Eucharist or the Holy Mass. The institution of the rite is first recorded by St Paul, c 55 AD (1 Corinthians, chapter 11) and is described, with variations, in the gospels of Matthew, Mark and Luke. The words of institution used by Christ gave the rite a twofold significance. The consumption by the faithful of bread and wine, specially consecrated as the body and blood of Christ, signified an act of communion with Christ effected by the taking into the body of the consecrated

elements. The symbolism of the broken body and outpoured blood implied sacrifice, thus making the rite commemorative or representative of the crucifixion of Christ, interpreted theologically as the atoning sacrifice offered for the sins of mankind. These implications inspired the development of two of the most notable doctrines of medieval Christianity: transubstantiation and the sacrifice of the Mass.

According to the doctrine of transubstantiation, the substance or essence of the bread and wine are transformed by the words of consecration into the body and blood of Christ, although they still retain their outward appearance of bread and wine. This doctrine led to the idea that, at Mass, Christ is present on the altar, and could be carried about in processions of the sacred host (the consecrated bread). The doctrine of the sacrifice of the Mass teaches that, at each celebration, Christ's sacrifice is represented to God the Father, often with some special intention. Thus at Requiem Masses, the sacrifice is offered for the repose of the souls of specified deceased persons.

The sacrament of confirmation was originally part of the rite of baptism. Its 'outward and visible sign' is the laying on of hands, administered by a bishop, on baptized candidates so that they may receive the gift of the Holy Spirit, according to the authorizing precedent recorded in the Acts of the Apostles (8. 14–17).

The sacrament of holy orders is essentially connected with the doctrine of apostolic succession, according to which the Apostles passed on to their successors the priestly power and authority which they had received from Christ. The 'outward and visible sign' is the laying on of the bishop's hands as the means of transmitting apostolic grace and authority. In the consecration of a bishop, an archbishop and other bishops impose their hands; the ordination of priests is performed by a bishop. In the Roman Catholic Church, the solemn delivery of a chalice and paten, the instruments for celebrating Mass, to a candidate for the priesthood is part of the ordination rites.

The sacrament of penance finds its divine authority in the gospel of John (19. 21–23), where Jesus is recorded to have commissioned his Apostles to 'remit' or 'retain' sins. The evolution of this sacrament is obscure; it would appear that the Church gradually developed a system of the private confession of sins to a priest, who gives absolution and some form of penance. In 1215 the Lateran Council decreed that every Christian should make sacramental confession of his sins at least once a year.

The establishment of the sacramental character of matrimony originally encountered the hesitation of certain theologians, because it was difficult to discern how the rite was productive of spiritual grace. The epistle to the Ephesians (5. 22–23) was generally accepted as authorizing its status as a sacrament. But, although the status has been accorded in Catholic Christianity, it is recognized that matrimony differs from the other sacraments in that the parties themselves are the ministers of the sacrament; the officiating priest at the marriage ceremony is only the Church's appointed witness, who pronounces the Church's blessing on the union.

In some of these sacraments the 'form' and 'matter' are difficult to discern, and their definition seems to be rather contrived. However, they have been integrated into the pattern of the Christian life, and interpreted theologically as an extension of the principle of the incarnation of Christ into the created world. Thus it is maintained that as God became incarnated for the salvation of man, so the sacraments are divinely ordained means whereby spiritual grace is mediated by material means to the human soul, indwelling a material body. But though legitimately evaluated thus in terms of Christian theology, the Christian sacraments are founded on a principle that has found expression in many other religions, both ancient and modern.

Left Part of the ritual of the 'Opening of the Mouth', from an Egyptian tomb: a bronze implement was used to 'open' the mouth and eyes of a mummy, so as to restore the corpse's ability to see, breathe, eat and drink *Opposite* Detail from a 15th century French painting of the People's Crusade, a disastrous mass pilgrimage of 1076, led by Peter the Hermit, to help free the Holy Land from the Moslems

Pilgrimage

In the most famous lines of the *Prologue* to the *Canterbury Tales,* Chaucer refers to the restless religious longing which overcomes the devout man in spring:

> When the sweet showers of April fall
> and shoot
> Down through the drought of March to
> pierce the root . . .
> Then people long to go on pilgrimages
> And palmers long to seek the stranger
> strands
> Of far-off saints, hallowed in sundry
> lands . .

These words express succinctly a feature of the religious life of man in practically all ages and all parts of the world – the desire to go on a pilgrimage.

The word pilgrim itself is derived from the Latin *peregrinus,* and means simply a wanderer or stranger. Although 'pilgrimage' *(peregrinatio),* means literally no more than 'wandering about', the word has come to mean wandering with a purpose, and a pilgrim is one who temporarily abandons his or her normal pursuits in order to seek the spiritual and moral benefits believed to be obtainable in some particularly holy place. A palmer, on the other hand, was one whose whole life was spent in wandering from place to place.

Wherever there have been holy persons or holy places, there have been pilgrims to visit them. Perhaps the first problem to

consider is why some places and some people are regarded as more 'holy' than others. It seems that in the religious history of mankind, the world of men and the world of the supernaturals – gods, spirits, demons, ghosts – have been believed to exist for the most part in parallel. However, there are certain points at which the parallel worlds meet, points at which supernatural power comes, as it were, to a focus. Sometimes the original reason for such belief in the concentration of power is unclear. But certain places – for instance, mountains, caves, rivers and springs – were very early thought of as dwelling-places of the supernaturals, where power was intensified; and when early man worshipped, he did so in such places. Later, when temples were constructed, they too were thought of as the homes of the gods to which they were dedicated, consecrated by the presence of the deity within them. Holiness – supernatural power – is contagious, and anyone wholly dedicated to the service of a deity partakes of this same quality.

There were also sites at which a deity was believed to have revealed himself or herself, sites connected in some way with holy history, shrines of the great departed and places at which oracles were delivered and interpreted. Any of these might serve to mediate the power of the supernaturals to ordinary people: hence they were sought out, and became places of pilgrimage.

The reasons which prompted people to become pilgrims doubtless varied greatly. On the one hand, there was the subjective desire to acquire power, merit and those other benefits (the expiation of past sins, for instance, and the healing of present diseases) which might be held to derive from exposure to the focus of holiness. On the other hand, there was the desire to worship and do reverence to the supernaturals themselves. Yet there were other motives than such purely personal ones. In some religious traditions, pilgrimage might simply be part of one's accepted religious duty; and although merit might well accrue the motive was social, rather than personal. Chaucer's pilgrims, for instance, had a collective, as well as an individual motive for making the journey in spring to the shrine of St Thomas.

In the ancient world, pilgrimages were very often connected with seasonal festivals, and especially with the New Year Festival, or its equivalent, at which atonement was made for the sins of the past year and the world was symbolically renewed for another cycle.

It is not known exactly who attended such festivals in the ancient Near East – in Mesopotamia, Egypt, Israel – but the later practices of Judaism and Islam make it clear that the custom of visiting holy places, and particularly the great temples, at certain seasons of the year has deep roots.

209

The pilgrimage to Jerusalem for the Passover ceremonies, for example, lasted until the destruction of the Temple in 70 AD.

Possibly the longest unbroken tradition of pilgrimage to one particular place is seen in the Moslem pilgrimage to Mecca. In pre-Islamic times the tradition of visiting the Kaaba was already well established, but under Mohammed pilgrimage *(hajj)* was elevated into one of the five pillars of the faith, and it has always been the religious duty of every Moslem who is able to do so, to go on pilgrimage to Mecca at least once in his or her lifetime.

Elsewhere in the ancient world, old places of pilgrimage now exist only as archeological sites – for instance, the hall in which the Mysteries of Eleusis were once celebrated, near Athens, and the sites of the oracles at Delphi and Dodona.

The subsequent function of some places of pilgrimage have been radically altered. The great pre-Christian temple at Old Uppsala in Sweden, for example, was once visited by great crowds of pilgrims at the seasonal festivals. In the 12th century the coming of Christianity led to the destruction of the temple with its images of Thor, Odin and Freyr, and the building of a church on its site; but the attraction had gone and, soon after, the capital of the Svea kingdom was moved elsewhere – an eloquent testimony to the secular significance of pilgrimage centres.

The Indian sub-continent has a vast number of sacred sites, which Hindus, Buddhists, Jains and others visit as often as circumstances permit. However, for the Hindu there is no qualitative difference between worship at the local shrine and the visit to a particularly important holy place. Worship, to the Hindu, is invariably a matter of individual concern, connected both with the reverence due to the gods or (more usually) the Supreme Being, and with the acquisition of individual merit. Pilgrimage raises both these concerns to a higher level, but does not really change them. To the Buddhist, although the motive of worship may in theory be unimportant (Buddhism denies the existence of a Supreme Being and classifies the gods as merely higher forms of universal life), the motive of the acquisition of merit is very much present. For Hindu and Buddhist alike, the gaining of merit leads to an improved status in the individual's next life, and thus ultimately to release.

Among the holiest of goals for Hindu pilgrimages are the seven great rivers, especially that to the Ganges; and of the cities on the rivers, probably the best-known is Benares (Varanasi), with its hundreds of temples, large and small, its ghats (places where the dead are burned), and its crowds of pilgrims at all times of the year. Every inch of the Ganges is sacred, but none more so than the holy places, Gangotri, Kedarnath and Badrinath, at the sources of the river's three main branches, the Bhagirathi, the Mandakini and the Alaknanda. The great Ganges pilgrimage begins at Hardwar, 'Hari's gate', and passes through Rishikesh, the town of ascetics, to the three sanctuaries. The entire pilgrimage, performed in May, June and July, covers over 600 miles, and although transport is available for much of the way, there remains a good deal which has to be undertaken on foot, often in very difficult conditions. Recently a Western youth who attempted the journey barefoot had to have both feet amputated as a result of frostbite. Of course, where there are difficulties to be surmounted, this only adds to the merit acquired, as well as serving as a necessary mortification and disciplining of the body. The best-known (though now seldom practised) pilgrim austerity is that which requires the seeker after perfection to measure his length along the entire road.

Other celebrated pilgrim cities of India include Mathura and Vrindaban, connected in legend with the boyhood and youth of the god Krishna, and Dwaraka, where Krishna left the world. Often there is a pilgrim route round the city, the following of which in its entirety *(parikrama)* brings especial merit. At individual shrines, it is common to circle them, keeping the shrine on one's right *(pradaksina)* – a custom which can be paralleled in the Christian West. Pilgrimages usually take place at festival times, though they may be undertaken whenever the time is auspicious. Certain festivals at certain places, such as

With the catacombs and the tombs of St Peter and St Paul, Rome became and remains a great centre of Christian pilgrimage *Above left* Crowds flock to St Peter's Square to receive the Pope's blessing *Below left* In this 19th century illustration, the faithful prostrate themselves before a statue of St Peter *Opposite* Papal cortège in Rome

G. Tomsich/Spectrum

Hardwar, Allahabad, Ujjain, Nasik, draw vast crowds, and it has been claimed that the *Kumbh Mela,* held near Allahabad every 12 years, attracts larger crowds than are to be found at any other religious festival anywhere in the world. Another festival is the *Jaggantha* car festival at Puri, where the image of the god, mounted on an enormous car (whence our word 'juggernaut') is dragged through the streets by worshippers.

The Buddha himself neither recommended nor forbade the practice of pilgrimage, but shortly after his death, his relics were distributed and placed in monuments (*stupas*), which very soon became centres of pilgrimage. Indeed, the technical term for the first stage in Buddhist ordination (into the order of monks, or *bhikkhus*) is *pabbaja,* meaning 'going forth from the world' or, in a sense, becoming a pilgrim.

Today, the main centre of Buddhist pilgrimage in India is Buddh Gaya, the place at which the Buddha gained enlightenment. Outside India there are many Buddhist shrines, the best-known among them being the Temple of the Tooth – a relic of the Buddha preserved in an inner chamber on a golden lotus flower within nine caskets of gold – in Kandy, Sri Lanka. Here also is perhaps the most universal of pilgrimage centres, Adam's Peak, with its sacred footprint, believed by Buddhists to be that of the Buddha, by Hindus to be that of Shiva, by Christians to be that of St Thomas, and

also by Moslems to be the foot of Adam.

In Christianity, the practice of going on pilgrimage began in the early Church, achieved great popularity in the Middle Ages, and is by no means forgotten – particularly by Catholics – in the modern world. The first goal of Christian pilgrimage was the Holy Land, and especially Jerusalem. Among the earliest records in post-biblical times is that of 'the Bordeaux pilgrim', who went to Jerusalem in 333 AD. Despite political difficulties in gaining access to the holy places (a factor which was one of the causes of the Crusades), the practice has continued to this day, though the modern pilgrim visits all the actual or supposed sites of sacred history, and not just the Holy City.

As the focus of Christendom shifted from Jerusalem to Rome, the presence in Rome of the tombs of Peter and Paul, and the catacombs, caused a corresponding shift in pilgrimage to these more specifically Christian sites. At the same time, the development of the doctrine of purgatory, and the belief that the individual's time in purgatory (or that of his relatives) could be lessened by acquiring merit, caused the growing practice of the granting of indulgences as a reward for faithful pilgrimage. Thus when the Papal Jubilee was celebrated in 1300, the indulgences offered on that occasion are said to have drawn more than 20,000 pilgrims to Rome. The early Christian Middle Ages also saw a vast – and frequently

dishonourable – trade in sacred relics, theoretically repositories of divine power, but often in practice nothing more than, as the cynical Chaucer expressed it, 'bones and ragged bits of clout, relics they are, at least for such are known . . .'

Pilgrimage and the viewing, touching or kissing of such relics were closely connected, and the superior centres of pilgrimage gradually acquired vast stores of relics. In 1446 a German pilgrim to the shrine of Thomas Becket at Canterbury recorded that '. . . we were shown the sword with which his (Becket's) head had been struck off. Then they also showed a remarkable piece of the holy cross, and one of the nails, and the right arm of the honourable knight Saint George and a single thorn from the crown of thorns, mounted in a monstrance.' Elsewhere in England, for instance at the celebrated shrine of Glastonbury, which was almost certainly a Celtic cult centre before being Christianized, stores of relics were kept and miracles of healing were recorded as late as the 18th century, long after the Reformation.

Pilgrimage for the purpose of healing was common in the Middle Ages. The Venerable Bede told of the place where Oswald, King of Northumbria, fell in battle against the Mercians: 'Many people took away earth from the place where his body fell, and put it in water, from which sick folk who drank it received great benefit. This practice

Popperfoto

became so popular that as the earth was gradually removed, a pit was left in which a man could stand . . .'

It has become a commonplace of Church history that the excesses of popular devotion to sacred places and the relics of holy persons were among the causes leading to the Reformation. In the 16th century a chorus of protest was raised by the reformers, with Martin Luther at their head. In 1510 Luther went to Rome, on Church business but entirely in the spirit of pilgrimage, intent on making the very best of whatever spiritual benefit the city could offer him. His sense of disillusion grew, largely as a result of the sheer levity of many of the sacred proceedings. He did not then doubt that merit was to be gained; what he did doubt was that it could be transferred to the dead. There is a story that he ascended Pilate's staircase on hands and knees in the approved manner, hoping thereby to extract his grandfather from purgatory. At the top he stood up, and said to himself, 'Who knows whether it is so?' On such doubt was the Reformation based.

But the doubt of the reformers led directly to the distress of the faithful. In England, the shrine of Walsingham, reputed to contain a few drops of Mary's milk, was suppressed at the Reformation. Although Protestantism has always looked with disfavour on the custom of pilgrimage and the religious views on which the practice was based, the Roman Catholic world has continued to believe in the efficacy of holy places. Many of the old shrines have disappeared beyond recall; but others have been reopened – Walsingham, for example – and new shrines have arisen. The most celebrated of these is certainly that at Lourdes, in the French Pyrenees, where in 1858 a peasant girl, Bernadette Soubirous, saw a series of visions of the Blessed Virgin. All the classical features of the pilgrimage centre are there: manifestations of holy power, a sacred spring, and healing miracles. There are also similar centres of pilgrimage on the American continent.

There are certain places which are felt to be points of contact between the natural and supernatural worlds, places where supernatural power comes to a focus and can be most effectively felt by worshippers. One of them is Jerusalem, a holy city in three different religions *Top right* Christian pilgrims in Jerusalem: 'the Bordeaux pilgrim' is known to have made the journey from France as early as the 4th century *Centre right* The Wailing Wall, which contains stones from the Temple *Bottom right* David's tomb *Opposite* The East abounds with sacred places: for both the Hindu and Buddhist the merit gained in the act of pilgrimage leads to an improved status in the next life and 'thus ultimately to release from the wheel of rebirth' *Opposite left* Pilgrims at Benares beside the Ganges – the holiest of Indian rivers *Right* The Temple of the Tooth in Ceylon where a relic of the Buddha is reverently preserved on a golden lotus flower within nine cases of gold

Ronald Sheridan

Picturepoint, London

Picturepoint, London

Above An early souvenir: pilgrims' badges like this one of the archangel Michael could be bought at holy shrines throughout Europe and were often worn on their clothing by the pilgrims, especially on their hats, to show the places they had visited, and also to demonstrate that they were bona fide in an age of brigandage. To molest pilgrims carried severe reprobation *Opposite* All forms of self-denial entail the development of the will, and by rejecting material and bodily pleasures the will can become the focus of tremendous power. Abbot John of Rila who died in AD 946 spent some 60 years of his life in the mountains of Bulgaria and founded the great monastery of Rila there: illustration from a 19th century mural *Below right* The Franklin and the Merchant, two of the pilgrims from Chaucer's *Canterbury Tales*, who made their way to the shrine of Thomas Becket at Canterbury. The canonization of the murdered archbishop was one of the most rapid on record, as was the devotion to him

Above Pilgrimages to shrines of the Virgin Mary have become popular in the Roman Catholic Church in Europe, and in particular at Lourdes in France, and in England a pre-Reformation shrine of the Virgin at Walsingham has been revived successfully. Similar devotion has been stimulated by the canonization of Thomas More, who died for his beliefs under Henry VIII, and already annual pilgrimages to the sites connected with Thomas More are becoming popular in London *Below* Mohammed with two followers on his way to Mecca, which has perhaps the longest unbroken tradition of any place of pilgrimage

Above 'The enemies of the Prophet had elephants, camels and horses, but he had none': the flight from Mecca to Medina, known as the Hegira, in AD 622, which became the year 1 of the Islamic calendar, was the turning point in Mohammed's career; in Mecca he had met fierce hostility but from Medina he strengthened his position by raiding Meccan caravans and subduing neighbouring Arab tribes. In AD 630 he conquered Mecca, which became the most sacred city of Islam and place of pilgrimage, although Mohammed himself went back to Medina. Every good Muslim must try and make the pilgrimage to Mecca

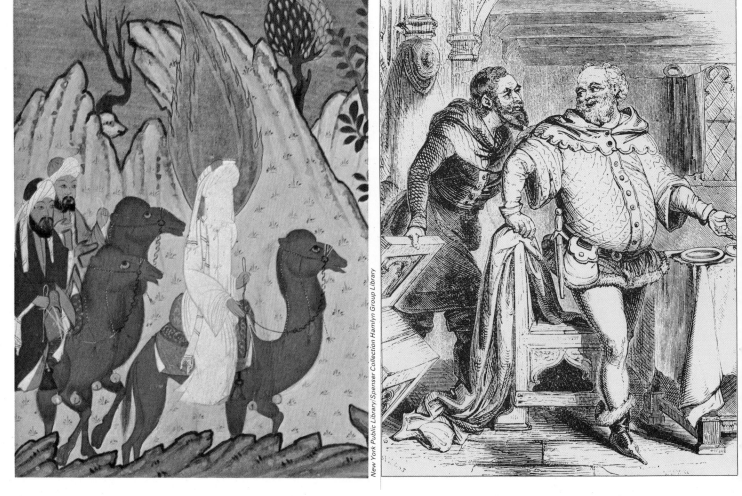

Self-denial

When Alexander the Great invaded India in 327 BC he was curious to see the famed Indian yogis, and he took the opportunity of visiting one of their retreats. He found them sitting motionless and silent, emaciated by long fasts and blackened by exposure to the elements. Through an interpreter the world conqueror asked them what they desired, and whether he could do anything for them. In answer, one of the naked sages, without deigning to look up, waved his hand to indicate that he just wanted Alexander and his entourage to get out of the way of the sun.

Such supreme contempt for worldly comforts was by no means confined to Hindu ascetics. Throughout recorded history men and women in all parts of the world have scorned contentment, luxury and fame, and have deliberately cultivated as virtues and adopted as part of their lives, practices that are by nature difficult, disagreeable and even painful. When it is within a man's power to enjoy what is pleasurable, it is strange to find that he often chooses the harsher alternative. Yet that, in the form of asceticism, has indeed been part of the religious ideal of many stalwart souls through the ages.

The term asceticism comes from a Greek word meaning training, discipline or self-denial, undertaken to acquire skill and stamina for victory in athletic games. The Roman philosophers known as the Stoics gave it a more austere significance. To them it implied a complete disregard for worldly success, for popular praise and physical pleasures. And they were not alone in recognizing the need for personal discipline and self-denial. The Spartans among the ancient Greeks, the Samurai warriors of medieval Japan, Tibetan monks sitting in solitude in icy Himalayan caves, are all representatives of this stern tradition.

All forms of self-denial entail the development of the will which is the motive element in human beings. Mostly the will prompts a man along the line of least resistance, for people generally prefer not to exert themselves more than necessary. They do not will, but merely wish, and their wishes are vague pleasurable day-dreams that do not call for undue effort of any kind. But when controlled and directed the will can become the focus of tremendous power. A will that is fixed on its goal, and inflexible and unwearying in its purpose, must attain what it seeks, for obstacles appear to melt away before its impetus. In confrontation with others it exercises a masterful and almost hypnotic power, so that few can resist its impact. But to develop such a will demands long preparatory training in self-denial, asceticism and self-punishment.

There have always been men and women who have willingly accepted pain and sought punishment; some from a sense of personal guilt, some in an endeavour to purify their souls, but many as a deliberate discipline to strengthen the will. When rigorously and consistently maintained, such disciplines are thought to increase man's spiritual strength and open up a world of limitless possibilities. The body becomes infused with a dynamic force and an attractive energy that irresistibly draws others.

The extraordinary means that men have resorted to in order to punish themselves are among the curiosities of religious history. In early Christianity these were the celebrated ascetics of the Syrian and Egyptian deserts of the 4th and 5th centuries. One of them loaded himself with so many chains that he had to crawl about on all fours; another never lay down, even to sleep; yet another lived only on seeds like a bird. One lived in a dried-up well, and one on the top of a pillar 60 feet high – in fact Simeon Stylites. Yet another, having in a fit of temper killed a troublesome mosquito, expiated the sin of his anger by spending the remainder of his life near a mosquito-infested swamp so that his body was bitten all over by the insects and was covered with lumps and ulcers.

Hindu ascetics have aroused the curiosity of travellers from earliest times. The *saddhus* or holy men remain half-immersed in water for weeks at a time; lie on beds of thorns or nails; keep one arm lifted up till the muscles stiffen and the limb is permanently immobilized in an upraised position. Others gaze upwards or downwards until the neck muscles stiffen in the same way. Yet others keep the fist permanently closed so that the nails grow into the flesh of the palm.

There have been fanatical religious sects whose members have subjected themselves to bodily torture, to starvation, mutilation, burning, burial alive, crucifixion, in order to secure the salvation of their souls. Occasionally some special form of self-punishment caught the popular imagination and caused an 'epidemic', as in the case of the Flagellants, who beat themselves. This Christian sect came into prominence in the 14th century and rapidly spread through Germany, France, Spain, Italy, Austria and Hungary. Large numbers of barely-clad people, young and old, men and women, nobles and serfs, rich and poor, used to go about in groups and lash their bodies with whips, rods and chains. They looked upon their self-punishment as a fresh baptism of blood. The sect died out in Western Europe but was revived in Russia among a group of people known as Khlysts, who danced ecstatic dances, beat themselves with whips, fell into trances and believed they were possessed by the Holy Ghost. A variant of this sect known as *Skoptsi* had a corps of elite leaders who even castrated themselves on occasion. Both sects practised complete abstinence from sexual relations.

In no part of man's life, it is thought, does self-restraint need greater vigilance than the

Sonia Halliday

sexual, for the sex instinct is the most pervasive, the most insistent, and the most difficult to control. In the Hindu tradition extraordinary virtues are claimed for *brahmacharya*, or continence. Great spiritual power is said to be raised by chastity. According to Hindu mythology nothing caused greater consternation in heaven than the knowledge that a *rishi* (sage) had started on a course of austerities involving abstinence from sex and sexual thoughts. The heavenly abodes were put into a state of turmoil, for the gods knew that with the power generated by the rishi vibrations were set up in the higher spheres that reverberated through the cosmos and disturbed the peace of the world order. The longer the rishi remained celibate, the more compelling became his power, and he could even bend the gods to his will. Vishvamitra, a famous yogi of Hindu mythology, once began creating universes of his own by means of the energy he had conjured up by sexual restraint. The usual counter to this manoeuvre was for the gods to send a heavenly nymph to tempt the ambitious celibate, which often proved successful and peace was restored again.

Among certain Christian denominations chastity has also been held up as an ideal and has often been made a prerequisite to the higher life, priests being forbidden to marry largely so that they might devote themselves wholly to their calling without the distractions and responsibilities of family life. Certain Puritan sects, while permitting marriage, advocated a strict control over the sexual act. The bond of marriage did not entitle a couple to indulgence in sex whenever they desired. In fact, excessive love for one's husband or wife, in their belief, constituted adultery.

Whenever any higher aspiration is sought, a tight reign on the sexual appetites is very frequently regarded as essential. The clamour for sexual expression can only be heeded, it is felt, at the expense of the spirit. The controlled sexual impulse, on the other hand, can be utilised for a variety of purposes and find expression in 'sublimated' form in religion, literature, art, science or philosophy. Gustave Flaubert, the French novelist, suggested that artists should subjugate their sexual instincts so as to lend a more intensive drive to the creative impulse in their work. Freud confirmed the view that people engaged in intellectual work would benefit by sexual abstinence.

Many men of high intellectual calibre have been driven to the same conclusion. Blaise Pascal, mathematician and philosopher, became convinced that carnal desires were pitfalls, the pleasures of the table a trap, and the joys of love-making a stratagem of Satan to lure people to destruction. So in order to develop the will-power to resist the temptations of physical pleasure, he actively sought pain and privation. He wore a belt with spikes, which were turned inwards, and if he found himself taking an undue interest or pleasure in food, in conversation or the company of others, he would secretly press the belt so that the spikes would prick his flesh. Pascal regarded wealth as one of the prime evils and poverty a

Michael Holford

blessed condition, since it limited the area of Satan's operations in his assaults on the body of man.

In religion the exercise of discipline over the bodily appetites is often found to arise from the belief that a twofold principle governs the universe – i.e. Dualism. A spiritual reality underlies the world, and this reality has a dual nature which is in constant opposition. The antagonism between these two principles is symbolized as a struggle between God and Satan, Good and Evil, Light and Darkness, and the opposition between the ideals of self-denial and self-indulgence may be said to represent the battle of these dualistic principles being fought out on the material plane. Sensuality springing entirely from the physical body represents evil, because in the earthly conflict the base or physical self is the enemy of the soul, which must be subjugated and denied expression.

Countless men and women, believing in this philosophy, have given up status and wealth to embrace the life of self-denial and harsh abstinence once they have been convinced of the shortcomings and indeed the incipient dangers of a life of ease and luxury. Material comfort and the satisfactions of the flesh can breed increasing appetites that are never satisfied and in their wake bring moral sluggishness and spiritual degradation. To such persons physical self-fulfilment, for all its so-called benefits, has serious drawbacks. It pacifies, soothes, and above all softens and weakens the spirit in its struggle against the powers of evil. Mystics have said that one of the greatest obstacles to the evolution of the soul is the pursuit of pleasure. Nothing so effectively obscures the interior mirror in which we might 'witness the Higher Self' as worldly success and sensuality. Not self-expression but self-denial should therefore be the aim, for the self that seeks expression may be, and usually is, the lower self, and the ways in which it seeks expression are spiritually injurious.

Besides sex there are several other desires that crave satisfaction, and all these must be carefully watched. In most ascetic and mystical cults the pupil is warned to resist the desire for fame and popular esteem. All good deeds should be anonymous. He should conceal his virtuous acts as if they were evil deeds. The 4th century Christian saint, Macarius, who settled in the desert to practise austerities, was accused by the nearby villagers of making a girl pregnant and was almost killed by them. He did not say a word and made no effort to defend himself. Later, when the real culprit was found, the villagers came to Macarius to apologize, and praised him for his saintliness. Again he said nothing. He had made it a rule of his life not to care one way or the other what people thought of him. He remained quite unmoved by praise or blame.

In ancient Greece the ideal aimed at was called *ataraxia*, freedom from all violent and disturbing emotions, a passionless indifference that leads ultimately to inner

harmony. The Roman Stoics too regarded it as one of the great virtues, and one that was sorely needed in their excitable age which sought satisfaction in vulgar appetites that were being progressively stimulated as Rome's wealth increased.

'He who is rid of desire,' says a Chinese classic, 'has an insight into the secret essence.' The ideal of the Hindu yogi was 'uncolouredness', the state of being untouched by the storms of passion and prejudice. The virtues he cultivated were patience, endurance, forbearance, and the acceptance of one's lot, and a total detachment unperturbed by pleasure or pain, fame or contempt, success or failure, poverty or plenty, sympathy or scorn, love or hate, praise or blame.

The Buddhists also regarded as sinful the encouragement of anything likely to excite envy, desire, anger, lust, greed, or even admiration. They sought to make no distinction between the world conqueror and the penniless beggar. They condemned any preoccupation with things that were beautiful or enjoyable. To take a literary example, a thesis presented in a beautifully-written style was suspect, for the manner of saying it might deceive one into believing that because it was well expressed it was also true, whereas in reality it might contain much falsehood. Again, the appreciation of beauty is largely a sensual matter and a concession to the lower self. Buddhist legend tells of the monk Chittagutta, who lived in a monastery adorned with beautiful murals of a religious nature, yet who never let his glance stray upward lest he be misled by the charm of the paintings and forget the message they were meant to convey. The Christian monk St Bernard shielded his eyes from the sight of the wonderful Swiss lakes and mountains lest he find too sensual a joy in their beauty.

The deceptive attraction of worldly success and power must also be avoided. Success can be degrading. Possessions can contaminate. Anthropologists have shown that when primitive peoples are suddenly brought into contact with an advanced culture they soon become demoralized. The cargo cults of the Melanesians, for example, provide a good instance of the progressive phases of perplexity, reaction and revolt against the good things imported into their islands from the Western world. Sociologists have not been slow to point out that in a sense even civilized man finds the impact of worldly abundance and the growing complexity of his own culture becoming more and more alien to him and more difficult to bear, and he ultimately suffers the same phases of bewilderment and demoralization as his brother in the South Seas.

Most observers of contemporary society

Left Head of John the Baptist, from Chartres Cathedral *Opposite* Grünewald's *The Temptation of St Anthony*: as a young man he overcame great spiritual and physical temptations and went away into the desert where he was followed by those seeking his advice

feel that there is a definite need to shed the excess baggage carried by the affluent, and not continually to strive for more and more. Probably no single book has expressed this idea with greater clarity than the *Tao Te Ching*, one of the great classics of Chinese philosophy.

Self-denial means learning to do with less, to thin out and attenuate. Henry Thoreau, the American backwoods philosopher, once said that a man should so live that he could flee a burning city and be none the poorer. So many people have far more than they can cope with, and the real need is to jettison some of the unnecessarily heavy loads we carry about with us.

From Greece, Rome, China, Arabia, North and South America, and many other places, we have records of the deliberate sacrifice of valuable possessions as part of a rite of liberation from material bondage. For example, the Celtic tribe of the Cimbri after a great victory in 105 BC destroyed their victory booty. A strange form of orgiastic celebration found among the American Indians is known to anthropologists as a potlatch, in which huge quantities of stores, money and property are wantonly destroyed after a ceremonial feast.

Perhaps the most vivid example comes from ancient Greece, when the people of Croton were having trouble with the neighbouring city of Sybaris, both in the Bay of Tarentum in Italy. The Sybarites were extremely wealthy and powerful. They had the distinction of being the first people to use chamber pots at banquets, and were responsible for introducing hot baths to the Western world. Luxury-loving in the extreme, they made a fetish of refined foods and

titillating wines, and the exciting rhythms of the most sophisticated music. They decorated their cooks with crowns of gold and presented their sexual partners with bejewelled sceptres. The philosopher Pythagoras, on the other hand, advised the people of Croton, who had hitherto tried to copy the refinements of the Sybarites, to surrender their luxuries if they wished to draw down from heaven the strength that would enable them to overcome their enemy. Costly urns full of jewels, beautifully wrought statues, priceless paintings and works of art, wonderful fabrics and carpets were brought from their homes and laid at the altar of Juno, and then systematically destroyed, burned, torn up, ground to powder, or sunk in the deep river. It was as though the people were purified from a feverish plague, relieved of an incubus that had settled its dragging load permanently on their shoulders. They went forth

against the Sybarites, conquered them, razed Sybaris to the ground, and diverted the waters of a nearby river so that it submerged the hateful city.

Two thousand years later, in May 1497, the Dominican monk Savonarola preached against the luxuries of the 'sybaritic' city of Florence. Like an Old Testament prophet he raised his voice against its decadence and its vices. As a result of his preaching the citizens carried to the marketplace of Florence hundreds of rare books of art, profane literature by the cartload, licentious poetry, precious manuscripts, ladies' ornaments and trinkets, costly pomades, lotions, eye salves and beautifiers of every kind, as well as musical instruments, chess boards, cards and hundreds upon hundreds of costly items of clothing. All this, forming the 'boils and sores' of Florence, was piled in a great heap. A trumpet was sounded and amid the acclamations of the mob, Savonarola applied a torch to this, perhaps the most expensive 'bonfire of vanities' ever.

In the view of the ascetic, men and women could always do with less. The barest minimum is the ideal possession, and poverty the ultimate aim. St Francis of Assisi, founder of the Franciscans, was one of that noble band who embraced poverty. He gave up his patrimony, exchanged his rich clothes for the rags of a beggar and mortified himself by severe penances. He was only one of countless numbers who have preferred self-denial to self-indulgence. Suffering is basic to asceticism. We do not know why suffering exists or who is responsible for it. Mystics regard it as having its roots in the cosmic process. Thomas à Kempis (d 1471) called suffering 'the gymnastic of eternity'. The mystics say that it is a great delusion to imagine that man is born for happiness, or that pleasure is his birthright. The fact is that no human life can be free from suffering, and its value can only be seen in retrospect. Human life is meant to be enriched by suffering. So we find through the ages that men and women have not only passively accepted suffering when it came, but actively sought it out. Ascetics have inflicted punishments on themselves, in order to strengthen or purify their souls.

Meditation

Once regarded almost exclusively as a preoccupation of mystics, saints and hermits, meditation is today an established feature of several popular cults. What it is all about, what it does, and how it is achieved, are matters of considerable interest to a growing number of people today.

Though common to Hinduism, Buddhism and Islam, meditation has not played a particularly prominent role in the Christian tradition. Now, as a result of an unprecedented upsurge of interest in achieving states of mind in which the consciousness is expanded by various means, meditation is being rediscovered as a useful plumb-line to the deeps of the mind.

But why meditate? In a busy world is the time spent pondering on abstractions worth anything at all? Is it not just a futile pursuit, at best another 'opiate' with no practical benefit to recommend it? For the majority, the occasional periods of introspection are of little help. Men only become more confused by what emerges from their deeper reflections. Instead of the restorative relief they seek from the muddled complexity of their lives, they find themselves thinking about their problems more than ever, and they are consequently much less likely to be able to solve them.

Those who advocate meditation, however, say that if it is approached correctly, the exercise can be rewarding. For one thing, a short time devoted each day to the cultivation of a tranquil mind cannot be without its psychological benefits. Confusion only comes with wrongful methods. Meditation does not imply an escape from reality, nor a loss of consciousness; after all, there is little purpose in having experiences which one cannot recall having had.

The first requirement is a 'sanctuary', a room where one can perform the daily ritual in peace and quiet. A trained practitioner can meditate on top of a bus in the midst of the city's hubbub, but such surroundings are hardly conducive to meditation for the average person. Any room will do where one can sit undisturbed for at least 15 minutes at a stretch.

The best position is one of complete repose. One can meditate even while lying in bed,

Opposite above **Buddha taught his followers that suffering ends when craving ceases as part of the Way to Enlightenment: the emaciated Buddha receives food from the daughters of Sana after undergoing extreme austerities** *Opposite* **A Hindu holy man lies in a trance on a bed of thorns on a Jaipur pavement: the ideal of the Hindu yogi was 'uncolouredness', being untouched by passion and prejudice** *Above* **'The next step is to empty the mind, slowly to eliminate from the consciousness every thought of a practical nature, domestic or business problem as it intrudes': bronze head of Buddha, 15th century, now in the Museo Nazionale di Arte, Rome**

but there is a danger of falling asleep. Sitting in an easy position is therefore recommended in most Eastern systems. Having assumed a comfortable position, one should let the whole body relax. All the muscles must be loosened; all tension let go. Among the many aids used for inducing relaxation are rhythmic breathing; a gentle humming; a slight swaying of the torso while seated. Easiest of all perhaps, is mentally going over the parts of the body in which tension is likely to occur, starting from the feet; then the toes, knees, stomach, neck, hands, shoulders, face, jaws, forehead, eyes, the back of the head, the scalp; ensuring that each part in turn is free from strain. With the body relaxed, it becomes easier to achieve tranquillity.

The next step is to empty the mind, slowly to eliminate from the consciousness every thought of a practical nature, domestic or business problem as it intrudes. This, it might be objected, is easier said than done. But ˙meditation requires patience and practice, and it is surprising how soon one can successfully fall into the routine.

One of the main problems confronting the beginner is to decide on a subject for meditation. Having put aside his worldly cares, what does he fill the vacuum with? Stray thoughts and day-dreams keep drifting in. It is precisely in order to prevent such aimless drifting that another factor is introduced at this stage: an objective device, a psycho-symbolic nucleus around which the thoughts are built up, or from which they are reflected or rebound. But the Mohammedan aspirant may not like to think in terms of Hindu symbols, nor the Christian of Buddhist. For that matter the agnostic or free-thinker may disdain any of the formulations of the theistic practitioner. The choice of a symbol to meditate upon therefore becomes of great importance. Just any symbol will not do, because the ramifications of every symbol can be traced by subconscious processes along lines traditionally inherited, or rationally accepted, by the practitioner. So each religion and each school prescribes its own meditative material. The following is a brief outline of some of the major disciplines and methods used in meditation.

Perhaps the most detailed and systematic presentation of meditative techniques can be found in Hindu writings, as exemplified in yoga. The aim of yoga is 'union' with the Absolute, achieved by progression through eight stages of development. The first two pertain to external and internal 'ethics', with stress on non-injury and the elimination of negative emotions like anger, acquisitiveness, lust, greed, and the practice of equanimity and peace of mind. After these two ethical prerequisites we come to the third stage, namely, bodily postures, to inure the physical frame to the various positions assumed during meditation, some

Spectrum Colour Library

of which are extremely difficult. Next comes breath control, also control of the *prana*, which is believed to be one of the basic potencies of the universe. The air we breathe contains it, and the yogi practitioner subtilizes the air for its prana content and sends it streaming through his subtle body. This is followed by control of the senses, that is, withdrawing attention from all external distractions, or, as it is called, 'silencing the traffic of the senses'. By the time this stage is reached the body should be properly conditioned, the emotions under control, and all the mental faculties ready to be directed to a single goal.

The sixth stage is devoted to concentration (*dharana*) or holding the mind firm and steady. Here the student concentrates on a spot on a blank surface such as a wall; a point of light; the flame of a candle; a flower; the picture of a deity such as Krishna or Shiva; a letter of the alphabet. Yogis sometimes begin their meditation by concentrating with closed eyes on some part of their body: the top of the head; the space between the eyebrows; the tip of the nose. The picture of the yogi wrapt in meditation while contemplating his navel is not entirely fanciful. The navel can also serve as a focal point of concentration, for an important *chakra* (plexus, or centre of psychic energy) is situated near it.

Concentration itself must not be confused with meditation. The former implies an exercise of the will: the mind centres its powers on an object or idea till it yields its essence. Concentration brings mental energy to bear on a certain point so that with its conquest further doors are opened to the mind. Meditation on the other hand does not require any forcible harnessing of the will. It is not a smash-and-grab raid on the storehouse of the Infinite; it is something that emerges from the cessation of thought.

The seventh stage of yoga concerns contemplation (*dhyana*), a turning within of the consciousness, a focusing of the mental faculties inwards. The eighth and last stage, called *samadhi*, is a state of superconsciousness, which is the supreme goal of yogic meditation.

Because of its stringency yoga can be a disheartening course for the average practitioner. The most that is generally attempted are elementary postures like the head-stand and simple exercises in breath control. Recent exponents have evolved their own variations on the theme, such as Transcendental Meditation, tailored to the needs of an age which demands instant results. Most of these variations entirely bypass ascetic doctrines and world-abnegation, and permit and indeed encourage a two-way movement between spirituality and worldly life.

The ancient Chinese system of meditation is best exemplified in the Taoist teachings. Taoism seems to go direct to the heart of meditation by the paradoxical method of not even trying to get there. 'The movement of the Tao (Way) is an easy return to within oneself.' Any anxious pursuit of the Tao will cause an impenetrable veil to fall across the aspirant's path and make him lose his bearings. He must cease from aspiring and reduce all striving, study, discourse, discipline, ceremonial and concentration, attenuating them till he arrives at the state of *wu-wei*, 'non-striving'. 'Doing spoils it', says the Tao Master. 'Grabbing misses it'. 'Reaching out on tiptoe you are unsteady'. 'The mighty Way is easy but people still choose the difficult little paths'. There is, in other words, no attempt to stir up consciousness by exhausting techniques, but a natural quiet process of allowing the mental sediment to 'settle down', resulting in a spontaneous revelation of the clear depths within.

The Zen method, again, presents a middle way between the stern practices of yoga and the methodlessness of Tao. Meditation here is largely a matter of 'Shut up' and 'Keep still'. But it also provides by means of question, parable, short poem, paradox, riddle, silence, or even a clout over the ear, a means of sudden illumination called *satori*.

The Sufis, or mystics of Islam, also adapted their meditative techniques to suit their religious temperament. In Sufism there are several stages divided into two main groups: *maqam*, or man's effort, and *hal*, God's grace. It is said, 'Maqam is earned; hal is gifted'. Man's effort calls for all the rituals of religious observance, almsgiving, fasting, pilgrimages, prayers. It presupposes dedicated intention and demands effort. In due time external rituals are abandoned and one devotes oneself to the contemplation of higher things. 'When the mirror of the heart is polished by contemplation, the difference between the transient wealth of this world and the infinite treasure of heaven become manifest. It is then easy to reject the transitory and cling to that which abides.'

Repetition of the name of God plays an important part in Sufi mysticism. The Sufi sits in solitude and repeats without ceasing the name of Allah, letting his mind dwell on the mercy and glory of God. He must persevere until his heart takes up the refrain,

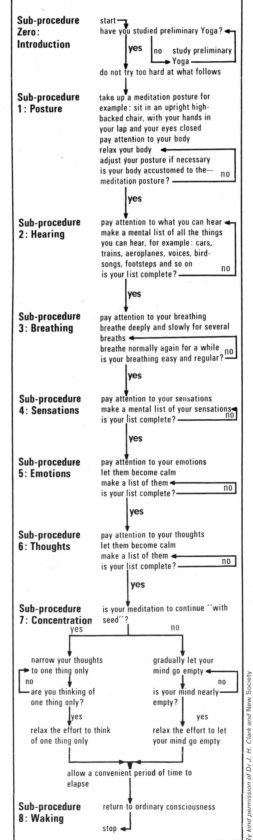

THE FLOW OF MEDITATION

Instructions in the 'Yoga Aphorisms of Patanjali' (2nd century BC) have been formalized by Dr John H. Clark of Manchester University in a flow diagram of the type prepared for computers: adapted from Dr Clark's article in *New Society* magazine (23 July 1970).

By kind permission of Dr J. H. Clark and New Society

and mind, heart and soul are suffused with the idea of God in the fullness of his mercy and power. Some Sufi teachers advocate progressive meditation during a period of retreat, every day of which is devoted to removing one 'veil' of the forty-fold veil covering the Face of God. The raising of the veils comprises graduated exercises in meditation, leading ultimately to ecstasy. The first step is 'watching the Watcher'; when one reaches the final stage of ecstasy, 'Everything perishes except his Face'.

Apart from these 'religious' methods, there exist a number of what might be called magical meditative techniques. Most of them involve recourse to a symbolic diagram. A common device employed by both Hindus and Buddhists is the *mandala*, in other words, an elaborate symmetrical, usually circular design, representing the abode of certain occult potencies who manifest as deities. The latter are invoked by special ritual acts and the intonation of magic versicles or *mantras* and are thus believed to come forth to occupy the places assigned to them in the diagram.

The mandala is regarded as a cosmic cross-roads where the physical and spiritual worlds intersect. The procedure requires deep concentration on the mandala pattern, as a result of which its configuration is imprinted on the psyche of the practitioner and he can clearly see, with his mind's eye, the whole maze depicted outside. For those who might find this difficult an easier way is used. They may look at the mandala, then shut the eyes, and continue this a hundred or a thousand times, until the pattern is clearly visualized with the eyes closed.

The mandala is spoken of as a psycho-cosmogram, a picture of the universe conceived in diagrammatic form and projected on the screen of the psyche. The experiences undergone in this manner become intuitive visualizations of the meditator's own psychodynamic process. Without a long period of correct training there is every likelihood of the imagination running amuck. Even under controlled guidance the apparitions that he encounters in the journey through the intricate pathways of the mandala can be frightening enough. The demon-guardians and the fearful monstrosities that lurk in the dark recesses are ever ready to block his path and hack him to pieces.

Another system of meditation, often resorted to in the West is that of the Cabala, which is basically a Jewish mystical teaching evolved in the Middle Ages, although a much longer history has been claimed for it. Quite early in the course of its development this system was taken over by Christian scholars of the 16th century, and it is not always easy to distinguish the Jewish elements from the later accretions.

There are ten centres, called *sefiroth*, in the meditative device used by the Cabalists, arranged roughly like a tree. When inscribed on paper, the tree is depicted as if on a single plane, but in reality it is believed to be operative on four separate levels or 'worlds'.

Meditation is being rediscovered in the West 'as a result of an unprecedented upsurge of interest in achieving states of mind in which the consciousness is expanded by various means': Maharishi Mahesh Yogi, one of many missionaries from East to West

In the cabalistic technique the aspirant performs a series of meditative exercises, sometimes known as 'rising on the planes', in which he carries consciousness along a predetermined path that links the centres of the sefirotic tree. Each point is a gateway to a new world which has its guardians and its terrorizing demons. The pupil advances

under proper tutelage from the simple to the more complex levels. He is conscious throughout his experience. This system is still practised but has achieved a certain notoriety as a result of its utilization by practitioners of the 'black arts'.

Meditation on the mandala and on the sefirotic tree represent the Eastern and Western systems which involve what occultists call the projection of the astral body through willpower. In both the same general goal is sought: an attempt to make a journey into another dimension and to retain full conscious awareness of it on return. Whether we believe in the actual

existence of the entities that are alleged to guard the zones or not, the fact remains that occultists of both schools, and practitioners of magic, black and white, have brought back vivid descriptions of their experiences while on such astral adventures. We may attribute them to the power of the imagination and the workings of a heightened faith, or dismiss them as hallucinations induced by some alchemy of the brain resulting from deep concentration on evocative archetypal symbols. But whatever the interpretation of such occult experiences might be, there can be no doubt that they are hazardous and can be injurious. The paths opened to the aspirant by encounters in a mandala trance, or on a limb of the sefirotic tree, are not to be ventured on lightly.

Buddhists, who practise meditation intensively, have been especially careful to emphasize the need not so much for meditation as for right meditation. This was thought to be of sufficient importance to be included as one of the eight fundamental principles of their religion. Misdirected or wrongful meditation can be worse than futile, it can be dangerous.

Against the background of all these methods that men have employed in their effort to attain enlightenment, beatitude or unity with the Absolute, it might be felt that the absence of a meditative regime in Christianity for the common man is a drawback to the contemplative life.

In fact, Christianity does not lack a tradition of the kind found in many other religions. First derived from ancient Greek and Jewish sources, this tradition developed along its own lines. Meditation was practised by the early monks who dwelt in the desert regions of Egypt and Syria from the 3rd century AD. Their disciplines were at times so severe as to be scarcely credible today, and their experience with 'temptations' by the Devil and elemental creatures are as vivid as any brought back by occultists from the astral planes. A system somewhat akin to yoga, with emphasis on breathing and concentration on the plexuses, was followed in Greece by the Hesychast monks in the Middle Ages. Many of the saints of the Roman Catholic Church, among them St Francis of Assisi and St Teresa evolved their own very successful meditative disciplines.

The *Spiritual Exercises* of St Ignatius of Loyola outlines a stringent procedure in a contemplative process that has led many to spiritual exaltation. Countless Christian mystics have experienced the sudden transports that betoken the touch of the Divine Breath, and their written works are replete with meditative aids.

But all such methods are meant primarily for the recluse. The Church, it would seem, does not normally advocate meditation for the layman, apart from the periods of retreat set aside for the purpose in the religious calendar, such as the days between Good Friday and Easter Sunday. Perhaps it is considered desirable to withdraw from general sanction the use of any 'device' that might bring one inadvertently into contact with what St Paul refers to as the 'Principalities and Powers, and the rulers of darkness in this world'.

For even the orthodox method can be a staggering experience for the untrained soul. Among mystics, one persistent phase in the more advanced stages is a period of spiritual privation that afflicts even the highest aspirants. St John of the Cross described it as the 'Dark Night of the Soul', St Teresa called it 'the great dereliction', and Mme Guyon 'the mystic death', while others referred to it as 'the descent into Hell'. These perils on the way are not easily borne, and the passage of meditation often lies through some such stage of black despair. When the untried student meditates he is cautioned to do so only on the acceptable patterns provided by long experience.

The posture of meditation for the Christian is not face to face, implying equality with the Creator, but on bended knees with head bowed in humility. For the ordinary Christian meditation is almost synonymous with prayer: in the words of the psalmist: 'Let the words of my mouth and the meditation of my heart, be acceptable in thy sight, O Lord my strength and my redeemer'.

Left Indian saddhu, or holy man, in deep meditation, supported by a crutch. In yoga, meditation involves numerous highly disciplined techniques, including breath control, bodily postures, control of the senses, concentration and contemplation, 'a focusing of the mental faculties inwards' *Opposite left* A Zen monk contemplates a garden made of raked sand; the spiritual exercises of Zen, a form of Buddhism, are directed towards attaining *satori*, 'enlightenment' *Opposite right* A devotee of Vishnu, one of the many thousands of Hindu mystics in India

William MacQuitty

R. K. Singh

Mysticism

Mysticism is a term that tends to be very loosely used; and so it will be as well to state at the beginning what it is not. In ordinary speech it is often associated with the occult and with paranormal phenomena such as thought-reading, telepathy or levitation. It is true that many authentic mystics have had such powers, but they are in no way essential to the mystical experience itself and often merely prove an embarrassment.

Etymologically the word mysticism derives from the Greek *mueo*, meaning to 'initiate' into a secret cult – into a 'mystery'. Among Christians, however, the word has come to mean a direct experience of God; and since, in theory at least, Christianity is the religion of love, the 'mystical' experience is spoken of as union with God or as a 'spiritual marriage'. During the Middle Ages and after, 'mystical theology' was recognized as a legitimate branch of theology beside 'speculative theology'. The difference between the two is clearly brought out by the 17th century French saint, Francis of Sales. What, he asks, do we talk about in prayer? What is our topic of conversation? God: nothing else. After all what does a lover talk about but his beloved? Prayer and mystical theology, therefore, are identical. Prayer is called theology, because it deals with God as speculative theology does; only there are three differences. First of all, speculative theology deals with God as the supreme Being – the divinity of supreme goodness; mystical theology deals with him

as supremely lovable – the supreme goodness of the divinity. Secondly, speculative theology is concerned with God and man, mystical theology with God alone. Thirdly, speculative theology leads to knowledge of God – turning its pupils into learned scholars and theologians; mystical theology leads to love of God – turning out intensely affectionate lovers. This is the traditional Christian point of view: mystical experience is the immediate experience of the love of God, and any experience in which neither God nor love were felt to be present would scarcely be taken seriously as mystical.

In the course of the last century or so, however, the word has taken on a wider meaning. There seem to be two reasons for this: the rise of the secular 'science' of psychology; and the dissemination of knowledge of the religions of India and China, in both of which the mystical element is prominent. And yet in neither Buddhism nor in Taoism does love, or indeed God, play a significant part. In what sense, then, are they mystical? Let us turn to the Oxford Dictionary for guidance. On 'mystic' it says: 'one who seeks by contemplation and self-surrender to obtain union with or absorption into the Deity, or who believes in the spiritual apprehension of truths inaccessible to the understanding.' And for 'mysticism' it gives a similar entry: 'belief in the possibility of union with the divine nature by means of ecstatic contemplation; reliance on spiritual intuition as the means of acquiring

knowledge of mysteries inaccessible to the understanding.' In neither entry is there any mention of love; and in both 'deity' has come to replace the more personal 'God'.

But these definitions are still perhaps not broad enough, if we are to include in the category 'mystical' the Buddhist concept of Nirvana, considered by many non-Christian writers on this subject to be the mystical experience above all others. At the risk of over-simplifying I should define 'mysticism' as 'a direct apperception of eternal being', whether this eternal being is conceived of in personal terms or simply as a state of consciousness. This may take many forms, but perhaps the characteristic lowest common denominator is the loss of the sense of personality or ego-consciousness in a greater whole. Tennyson seems to have put it very well when he said: 'All at once, as it were out of the intensity of the consciousness of individuality, individuality itself seemed to dissolve and fade away into boundless being, and this not a confused state but the clearest, the surest of the sure, utterly beyond words – where death was an almost laughable impossibility – the loss of personality (if so it were) seeming no extinction, but the only true life.' Again, not a word about either love or God.

This kind of experience is usually called 'Nature mysticism'. It is as if one's everyday personality – one's ego – were dissolved and merged into the 'All'; and through this merging into the totality of existence the mystic

223

now feels that he lives with the life of the All and therefore cannot die. This experience is perhaps not so uncommon as is often supposed: it comes unheralded, lasts only for a short time, but brings with it an absolute conviction of its reality. Examples of it turn up in the mystical traditions of Christians and Moslems but on the whole it is not central to them. On the other hand, it seems to constitute the core of the experience which the Zen Buddhists call *satori*, though it is quite different from what the early Buddhists called *nirvana*.

This Nature mysticism which R. W. Bucke, a Canadian doctor who wrote at the turn of the century, called 'cosmic consciousness' and which Freud called the 'oceanic feeling', can strike anyone at any time; and it can also be induced by yoga techniques and by drugs. It is not necessarily associated with religion of any kind but is liable to infiltrate the mystical tradition of any religion. Its most disturbing characteristic is that through it the mystic feels that he has transcended all the 'opposites' and contradictions of life, including good and evil. Bucke himself had such an experience and (as is the custom of most Nature mystics) he drew from it the most unwarrantable conclusions. According to him, cosmic consciousness 'shows the cosmos not to consist of dead matter governed by unconscious, rigid, and unintending law; it shows it on the contrary as entirely immaterial, entirely spiritual and entirely alive; it shows that death is an absurdity, that everyone and everything has eternal life; it shows that the universe is God and that God is the universe, and that no evil ever did or ever will enter into it; a great deal of this is, of course, from the point of view of self-consciousness, absurd; it is nevertheless undoubtedly true.'

This is typical of the attitude of the Nature mystics. Their experience is usually momentary, but it is overwhelming in its impact: they simply cannot doubt that they have entered into a totally new and different form of consciousness which represents a truth of which they had never dreamt before and which they find it almost impossible to describe. Their attitude is that they have seen the truth and that they therefore know. They are, however, the amateurs at this very hazardous game and unfortunately they rarely think it necessary to consult the professionals. The professionals are, of course, the religious mystics; and of them the Indians are without doubt the most important. They are important because (unlike believers in Judaism, Christianity and Islam) they are not bound by dogma. Hence they feel no obligation to express their experience in terms of any given religious framework. Thus if love does not form part of their experience, they will not speak of love, the idea of love being only peripheral in their sacred texts.

It is a common error to suppose that 'mysticism is essentially one and the same, whatever may be the religion professed by the individual mystic', for any study of the Hindu and Buddhist mystical texts will very soon

convince us that this is not true. There are varieties here which it is simply not possible to overlook: it is not a question of interpretation but of the experience itself. And it would seem that there are three recognizable types of mystical experience, all of which are to be found in the Hindu and Buddhist classics. The first is 'cosmic consciousness'; the second is the realization of eternity and 'deathlessness' within oneself from which the whole universe of change and time and space is excluded; and the third is the experience of the union of the soul with the Absolute or God in a supreme act of love. The first is typical of the *Upanishads*, the sacred mystical texts of the Hindus; the second is typical of early Buddhism; and the third is characteristic of Christianity, Islam and later Hinduism.

The classic formulation of 'cosmic consciousness' occurs in a very ancient Hindu text which says that, 'The whole universe is Brahman' who is also 'my Self within my heart', smaller than a grain of rice yet also 'greater than the earth, greater than the atmosphere, greater than the sky, greater than all these worlds . . . This my Self within the heart is that Brahman'.

This means that the inmost self of man is identical with the Absolute, with the unchanging power over against which the whole changing universe must be seen. One lives not with one's own life but with the life of the whole universe, which is founded in a changeless Being which is at the same time one's own eternity. It was this experience which made it possible for Tennyson to say that death was 'an almost laughable impossibility'. As Hugh of St Victor said in the 12th century: 'This one is all, and this all is one.' This is the experience of cosmic consciousness.

The Absolute is also commonly called the One, and you and I are in some sense that One: 'This finest essence – the whole universe has it as its Self: that is the Real: that is the Self: that you are.' The manifold universe is unified in the One, and so far as each conscious soul is aware of the One behind the many, he feels himself to be that One and through it interconnected with all the manifold existences that formerly had seemed to be separate from it. All things cohere in the One as spokes 'cohere' in the hub and felly of a wheel: there is identity of Being but not of function or of power.

There is identity in Being but at the same time diversity in function, power and relationship; and the identity does not exclude the relationship. This is, of course, a paradox. So be it, but paradox is of the very stuff of mysticism, particularly where cosmic consciousness is concerned. Thus though I may realize myself as the Infinite and the universal Self, this does not prevent me from having a passionate love-affair with that universal Self. This comes out clearly in another passage taken from the *Upanishads:*

> The Infinite is below, it is above, it is to the west, to the east, to the south, to the north. Truly it is this whole universe.
>
> Next the teaching concerning the ego.

I am below, I am above, I am to the west, to the east, to the south, to the north. Truly I am this whole universe.

Next the teaching concerning the Self.

The Self is below, the Self is above, the Self is to the west, to the east, to the south, to the north. Truly the Self is this whole universe.

The man who truly sees and thinks and understands in this way has pleasure in the Self, plays with the Self, copulates with the Self, and has joy with the Self: he becomes an independent sovereign. In all the worlds freedom of movement is his.

Here cosmic consciousness merges into the mysticism of love – and frankly sexual love at that. The essence of cosmic consciousness, however, is the realization of oneness in and through diversity, 'that kind of knowledge,' as the *Bhagavad Gita* says, 'by which one sees one mode of being, changeless, undivided in all contingent beings, divided though they be.' It is to see the eternal in and through the transitory, and to see the transitory as itself eternal: no clear distinction can be made between the two. Clearly this is very different from our second type of mysticism, 'the realization of eternity and "deathlessness" within oneself from which the whole universe of change and time and space is excluded'.

Unlike the *Upanishads*, early Buddhism draws the sharpest distinction between the world in which we live and eternity. Our world is in a state of continual flux. Nothing in it is permanent, nothing remains the same for two moments on end, and this applies just as much to mind as it does to matter. The man I am today is different from the man I was yesterday, and this means that I have no self, no permanent substratum which I can legitimately call 'I'. This applies to everything. Everything lacks substance, and because it lacks substance it is in a permanent state of unease. Hence no one can truthfully say 'I am', or 'this is mine', or 'there is a self', or 'this belongs to a self'. There is no means of deliverance from the unease of this world except by realizing that we have no individual and personal existence; and since we consider that we belong to the world of flux we have to detach ourselves completely from that world and everything which attaches us to it.

Only so can we realize Nirvana, which is a deathless state of being, totally separate and distinct from this world of flux, utterly at peace, not born, not become, not made or compounded, the cessation of phenomenal existence, the extinction of becoming, craving and pain, perfect peace, wisdom and enlightenment. In Christian terminology, it is *requies aeterna*, 'eternal rest', the peace of death. This would appear to be literally true, for life is flux, and it is therefore life as such that the early Buddhists

would put an end to. This is not surprising, given their premises; for the Buddhist idea of salvation is conditioned by their unshakable belief in transmigration – what they call *samsara*, an endless process of birth and death, re-birth and re-death, in a form of existence which is forever impermanent, unreal and fraught with suffering. To put an end to this is very heaven – it is Nirvana. It is, as one of the Moslem mystics puts it, 'to isolate the eternal from the originated', perfect, static, timeless peace.

The guarantee that such a state of timeless peace exists and can be found is the Buddha's own Enlightenment. Once he had found it, however, he did not consider it expedient to define it in concrete terms. One thing only would he assert, and that is that Nirvana puts a stop to all becoming. In cosmic consciousness, eternal Being is seen as the cement that holds the whole world of becoming together: in early Buddhism, Being and becoming are forever and unalterably separate.

Neither the Hindus nor the later Buddhist schools (the so-called Mahayana), however, were prepared to leave things so uncomfortably vague. On the Hindu side one of the late *Upanishads* defines what seems obviously to be the same as the Buddhist Nirvana in these terms: 'Conscious of neither within nor without, nor of both together, not a mass of wisdom, neither wise nor unwise, one with whom there is no commerce, impalpable, devoid of distinguishing mark, unthinkable, indescribable, its essence the firm conviction of the oneness of itself, bringing all development to an end, tranquil and mild, devoid of duality, such do they deem this fourth (and ultimate state

of consciousness) to be. That is the Self: that is what should be known.'

This 'fourth' state of consciousness is beyond the other three states of dreamless sleep, dream, and our ordinary waking state. What is strange is that this fourth state which is really total unconsciousness is regarded as being the one Reality – the Absolute which is beyond the personal God himself; for in man, the microcosm, it is dreamless sleep, not the 'fourth state', which corresponds to the creator God in the macrocosm. It is considered that just as dream emerges from dreamless sleep, so does the phenomenal world emerge from God: but beyond God and beyond dreamless sleep there is the totally static One which is beyond change of any kind. In this 'fourth state', then, the mystic realizes himself as the Absolute. Plainly, if this is really so, this is the one Reality beyond which one cannot go. Insofar as the mystic realizes himself as this One, he is superior to God, so far as God is operative in the material world. This, of course, makes nonsense of all religion.

But this is not the only way in which this experience of 'isolation' can be interpreted. According to another Hindu school of philosophy, this oneness which the mystic experiences is not the Absolute but only the incommunicable essence of one individual soul. These 'souls' or spiritual monads are innumerable, each one being exactly like the others, each being a unit of pure consciousness, eternal, beyond space and time, isolated from all other spiritual monads and from matter. It is the misfortune of these monads, however, that they 'fall' into matter and are there imprisoned until, after count-

Above A kind of mystical experience has been recorded in certain forms of Hinduism: the loves of Krishna and the *gopis* could be allegorized to represent the love between God and the soul *Opposite* Drugs are sometimes used as aids to mystical illumination: an 18th century painting shows dervishes meditating while they smoke *ganja*, the dried leaves of the hemp plant, and drink *bhang*, also made from hemp

less more or less miserable incarnations, they are finally released by the evolutionary processes at work in matter itself. The experience again is the same – the Buddhist Nirvana, the final and definitive isolation of spirit from matter. Thus what the Buddha had refused to define in positive terms – the isolation of spirit from matter – is interpreted by the 'monist' Hindus as meaning that the mystic realizes himself as the sole Reality, as the Absolute 'One without a second', but by the 'pluralistic' Hindus as meaning the realization by one out of countless spiritual monads of its own timeless essence. The experience is the same, and it is the very reverse of cosmic consciousness, for the 'cosmos', the phenomenal world of change and life and self-consciousness, is totally excluded and transcended.

In the mysticism of 'isolation' there can by definition be no question of love. In that of cosmic consciousness a feeling of love may or may not be present. In the passage from the *Upanishads* quoted above the mystic feels himself to be present everywhere throughout the whole wide universe. There is no difference between him and the infinite 'Self' of all things, and yet he is able to 'have pleasure in the Self, play with the Self, copulate with the Self, and have joy with the Self'. The 'Self', then, is both an all-pervasive Absolute and a personal God with whom the mystic experiences the spiritual equivalent of sexual union.

Christianity is, in theory, the religion of love, and its mysticism therefore naturally expresses itself in terms of love. But Christianity also exalts virginity as one of the greatest virtues, and virginity is not compatible with human love as it expresses itself in wedlock. This is rather awkward for Christians, the more so in that their mystics *experienced* the love of God as a spiritual marriage, the consummation of which bore an uncomfortable resemblance to the sexual act in the physical world. Origen, who had castrated himself for the love of God, was painfully aware of this, but it did not prevent him from writing a commentary on the frankly erotic Song of Solomon. He knew very well that the spiritual espousals of which he wrote would be misinterpreted by the profane, and so he wrote:

If any man who lives after the flesh should approach this subject, to such a one the reading of this scripture will be the occasion of no small hazard and danger. For he, not knowing how to hear love's language in purity and with chaste ears, will twist the whole manner of his hearing of it away from the inner spiritual man and on to the outward and carnal; and he will be turned away from the

spirit to the flesh, and will foster carnal desires in himself, and it will seem to be the divine scriptures that are thus urging and egging him on to fleshly lust.

Love and marriage, of course, are only possible between two *persons*. The God of the pantheists — of cosmic consciousness — must therefore also have his personal side. In the *Upanishads* this is only occasionally recognized. In one of the later *Upanishads*, however, the existence of God as creator and sustainer not only of the physical universe but also of the timeless eternity called Brahman, is admitted.

In the imperishable, infinite city of Brahman
Two things there are —
Wisdom and unwisdom, hidden, established there:
Perishable is unwisdom, but wisdom is immortal:
Who over wisdom and unwisdom rules, he is another.

This distinction between the personal God and the impersonal Brahman and the relationship between the two becomes even more apparent in the text of *Bhagavad Gita*. The *Gita* is in element a dialogue between Krishna, who is God incarnate, and his friend Arjuna. It is, then, in the eyes of the Hindus the spoken word of God. The *Gita* starts where the *Upanishads* leave off, but it also takes for granted the Buddhist

Nirvana, which it sometimes also calls Brahma-nirvana. Salvation or rather 'liberation', that is, the escape from matter, time and space, into a condition of timeless eternity, is taken for granted. This the *Gita* calls either 'to become Brahman' or 'to enter Nirvana'; but this is no longer the end of the affair, for Krishna, the personal God, is beyond and above both Brahman and Nirvana. Nirvana 'subsists' in him, and he is 'the base supporting Brahman — immortal Brahman which knows no change — supporting the eternal law of righteous and absolute beatitude.' This, then, is a personal God with whom it is possible to have personal relations and whom it is possible to love.

And then comes the final revelation which is, in essence, the Christian revelation too. Not only is man required to love God but God on his side loves man in return: 'And now again listen to this my highest word, the most mysterious of all: I love you well. Therefore will I tell you your salvation. Bear Me in mind, love Me and worship Me, sacrifice, prostrate yourself to Me . . . Give up all things of law, turn to Me, your only refuge, for I will deliver you from all evils; have no care.'

The development of mysticism is illustrated in Hinduism as it is nowhere else, largely because Hinduism has no fixed dogmas. First comes cosmic consciousness, then the experience of the 'isolation' of man's innermost spiritual essence which is

beyond time and space, and finally the union of this essence with God who is the essence of all essences.

Much the same happens in Buddhism, for with the development of the Mahayana, the 'Great Vehicle', some 500 years after the Buddha's death, the ideal of Nirvana is denounced as being only a stage on the road to absolute beatitude. The goal is now to realize the 'Buddha-nature' in oneself, and the Buddha-nature is not just perfect peace and infinite wisdom but also boundless compassion, which makes the salvation of all mankind the primary concern of all who have experienced the bliss of enlightenment.

In all traditions, however, even in those which start from the love of God, there is a tendency to mistake the stage of 'isolation' for identity with the Absolute and therefore beyond all relationships of any kind including the consummation of the spiritual marriage. This tendency becomes the official teaching of the non-dualist Vedanta in India. But as the *Gita* makes it perfectly plain, what is taken to be identity with the godhead turns out to be only the experience of the oneness and eternity of one's own soul. The modern Jewish mystic Martin Buber discerned this and warned against it in words that reflect the teaching of the Gita: 'Now from my own unforgettable experience, I know well that there is a state in which the bonds of the personal nature of life seem to have fallen away from us and we experience an undivided unity. But I do not know – what the soul willingly imagines and indeed is bound to imagine (mine too once did it) – that in this I had attained to a union with the primal being or the godhead. That is an exaggeration no longer permitted to the responsible understanding. Responsibly . . . I can elicit from these experiences only that in them I reached an undifferentiable unity of myself without form or content. I may call this an original pre-biographical unity and suppose that it is hidden unchanged beneath all biographical change, all development and complication of soul. Nevertheless, in the honest and sober account of the responsible understanding, this unity is nothing but the unity of this soul of mine, whose "ground" I have reached, so much so that . . . my spirit has no choice but to understand it as the groundless. But this basic unity of my own soul is certainly beyond the reach of all the multiplicity it has hitherto received from life, though not in the least beyond individuation, or the multiplicity of all the souls in the world of which it is one – existing but once, single, unique, irreducible, this creaturely one: one of the human souls and not the "soul of the All"; a defined and particular being and not "Being"; the creaturely basic unity of a creature.'

There is, then, a mysticism of the soul as it is in itself and a mysticism of the love of that soul for God. In the Christian tradition the two are rarely distinguished, for love is God, and God is timeless eternity. The exceptions are, among others, Ruysbroeck and Richard of St Victor. The case of Richard is particularly interesting, for he reads

Museum für ostasiatische Kunst, Cologne

like a Christian version of the *Bhagavad Gita*.

His predecessor, Hugh of St Victor, too was perhaps the most 'Buddhist' of the Christian mystics. Little concerned with love, he had a positive terror of time and regarded absolute changelessness as the ultimate goal of the mystic. 'The more a man gathers himself together in spirit, the more . . . is he raised in thought and desire; until, at last, when he comes to that supreme changelessness, he is altogether unchangeable.' This is to 'become Brahman' and to enter Nirvana. Richard, however, like the *Gita* goes further than this. This changelessness he calls self-knowledge, as does the *Gita*. Self-knowledge, however, is only the first step on the way to the knowledge of God. And so he says:

> The soul which is attempting to rise to the height of knowledge must make self-knowledge his first and chief concern. The high peak of knowledge is perfect self-knowledge. The full understanding of a rational spirit is as it were a high and great mountain. This mountain rises far above the top of all earthly learning and looks down from on high upon all philosophy and all the learning of the world . . . By as much as you make daily progress in self-knowledge, by so much you will be reaching out to higher things, for he who attains perfect self-knowledge has reached the top of the mountain.

What Christian mystics call the apex of the soul is the top of the mountain; and standing here the soul looks down and contemplates all the transitoriness of the world, realizing its own changelessness. Men, however, are not angels: they do not have wings. Hence it is impossible for the soul to rise higher than the top of the mountain. If it is to go further, then it must receive wings, and this can only come about by the grace of God. And so Richard goes on to say:

> Let a man rise up by himself above himself, and from self-knowledge to the knowledge of God. Let a man first learn from the image of God, let him learn from the likeness of God what he ought to think about God . . . A mind which does not raise itself to consideration of its own nature, how can it fly away on the wings of contemplation to that which is above itself? . . . If the mind has not yet been able to gather itself into a unity, and does not yet know how to enter into itself, when will it be able to ascend by contemplation to those things which are above itself?

It must, however, beware of resting content on the mountain-peak under the delusion that this is the journey's end, for this may lead to complacency and spiritual pride, as the Mahayana Buddhists had also seen.

A Japanese scroll of the 14th century shows Shakyamuni's entrance into Nirvana: the Buddha, Shakyamuni, dies surrounded by a mourning creation ranging from gods and human beings to animals, birds and insects. Nirvana, the Buddhists' ultimate goal, was a deathless state of perfect peace, wisdom and enlightenment

Left The 17th century French saint Francis of Sales described in his treatise *On the Love of God* the effects of divine love on the hearts of men: in the Christian religion mystical experience is equated with the immediate experience of the love of God *Below* Krishna, who is God incarnate as the charioteer of Arjuna, delivers the message of the *Bhagavad Gita*. This work, one of the later developments of Hindu mysticism, presents a personal God with whom it is possible to have personal relations: 'And now again listen to this my highest word, the most mysterious of all: I love you well'

Opposite The empty chair here represents Buddha, under a tree whose shape shows that, like the Christian cross, it symbolizes the world. The God of the East is not a person but a principle, 'the principle of unchanging Being, which is yet the source of all becoming' *Opposite right* One of the important general differences between western and eastern religions is the contrast between the western picture of God in human form, as *he*, and the eastern idea of God as abstract, an *it*. The death of God – man on the cross, often seen as a symbol of the world; by El Greco

Michael Holford

Michael Holford

On this too the 14th century Flemish mystic, Ruysbroeck, is most emphatic in his denunciation:

> All those men are deceived whose intention it is to sink themselves in natural rest, and who do not seek God with desire nor find him in delectable love. For the rest which they possess consists in an emptying of themselves, to which they are inclined by nature and by habit . . . In this emptiness rest is sufficient and great, and it is in itself no sin, if, however, they know how to make themselves empty.
>
> But when they wish to exercise and possess this rest without the works of virtue, then they fall into spiritual pride, and into a self-complacency from which they seldom recover. And at such times they believe themselves to have and to be that which they never achieve.

This was directed against the Brethren of the Free Spirit, who were almost certainly Nature-mystics and held, like some early passages in the *Upanishads*, that their spiritual experiences exempted them from both the religious and the moral code. This antinomianism we meet with in all the mystical traditions, and it is also true that mystics are on the whole not conspicuous for love of their neighbour. There are exceptions, of course, and Richard of St Victor was one of these. For him there are four stages in the mystical ascent – knowledge of self as changeless (and this would include cosmic consciousness as well as spiritual 'isolation'), ascent to God, absorption in God, and finally going forth from God – the infinite compassion of the Mahayana Buddhists as it is ultimately realized.

This is how he eventually sums up the mystical quest: 'In the first degree God enters into the soul and she turns inward into herself. In the second she ascends above herself and is lifted up to God. In the third the soul, lifted up to God passes altogether into him. In the fourth the soul goes forth on God's behalf and descends below herself. In the first she enters into herself, in the second she goes forth from herself. In the first she reaches her own life, in the third she reaches God.

'In the first she goes forth on her own behalf, in the fourth she goes forth because of her neighbour. In the first she enters in by meditation, in the second she ascends by contemplation, in the third she is led into jubilation, in the fourth she goes out by compassion.'

NEW MOVEMENTS

Communistic Religions

Holding all property in common has never been a widespread practice among religious movements. It is an interesting variant of the much more frequently found monastic arrangement, in which the monk abandons all his goods on entering the order. Orders of monks, nuns and friars, as they are found in Christianity and Buddhism, differ from communistic religious movements principally in being constituted of members of only one sex; in accepting a hierarchic system of authority; and in emphasizing personal poverty rather than communism of possessions. Most important of all, these orders are part of a wider religious organization and tradition. By contrast, communistic movements are total social systems, which usually do not admit those outside the commune to any place in their religious scheme of things.

Communistic movements are necessarily communitarian, that is, they establish communities, in which the principles of communism are applied. Without the total control of the activities of everyday life possible in a separate community, communistic principles would be difficult, if not impossible, to implement. The initial aim of many of these sects has been to create a community, rather than to establish communism, and the principle of common ownership has often been adopted only after the community has been established.

Communistic sects have sought isolation from the rest of society to enable them to safeguard their beliefs *Opposite, above* The Shakers, who got their name from the ecstatic trembling which took place at their religious meetings, fled to America in the 18th century to escape persecution; there they organized themselves into strictly disciplined celibate communities *Opposite* In Paraguay Mennonite communities often recruit new members from the local Indians; communal baptism of Lengua Indians

Although many Christian communities have existed which have not been communistic, when sects set up separated communities, their basic principles of brotherhood, equality in the love of God, and the shared prospect of salvation, predispose them to communistic arrangements. When a group has drawn together as a fellowship, any disparities of wealth among them are irrelevant to their new hopes, a hindrance to their common purpose, and a symbol of the vain and corrupt values of the world.

So communism may be adopted as a matter of expediency, as an outgrowth of the movement's new circumstances once it has established a separated colony. In this case, the new system may be justified by inspiration or revelation, as among the Community of the Truly Inspired (the Amana Society), who adopted communism of goods after they had emigrated to America and whose new practice was made legitimate, after some members had challenged it, by revelation of the Holy Spirit to their leader.

In other cases, as among the Oneida Community, or the Tolstoyans, communism is prescribed as part of the way of life of the saints and is a basic principle, to be realized by the establishment of a colony. Sometimes there is explicit reference to the early Church at Jerusalem, as described in the Acts of the Apostles, which provides scriptural justification for communism.

Religious communism differs from the communism of political Utopians, such as the followers of Robert Owen at New Harmony or the disciples of Fourier, who set up many colonies in the United States during the 19th century. Religious groups are not necessarily, and not usually, attempting to provide a model of social organization for other men to imitate – at least not until other men learn the spiritual truths which they know. In the event, political communities have always failed, usually very soon after being founded.

Religious communistic colonies have had more varied fortunes and some have flourished for decades.

One of the necessary conditions for the establishment of sectarian communism is the possibility of finding a place in which the sect can be sufficiently isolated from the rest of the world. This is essential, to prevent the contamination of the group by outside influences and to provide a stable context in which children can be brought up in the values of the sect. Since such groups come out of the wider society, the colony is both a place of refuge and a heavenly community.

It is not every society that allows men to congregate in this way. The Levellers and Diggers of 17th century England were seen as a threat to the social order, and when this is the response of the political authorities such groups are not permitted to establish themselves. Only where royal or aristocratic patronage was gained, as the Hutterian Brethren gained it successfully in Moravia, Hungary and Russia, were sects able to practise communism, at least until late in the 18th century. More often, the sects fled from persecution, usually to North America where land was abundant and diligent settlers were welcomed.

The principal religious communistic sects have come from central Europe and have usually been German-speaking. Some semi-communistic sects have arisen in England but the groups like the Girlingites in the New Forest met with opposition.

An important factor aiding the success of communistic sects has been their isolation from the wider society, and one of the most important insulating mechanisms has been the use of a language differing from that of the surrounding people. The Mennonites in Brazil, who were not always communists though they always lived in segregated communities, were well aware of the importance of retaining their native German as

Above In the 16th century, Protestant revolutionaries known as Anabaptists established a 'kingdom of the saints' at Münster in Germany; they were accused of all manner of atrocities *Opposite* Drop-Out City in America is a haven of refuge for hippies, and others who feel themselves at odds with the highly organized world around them; they share their goods in common and practise free love *Below* The pacifist Russian Doukhobors, who emigrated to Canada at the beginning of the century, practised communism for a time; they caused embarrassment by parading in the nude as a protest against government interference

a defence against assimilation to the society outside. In those communistic groups which have permitted sexual relations and have raised children, difference of language has been of great importance in preventing young people from learning too quickly about the all too vociferous attractions of the world outside.

The Shakers are perhaps most celebrated of all the communistic sects. This sect owes its origin to the preaching of refugee French Camisards who were active in 18th century England. They converted some Quakers in Lancashire to belief in the imminent return of Christ, with the unusual feature that the returning Christ was expected to appear as a woman. The Shakers got their name from the ecstatic shaking that occurred in their noisy religious meetings.

In 1770 a woman named Ann Lee became their leader, after she had experienced a vision in which she clearly saw that sexual intercourse was the source of all the evil in the world. Her preoccupation with this subject may no doubt be explained by the fact that she had had several stillborn children. She now saw that redemption was to be gained by renouncing sex and reproduction. Although scarcely literate and given to shaking and speaking in tongues, Ann Lee was undoubtedly an impressive leader of considerable intelligence. She declared that to escape persecution the sect should go to the New World, where they expected to make converts in what they thought of as the last days of the existing order of things. Eight Shakers made the journey to America in 1774.

In the following years Shakers came into being in various places, scattered over several states. Perhaps as a defensive measure, and as a way of establishing the appropriate control of the godly life, the leading Shakers, after Ann Lee's death in 1782, decided to organize themselves in segregated communities. From 1787 Shaker communities were set up. Within them were organized large groups known as 'families', each with its male and female head. Celibacy was the absolute rule and each man was provided with a 'sister' who undertook a variety of household tasks for him. Care was taken never to leave individuals of opposite sex alone with each other, and there is no record of scandal in any of the 18 Shaker communities that were eventually established.

To become a Shaker was no light undertaking. New members, on entering a community, gave up all their possessions for the good of the fellowship. Thereafter they received a share of what was termed 'just and equal rights and privileges, according to their needs.' Should anyone leave the community — and inevitably some did — he received an agreed sum on discharge.

Practicality was a much prized Shaker virtue, their organization was a model of efficiency, and although agricultural work was the basis of their economy they were from the outset interested in a wide range of craft and industrial activities. Since no wages were paid, and each received simply what he needed according to the modest assessments that their religious dispositions dictated, the Shakers could devote all their energy and ingenuity to the work that they saw as the testimony to their faith. Among the many useful devices that they produced were a new type of circular saw, a much improved washing machine (this in the early 19th century), a tilting chair, and new designs in sewing machines and brooms.

Industry and inventiveness were principal outlets for Shaker enterprise, facilitated by the fact that they were a celibate community, in which no one had family problems or sexual distractions. Visitors were generally impressed by the spirit of harmony that prevailed among the Shakers. This harmony, and their successful economy, have been attributed to the simple principles of faith on which they based their way of life, and the intensity with which these were inculcated. Order, neatness, cleanliness, frugality and sobriety were the pervasive demands.

The discipline of the daily lives of the Shakers was informed by the joy that they expressed most fully in their worship, particularly in their ecstatic dancing, which in time was organized along a wide variety of set patterns. They believed in communications from spirits (though they found nothing in common with Spiritualism when that movement arose), in direct revelation from God, in faith healing and in speaking in tongues. They gave a good deal of time to religious exercises and, like other communistic sects, they did not have to give too much time to labour, because their needs were very limited.

Despite celibacy, the Shakers recruited sufficiently from the outside world to

Mary Evans Picture Library

Keystone Press Agency

continue through the 19th century and into the 20th. They can rarely have numbered more than 3000 at any one time and there probably cannot have been more than about 16,500 of them altogether during the movement's entire life. By the mid-1960s only a few old ladies remained, still living together in the last surviving Shaker community. Shaking as such had ceased to be practised and so had the dancing, which had been so developed in the 19th century.

A strong injunction to celibacy and community of goods were the distinguishing features of another sect that flourished in 19th century America, the Harmonists, or Rappites. This sect built successively, at ten-year intervals, three substantial villages in the states of Pennsylvania and Indiana. Initially the sect was composed of the personal following of its remarkable, autocratic and impressive leader George Rapp, a weaver, who in the 1780s began to conduct his own religious meetings in his native village in Württemberg, Germany, expressing severe disapproval of the outward show and ritual of the Lutheran Church. Württemberg was a strong centre of sectarianism at this time, and Rapp soon acquired a significant following from his own and neighbouring villages. His separatism and the emptying of the Lutheran churches caused the Lutheran authorities to seek the intervention of the state to discourage Rapp, and periodically he was called to account for his teachings and activities.

In the earliest known formulations of Rapp's beliefs there was no explicit demand for celibacy among his followers, although he himself – in spite of being married – was known to be leading a celibate life. Nor, in the first two decades of his movement, was there any direct assertion that there should be community of goods among the faithful. Perhaps, however, in those circumstances, such a demand would have been scarcely practicable for the farmers and artisans who were among his following. They believed that withdrawal from the world was necessary, in preparation for Christ's reappearance, which they believed to be imminent – as indeed did many quite orthodox Protestants in Europe and America at the time of the Napoleonic wars.

It was after the keenest members of the sect had emigrated to America, in 1804, that communism proper was adopted by them. Migration itself tested the faith of the Rappites, since they all gave what they had to support the costs of the journey for themselves and others, and for their initial expenses in America. The Harmony Society, as the sect called itself, bought land and, after considerable hardship in the early days built a model village on the Connoquenessing Creek, near Pittsburg in Pennsylvania. The community regarded itself as a Church, in which all members surrendered their property to the society and pledged themselves to its laws. In return, they were ensured all the necessities of life, education and religious instruction, and insurance for their dependants.

Eve Arnold – Magnum

The productivity, inventiveness and social usefulness of the communistic religious societies is again illustrated in the history of the Amana Society, the Society of the Truly Inspired, which eventually settled in Iowa. The Amana Society which numbered some 1500 people at the height of its success also came from south Germany. It had originally arisen early in the 18th century, at the instigation of two inspired preachers, Rock and Gruber, who had travelled to various places at the bidding of the Spirit, preaching the word. The sect which they founded was pacifist and committed to the view that God still inspired men through the Holy Spirit, whose instruments some men were called to be.

After Rock's death, no new 'instrument' appeared for some time, but a number of prophets arose in the sect at the beginning of the 19th century in various parts of Germany. In 1842, under the leadership of Christian Metz, it was revealed that they should emigrate to America. Initially, the sect settled near the city of Buffalo and called their community Ebenezer. They were not, at this stage, communists: their intention had been to find a place where they could live the life of faith in peace.

Trouble with the Seneca Indians and fear of encroachments on their withdrawn way of life from the growing city of Buffalo, induced them in the late 1850s to sell their land and move to Iowa, where they settled in seven villages. They took the name Amana from the Song of Solomon (chapter 4, verse 8). Force of circumstances caused them to become communists, and this was an understandable development for a group that had already committed itself to a common destiny in this world and the next. Their adoption of the communistic principle was conveniently reinforced and made legitimate by the inspiration of the Holy Spirit, speaking through Metz, the leader of the community. The regulations concerning the entitlements of individuals and the responsibility of the community were similar to those of the Harmonists. They ate as a community, in common dining halls, the two sexes being separated.

The Amana Society did not impose celibacy. It was approved, but was not so strongly enjoined as among the Harmonists and the Shakers. Even as children, the sexes were kept apart, and marriage was permitted only when a man reached the age of 24: ideally, however, the faithful should not marry. This had been an early injunction, long before the sect became communistic but, of course, the virtual elimination of the family unit predisposes a sect to communism of goods and mutual help.

The sect had three orders of piety, and those who married revealed by so doing that they were of the lowest order. Only by leading a conscientious life could a couple who married rise again in spiritual status. Families did, however, dwell in individual homes in Amana, which suggests that marriage continued to be a common, if disapproved arrangement. In contrast with the Shakers, whose way of life allowed for considerable elements of recreation, the Amana Society frowned on entertainments and all levity.

The Amana Society was governed by trustees under the inspired instruments of the Holy Spirit. After Metz died, Barbara Landmann was the leader of the community,

but she was the last of the 'instruments' and long before the end of the 19th century the Society ceased to have a spiritual head with inspired power. The villages were organized by elders, who were not necessarily old, but who were recognized as spiritually advanced. They were in charge of industrial and agricultural activities. In their dealings with the outside world, the Amana Society gained a reputation for honesty and shrewdness, neither cheating others nor letting themselves be cheated.

The religious beliefs of the sect were simple. They accepted the Bible in a literal way, believed in the Trinity and in the resurrection of the dead, but not in eternal punishment, since hell would purify even the most wicked in time. They sought to avoid the world in every way, and to lead retired, withdrawn lives in humility and simplicity, eschewing anger, impatience, criticism, levity and idleness. They were exhorted neither to desire nor to grieve. The men were to 'fly from the society of womenkind'.

Without an inspired leader, the Amana Society continued, although in decline, until in 1932 they decided to abandon their communistic organization. They reconstituted themselves, abandoning the old restrictions on dress and in other matters. In time their settlements became tourist attractions.

Perhaps the most thorough-going of all communistic religious societies was that founded by John Humphrey Noyes, which

was eventually established at Oneida, in the state of New York. Its thoroughness consisted in its adoption not of celibacy, or preferred celibacy, but of communism of sexual relations.

The Oneida Community were known as Perfectionists, because they taught the possibility of perfection in this world. This was an extreme version of the Holiness teachings that had developed among some Methodists, Presbyterians and Congregationalists in the eastern United States in the second quarter of the 19th century. The principal idea of Holiness teachings was that men might, after their conversion, experience a second blessing of sanctification; the more extreme advocates held that sanctification might be instantaneous. Although the majority of Holiness believers took the doctrine to mean that the converted person who was 'born again' should lead an exemplary life, others believed that, being sanctified, they could no longer sin, no matter what they did. In consequence, promiscuity occurred among some as a 'proof' of perfection, and theories of 'spiritual wivery' opened the way to sexual licence. The Oneida Community were frequently condemned on this score.

A number of other communistic religious sects have flourished, some of them, such as the Russian Doukhobors, who settled in Canada at the turn of this century, espoused communism in part and for a period, but

Above Common beliefs and interests have led members of the Amish sect, an offshoot of the Mennonites, to set up segregated communities in the United States, where they pool their resources for the welfare of the group **Opposite above** Louwrens van Voorthuizen declared himself to be God in 1950: the Bible was superseded and salvation was to be attained only through him. Despite his claim to immortality, the former fisherman died in 1968 **Opposite** Drawing of a Ras Tafarian. These Jamaican extremists, who reject Christian ideas, are united by their belief that Haile Selassie, the former Emperor of Abyssinia, is the messiah who will lead black men to victory over the whites and into their rightful heritage – the ownership of the African continent

without particular success. An outstanding case from Africa is the Aiyetoro Community in Nigeria. This sect was constituted by seceders from the revivalist movement known as Cherubim and Seraphim. They established themselves on the coast, and organized a communist system of production. Within a few years, their fishing enterprise had produced considerable profit, and the plain uniforms of the early days were abandoned for dress of individual choice. The community is essentially religious, and although it has a living standard far higher than the Nigerian average, it has maintained its collective services and its community structure.

Messianic Religions

The distinction between a messiah, or saviour, and a prophet who foretells doom and offers ways of escaping it, is not always easy to draw, but in the strict sense the term 'messianic' is confined to movements whose leader claims to be God or a representation of God, or which arise in firm anticipation of such a god-man's appearance. The term is often used loosely for religious movements which expect the end of the world and the establishment (usually for believers only) of a new dispensation of peace, plenty and pleasure. These are more accurately called millennial movements but some movements, of course, are both messianic and millennialist, when the messiah's role is to lead the faithful into the millennium. Early Christianity, and all movements expecting the Second Coming of Christ as a reality, can properly be called messianic but current usage tends to restrict the term to groups whose messianic beliefs are outside the Bible.

Claimants to messiahship were common in Jewish history before Christ, and were by no means uncommon in the Middle Ages among Jews, Christians and Moslems. In modern times, the messianic figures who have commanded the greatest following have appeared in non-Christian countries or among underdeveloped peoples. An example is Hung Hsui-chuan, the son of a Chinese peasant household who emerged as a visionary, after repeatedly failing the Civil Service examinations, and inspired the

Sheila Kitzinger

Taiping rebellion which began in southern China in 1851 and lasted until 1864, with Nanking as its capital for most of this period.

Hsui-chuan has been influenced by an American missionary and the content of his visions was in many respects Christian, but he became convinced that his destiny was to restore the true faith to China, and that this would be achieved only with the overthrow of the Manchu imperial dynasty. Thereafter Ta'i-p'ing t'ien kuo, the heavenly kingdom of great peace, would be established. The name *ta'i-p'ing* had been used to describe an era of peace in the Chinese past, but the rest of the title was coined to express the Christian concept of a heavenly kingdom. Hung Hsiu-chuan did not make outright claim to be God, but rather to be the younger brother of Jesus; however, some scholars believe that he produced, in place of a trinitarian system, a fourfold concept of the deity. His followers were seen as a Chinese version of the children of Israel seeking the Promised Land.

As the movement grew and drew around it more conventional rebellious elements, Hung Hsiu-chuan's role was overshadowed by more militant and political leaders. He had been the early focus of attention for many who were discontented in southern China, where the peasantry had been reduced to the status of tenants, where population growth had produced new pressure on arable land and where, in Hunan province in particular, famines and catastrophes had been frequent. Hung Hsiu-chuan's ideas were alien to Chinese thought, and this has been seen as a factor which may have limited the support that he commanded. His message combined the unreconciled elements of Christian eschatology, promising both a new kingdom on earth with resurrection of the dead, as well as the prospect of salvation in the otherworld. He is reputed to have dwelt very much on sin and to have made men anxious about its consequences, demanding regular prayer for forgiveness, and obedience to the Ten Commandments. In the early days of his activity some of his followers had ecstatic and convulsive experiences. In spite of the unfamiliarity of these things, the new ideology mobilized an effective following who rose in armed rebellion on an impressive scale, until the movement suffered defeat largely through the agency of General Gordon.

Gordon's role in life seemed destined to be that of opponent of messianic claimants, for he is linked more intimately in the public mind with the struggle against another modern messiah – Mohammed Ahmad, the Mahdi who inflamed the Sudan in the 1880s. Despite the rigorous monotheism of Moslems, messianism has played a powerful role in Islam. Ahmad proclaimed himself the Imam, successor of the Apostle of God, the expected saviour, the chosen one who would reconquer the Moslem world and restore the community that Mohammed the prophet had

Foto Anefo

brought into being. He took the title Mahdi, the 'guided one', although, since the Sudan was of the Sunnite division of Islam, he did not claim to be the Hidden Imam, long awaited by Shiite Moslems. Ahmad was widely accepted, and his personal piety and high reputation made plausible his claim to be the Mahdi. He quickly built up a new state which was a theocratic despotism, the success of which lasted for more than a decade after his own death in 1885, even though there were strong tensions between the different groups among his followers.

No messianic figure of the last century can equal the Mahdi in terms of worldly success, but there have been many men who have claimed to be God both in underdeveloped countries, where they have been more successful, and among more advanced peoples. In modern society, where rational bureaucratic systems regulate life, and where there is heavy reliance on technical skills and well-defined roles, claims to superhuman competence are far less credible than in the more personal world of simpler societies. Miracles are not believed in by people who are used to explanations of a scientific and strictly causal kind, and successful modern religious figures, in America and Europe, tend increasingly to claim to be 'scientific' rather than to be workers of miracles that defy the laws of Nature. Where technology is less advanced, where rational principles of organization are less understood and, above all, where abstract concepts and empirical inquiry are less developed, the messianic claimant can still gain a hearing among those who dream of personal saviours who will solve men's problems. But messiahs have arisen from time to time in advanced countries, not only among underprivileged ethnic groups, in culturally retarded areas or among severely isolated and unworldly groups, but among much less easily identified groups of the population including well-to-do and educated members of society.

One of the most colourful of these was Lou, who was born Louwrens van Voorthuizen in north Holland, and who spent the middle

years of his life as a fisherman. Lou, as he preferred to be called, declared himself to be God in 1950, and drew around him a small and somewhat contentious body of followers, *Lou-mensen,* who were united essentially by their complete devotion to him. Lou maintained that his role was the equivalent of that of Christ, but whereas Christ had won a spiritual victory over the Devil, he, Lou, would defeat the Devil in the body.

Lou rejected conventional moral obligations, as having no relevance for salvation. (He made much of his liking for cigars: 'Why shouldn't God smoke?' he asked.) Salvation was to be attained only through him. His followers were to regard themselves as the sons and daughters of God, and needed no wills of their own. They should surrender themselves gratefully to Lou, God. The Bible was entirely superseded now that God was on earth again incarnate, and in the pamphlets which some of his middle-aged women votaries sold on the streets of Amsterdam, Lou derided both the Bible and the clergy who preached it. He preached that the time of the end was at hand, when all his followers would triumph over death. Despite the claim to immortality, Lou died in 1968. For a time his followers continued as a group, but recent inquiries at their address have not been answered.

A figure about whom even less is generally known is Georges Roux, the Christ of Montfavet, near Avignon in France. Roux was a postmaster who had practised as a faith healer for some time when, in the early 1950s, he announced that he was Christ. To read his works in simplicity of heart, it is claimed, is to accept his mission as the reappearing Christ. Roux's followers, whose churches

take the name *L'Eglise chrétienne universelle,* are reputed to number more than 5,000, principally in Paris and southern France.

The 19th century produced the most spectacular recent claimants to messiahship in Britain. Among these were two men, one of whom 'inherited' this claim from the other. Such a transfer of a status as unique as that of messiah must be unprecedented (short of a belief in the transmigration of souls) and yet the group known as Agapemonites, brought into being in the 1840s by an Anglican priest, Henry James Prince, accepted after his death a new immortal messiah in the person of John Hugh Smyth-Pigott. Prince had been renowned at St David's, Lampeter, where he had studied for the Anglican priesthood, as a particularly pious student, and soon after taking up his first curacy at Charlinch in Somerset, he gained a reputation for powerful sermons and strong personal magnetism, particularly for women. Believing himself to be possessed of the Holy Spirit his sermons became increasingly heretical, and after some time his relations with the Church of England became strained, and he opened his own chapel in Brighton. With donations from his supporters, among whom were a number of wealthy women, he bought a large house and grounds and a farm at Spraxton in Somerset, and there established his community, the Abode of Love. He had set forth his teachings in a number of tracts, and styled himself 'the Beloved One' and 'the Messiah'.

At Spraxton Prince assumed complete control of his followers, making it clear that his will was the will of God which none must question. Some of the women who joined the community bestowed all their

property on Prince, and well-wishers in Brighton, Weymouth and elsewhere contributed to its support. From the beginning a luxurious style of life was adopted, with emphasis on recreation (the chapel itself was furnished with a billiard table). Prince drove a carriage with footmen, and was later remembered as having driven through the neighbouring town of Bridgwater with his footman sounding a trumpet and announcing him as the messiah. The most distinctive feature of Agapemonite life was Prince's teaching of 'spiritual wivery'. Surrounded by 'sisters', he took a bride of the Lamb from among his following, declaring that 'in me you see Christ in the flesh, in my flesh'. The successive sexual adventures of Prince, undertaken in the name of the highest spirituality, caused some of his followers to withdraw, but those who stayed at Spraxton, other than his own paramours, led chaste and upright lives. The teaching which allowed Prince to affirm that he was above sin, no matter what he did, was a teaching for the leader not for the following.

Prince fathered several children and also found himself involved in a number of lawsuits when female adherents sought to recover their surrendered property. Although his practices were exposed in these proceedings, and although Prince was unfrocked as an Anglican priest, the community continued; undoubtedly most of its members had implicit faith in their messiah. Prince preached that he and his followers were immortal and deaths within the community were explained as the consequence of lapses into sin. His own death, in 1899, might have been expected to see the collapse of the Agapemonites: instead it

238

produced yet another messianic claimant.

Shortly before his death, Prince had sponsored the building of a church in Clapton, London, known as the Church of the Ark of the Covenant. This development was all the more surprising since in Prince's later years the Agapemonites had done little in the way of evangelization. It is uncertain whether the founding of this church, at which non-resident sympathizers of the Spraxton community occasionally met, had any direct connection with the choice of Prince's successor, or whether Prince had any interest in the continuance of his sect after his death. But it was at this church that, in 1902, John Hugh Smyth-Pigott declared himself to be the messiah.

Smyth-Pigott had been ordained an Anglican clergyman in 1882 and for a time had been curate at St Jude's Church, Mildmay Park, not far away from Clapton. In the period following Prince's death he was leading a mission in Dublin. By some means he came, or had come, into contact with the Agapemonites, and after his pronouncement at the Church of the Ark of the Covenant was accepted by them as their new leader. Some among them came to believe that he had been specifically designated as such by Prince himself – improbable, in the nature of messianic claims, as that must seem. At Spraxton, Smyth-Pigott quickly established himself over the community, continuing many features of Prince's regime. He retained the division of the community into three classes: the lowest comprised those who were the domestic servants of the rest, and the highest were the most spiritual group from among whom he would choose his soul brides.

Young women were still recruited to the community, and in 1904 Smyth-Pigott brought in a 'chief soul bride', a Miss Ruth Preece. He had three children by Ruth. His wife, who had borne him no children, appears to have accepted the situation with equanimity as indeed did most members of the community. The local Anglican bishop, however, eventually felt constrained to have the Spraxton messiah unfrocked. Producing illegitimate children, rather than the well publicized claim to messiahship, was what finally brought the Bishop of Bath and Wells to have Smyth-Pigott's case brought before a Consistory Court. In later years, the messiah took other brides and Ruth was displaced at an elaborate ceremony, for disobeying the messiah's will.

The numbers at Spraxton, sometimes reinforced by visitors from a Norwegian sister house which Smyth-Pigott frequently visited, steadily declined, and the messiah's death in 1927 reduced the numbers further. Without a leader the community slowly dwindled, until in the 1950s Sister Ruth also died and within a short time the community disappeared.

Movements that arise around a self-styled messiah are, in the modern age, unlikely to be revolutionary movements in any militant sense. The legal monopoly of coercive force in the modern state virtually precludes the

possibility of a messiah actively fulfilling the implications of his claims to super-natural and omniscient power. In effect, therefore, the messianic leader operates more as if he were simply a wonder-worker. His miracles tend to be small miracles, tokens of power rather than manifestations of power in anything like the dimensions in which it is claimed. The reputation for small miracles is often enough for the faithful, and on such miracles rested a great deal of the reputation of one of the best-known of modern messiahs.

Like many other claimants to messiah-ship, Father Divine had behind him a career of active religious evangelism before he accepted the title of God. As George Baker, he had been a missionary among Negroes in various parts of the United States, but in 1930 at Sayville on Long Island, New York, Baker took the suggestive title, Father Divine. It was one among a number of such names assumed by Negro revivalists ('Daddy Grace' was a contemporary rival of Baker's). At Sayville he established the first of his Peace Missions, communities which became known as 'heavens' for those who lived in them. They were organized along co-operative lines, and to them were attached members who were non-resident but who joined the residents for religious services. Father Divine conceived the idea of a well-organized social service for his adherents. He found jobs for the un-employed and cared for the poor, and since many of those who joined the sect were incapable of much organization on their own part, there was a very real sense in which Father Divine was their saviour, in this world if not in the next. Like most messianic leaders, Divine had no developed eschatology: salvation was indeed here and now, since God was here and now. In common with other messiahs, he taught that his members should not and would not die, and death was a shameful thing within the movement and not to be spoken about. Nor had Father Divine much use for the Bible, which was clearly a superseded book. Since God was available to speak for himself, the written record of his acts long ago and for a remote people was of little specific interest.

The Peace Mission espoused a rigorous ethical code and this may in itself have been part of its formula for success. Members were weaned away from those habits which caused debility and degeneracy among large sections of the population. Smoking and drinking were prohibited. Honesty was a strict requirement. Sexual continence, even between those who were married, was

Opposite 'Father Divine', formerly George Baker, had behind him a career of active evangelism before he accepted the title of God. He taught his many thousands of followers to accept his will as their supreme good: he himself could work all the miracles that they needed **Right** Beneath a placard proclaiming him as God, Father Divine addresses a meeting in a Harlem Peace Mission or 'heaven'

Keystone

rigorously enjoined and the ill consequences of a large progeny were in this way avoided. Father Divine taught his followers to accept his will as their supreme good, and he forbade them to accept government welfare or to take out insurance policies. He himself could work all the miracles that they needed. He gave lavish banquets on a scale and in a style far beyond the previous experience of his adherents, and since they did not pay for these directly, his provision appeared as a miracle. He could pour innumerable cups of coffee from one small coffee pot, so it was frequently affirmed of him. His followers believed that anyone who spoke or acted against him would surely suffer, and took this as certain evidence of his divine power.

It is not easy to assess the numbers who believed in Father Divine when he was on the tide of success in the late 1930s, but there were perhaps hundreds of thousands, almost all Negroes. After the Second World War the movement seemed to have passed its peak, as more militant forms of Negro religion, in particular the Black Muslim movement gained strength and displaced the essentially peaceful Father Divine cult. The movement may have suffered after Divine took a white second wife towards the end of his life, and because he was gradually less and less disposed to appear in public. He died in 1965, but the movement continued, although at a less impressive level than formerly.

Much more propitious circumstances for claimants to deity exist in Africa than exist even among the least educated and poorest groups in advanced societies, and it is there that the most dramatic among modern messianic movements are to be found. Belief in a personal and visible God is much more acceptable to illiterate natives, lost between tribal and urban styles of life, than in any other community. Black Christs have emerged from time to time, most notably in the Congo, but in South Africa, too, there has been no shortage of claimants to the role. Edward Lekganyane is a contemporary self-styled messiah who commands the devotion of between 40,000 and 80,000 followers from his headquarters at Zion City, Moria in the northern Transvaal.

Lekganyane was one of two sons of the leader of a religious movement known as the Zion Christian Church. Although the brothers quarrelled after their father's death in 1949 or 1950, a large proportion of the movement followed Edward. His capital is a village of about 300 persons in which strangers are not welcomed; from here he rules the movement, which has churches as far away as Johannesburg and Pretoria. Lekganyane's precise claims are difficult to discover, but his followers believe that he has power to prevent or create unemployment, to work miracles of healing, to destroy his enemies, and that he will soon have nations bowing down before him. His power is thought to destroy witchcraft, and in part he acts as the traditional witch-purger. But he is also the focus for intense hatred of white men, and it may be in the anticipated victory of Zion over the world that his messianic quality is most significant.

As with other African religious movements, a mixture of traditional and Christian ideas prevail in Zion City, together with some innovations of unknown origin. Followers must not take medicines, since that would be to accept rival claims to power. They are to abstain from alcohol and tobacco. They are forbidden to eat pork, a taboo which may stem from the Old Testament influence of the Protestant 'Zionist' sects which formed missions among South African natives at the end of the last century. Paper which Lekganyane has blessed is burned as a way of liberating its potent virtue against witchcraft and illness. The ceremonial adopted at Zion City is like that connected with an African chief, and part of the appeal of the movement may be its function as a substitute for tribal identity among peoples who have become detribalized. Since chiefs have little power, messianic claimants who behave like chiefs but who, from the point of view of the authorities, do not pose an overt political threat, are the most powerful native figures in South Africa, exercising authority in the one sphere in which Africans are permitted considerable freedom – religion. Lekganyane combines the appeal of the traditional chief,

presiding over ceremonies in which dancing, drumming and processions are all significant, with that of the modern tycoon, living in a modern house, dressing like an army officer and maintaining two Cadillacs and other cars.

In some ways a not dissimilar movement is that of John Galilee Shembe, whose organization is known as the Nazareth Baptist Church. This Church, too, was founded by the father of the present messiah, and the father was in his own lifetime also deified by his Zulu followers. The present messiah is in some respects a reluctant messiah. He is a man who has had a university education, who maintains in the name of his Church active business interests, and who finds himself not wholly at home in the role he has inherited. Some of his followers see J. G. Shembe as the god of the blacks, just as Jesus was the god of the whites, and others regard him as the incarnation of the Trinity. Shembe himself tends to refer messianic claims to his father. The ethical and ritual code of the movement is based largely on Old Testament precepts: pork is tabooed; circumcision is practised. Before the great festivals of the sect's year, sexual abstinence is to be practised between spouses. Beards are worn by men, and women are forbidden to cut their hair. All medicine is to be avoided, since illness is attributed to witchcraft, from which Shembe alone can rid his followers. Healing is in many ways a central concern of the movement, but Shembe is an undramatic person and his 'laying on of hands' tends to be undertaken in a perfunctory fashion, whilst he attends to other business. He also holds mass healing sessions.

In many respects the Nazareth Baptist Church resuscitates the richness of Zulu tribal and ceremonial life. Shembe is often referred to as a chief, and has in the modern world more prestige than any of the actual Zulu chiefs, some among whom worship in his Church. Ceremonies are extremely complex, and traditional dancing in elaborate costume is practised. Like a chief, Shembe receives tribute from his followers, who are largely uneducated people. They have good reputations as workers and as orderly and law-abiding people. For them the movement provides community, offers possibilities of healing and fertility (a strong preoccupation among African women), and provides some type of security for individuals who feel endangered by life in the towns. It gives them a sense of belonging to a powerful deity who can protect them, and maintains strong links with the dignified tribal life of the past. A tract of land is maintained at which principal festivities are enacted and this serves, at least symbolically, as a type of tribal homeland for the Shembe-ites.

Opposite The storming of the Pai-how forts by the French in 1860; the Taiping rebellion was not finally put down until 1864 **Right** Hung Hsui-chuan, whose visions inspired the Taiping rebellion which began in southern China in 1851: he preached the foundation of a heavenly kingdom and claimed to be the younger brother of Jesus, though not God himself

Not every messianic movement arises round a self-styled messiah. Some are anticipatory, and others select as their god an individual who makes no such claims on his own behalf. One of the most extraordinary movements of the latter sort is the Ras Tafari movement of Jamaica. Like some other movements in less-developed societies, the Ras Tafarians are not a distinct sect with a coherent organization, but a collection of groups of greater or lesser degrees of permanence, centred around a number of spasmodically emerging leaders, who proclaim a broadly similar set of beliefs. These leaders have often been rivals, and there have been sharp differences between them, but their central ideas, and in particular their faith in an unwitting messiah, are common ground. Their central theme is hatred of the white men who have dominated, first politically and still economically, the life of the West Indies.

In the now deposed Emperor of Ethiopia, Haile Selassie, they acclaim a saviour who will bring black men into their heritage.

The reason for such faith in Haile Selassie is a curious one. Many Jamaicans were impressed, during the period following the First World War, by the pronouncements of Marcus Garvey, a militant pro-Negro Jamaican who was active in the United States. Not long afterwards, in 1930, Ras Tafari, as the Crown Prince of Abyssinia was known, became Emperor, and West Indian Negroes, recalling Garvey's prophecy, became excited about their prospects.

The Italian attack on Ethiopia in 1935 inflamed the enthusiasm of the Ras Tafarians in Kingston, for this clearly represented a struggle of black men versus white, the worshippers of a living God against the worshippers of a dead God. Christian ideas were now completely abandoned by the

241

various groups of supporters of Ras Tafari, and the movement became a semi-political religious belief in the power of a black saviour, Haile Selassie. Different local leaders elaborated their variants on this theme in different ways. Some were more avowedly religious and maintained services of worship. Others were more explicitly political. Some, the most extreme groups, withdrew to the plantations, grew 'ganja' (marijuana) and established a colony of militant anti-whites. Later a number of leaders arose who traded on the bizarre fantasies of some of the believers, promising that airplanes would arrive on specified dates to take them all to Africa and making a great deal of money by the sale of worthless 'passports'.

Despite such trickery, belief in Ras Tafari persisted. Some groups rejected European titles and some came to reject food cooked by anyone but a true believer. They became distrustful of hospitals, and in particular of birth control propaganda which was seen as an attempt by white men to destroy the black people. For similar reasons they condemned blood transfusions. The most extreme group of Ras Tafarians called themselves Niyamen, used ganja and grew their hair into long spiky locks, becoming known as 'dreadlocks'. The intention was to imitate African warriors. The name Niyamen appears to have been adopted during the Italian-Abyssinian war, when a newspaper article appearing in Jamaica described a

secret organization, said to be led by Haile Selassie, the aim of which was the total destruction of all white men in Africa. A movement had existed in Rwanda and Uganda some years earlier, known as Nyabingi, which had had something like this aim, but the imputation to Haile Selassie of leadership of such a movement (which had no connection with Ethiopia and which had been extinct for years before the Italian-Abyssinian war) was no doubt an embellishment of Italian propaganda agencies. Nonetheless the article had a powerful effect on the Ras Tafarians, who were well disposed to believe it. The Niyamen swore an oath promising death to the white oppressors and to all those Negroes who collaborated with them. It is this group of extremist Ras Tafarians that have come most to public notice, although the periodic craze for a ship or a plane to take Jamaicans to Africa has also brought the cult into the public eye.

Towards the end of British rule in Jamaica, there was an incident which made it evident that some Ras Tafari leaders were using the movement to foster political revolution on the island and, in a skirmish with one of these leaders, two British soldiers were murdered in the late 1950s. There was evidence that this particular Ras Tafarian, the Rev. Henry, had been in communication with the government of Fidel Castro in Cuba. It may well have been that the religious aspects of Ras Tafari

practice were, in this instance, a front organization for a political group. Other groups of cultists have remained quite explicitly religious however. Some settled on the rubbish dumps outside Kingston and rejected white ways by deliberately being dirty, scavenging, periodically insulting tourists, and coming into riotous conflict with the police. Others are described by their fellow cultists as those who 'go tidy', who lead orderly peaceable lives and observe traditional dietetic taboos (the rules of the Old Testament for the Jews again apply, and there is conscious identification with the children of Israel in bondage). Some of these sectarians are described as good craftsmen and model citizens, who wait patiently for the airlift to Africa, which is the Utopia to which their messiah will in due time deliver them.

A government inquiry into the activities of the Ras Tafarians, in the late 1950s, led the newly independent government of Jamaica (to which the Ras Tafarians were as much opposed as to the whites) to permit a delegation of Ras Tafarians to visit Africa. They visited Liberia, Nigeria and Ethiopia, and were received by Haile Selassie, who gave them a token plot of land in his country. The Ras Tafarians were, however, disappointed by the possibilities of migrating to Africa and seem to have received no positive encouragement from any of the governments they visited. In 1965 Haile Selassie paid a state visit to Jamaica and this very much excited the Ras Tafarians. He received some of them at a formal garden party, where they mixed with official guests, despite their dirty condition. Although the messiah of their choosing gave medals to these would-be subjects, it appears that little or nothing could be done to satisfy the Ras Tafarian dream of settling in Ethiopia under the leadership of the messiah.

The militant and ecstatic type of messianic movement is probably a waning phenomenon in the modern world. Whilst in countries undergoing dramatic social change from primitive to modern technological conditions, such outbreaks may still occur, in advanced societies social disorder is likely to arise around different symbols. Few modern men believe that their problems, and those of their society, can be solved by the agency of any one person. Few believe that there is superhuman power available to any man, much less divine power. Messiahs are perhaps a dying species, even though disruptive movements, similar to those which arose around messianic figures in the past, may continue.

Radio Times Hulton Picture Library

Left The final defeat in 1898 of the followers of Mohammed Ahmad, the Mahdi: the theocratic state which he had established in the Sudan had lasted more than a decade after his death *Opposite* The robes of these priests are black because that is the colour their black god prefers: new religions in underdeveloped countries tend to combine Christian and pagan elements, and show 'the problems of people dramatically strung between two cultures'

New Religions

An almost invariable accompaniment of processes of rapid and intense social change is the emergence of new religious movements. They are particularly conspicuous in periods of urbanization and industrialization in advancing countries, but are perhaps most spectacular and prolific at times of sudden and disruptive cultural contact between advanced and primitive societies. In such circumstances the clash of cultures gives rise to profound disorientation of the lives, customs and comprehension of simpler peoples. Since it is usually a principal function of religion to interpret the world, in both the cosmological and moral sense, for its followers it is understandable, when a particular view of the world is disrupted, that new attempts to make sense of things should occur.

It is sometimes the existing religious specialists in a society who offer these new religious orientations, but more usually it comes from new prophets. Inevitably what they offer is not entirely new. It tends to be an amalgam of many old ideas and some new ones, a syncretic system of myths, procedures and rituals. Because the disruptions of social life often produce intense anxiety, particularly when they are sudden, new movements frequently manifest patterns of behaviour that approximate to anxiety symptoms. Delusions, institutionalized obsessions, fantasy and escape from reality into a dream world of wish-fulfillments, are frequently found in new movements, particularly at their beginnings. Visions, shaking, hysteria and orgies of sexual indulgence sometimes occur. In some cases

they have arisen in close association with military activity against the colonial settlers or the colonial government, and sometimes against the governments of newly independent nation-states in underdeveloped territories. In such circumstances they have often been short lived or sporadically recrudescent. In other cases, we find movements that offer new prescriptions for purely personal anxieties, and sometimes there is a succession of such movements, each of which differs in specific cultural content and in intrinsic myth and ritual, but the goals of which are precisely the same.

Broadly two types of response to disturbed social conditions can be discerned among these movements. Some are militant and revolutionist, providing religious justification for resistance to the intruders who bring a new culture. Others, and there is some reason to suppose that these tend to arise earlier in the process of cultural contact, are basically concerned with providing better magical means to meet the needs of their followers. These latter movements are usually more emotionally and expressively oriented: they are less explicitly concerned with the preservation of the tribe or its culture. Movements also differ in the direction of their concern. Some arise in the name of the preservation or restoration of traditional ways of life. They resist the attrition of native values, and often the ancestors are invoked as the guardians of past culture. Whatever is new, whatever the white man has introduced, are rejected. Other new religions promise their adherents

exactly the opposite: the full benefits of modern civilization, the power of the white man's knowledge, and enjoyment of his luxuries, and sometimes they envisage a reversal of roles – a millennial society in which black men are clever and commanding, and white men are ignorant workers. These movements sometimes avowedly reject the culture of the native past, and their leaders promote the imitation of European practices.

New religious movements necessarily exhibit the cultural preoccupations of the particular societies in which they arise. Thus African movements are frequently concerned with the elimination of witches: whilst movements in Melanesia, on the other hand, reveal the preoccupation of tribal cultures in that part of the world with the acquisition of trade goods. Some movements function particularly as agencies of cultural identification for groups whose traditional way of life is in decay, and whose position is acutely uncertain in a rapidly changing social situation, and this has been very much the case with the peyote cult among some of the North American Indian tribes and some Maori religious movements in New Zealand.

Similar cultural continuities are to be observed in the new religious movements in contexts other than purely tribal societies. The cults that flourish among Negroes in Haiti and Brazil bear very evident traces of their antique African origin. The Negro populations of the Brazilian coastal cities such as Recife, Bahia and Rio, maintain shrines in which the deities who are

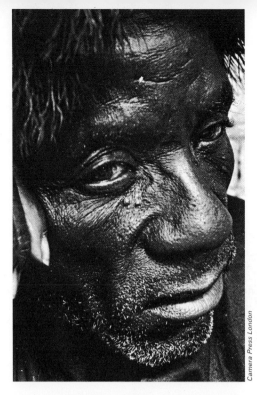

Camera Press London

Many new sects in Africa link Christian doctrines with African beliefs in witchcraft, magical healing and direct contact with a god through spirit-possession. The chief acolyte *(above)* and the wife *(below)* of the Rhodesian prophet Muchetera, who becomes possessed by the spirit of the god Chaminuka and transmits through his acolytes the words of the god to the worshippers *Opposite* Alice Lenshina, who was originally a member of a Church of Scotland mission in Rhodesia: people flocked to her to be baptized after she claimed to have met Jesus during a period of three days and three nights when she was 'dead', and she founded her own Lumpa Church. Such manifestations upset Christian missionaries, who saw their own congregations – and influence – diminishing, and for a time her church was prohibited

Camera Press London

worshipped are, despite the Christianization of their names, readily identifiable as gods worshipped at one time by their ancestors in Nigeria and Dahomey. Even in movements that have developed considerable sophistication, such as the new Christian denominations in West Africa, traditional cultural concerns are recognizable behind the organizational forms that have been acquired from Western Christianity and modern styles of denominational structure.

Some of the most dramatic new religious movements have arisen in the Congo, where prophetism had flourished from the very early days of European contact. Most outbursts have been of limited duration until recent times. The prophet whose name is associated with the most important group of movements is Simon Kimbangu, who had been a catechist (trainee member) with a Baptist mission, later claiming to have been called to prophesy, and in particular to undertake healing work. In the prevailing conditions of a society disrupted by the collapse of markets following the end of the First World War, there were many who were ready for some new dramatic development. People travelled long distances to listen to Kimbangu preaching, and although there is no reliable evidence that healings actually occurred, his reputation spread rapidly. Hospitals were deserted, and although he preached against *minkisi* (spirits) and fetishes, and as a consequence of his exhortations the demand for Bibles grew, nonetheless Kimbangu quickly fell foul of the Belgian colonial authorities and of the Roman Catholic missionaries. Natives were leaving their work and journeying to see him, and this excitement was enough to convince the authorities that Kimbangu was a threat to public order. To the natives he was a powerful destroyer of witches: among those who set out to hear him some died on the way, and this was taken as sure evidence that these people were involuntary witches who had died as they approached the counter-witchcraft influence of Kimbangu.

As the authorities became more alarmed, Kimbangu was arrested, but escaped and thereby established even more prestige with his fellow natives. The movement now acquired a strong anti-white impulse which had not been part of its original character. His village was plundered and Kimbangu preached in the bush. The idea of this new folk-hero as a ruler now took root, and what had been an essentially magic, miracle-working movement became a millennialist and revolutionist one. Some of his followers were arrested and in a dramatic gesture, Kimbangu returned to his own village in the fashion of Christ entering Jerusalem, to face arrest, trial and condemnation to death. The death penalty was commuted to life imprisonment, and Kimbangu remained in prison until his death in 1950.

The movement to which he gave his name had only just begun at the time of his arrest, however. Thereafter it thrived on recurrent rumours and expectations of the return of Kimbangu, which was now awaited, much as second adventists await the return of Christ. Indeed Simon Kimbangu became identified with Christ and was regarded by many as the third member of the Trinity. Periodic outbreaks of enthusiasm occurred. Kimbanguists began to celebrate the third day of the week as their special day of religious observance. In some places the movement remained avowedly anti-white and adventist: in other places sympathetic Lutheran missionaries directed it into a more conventional type of revivalism. But periodic government repression and the influence of local prophets in many districts led the more extreme groups to take refuge in the bush where some of them engaged in new and bizarre rites directed towards the eradication of witchcraft. Missionaries reported that at some of these ceremonies, shaking, frenzied dancing and ordeals of lying down in the fire occurred. In response to government action against them, the various local groups tended to become more anti-Christian and pagan. Attempts were made to resuscitate the dead and some of the dances were lecherous and orgiastic. Such practices reverted to traditional preoccupations – healing and the purging of witches and concern with the ancestors – and represent an alternative response to the millennialist expectations of other branches or phases of the movement.

Two prominent prophets arose in the 1930s claiming to have inherited the mantle of Kimbangu. They were Andrew Matswa, who was active in the (then French) Congo, and Simon Mpadi. Matswa served in the French army in Morocco and later lived in Paris where he moved in left-wing circles. There he was successful in getting a government subsidy for a welfare organization to help Africans in Paris, and through this association, Matswa sent agents to collect funds in the Boko district of French Equatorial Africa, although those who contributed had widely divergent ideas of the purpose of their donations. Matswa may have been a crook, a political agitator or even a religious leader. He was prosecuted and this was enough to make him a martyr, and his movement, variously known as 'the religion of the candle' and 'the religion of the sacred wood' flourished after his death after a few years of imprisonment. It remained a potent force in the French Congo, and the Matswaists were an important group in the period leading to independence in the late 1950s.

Mpadi rose into prominence largely through his association with the Salvation Army. The Salvationists arrived in the Congo in 1934–5 and had immediate success with the natives. Unfortunately, what the Salvationists took to be Christ touching the hearts of savages, was an experience with quite a different interpretation for the natives. The Salvation Army taught religion in a context of emotional freedom and joyousness; they wore a uniform; and they were prepared to shake hands with natives. They offered them a new flag. Above all, on the lapels of their coats they wore the significant letter 'S' for 'salvation', which the half-literate natives took to be a symbol for the sacred name, Simon. To the natives, the Salvationists were the new whites, the army which would lead to salvation and the return of Simon Kimbangu.

Once the natives were disillusioned about the Army, a separatist movement grew up from among those who had joined it. It now provided the model for a new style of religious movement. Simon Mpadi had been a regular Salvationist sergeant for about a year, and the movement which he founded during the intervals between periods of imprisonment, was known as the Khakists, from the uniform it adopted. Later other leaders took over, but not before, in his own area, Mpadi had established a reputation as a prophet whose return, during his imprisonment, was awaited like the advent of a new age.

In 1951 the Belgian authorities granted greater freedom to natives to establish religious organizations, and in 1956 one of Kimbangu's sons established the *Eglise de Jesus Christ sur la terre par le prophète Simon Kimbangou* (the Church of Jesus Christ on Earth through the Prophet Simon Kimbangu). The movement has many Protestant elements, including baptism by immersion, use of the Bible, public confession and a Protestant type hymnology. A few years later Simon Mpadi was released from prison and returned to lead what continued as a more exotic adaptation of Christianity to African conditions.

More recent religious movements, whilst continuing to manifest concern with witchcraft, have tended to espouse the organizational forms of the Christian missions and churches. They have thus persisted better, and have been more immediately visible than were the older cults that centred on the self-claimed power over witchcraft of one prophet. Among the most dramatic of anti-witchcraft movements has been the Lumpa Church of Alice Lenshina in Zambia.

Alice Lenshina was a simple tribeswoman who belonged to the Church of Scotland Lubwa Mission in (then) Northern Rhodesia. In 1953, Lenshina claimed to have received visions, to have entertained angels, and to have met Jesus during a period of three nights and three days when she was 'dead'. Initially she remained in the mission where a wise missionary sought to use, rather than to suppress, her religious impulses. She testified against hatred, stealing, swearing, lying, adultery and other sins, and she soon acquired a name as a prophetess among the natives. After a little time she began to baptize people, and called them to surrender to her their horns, charms and other implements of witchcraft. Her fame spread, and pilgrims came from as far away as Lake Tanganyika and Nyasaland. She taught the pilgrims songs, and after a time began to authorize teachers. Up to this point her message was by no means out of harmony with Christian teachings – despite her dramatic visionary claims.

But the accommodation of such a powerful teacher to mission Christianity proved

Associated Press

difficult. In particular, the Roman Catholic missions in the area were denuded of their following and Lenshina began to incur the hostility of the missionaries. Some declared that she had been given to spirit-possession when young, and others asserted that the new movement was an African nationalist and racist organization. There is, however, no evidence that Lenshina taught anything about an impending cataclysm which would overtake the government or the whites, even though – in common with Christian Churches – she had some teachings about the millennium. The central concern of the Lumpa Church was the elimination of witchcraft, but even this was misrepresented. Press reports by journalists, who understood little of African cultures, mistook witchcraft-elimination for witchcraft itself.

Inevitably, a quickly-growing movement of this kind met antagonism; her popular strength was great, and this emboldened her followers to defy the government on certain issues. She held court rather in the traditional style of a chief; thus prophetism here, as elsewhere in Africa, was an avenue of social mobility. Nonetheless, district officers conceded that in the Chinsali district where the Lumpa Church was strongest, morality had greatly improved. In 1963 the followers of Lenshina became involved in politics, despite her exhortations, and in the last days before complete independence a clash occurred between Lumpa churchmen and the authorities in which some hundreds of

her followers were killed. Alice Lenshina, although perhaps not responsible for this conflict, was arrested and for some years the government prohibited the movement.

One of the most famous anti-witchcraft movements was that of the Tigari cult which spread throughout Ghana and neighbouring territories in the 1940s, and which was directed to the elimination of witches, the procuring of health, fortune and children. Tigari ceremonial was enacted for 'clients' who had particular requests to make at the shrine, and Tigari priests manipulated their equipment to bring the semi-magical forces that they claimed to command into operation. To the accompaniment of drums, sacrifices were performed by which the priest claimed to exorcize witches or the effect of witchcraft. Malefactors were condemned and fines were levied against them: the system worked because those condemned feared the power of the Tigari priest and his medicine, and so yielded up whatever was demanded of them.

As long as the cult was popular, Tigari provided a swifter avenue of social mobility than had the older religious system. In a society where men were just beginning to recognize the possibilities of 'getting on in the world', of leaving tribal and village associations and traditionally ascribed roles, it is not surprising that religion should become a field of endeavour both for those seeking wealth and success and those attempting to exercise power.

A decline in the Tigari cult occurred in the 1950s, because changing circumstances demand new magical responses. What followed Tigari was an interesting development which illustrated a continuance of traditional preoccupations, the intensification of demand for reassurance from the insecurities with which Tigari had sought to cope, and the growing capacity to adopt Western forms of organization. The new movements resembled very much more the mission churches and, increasingly, the more modern among the denominational organizations in Western countries that supported missions. They also incorporated, along with these forms of organization, an explicit commitment to Christianity. The origin of these movements was the Christian missions, and their leaders were all men trained in, and often occupying minor ecclesiastical roles within, the mission churches.

Characteristic were the group of revivalistic movements that sprang up in Nigeria just after the First World War. In some respects the leaders of these movements were looking for a more emphatic, more compelling and more powerful religion than the missions offered, and they became the native equivalents of fundamentalist revivalists in 19th century America. African movements necessarily embraced concerns and preoccupations that were of distinctly African provenance and they wanted a religion that could deal with the magical and evil power which Africans almost all believed in. The Churches that were spawned by these revivals were avowedly committed to faith-healing, to a generally Christian standard of morals, but also to the reassurance of individuals about their most compelling concerns – health, fertility and worldly success. The ecstatic character of services, with drumming, dancing, revelations and the outbreak of inspired utterance, reflects the intensity of concern.

Typical of these movements is the Aladura Church of the Lord, founded by J. A. Ositelu, a disappointed Nigerian catechist in an Anglican mission, who in 1926 received divine inspiration to set up his own Church in Western Nigeria. Today that Church has branches in various West African countries, working under an elaborate written constitution, with a well-regulated hierarchy of officials from its Primate down to local 'Captains' and ministers. The insistence on prophecy is underlined by the institution of the office of 'Prophet' and 'Assistant Prophet'. The thousands who attend Aladura services regard themselves as Christians, but emphasize that they belong to 'spiritual Churches'. The term spiritual refers to the belief in the continued operation of spiritual power in the Church, and the expectation of revelations to the congregation at large through its inspired agents. Among bodies which prefer to be collectively known by this term is the Church of the Lord, the Cherubim and Seraphim movement, which is also found in other West African countries besides Nigeria, where it originated.

The spiritual Churches draw in large numbers of West Africans, mainly from the new lower middle classes in rapidly growing cities such as Lagos, Accra and Freetown. The services have the form of Christian worship, with hymns and choruses borrowed from the missions. In the Church of the Lord, hymnology is evangelical, liturgy is closer to that of the Roman Church, whilst the central preoccupations are emphatically African. Drumming, dancing and repetitive choruses continue for three or more hours at Sunday and week-night 'watch services'. Members of the congregations are exhorted to dress in white. Like Moslems they are barefoot, and for their prayer exercises they also adopt the Moslem practice of kneeling and bowing to the ground. Occasionally an individual becomes possessed during the dancing, or is afflicted by strong pangs of conscience; in writhing agony he is taken out to the 'mercy ground' – a sandy enclosure – outside the church to wrestle in the Spirit, shouting and rolling in the sand, until, calm again, he rejoins the congregation.

During the principal services individuals will sometimes announce visions they have seen during the period of collective prayer, and these are usually interpreted by the officiating minister. Even more important, however, are the institutionalized revelatory

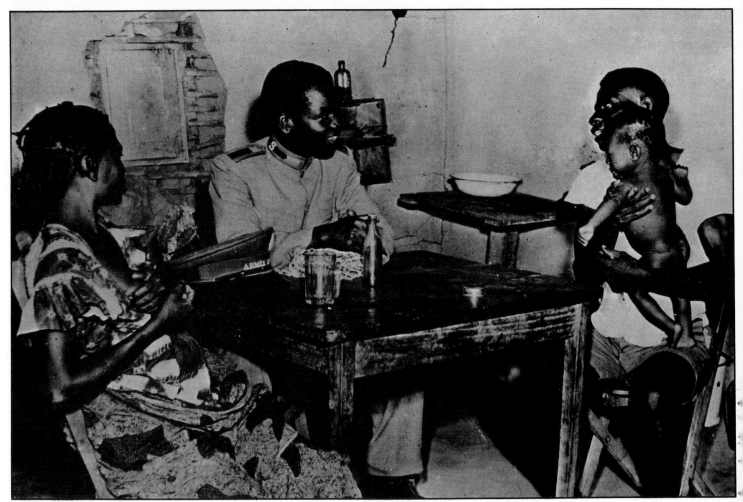

interviews between (in the Church of the Lord) the lay officials known as 'the Army of Jesus' and the rest of the congregational participants.

The officials move about among the crowd, halting in front of an individual who then goes down on his knees whilst the official intones, 'Oh Brother, the Lord has revealed unto me . . .' and then continues to indicate what is likely to befall the particular member and how he might ward off evil, induce goodwill from God and protect himself and his family from illness and witches.

New religious movements in Africa illustrate the problems of people dramatically strung between two cultures and two sets of assumptions about the world and its religious interpretation. The same is true, in even stronger measure, of the less developed tribal peoples of Melanesia. But such movements there reflect distinctive cultural concerns which differ significantly from those to be found in Africa. The common element is the demand for prosperity, but in Melanesia there is a much more emphatic demand for power which will bring the benefits of white technology and white material equipment to natives in the so called cargo cults.

Even among peoples much more used to the facilities of modern life than the Melanesians, as for example in Brazil, the problem of interpreting social experience persists. Insecurity in the cities and ignorance in rural areas give rise to strong desires to manipulate spiritual forces and wrest some good from a recalcitrant world. Brazil is a country of dramatic religious expression and a wide variety of movements exist side-by-side there, representing completely unreconciled conceptions of the divine and the supernatural.

There has been, for example, a rapid growth in Brazil of modern Pentecostal movements, both in consequence of the work of the missionaries of such sects in the United States, and as a local spontaneous development among some groups of Brazilians, particularly Italian immigrants. Apart from growing branches of other American sects, such as Jehovah's Witnesses, active in many parts of the world and particularly in underdeveloped countries, there is also a stronger body of Spiritualists in Brazil than anywhere else in the world. There have been several vigorous millennial movements.

Brazilian Spiritualists are of two principal kinds, those known as Kardecists, so called because their religious views derive from the writings of Alain Kardec, a French 19th century Spiritualist who acquired a significant following in Brazil; and those known as Umbandists. The Umbandists represent a more primitive type of Spiritualism, the inspiration for which is originally African, and which in some respects is rather closer

Camera Press London

as a religious phenomenon to the beliefs and practices of the *candomblés* of Bahía and Recife than to the more sophisticated, metaphysical system espoused by the Kardecists. The Kardecists believe in reincarnation, the remoteness of God and therefore the necessity of appealing to lesser spirits for assistance in one's worldly concerns. There is some emphasis among them on general ethical principles and they have also steadily developed a programme of social service. Some of the more intellectual among the Kardecists are openly contemptuous of the crude performances, spirit-possession and the search for spectacular manifestations that are common among the Umbandists.

The candomblés are in themselves not an organized religious movement, but rather a collection of independent shrines presided over by a priest or priestess, upon whom wait a group of acolytes, usually women. At services in the candomblés the young women, most of whom are dedicated to a particular god, dance until they become possessed by the deity, in whose special robes they are then dressed. They then dance and behave entirely according to the character of the deity to whom they are dedicated. They may act quite licentiously and impertinently to those who come seeking their aid, but they also provide advice, inspiration and evoke faith among the crowds of believers who flock into the candomblés every night. The clientele is largely Negro, but in recent years the spectacular performances of some priestesses whilst possessed have begun to command the attendance of more sophisticated Brazilians, and perhaps also their belief.

The deities, although taking Christian names, are the gods of West African religions, or, in some cases, combine attributes of the gods of the indigenous Indian population of Brazil.

Many hundreds of new religious movements, some of very brief duration, have been recorded in the underdeveloped countries of the world.

In Africa, for example, it is now virtually impossible to determine what the truly indigenous religion in most areas really was. In South America, too, with the onslaught of Western-style civilization, not only is the native religion assimilated, but also the whole way of life. Sometimes the impact is, literally, too great for the natives to bear, and whole tribes have disappeared. What the Christian Church at last seems to have realized is that if it is to survive at all in the face of a rising tide of nationalism in the underdeveloped countries, it must radically modify its whole approach and pioneer a different brand of Christianity outside the exclusively Western tradition imparted by missionaries hitherto.

As the peoples of such countries acquire greater organizing ability, learn to imitate the forms and systems of white men, and benefit from education, so their indigenous religious movements can acquire, as among the Aladura Churches of West Africa, the necessary structure for more permanent operation. Inevitably, as this process of learning occurs, so too the intrinsic religious conceptions of a people steadily undergoes transformation and increasingly such new movements as persist come to show closer approximations to the religious forms common in the Western world.

Opposite **The Salvation Army's S Symbol aroused enthusiasm among Africans who mistook it for an emblem of the prophet Simon Kimbangu** *Above* **Mock magical rite performed before an audience of 'witches' in Kenya**

Index

Index

Index

ACKNOWLEDGEMENTS

Front of jacket: Temple banner showing scene from the life of the Buddha (Asia Museum, Bad Wildungen/Werner Forman); back of jacket: God looks down from Heaven while St John supports the Virgin Mary who mourns over the dead Jesus; inset: The saints in Heaven (detail from the Judgement of the Dead) (Roger Wood); front flap: Emma-O, ruler and supreme judge of the dead in Japanese Buddhism (Michael Holford); back flap: Abbot John of Rila (Sonia Halliday); endpapers: Figures of the Shongo cult from the Shongo shrine of the Temi of Ede in Northern Nigeria (Werner Forman); page 5: The reading of the Torah in the synagogue (Keystone); pages 6–7: Woman praying, Notre Dame Cathedral, Paris (Sonia Halliday); pages 8–9: Gilded-bronze statue of a Hindu monk (Collection Philip Goldman/Werner Forman).